"While the topics of leadership and sexuality have each received much attention, unfortunately, their intersections have not. Conversely and fortunately, concerning leadership and sexuality, this volume successfully moves the scholarship needle on those understudied intersections. From education and activism to mentoring and more, this volume masterfully reviews what we know, describes what we don't know, and prescribes what we should know. Kudos on a complex job well done!"

– *Juan Battle, Ph.D., Presidential Professor,*
Graduate Center of CUNY, USA

"The Handbook of Sexuality Leadership is a powerful collection of works. It provides a comprehensive and innovative view of what we need to know now in order to advance empowered thought and activism in the fields of sexuality and relationships. It is particularly timely in relation to intersectionality studies, moving scholars and educators concerned about multilevel justice to new revelations about what comes next in personal, partnered, and communal visibility and liberation."

– *Jeanine M. Staples, Associate Professor of Literacy*
and Language, African American Studies, and
Women's, Gender, and Sexuality Studies,
The Pennsylvania State University, USA

"The field of sexology finally has an extraordinary compilation of scholarly essays devoted to various perspectives about leadership. This book has been needed for decades and carves out a new and definitive direction for emergent professionals to consider. Each chapter highlights the complexities of serving as a sexuality professional, and this book will be of great use to leading a variety of populations in a myriad of settings."

– *Monique Howard, Ed.D., Executive Director*
of Philadelphia Center Against Sexual Violence, USA

"By brilliantly introducing (or simply reflecting) leadership into sexology, Dr. James C. Wadley has created a treasure map for 21st century approaches to not only bridging the perpetual divides between sexology and the larger medical and mental health fields, but more importantly, for laying out paths toward the critical social justice ideals sexologists have traditionally championed and struggled to spread. Furthermore, I don't recall ever being moved so emotionally by an 'academic' text – the chapter authors' passion is gripping and contagious. I believe the impact of The Handbook of Sexuality Leadership on all related sexology fields will be seismic."

– Richard M. Siegel, Ph.D., LMHC, CST, CSTS, Co-Founder Modern Sex Therapy Institutes, USA

"Many of us working within the field of human sexuality deal with daily frustrations which are mostly due to lack of effective leadership in our communities. Acquiring leadership qualities and skills are not limited to a few with specific social locations. We can all become visionary leaders, inspire others, and be the change we want to see in the world. Any successful leader will tell you that having a generous and insightful mentor has been invaluable in their career. The Handbook of Sexuality Leadership brings multiple perspectives to the mix, which are liberating, inspiring, and packed with wisdom that everyone could benefit from. To our colleagues who have a passion to make our world a better place, I would say, don't just read this book, study it!"

– Sara Nasserzadeh, Ph.D., Senior Cultural and Technical advisor to the United Nations and Author of Wheel of Context for Sexuality Education

"This edgy, unique book offers a stunning array of perspectives on the intersection between sexuality and leadership. Recommended – or perhaps necessary – reading for professionals in the sexuality field as well as for students and others considering a career in sexuality."

– Inge Hansen, Psy.D., Clinical Psychologist, Director, Weiland Health Initiative, Stanford University, USA, and Coauthor of The Ethical Sellout

Handbook of Sexuality Leadership

This interdisciplinary book bridges the gap between sexuality and leadership studies and serves as a blueprint for professionals seeking to understand the rationale behind leadership styles, particularly those which facilitate conversations that educate or liberate individuals, couples, families, and communities.

The *Handbook of Sexuality Leadership* brings together education, clinical, research, and advocacy experts from the field of sexology, who each speak of their unique leadership experiences – with diversity and inclusivity in mind – and serve as a medium of empowerment and transformational influence. This innovative compendium illuminates strategic planning, community engagement, and the necessity of working with underserved or marginalized communities using a combination of leadership styles. Chapters provide tools for risk taking, organizational improvement, collaborative leadership, and cultural intelligence, as well as strategies to emancipate underrepresented groups and lead systemic change.

With questions for further thought included to provoke critical thinking and initiate transformative conversations, this book will be an essential read for anyone interested in becoming a sexuality consultant or serving in a leadership position.

James C. Wadley, Ph.D., CSTS, is Professor and Chair of the Counseling and Human Services Department at Lincoln University in Pennsylvania, USA. He is a licensed professional counselor and AASECT-certified sex therapist and supervisor. Dr. Wadley also maintains a private practice in Pennsylvania and New Jersey.

Handbook of Sexuality Leadership

Inspiring Community Engagement, Social Empowerment, and Transformational Influence

Edited by James C. Wadley

Routledge
Taylor & Francis Group

NEW YORK AND LONDON

First published 2020
by Routledge
52 Vanderbilt Avenue, New York, NY 10017

and by Routledge
2 Park Square, Milton Park, Abingdon, Oxon, OX14 4RN

Routledge is an imprint of the Taylor & Francis Group, an informa business

© 2020 Taylor & Francis

The right of James C. Wadley to be identified as the author of
the editorial material, and of the authors for their individual
chapters, has been asserted in accordance with sections 77 and 78
of the Copyright, Designs and Patents Act 1988.

Library of Congress Cataloging-in-Publication Data
A catalog record for this book has been requested

ISBN: 978-0-367-22360-1 (hbk)
ISBN: 978-0-367-22361-8 (pbk)
ISBN: 978-0-429-27450-3 (ebk)

Typeset in Sabon
by Apex CoVantage, LLC

This book is dedicated to my sons Corbin and Cairo; my nephews Jordan, Devin, and Darius; and my niece Savannah. The book is also dedicated to my Lincoln University counseling students Sarah, Silvine, Walton, Guy, Nancy, Donna, Mia, Jessie, Elizabeth, Shaneequa, Nicole, and Gregory whom I expect to become leaders in their communities.

Contents

Biosketches

Editor

James C. Wadley, Ph.D. is Professor and Chair of the Counseling and Human Services Department at Lincoln University. As a scholar-practitioner, he is a licensed professional counselor and maintains a private practice in the States of Pennsylvania and New Jersey.

He is the founding editor of the scholarly, interdisciplinary journal, the *Journal of Black Sexuality and Relationships* (University of Nebraska Press). He is also the founder and Principal of the Association of Black Sexologists and Clinicians and his professional background in human sexuality education, educational leadership, and program development has enabled him to galvanize scholars and practitioners in the field of sexology across the world.

His research and publication interests include sexual decision-making among young adults, masculinity development and conceptions of fatherhood by non-custodial fathers, and HIV/AIDS prevention. He has written undergraduate and graduate courses and authored 22 courses for the Master of Science in Counseling program for Lincoln University (Pennsylvania). In addition, he recently coauthored 13 doctoral-level courses for the Theological Seminary of Puerto Rico. In 2015, Dr. Wadley earned his NBCC-International Mental Health Facilitator certification after spending time with Rwandan therapists discussing the impact of genocide and trauma in the early 1990s. In 2016, he helped develop curricula and conducted a sexuality education course at the University of Muhimbili in Tanzania for the nursing and midwifery program. Later that year, he developed and taught an applied research methods course at Cape Peninsula University of Technology in Cape Town, South Africa. In 2017, Dr. Wadley's work and advocacy domestically and abroad enabled him to complete his first documentary, *Raw to Reel: Race, Drugs, and Sex in Trenton, New Jersey*, which captures some of the challenges that emerge in addiction and recovery. Finally, in 2018, Dr. Wadley co-edited *The Art of Sex Therapy Supervision* (Routledge), which is a book devoted to the clinical experiences of supervisors and supervisees in the field of sex therapy. The book received AASECT's 2019 Book of the Year Award. Dr. Wadley received his Doctorate of Philosophy degree in Education from the University of Pennsylvania with a concentration in Educational Leadership and Human Sexuality Education. He earned a Master of Science in Education degree in School Psychology from the University of Kentucky after completing his B.A. in Psychology from Hampton University. Finally, he holds a clinical postgraduate certificate from Thomas Jefferson University/Council for Relationships in Philadelphia and is an AASECT Certified Sex Therapist Supervisor. These credentials and a wealth of domestic and international clinical experiences have catapulted him to be one of the nation's best marriage, family, and sexuality clinicians.

Tanya M. Bass, MS, MEd, CHES®, CSE is the founder of the North Carolina Sexual Health Conference (NCSEXCON). She has over 20 years of experience in health education, pregnancy prevention, HIV/STDs, reproductive health, and sexual health. Tanya is a member of the Women of Color Sexual Health Network (WoCSHN), the Association of Black Sexologist and Clinicians (ABSC), the American Association of Sexuality Educators, Counselors, and Therapists (AASECT), and the North Carolina Society for Public Health Education (NCSOPHE). She is a Certified Health Education Specialist (CHES) and an AASECT Certified Sexuality Educator (CSE). She is a current member of the Editorial Board for the *American Journal of Sexuality Education.* Tanya is an alumna of North Carolina Central University's (NCCU) Department of Public Health Education, where she has served as an adjunct instructor for the past 15 years. Currently, Tanya is the lead instructor for Human Sexuality. Tanya is committed to sexual health equity and has a Master of Education and completing doctoral studies at Widener University in Human Sexuality Studies. She is a member of Alpha Kappa Alpha Sorority, Incorporated®.

Jenna Benyounes always had a passion for improving the lives of women. After completing school as a Certified Nurse Midwife (CNM) and Women's Health Nurse Practitioner (WHNP) she continued her education in the field of sexuality. Her clinical specialty includes painful intercourse, recurrent vaginitis, low libido, and menopause. She is current faculty at Georgetown University and believes that knowledge is potential power. She serves as a consultant to other providers and creates educational programs, providers, and patients about their sexuality.

Denise Ford Brown earned her Ph.D. in the field of Human Services with a specialization in Clinical Social Work. After working in Social Work and Mental Health for seven years, Dr. Brown starting teaching part time at Delaware Community College and then onto Lincoln University as an Assistant Professor in the Psychology and Human

Services Department. Dr. Brown is also the Field Placement Coordinator for Lincoln's Human Service students and co-runs a Lincoln grant for opioids research. Dr. Brown is a mentor for students who are doing research in traumatic brain injury during the summer. Recently, Dr. Brown has been involved in research surrounding the LGBTQ community involving the issues of discrimination and bullying which is a continual process. Currently, Dr. Brown has seven years of teaching experience at the college level.

Carole Clements serves as Dean of Undergraduate Education and Associate Professor of Contemplative Psychology at Naropa University in Boulder, Colorado, teaching courses in Dynamics of Intimate Relationships, Erotic Intelligence, and Sexual Narratives. Carole is also a mindfulness-based, LGBTQPIA+ inclusive psychotherapist specializing in issues of gender and sexuality for conventional and alternative, monogamous, and consensually non-monogamous partnerships and relationship constellations. With a B.A. in Political Science from Syracuse University, a Master of Arts in Psychology – Contemplative Psychotherapy and a Master of Fine Arts in Creative Writing (both from Naropa University) Carole's research interests and scholarship in erotic justice, sexual narration, whiteness, intersectionality, critical race theory, and queer temporality are informed and enlivened. Carole has presented on "Queering Time and Space: Beyond the Binary of Gender and Sexual Orientation in Group Psychotherapy" and "Minding the Gap: Gender and Sexuality in the Group Context" at the Annual Meeting of the American Group Therapy Association. Carole's article "The Erotic Academy: How Mindfulness Misses the Mark" was published in *Naropa Magazine* in November 2016. Carole identifies as queer and uses the pronouns they/them/theirs or "Carole." Carole is pursuing a doctorate in critical sexual studies at the California Institute of Integral Studies.

Melanie Davis, Ph.D., CSE, CSES, is a founding partner in the New Jersey Center for Sexual Wellness. She is a professional development provider and speaker on sexuality, and she been on the adjunct faculty of Widener and Drexel Universities and the American Medical Student Association's Sexual Health Leadership Program. She is a Certified Sexuality Educator and Supervisor through the American Association of Sexuality Educators, Counselors and Therapists. She is the Our Whole Lives Sexuality Education Program Associate for the Unitarian Universalist Association and author of *Sexuality and Our Faith: A Companion to Our Whole Lives Sexuality Education for Grades 7–9* (2nd ed.) and *Our Whole Lives Sexuality Education for Older Adults* and was a developmental editor for *Our Whole Lives Sexuality Education for Grades 7–9* (2nd ed.).

Richelle Frabotta has been a professional community-based Sexuality Educator since 1992, certified as an Educator by the American Association of Sexuality Educator Counselors and Therapists since 1996 and as a Supervisor since 2015. She teaches a multitude of subjects that are Human Sexuality to 4th–12th grades in schools, institutions of higher education, public, private, and nonprofit organizations, faith communities, alcohol and drug rehabilitation facilities, jails – anywhere she is invited – for a cumulative number of students in the thousands. When training colleagues and those working in human services, she emphasizes that sexuality education should be taught from a medically accurately informed, compassionate, and person-centered perspective with methods that are developmentally relevant, culturally appropriate, grounded in research, and informed by a code of ethics. She never forgets that teaching also means learning from her students.

Richelle is proud of her focus on individuals with atypical and divergent learning styles. In specific, she has authored curricula, trained staff, provided group education to parents, caregivers and self-advocates, and offered consultation for those in the Intellectual/Developmental Disabilities, Learning Disabilities, Autism Spectrum, and Traumatic Brain Injury communities. Most notably in 1997, she established a full-service sexuality education program for the Butler County Board of DD (Ohio) that is still operating today under the leadership of one of her former students. Since 2009, Richelle has worked with Council of Governments (COGs) and respective Superintendents to offer multiple on-going sexuality education services throughout Ohio. In 2017, she was invited by the Ohio Department of Developmental Disabilities to present throughout the four regions and continues to provide support, resources, and consultation to the DODD Regional Liaisons. She is happy that a historically underserved population and those whom assist are finally getting and giving attention to these quality of life and equity-based topics.

Currently, Richelle is at Miami University, Oxford, Ohio, where she serves as an Instructor in the Family Science and Social Work Department; Directing the Dennis L. Carlson Sexuality Education Studies Center, and wrapping up her doctoral program, Leadership, Culture and Curriculum, in the first Educational Leadership department in the United States. Her two-plus-decade experiences in community-based education informs her research. Richelle's scholarship challenges contemporary sex ed curriculum standards (centering on the benefits of a comprehensive curriculum) and teaching preparation practices (supporting those who want to be/are credentialed and trained). She is an active volunteer member for AASECT having served in numerous leadership roles. She also has served Look Both Ways (Colorado), Health Care Education and Training (Indiana), and Parents Families/Friends of Lesbians and Gays (Ohio), state of Ohio maternal and child health committees, teen pregnancy prevention groups, and is a singer for a classic rock band. Raised in a traditional Catholic home and strongly influenced by education professionals who value the power of progressive teaching pedagogy, Richelle has a profound respect for diversity of all kinds, believes in prevention education and endeavors to empower people to make healthy choices for sexual pleasure, health, and wellness. Teaching about Human Sexuality is Richelle's passion . . . she loves her work and can think of nothing else she'd rather do than talk about sex/ual/ity!

Shadeen Francis, LMFT is a marriage and family therapist, educator, and author specializing in sex therapy and social justice. She has been featured on platforms like 6-ABC, the *New York Times*, *Reader's Digest*, and NBC to share her expertise, and she speaks internationally on topics such as self-esteem, sexual intimacy, and pleasure. Her curricula on healthy relationships are implemented nationally, and her signature combination of warmth, humor, and compassion has allowed her to develop interprofessional training programs that raise the bar for humanistic healthcare.

Shadeen's belief is that the world is built on the strengths of communities. This worldview has propelled her to focus on underserved populations: ethnic and cultural minorities, the kinky/poly/queer communities, and victims of economic hardship. Her work allows people of all backgrounds to improve their relationships and live in peace and pleasure.

Sydney Fowler identifies as genderqueer and uses "They and Them" pronouns. They are the Administrative Assistant for the Gender Institute for Teaching and Advocacy (GITA) at Metropolitan State University of Denver. Sydney has worked with LGBTQIA communities since 2010 in professional, academic, and community settings. As the former Program Coordinator of LGBTQ Student Resource Center, they personally trained over 600 people to become stronger advocates for our communities. They have presented at local, state, and national conferences including Creating Change on subjects including LGBTQIA activism and leadership, intersectionality of identity, Non-monogamy, and surviving interpersonal violence. In 2016 they published their first academic article in *New Directions Folklore* titled "More Different Than the Same: Customary Characterization of Alternative Relationship Groups and Types."

Kirsten deFur is a sexuality educator and trainer specializing in utilizing sex-positive educational approaches, teaching about healthy and unhealthy relationships, and preventing sexual and intimate partner violence. A contributing author to the curricula *Teaching Safer Sex*, *Sex Ed in the Digital Age*, and *The American Journal of Sexuality Education*, Kirsten is the editor of the 4th edition of the Center for Sex Education's curriculum *Unequal Partners: Teaching About Power, Consent, and Healthy Relationships*.

Kirsten has been facilitating workshops since 2001 in a variety of settings for participants of all ages, especially as an Our Whole Lives Facilitator and Trainer with the Unitarian Universalist Association.

Kirsten is the coauthor of the 2nd edition of Our Whole Lives for grades 4–6 and the accompanying Parent Guide.

Kirsten received her Master of Public Health from Columbia University's Mailman School of Public Health in Sexuality & Health and is currently pursuing a Business Certificate at Columbia University's School of Professional Studies. She enjoys the critical analysis of social and cultural constructs of sexuality with her sexuality-based book club, made up of sexuality professionals throughout NYC. She shares insights on topics related to sexuality education on her blog, fearlesssexualityeducator.com, and tweets with the handle @FearlessSexEd.

Kirsten lives in Brooklyn, New York and brings as much enthusiasm to cooking, biking, and cats as she does to sexuality education.

Dr. Jayleen Galarza is a licensed clinical social worker (LCSW) in Pennsylvania and an Associate Professor within the Social Work department at Shippensburg University. She is also a certified sex therapist through the American Association of Sexuality Educators, Counselors, and Therapists (AASECT). She completed her Ph.D. in Human Sexuality at Widener University with a focus on exploring the intersections of queer, Latina identities and experiences.

In addition to her academic and clinical work, Dr. Galarza is involved in various national service initiatives. Some of her service work includes being appointed to the Council for Social Work Education's (CSWE) Council on Sexual Orientation and Gender Identity/Expression. Most recently, she also completed a two-year term as cochair of AASECT's annual conference.

Katherine Glick, LPC, LCADC, ACS, MAC, SAP is the founder of Personal Evolution LLC & Fishtown Wellness Center, a holistic and integrative psychotherapy and education practice. Her professional background includes 11 years of clinical and management experience working in clinical mental health and addiction treatment. She also has held adjunct and part-time instructor positions in higher education for the past eight years, teaching psychology, addictions, social work, and counseling courses at the undergraduate, graduate, and continuing education level. Her recent clinical and educational foci have included sexuality- and gender-based counseling, education, and therapist trainings.

Patrick Grant, M.A., MPH is a fourth-year Doctor of Clinical Psychology (PsyD.) candidate at LaSalle University, whose interests include examining the intersections of sexual health, mental wellness, and religiosity among Black sexual and gender minorities. As a sexual health educator in St. Louis, Missouri, Grant worked to promote sexual wellness among young Black men who identified as gay, bisexual, and queer; as well as among individuals of varying sexual identities with cognitive disabilities. As a sexual health educator in Philadelphia, Pennsylvania, Grant collaborated with self-identifying Black LGBT youth to develop a teen pregnancy prevention curriculum for sexual minority emerging adults.

A podcaster, presenter, and group facilitator, Grant has provided an array of domestic and international presentations. His liberation-focused presentations, such as "We Should All Be 'Finger in the Boo-tyhole Ass Bitches,'" has afforded him the opportunity to engage with audiences in Chicago, Illinois, St. Thomas, and Cape Town, South Africa. His recent published works have focused on the ethnographic and autoethnographic study of Black same sex attracted men; and have examined various topics related to this cohort, such as the availability of truly sexually liberating spaces for Black queer men in metropolitan areas. Grant is currently working on his dissertation, which will center on Black queer men's experiences with internalized homonegativity. In his downtime, Grant enjoys food, wine, and singing.

Leah Hollis is a noted national expert on workplace bullying. She has conducted lectures at Oxford University, the University of Milan, for the American Council of Education (ACE), and for National Confer-ence on Race and Ethnicity (NCORE). Her most recent book, *The Coercive Community College; Bullying and Its Costly Impact on the Mission to Serve Underrepresented Population* (2016) is an exten-sion of her work on bullying in higher education. Other notable work includes, *Bully in the Ivory Tower: How Aggression and Incivility Erode American Higher Education* (2012), which is based on inde-pendent research on 175 colleges and universities.

Dr. Hollis has taught at Northeastern University, the New Jersey Institute of Technology, and Rutgers University. She earned her Doc-torate of Education from Boston University, as a Martin Luther King, Jr. Fellow. Also, Dr. Hollis continued her professional training at Harvard University's Graduate School of Education, Higher Educa-tion Management Development Program. With certification in Project Management and Executive Leadership at Stanford University and Cornell University, respectively, she is also the president and founder of her own consultant group, Patricia Berkly, LLC, a healthy work-place advocate at www.diversitytrainingconsultants.com. She is cur-rently on the faculty at Morgan State University.

Jeanae Hopgood-Jones is a couples and family therapist, clinical sexolo-gist, and sexuality educator in the Philadelphia area. She originally hails from Brooklyn, New York and holds two Master's degrees in Marriage & Family Therapy (MFT) and Human Sexuality Education (M.Ed.). She is currently a doctoral candidate at Widener University working on her dissertation for a Ph.D. in Human Sexuality Stud-ies. Her professional memberships and affiliations include WOCSHN (Women of Color Sexual Health Network), AAMFT (American Asso-ciation of Marriage and Family Therapists), ABSC (Association of Black Sexologists & Clinicians), AASECT (American Association of Sexuality Educators, Clinicians and Therapists), and the Black Schol-ars in Human Sexuality (Widener chapter). In addition, she is also a member of Gamma Eta Rho – the Human Sexuality Honor Society. She is the founder of the blog www.blackangelmom.com which focuses on perinatal loss in the black community as well as family creation. Her passions include working with LGBTQ+ black couples, individuals, parenting, family of origin challenges, fertility issues, femme empowerment, processing grief and loss, black feminism, racial justice, and healthy sexuality.

Dr. George James, LMFT speaks, counsels, consults, coaches, and teaches people how to overcome everyday relational struggles to build successful connections in love, family, and career. With a practical approach to relationships and life, Dr. James helps bring success within the reach of those he influences! Dr. James has been a reoccurring expert guest on radio, TV, and online programs including The TODAY Show on NBC, Good Day Philadelphia on FOX29, NBC10, CBS3, and many others. He is also a reoccurring relationship contributor to *Ebony* magazine. He is a licensed marriage and family therapist who specializes in helping couples improve the quality of their relationship, reconcile conflicts, and overcome intense situations such as affairs, lack of communication, parenting struggles, and much more. He also works extensively with professional athletes, adult men, and young adult men on various issues including defining manhood, career, and work-life balance. His expertise also includes treating actors, entertainers, college students, faith-based concerns, anxiety, and depression. In addition, he speaks and consults with universities, for profit and nonprofit organizations, and family-owned businesses. Dr. James is devoted to helping people improve their quality of life, and to be involved in the healing of their wounds and the enrichment of their relationships. Dr. James is a staff therapist and an AAMFT Approved supervisor at Council for Relationships. In addition, Dr. James is the Program Director for the Couple & Family Therapy Program at Thomas Jefferson University. Dr. James is president and CEO of George Talks, LLC, a communication and consulting company. Dr. James is a nationally recognized speaker, seminar presenter, and lecturer on various topics. Dr. James has taught, presented, spoken, and consulted with multiple businesses, organizations, universities, and places of faith. Dr. James is a recognized media personality, speaker, workshop leader, and lecturer on various topics. He has had over 400 speaking and media appearances in the past seven years. His breadth of expertise includes a special emphasis on topics geared towards couples, men, professional athletes, actors/entertainers, musicians, college students, family-owned businesses, and people of color. Dr. James is devoted to working with people to help them improve their quality of life, to be involved in the healing of their wounds and enrichment of their relationships. Dr. James attended Villanova University as a Presidential Scholar, and majored in Psychology and concentrated in Africana Studies. He received his Masters of Family Therapy degree from Drexel University and his doctorate in Clinical Psychology from Immaculata University. He is married to Candace and they are parents to their beautiful daughter, Nalani, and cheerful son, Alexander.

Bianca I. Laureano is an award-winning sexologist, educator, and revolutionary lover. She identifies as a LatiNegra, Black Puerto Rican, queer, fat, femme. Bianca's focus has been on creating intersectional and inclusive curricula for trans and queer youth, immigrant youth, and supporting seasoned professionals in evolving their practice. She is the foundress of ANTEUP! a professional development virtual freedom school. Women of Color Sexual Health Network (WOCSHN), The LatiNegrxs Project. She's been in the U.S. sexuality field for over two decades and has written several curricula and lesson plans including the New York City Department of Health and Mental Hygiene's *Sexual and Reproductive Justice Discussion Guide*, Planned Parenthood's Peer Education Institute Curricula, *What's the REAL DEAL about Love & Solidarity* (2015), and *Communications Mixtape: Speak on it! Vol 1.*

Satori Madrone has been a holistic practitioner in private practice for 23 years, having received a B.A. in American Indian Studies and Sociology from the University of Minnesota, Twin Cities, a M.A. in Transpersonal Counseling Psychology from Naropa University in Boulder, Colorado, and is currently pursuing a Ph.D. in critical sexuality studies from California Institute of Integral Studies in San Francisco. The founder of Boulder Sexuality and Relationship Counseling, Satori identifies as queer and is an Applied Existential, sexuality, gender, and relationship therapist with a focus in LGBTQPIA+ populations and diverse relational orientations. Satori is Adjunct Faculty at Naropa University and teaches Feminist and Queer Theory Methods of Inquiry.

Katherine Martinez is Associate Professor and Interim Chair of Gender, Women, and Sexualities Studies and the Interim Director of the Gender Institute for Teaching and Advocacy (GITA) at Metropolitan State University of Denver. Having received their Ph.D. in Sociology from the University of Colorado at Boulder, with additional certification in Women's Studies and Ethnic Studies, they teach on a range of topics relating to bodies/embodiment, queer theory, and multicultural genders and sexualities. Katherine's research interests are in queer identities, practices, and activism, as well as family violence. They have published their BDSM research in the *Journal of Sex Research* and *Journal of Homosexuality* and copublished their sibling violence and trauma research in the *Journal of GLBT Family Violence* and the *Journal of Interpersonal Violence.*

Melina McConatha is Assistant Professor of Human Services at Lincoln University. Her research includes gender, sexuality, eco-feminism, and sustainability. Dr. McConatha is the faculty advisor for a student powered LGTBQ Ally group at Lincoln University and is currently creating a LGTBQA Resource Manual from a collection of data gathered from 25 of the nation's most attended Historically Black Colleges and Universities. She lives with her daughter on a small sustainable farm on the Brandywine River in Pennsylvania.

Dulcinea/Alex Pitagora holds a Master of Arts (M.A.) in Psychology from the New School for Social Research, a Master of Social Work (MSW) from New York University, a Master of Education (MEd) and a Doctorate in Clinical Sexology (Ph.D.) from Widener University, and is an AASECT Certified Sex Therapist (CST). Pitagora has a practice in New York City that includes individual, couples/dyads, and multipartner therapy. Pitagora's practice is person-centered and strengths-based, focuses on self-determination and empowerment, and is LGBQ, trans, poly, and kink affirmative. Pitagora is an adjunct professor of sexual health at New York University, has published articles and chapters in peer-reviewed journals and books, and presented at conferences on the topics of alternative sexuality and gender diversity. Pitagora conducts research, lectures, and seminars pertaining to these communities; is the founder ofManhattanAlternative.com, an alternative lifestyle affirmative provider listing; and is a co-organizer of the AltSex NYC Conference. Pitagora is Kink Doctor in the Web series by the same name.

Candace Robertson-James, DrPH is an assistant professor and director of the Master of Public Health Program at LaSalle University. Dr. Robertson-James' research interests include health disparities. She has led and evaluated community participatory research initiatives involving multiple sectors (health, community, school, faith, etc.) promoting health in diverse and underserved communities for over 10 years. Dr. Robertson-James has participated in research exploring the role of discrimination in health risk as well as the role of faith institutions in sexual and relationship violence risk reduction and prevention interventions. She has also served as the program evaluator for programs assessing the role of gender in health, programs integrating HIV risk reduction into domestic violence services, health education initiatives targeting women with a history of incarceration as well as other groups of women and heart health initiatives. In addition, she also teaches on a variety of public health, health promotion and research topics.

Her ultimate goal is to serve passionately, promote endearing change and to leave a lasting impression that will inspire action. Dr. Robertson-James received her Bachelor of Science in biology from Villanova University, her Master of Public Health from MCP Hahnemann University, and her Doctor of Public Health from the Drexel University School of Public Health.

Bill Taverner, M.A., is the executive director of The Center for Sex Education and is the editor-in-chief of the *American Journal of Sexuality*

Education. He is the author or editor of more than 75 publications, including teaching manuals and curricula, college readers, journal articles, chapters, lesson plans, and other contributions in sexuality education. Bill is the chief editor of the third edition of *Teaching Safer Sex*, which received the prestigious AASECT Book Award, given by the American Association of Sexuality Educators, Counselors and Therapists. He is the coauthor of *Making Sense of Abstinence*; associate editor of *How I Got Into Sex . . . Ed*, and editor or coeditor of eight editions of *Taking Sides: Clashing Views in Human Sexuality*. Bill served on advisory boards for a number of organizations, including the inaugural board for the graduate Sexual Health Certificate program at the University of Michigan, and on an advisory panel convened by former U.S. Surgeon General David Satcher to provide input on the development of a curriculum to help parents talk with their children about sex. A trainer of thousands throughout the United States, who has twice advocated for sexuality education at U.S. Congressional briefings, Bill has received other national awards recognizing his leadership in sexuality education: the first "Schiller Prize" given by AASECT for best workshop using interactive strategies; Planned Parenthood's "Golden Apple Award" for leadership in education; a Sexual Intelligence award naming him named "one of the country's pre-eminent sex educators, trainers, and sex education theorists," and the AASECT Sexuality Educator Award.

Dr. Tralonda Triplett currently serves as Director of Operations at the Institute for Successful Leadership, Inc. and uses her varied expertise to examine cultural influences on health-seeking behaviors in vulnerable populations. In addition, Dr. Triplett advocates for fair and ethical treatment of public health research participants nationally and worldwide. Dr. Triplett's commitment to comprehensive wellness and HIV/AIDS prevention in racial and ethnic communities, emerging adult populations, adolescents and women continues to drive her efforts to design, implement, and evaluate health promotion strategies. An internship at the Centers for Disease Control and Prevention-Office of the Director for HIV/AIDS Prevention solidified public health as her professional passion. It is that passion that she saw reflected in professionals at UM that encouraged her to complete both her Master of Public Health and Doctorate of Philosophy in Epidemiology from the Miller School of Medicine. Dr. Triplett came to the UM Graduate Programs in Public Health after completing degrees in Business Administration and Industrial and Systems Engineering at Clark Atlanta University and Georgia Institute of Technology and eagerly anticipates contributing to public health policy, planning, and practice.

Dr. Daniel N. Watter received his doctoral degree from New York University in 1985, and has also earned a post-graduate certificate in Medical Humanities from Drew University. He is licensed as both a psychologist and a marital and family therapist. In addition, he is

Board Certified in Sex Therapy by the American Association of Sexuality Educators, Counselors, and Therapists (AASECT), and the American Board of Sexology (ACS), of which also holds Fellowship status. Dr. Watter is an AASECT certified sex therapy supervisor, and has been elected to Fellowship Status in the International Society for the Study of Women's Sexual Health (ISSWSH).

In addition to his clinical practice, Dr. Watter has held several faculty appointments. He has served as an adjunct professor of Psychology at Fairleigh Dickinson, Drew, and Seton Hall Universities, a clinical instructor of OB/GYN and Women's Health at University of Medicine and Dentistry of New Jersey-New Jersey Medical School, and a clinical assistant professor of psychiatry and behavioral medicine at the New York College of Osteopathic Medicine. Dr. Watter is also a former member of the medical staff of the Saint Barnabas Medical Center in Livingston, New Jersey, and served on the Medical Center's Ethics Committee.

Dr. Watter is a member of several professional organizations, and has been elected to leadership positions in many. He has completed two terms on the New Jersey Psychological Association's Ethics Committee where he spent two years as the Committee's chairperson. He has also served two terms as the Secretary/Treasurer of the Society for Sex Therapy and Research (SSTAR), where he previously served as Membership Officer. Dr. Watter is also the former chair of the Diplomate Certification Committee for the American Association for Sexuality Educators, Counselors, and Therapists (AASECT). Currently, he is serving as the Immediate Past-President of SSTAR. In 2009, Dr. Watter was appointed by New Jersey Governor Jon Corzine to the State Board of Psychological Examiners. He was reappointed by New Jersey Governor Chris Christie in 2017.

A frequent lecturer at professional meetings throughout North America, Dr. Watter is also the author of several professional articles and book chapters on topics such as sexual function and dysfunction, and ethics in healthcare practice. He is currently writing a textbook on Humanistic/Existential Approaches to Sex Therapy Practice.

Kamilah Marie Woodson, Ph.D. As a licensed Clinical Psychologist and the former Associate Managing Director of the Association of Black Psychologists, Dr. Woodson has over 20 years of experience working with individuals, couples, and groups. Her clinical interests include, but are not limited to, sexual victimization, sexual orientation concerns, interpersonal relationships, trauma, and depression. She is a graduate of the California School of Professional Psychology, Los Angeles, where she received the Ph.D. and M.A. degrees in Clinical Psychology and earned her Baccalaureate degree in Psychology from the University of Michigan, Ann Arbor.

Dr. Kamilah M. Woodson is the former Associate Dean/Director of Graduate Studies and a Professor in the Howard University School of

Education, Department of Human Development and Psycho-educational Studies, Counseling Psychology Ph.D. Program. Dr. Woodson is also a Professor in the Department of Psychiatry at the Howard University College of Medicine/Howard University Hospital. In addition to her dual appointment at Howard University, Dr. Woodson was an adjunct professor at the Chicago School of Professional Psychology, D.C., served on the Editorial Board of the *Journal of Negro Education* as the Book Review Editor for the last seven years, is the program evaluator on several NSF-Sponsored research projects, and works as a consultant with the QEM Network, Washington, D.C. She was previously the Director of Training for the Counseling Psychology Ph.D. Program (seven years), Director of the Howard University Office of Nursing Research, Division of Nursing, College of Pharmacy, Nursing & Allied Health Sciences, and the Director of the NSF sponsored (AGEP) Alliance for Graduate Education and the Professoriate Program at Howard University.

Dr. Woodson conducted research as a MHSAC Research Fellow at the Morehouse School of Medicine, Atlanta Georgia and works with the Howard University College of Medicine, Department of Psychiatry as a Research Associate, Professor, and Clinician. Her research is in the areas of health disparities, including the factors that impact health-related risk behaviors (HIV/AIDS and Substance Abuse) among people of color, including incarcerated populations, LGBTQIA identity research, and STEM leadership among women of color. Dr. Woodson also conducts research on the impact of global colorism and will further this research as result of being a recent Fulbright-Hayes Fellow (Brazil, South America).

Introduction

James C. Wadley

Colleagues at a local small college recently asked me to help them develop a graduate-level program that was devoted to leadership studies. The invitation to do the course construction emerged from the institutional recognition that their students could benefit from learning about an array of leadership theories and experiences as well as engage in reflective discourse that allowed for them to consider how individuals position themselves across a variety of contexts (e.g., community, academic, governmental, corporate, legal, medical, etc.). In addition, we conceptualized that the program could help students think critically about how leaders emerge in their respective fields and how those professionals are asked to make critical decisions that may impact present functioning and possibly the trajectory of future growth.

The intended program would be interdisciplinary in nature and serve as a bridge between some of the disciplines that were already a part of the college. The integrative nature of the program would allow the college to refine but enhance the tentacles of their engagement within and beyond the greater Philadelphia area. It was assumed that once the program was completed, the university's mission and ideas could reach communities around the world through the work of its faculty and its students.

I took several months exploring other graduate programs dedicated to leadership studies and reviewed various theoretical models that discussed the nature of leadership. During my research and reflection, I realized that my journey within the field of human sexuality, I had relatively few conversations about the use and application of leadership in communities and how positioning oneself in various spaces requires flexibility, adaptation, and patience. There may have been dialogs that applied some of the principles of leadership, but I had not been a part of a discussion that intentionally centered the concept of leadership.

With the thought of centering leadership and sexuality in mind, I decided to pursue writing a book that highlighted my professional journey. It didn't take long to think about how my social locations (e.g., Black, male, able-bodied, heterosexual, cis, middle class, etc.) influenced or disrupted my advancement at my institution, private practice, or consultative efforts. I quickly realized that, for this project dedicated to leadership, there were a multitude of experiences that could be shared from respected colleagues who may have taken a different path to become influential towards their peers and communities.

When the call for manuscript proposals was sent out, I had no idea if anyone would be interested in addressing the concept of leadership in the field of sexology. For some professionals I asked in person or by telephone, I simply asked the question, "How did you know what path to take to get to wherever you may be at professionally?" More often than not, there was initial silence for a moment or two. After the silence, these professionals started telling their story of how they figured things out on their own or they happened to advance from one level to the next because of the support they had. For some, their eyes widened as they considered the possibility of offering their personal experience and insight into how to grow within the field. For others who were unsure, I merely rattled off some of their professional accomplishments and experiences and the possible contribution they could make to a project like this.

The Handbook of Sexuality Leadership: Inspiring Community Engagement, Social Empowerment, and Transformational Influence is an interdisciplinary book that serves as a bridge between the fields of human sexuality and leadership studies. It is a blueprint for professionals who seek to understand how, when, where, and the rationale for selected leadership styles in a variety of circumstances and populations. As a professional map, this book empowers professionals who want to learn how to engage or serve communities who seek solutions to multifaceted and sensitive challenges. Emergent complex issues sometimes require time and resource-efficient responses in environments that are constantly evolving.

Recent conservative political shifts have galvanized leaders in the field of sexuality to think differently about how to confront long-standing traditions and paradigms (e.g., heterosexism, gender binaries, notions of privilege, etc.). Thus, this book includes discussions about the utility of collaboration, strategic decision-making and networking, access, and initiating and enduring systemic change. It explores risk taking, organizational change, the importance of various leadership styles, cultural intelligence, and engagement with underserved or marginalized populations. This book is divided into four sections. The first part of the handbook addresses leadership in sex education; the second segment is devoted to leadership in sexuality activism, counseling/therapy; the third section focuses on sexuality leadership and mentoring; and the final portion of the handbook focuses on leadership in sexuality consultation and special issues.

The chapter authors and I are proud of this work because of its spirit of inclusion, diversity, and depth. The field of sexuality is comprised of a variety of professionals who represent many disciplines and the contributions to this initiative reflect that range. This compendium of research, essays, and narrative experiences is a necessary read for anyone who seeks to become or evolve as a sexuality consultant or serve in a leadership position because of the contributions that are made by chapter authors who are recognized experts in the field. Finally, we hope that this book allows for a different conversation about the many facets and diverse faces of sexuality leadership.

Section I

Leadership in Sexuality Education

1 So, Exactly What Is "Appropriate"?

Sex/ual/ity Education and Developmental Disabilities

Richelle Frabotta

2019 . . . Sex Ed Right This Very Minute

Teaching about human sexuality in the United States can be a daunting task for numerous reasons. Given the traditionalist cultural climate, an essentialist approach to public education, attacks by social conservatives on "appropriate" values and behaviors while adding to the rampant misinformation about what is sexuality education, offers challenges of a monumental proportion that no math educator has ever experienced. Sexuality education is very much a matter of national discourse and public policy and includes political platforming and personal agendas. Disability complicates this multifaceted conversation even further.

Accruing information about one's sexuality is a lived experience. From birth to death, people are inundated with feelings, experiences, desires, and consequences from conscious behaviors and nonconsensual situations. Many people think that their unique way of interpreting and understanding sexuality is the right way, perhaps the only way. Plenty of ideologies and religious doctrine clearly spell out the right and the wrong, the black and the white of sex, sexual feelings, and identity. It would seem that society produces and is inundated with "sexperts" who are simply informed by perceptions and values informed mandates. Sexuality is personal and, therefore, familiar, so many people disregard the science, the data. Societally platformed or even personally platformed "sexperts" often fail to acknowledge that sexuality education is an interdisciplinary, research-informed area of instruction teeming with ethical dilemmas, diverse pedagogy and praxis. In fact, quality sexuality education is transformative at least and liberating at most – especially for the oppressed and marginalized.

There are numerous curricula written for teaching about human sexuality. The best of these are student-centered, culturally relevant, medically accurate, and focus on being socially just and inclusive. Quality curricula are designed to teach topics in an age-appropriate and developmentally relevant manner with an emphasis on prevention of unwanted outcomes, self-reflection, and skills building. Ultimately, the enduring understanding is about sexual health and well-being. Topics are varied and lesson plans are constructed in a goal-oriented and outcomes-dependent manner. The philosophy behind (pedagogy) and how those topics are taught (praxis) are key to a successful student learning experience. Current best practices encourage reflection about personal values and beliefs, effective communication skills, and opportunities for decision-making that affirms and empowers the learner for personal agency, autonomy, and pleasure.

Sex/ual/ity, written in this form with forward slashes, is a visual reminder that the word contains additional words and many concepts. *Sex* refers to a label assigned at birth based on genital presentation as well as a multitude of behaviors in which one may choose to engage throughout the lifespan. *Sexual* pertains to one's capacity for feelings and sense of erotic energy. And *Sexuality* is about identity: how one presents, represents, and walks through the world at any given moment. Sex/ual/ity is understanding that there is a continuum of identities that is not necessarily restricted to a binary. Sex/ual/ity education recognizes that communication, connection, and community are a few important "C" words that are relevant throughout the lifespan. Sex/ual/ity is facts, statistics, physiological functions and responses, *and* integral core values, beliefs, and perceptions. In short, sex/ual/ity is about being human. Thus, sexuality is a connecting factor among humans and may be considered universal.

Teaching about sex/ual/ity is actually teaching about humanity, health, and well-being and what is so controversial about teaching about those topics? Perhaps it is the idea that sex/ual/ity education promotes and encourages the development of personal agency and is therefore not relevant to certain populations. For example, some people prefer to think of children as "innocents" who can/will be corrupted in the classroom if exposed to "sexual ideas" too soon. This notion is cited frequently when those in society want to protect or to preserve a particular way of living complete with ideologically informed values. It makes learning anatomy and correct names for those body parts (genitals) or exploring physiological processes such as sperm production, menstruation, pubertal development, and baby making, taboo. It disallows body autonomy by teaching that private parts are where the bathing suit goes or that declining a hug from a caring adult is an afront. Some believe that keeping information and resources away from young people is the safest option to maintain a child-like view of the world. This approach is short-sighted, naïve, and does not allow for self-protection against violence. This approach has also been used for decades to further marginalize people of all ages with disabilities.

The United States has a long history where people with disabilities are viewed as child-like innocents, unteachable, and without social value. Particularly individuals who are cognitively, intellectually challenged are often overlooked and not considered to be capable of intimate partner relationships, controlling their own fertility, or setting boundaries effectively. According to Terri Couwenhoven, society characterizes the sexuality of the intellectually disabled in three ways:

1. As invisible and not a naturally occurring human experience
2. As asexual, lacking capacity for or interest in sexuality; therefore, sexual desires, need for intimacy, physical touch, and potential for partnering or even reproduction are not considered possibilities or options
3. As binary or extreme sexual identities, such as perpetual victims in danger of sexual aggressions; or promiscuous, over-sexed, and animalistic; or as perpetrators and predators

(2007, p. 2)

These three perspectives most certainly do not apply to the majority of individuals assigned the diagnostic label of Intellectually Disabled (ID). This unfair, biased, and prejudicial categorizing has resulted in an exponential amount of rights violations and horrific abuses by familial, private provider, and state supplied "caregivers." Often these perpetrators of abuses maybe be well intentioned by acting in the spirit of protection, prevention, or intervention. However, history is full of the well-intentioned perpetrating "treatment protocols" (i.e., mandated sterilization, anti-masturbation measures, withholding education about body functions, etc.) and abuses in manner that support marginalization and isolation. This includes forcing people with disabilities to adopt values and perform behaviors that are not authentic, intuitive, comfortable, or genuine.

The invisibility and dismissal of people with disabilities as sexual beings is perhaps the most problematic of the abuses as it completely denies the basis of being human. It disallows any conversation about identity or sexual autonomy. These hostile, negative, and devaluing atrocities makes people with disabilities' developmentally relevant struggle for sexual agency a challenge and hence, moves each chronologically, naturally occurring event to the problematic. Frabotta, Baldwin, and Daugherty (2013), referring specifically to ID people as individuals, writes in the *Invested in Being ME!* curriculum:

Individuals are typically excluded from educatory discourse and programming so lack of info, insight, and safe space leaves Individuals at a great disadvantage for feeling comfortable with their sexual selves . . . AND it may leave folks who care for Individuals a bit stymied as well. Talking frankly, honestly and openly about the topics in this curriculum . . . is progressive, affirming, empowering and just the right thing to do.

(p. 5)

People with disabilities, of any age, are rarely included in sex/ual/ity education programs in any venue, including their homes. How do chronological age discordant to developmental abilities Individuals recognize and embrace their sexuality when they experience a lack of visibility and opportunity as sexual persons? How do these Individuals, who are often atypical learners and have limited access to accurate information, manage the physiological challenges of a growing, aging body? How do people with disabilities, often subject to punitive consequences for "inappropriate" sexual behavior, receive affirming, personal agency encouraging supports?

The following modified literature review examines articles and expert voices from the 1970s–2015 that question and explore the value and implementation of sex/ual/ity education for people with disabilities by considering language, theoretical and pragmatic concepts, service provision, and identified expectations.

1974

"Sex Education for the Handicapped" is a paper that was originally presented at the National Council on Family Relationships (NCFR) in 1972. Medora S. Bass at first appears to be a visionary and an advocate for sexuality education for people with disabilities. For example, she asserts that "sexuality education for the handicapped is particularly important at this time" and uses studies (her own and two others) that demonstrate better adjustment of handicapped students after completion of classes as proof for the value of sexuality education (1974, p. 27). But Bass identifies as a Consultant at the Association for Voluntary Sterilization in Pennsylvania. And she writes, "The rights of the retarded to live as a normal a life as possible is bringing up for serious discussion their rights to live together, to marry, and to have children" (1974, p. 27), while using the term *Adjustment* for an achieved positive outcome from what were the major goals of the late 1960s–1970s for handicapped people: normalization and humanization.

With rights comes realization, relationships, and responsibility which Bass identifies as important factors in sex education (1974, p. 29). She distinguishes "sex education" from "sex education for the handicapped" by first suggesting that there are similarities as the goals are the same and young handicapped students are curious to learn as well. Bass then goes on to bullet point numerous differences that, frankly, read as concerns, dangers, and warnings. Paraphrasing Bass' bullet points, the list reads that the handicapped are ignorant, socially inappropriate, but willing learners who are more inhibited and prone to homosexuality (1974, p. 30). She calls out homosexuality specifically, which is a condition that can be addressed by "severe correction and punishment . . . almost always decreases when heterosexual interests develop" (1974, p. 30). It is relevant to note that homosexuality was eliminated from the Diagnostic and Statistical Manual (DSM) as a mental health diagnosis in 1973.

Bass goes on to write that marriage may be unlikely and inadvisable as, "severe handicaps may make the chances of marriage unlikely." She continues, "these individuals must be helped to understand that it is not necessary to marry to be happy; many persons choose not to marry – many others wish they had never married" (1974, p. 30). Bass finalizes her bulleted items list by noting that "competency for parenthood should be considered by all young persons" however, it may prove burdensome for individuals who can't even take care of themselves, which merits explanation for substitute parenting (1974, p. 30). Bass, who practices a direct communication style with little reference to credentialed authors or research, further articulates her assertions about marriage and parenting education for the handicapped:

> The reasons for wanting a baby are often neurotic; while we hear much about the joys of parenthood, the sacrifices and disappointments are seldom mentioned. Marriage and parenthood have been over-romanticized; we should be honest about this. . . . Marriage is a difficult adjustment for the retarded; it is especially important that they wait about two years before having a baby. Genetic factors must be explained and they should know what their chances are of passing on their handicap.
>
> (1974, p. 30)

Wrapping up her list of differences in sexuality education for the handicapped, Bass notes that the content should be simple, repetitive, use pictures, and begin with reproductive education with "humans because it may be confusing for them to shift from the birds to people" (1974, p. 30). She also uses statistics from 1960 to define who the handicapped are and notes that special education is required "to develop their maximum capacity" (1974, p. 30). The rest of her article presents sex education ideology for the blind, the deaf, and the physical and neurologically handicapped as well as identifies seven resources to support sex education services for the handicapped.

Although Bass' differentiation and characterization of the handicapped are outrageous by today's standards, it seems important to note that Bass *does* appear to be a visionary who espouses cutting-edge, progressive ideas for her time. She coauthors with and cites historically notable sexuality educators and advocates such as Winifred Kempton and Sol Gordon. Bass also identifies Planned Parenthood and the Sex Information and Education Council of the United States (SIECUS) as quality resources for sex education of the handicapped. Although Kempton and Gordon have passed, they and the organizational resources cited continue to have a positive influence within the field today.

1979

Barbara Edmonson, from The Ohio State University, along with two colleagues, McCombs from the Cuyahoga County Board of Mental

Retardation and Wish from the Milton S. Hersey Medical Center, conducted a research study to discern, "What Retarded Adults Believe about
Sex." Edmonson et al. write:

> After administering the Socio-Knowledge and Attitudes Test to
> retarded persons aged 18–41. . . little was found between subjects'
> ages and response scores, but . . . there were significant relationships
> between sex-knowledge score and subject's IQ, adaptive behavior
> level, sex, and/or place of residence.
>
> (1979, p. 11)

This research study was especially interesting because the authors posit
that quality of life was defined more by "the universal need for social
approval, acceptability, companionship, and love" (Edmonson et al.,
1979, p. 11). This implies that matters of dating, love, marriage, sex,
and reproduction are indeed relevant to the autonomy of the retarded,
which was counter to the popular belief of the time. The research study
advances the notion that testing for sexuality knowledge is primary and
necessary to determine a starting point for sociosexual instruction. Also,
the "test first" approach offers a baseline so that knowledge gained can
be noted, therefore, literally measuring the benefit of providing sexuality
education.

The authors conclude the research study with several discoveries based
on data evaluation. The most notable conclusion and implication was
that the research lead to an advancement in actual provision of sexuality education services to intellectually disabled folks as "IQ level was
not a limitation on sexual knowledge" (Edmonson et al., 1979, p. 17).
Edmonson's final thoughts are indicative of the decade's ideas regarding
the intellectually disabled and sexuality education:

> There is still conflict over whether to instruct retarded individuals in
> socio-sexual outlooks and practices to help them function responsi-
> ble or whether to preserve a state of naiveté. In view of the sexual
> stimuli from television, magazines, acquaintances in schools and
> workshops, and even from people in the neighborhood, it should be
> clear that naiveté is not a reasonable option. Our data indicate that
> moderately and even severely retarded individuals can acquire facts
> and attitudes that are components of self-sufficient and responsible
> behavior but that most individuals were poorly prepared.
>
> (1979, p. 17)

1980s

The 1980s brought continued research and writing about how and what
to teach "mentally retarded adults." At this point, educatory and training

programs were in place in some institutions. Retrospectively, this was fortunate as the "deinstitutionalization boom" allowed the disabled, who lived long-term in isolation from larger society, to engage the community (perhaps) more prepared. The notion is that *some* education about sexuality is better than *no education*. This does not imply that the breadth, depth, quality, or best practices of those institutional programs was reflective of an accepted sexuality education standard.

Foxx, McMorrow, Storey, and Rogers (1984) in his article, "Teaching social/sexual skills to mentally retarded adults," reiterates that indeed mentally retarded folks can learn and that socio/sexual skills training is helpful; however, he criticizes that:

> most of the research related to the sexual behavior of retarded persons has focused on discovering how much they know and do sexually, rather than helping them obtain skills that may facilitate normal sociosexual development . . . developmental progress may be thwarted by illegitimate births, premarital pregnancies resulting in job loss, financial exploitation and a variety of dysfunctional sexual behaviors.
>
> (p. 9)

Foxx goes on to promote the idea of teaching interactional skills for prevention of identified negative outcomes. He advocates for a standardization of curriculum that focuses on skill building and prevention that disallows staff to add in or teach from their personal values.

Chapman and Pitceathly's (1985) contributions in their article, "Sexuality and mentally handicapped people: Issues of sex education, marriage, parenthood, and care staff attitudes," are notable for two reasons: 1. He underscores and supports Foxx's ideas. 2. He provides continuity in progressive ideas about teaching from a larger, multicultural perspective. Chapman's research is from New Zealand. Chapman asserts that "active sexual life requires a degree of responsibility and maturity that such people do not possess" (p. 227) and goes on to cite American pioneer of sexuality education for the intellectually disabled, Winnifred Kempton by noting that "it is unrealistic for normal society to demand responsible sexual behavior from people who have never been taught what constitutes responsibility and irresponsibility in sexuality" (p. 227). Chapman continues to present ideas that fortify his call to sexuality education for the disabled by noting that socially appropriate behavior, i.e., normalization, cannot occur without improving living conditions, allowing for self-determination via personal decision-making, monitoring and improving staff (caregiver) attitudes, and creating guidelines for sexuality education programs. Chapman and Pitceathly (1985) states:

> It is clear that much remains to be done if the rights of the mentally handicapped are to be realized. Parents, guardians, and care staff

can have a significant positive impact in assisting mentally handi-capped people attaining those rights. Planned programs dealing with all aspects of psycho-sexual development, marriage and parenthood and sexual problems and dysfunctions would contribute significantly to such a goal.

(p. 234)

This brief historical recounting of sexuality education for people with disabilities would be remiss if it did not include the work of the vision-ary, Winifred Kempton (June 18, 1918–August 4, 2010). By the mid-1980s, Kempton had amassed a vast and impressive amount of research and writing about the importance of quality sexuality education, spe-cifically, the design, implementation, and teaching of curricula. *Sex Edu-cation for Persons with Disabilities that Hinder Learning: A Teacher's Guide* (1988) and *Socialization and Sexuality: A Comprehensive Train-ing Guide for Professionals Helping People with Disabilities that Hinder Learning* (1993) although dated, continue to be a resource for sexuality professionals. Mrs. Kempton advocated for trained educators to deliver sexuality education services. This is an excerpt from her obituary:

> Mrs. Kempton was an educator/advocate in the field of socializa-tion, sex education and reproductive rights for persons with men-tal and physical disabilities. She lectured worldwide and published many books and articles on the subject of rights of the disabled. She received many awards for her pioneering work on behalf of the disa-bled. In addition to consulting at Elwyn Institute, Mrs. Kempton was Education Director of Planned Parenthood of Southeastern PA for many years.
>
> (www.stretchfuneralhome.com/obituary)

Mrs. Kempton understood the value of best practices and a strong ethical foundation from which to provide quality sexuality education services. Her influence for future decades of work in creating equity for the devel-opmentally disabled cannot be overestimated. A leader in the field of sexuality education, indeed.

1990s

The Association for Retarded Citizens (ARC), a state-based national advo-cacy group consisting mostly of parents, released a page-long document in 1990 simply titled, "Sexuality." This document is monumentally signifi-cant because it spells out the issue quite clearly and in no uncertain terms:

> Sexuality is a natural part of every person's life. Sexuality and sexual expression of people with mental retardation cerates diverse reactions.

This issue requires respect, understanding, caution, and an awareness of the wide array of human rights. Current social trends make the issue more urgent and complicated. The commitment to full integration into the community has given people with mental retardation new experiences, more risks, and more opportunities to make choices. The ability to make educated choices in the area of sexuality is especially critical.

(Adopted by Delegate Body, November 1990)

The document continues to relay the position of the organization complete with enumerated rights and

support for programs that encourage people with mental retardation to develop expressions of their sexuality that reflect their age and social development, acknowledge the values of their families and are socially responsible.

(ARC, 1990, p. IX)

It seems that when parents proclaim it, back it, and fight for it, change happens quickly! Such is the progress and status of sexuality education services for intellectually disabled people in the 1990s.

This decade brought with it not only an increase is researching psychosocial sexual behaviors, but also adoptable curriculum and more programming. There are notable scholarly works identifying the positive outcomes associated with treating people with intellectual disabilities as typically sexual folks with learning challenges. For example, "Before sex education: An evaluation of the sexual knowledge, experience, feelings and needs of people with mild intellectual disabilities," by Marita McCabe (1992), calls into account the challenges that people with intellectual disabilities face when their sexual selves are blatantly ignored and repressed. McCabe rang the clarion bell – from Australia – to get sexuality education curricula to focus on general sexuality topics that all learners have a right to know. It is especially important to discern the basics of sex/ual/ity (sex, sexual feelings, and identity) when one is living in the community. The assertion is that knowledge increases and skill-building eliminates "the problematic" approach that informed institutionally utilized curricula.

Another example is Crocker (1992) who authored a research study, "Data collection for the evaluation of mental retardation prevention activities: The fateful forty-three," that produced a schema for measuring the effects of prevention programs. Crocker uses "items that are quantifiable, accessible, and pertinent to disability outcomes" (p. 303). This relevant work created service indicators, risk indicators, and incidence/prevalence information that aided agencies in providing services to people with disabilities as well as those curricularists and educators who were attempting to meet the needs of this population. Although no federal standards were forthcoming, it was this work that "encouraged cooperative measures among state agencies, academic centers, service providers, and consumer organizations" in order to "reinforce our capability to achieve prevention policies and goals" (p. 316).

Marita McCabe (1993) clearly denotes that the attitude of caregivers and parents were absolutely influential in allowing adults with intellectual disabilities access to sexuality education programs. In "Sex education programs for people with mental retardation," she references data from the 1980s that suggests a real separation between what academics proposed as ideal learning opportunities and what caregivers/staff felt were necessary services to provide daily. In other words, given the unique challenges that people with intellectual disabilities face, caregivers/staff chose to attend to other concerns that they felt trumped the stated benefits of taking their client to "sex class."

David Hingsburger, an undisputed legend in the field of providing quality sexuality education theories and principles for people with disabilities, recounts a conversation with John Money in the book *I Witness: History and a Person with Developmental Disability* (1992). Money, not a fan of staff who provided service to people with disabilities, asked Hingsburger to tell the history of disabilities. Hingsburger waxed poetic for quite a while. Money then said, "David, that is the history of service provision. That is your history. It is certainly not the history of disabled people" (Hingsburger, 1992, prologue). Money went on to point out,

> minorities are demanding more of those who would provide service. They are demanding that service providers be aware of history and how history has shaped both the provider and the service recipient. The same demand should be placed on those who work with people with disabilities.
>
> (Hingsburger, 1992, prologue)

David Hingsburger recounts how he began his most rewarding and challenging work: to listen, hear, and tell individuals' stories directly, unabashedly, and with the utmost respect for autonomy.

Sexuality education services funded by the government came to a screaming halt in 1996 when President Bill Clinton signed into effect The Temporary Assistance for Needy Families Act (TANF). Better known as "welfare reform," this law enacted Title V, Section 510(b) of the Social Security Act which established a new federal funding stream to provide grants to states for abstinence-only programs (SIECUS, 2018). Many sexuality educators doing work at Planned Parenthoods and other community-based, federally funded organizations were challenged to continue ed services. This moved the burden of such services to organizations that valued sexuality education, but may not have specialized or directly offered such.

In 1997, I had the unique challenge and pleasure to co-construct and deliver the first sexuality education program for people with developmental disabilities in Butler County, Ohio. The Social Training and Education Project (STEP), a well-planned collaborative effort initiated by the Butler County Board of Mental Retardation/Developmental Disabilities (BCBMRDD) administration, partnered with Social Health and Education (SHE, an original social hygiene nonprofit from the early 1900s) and parents. Sexuality education services, grounded in prevention philosophy and sexual wellness values, became available to referred adults in five services options: 1. assessment of knowledge, 2. individual education, 3. group education, 4. staff training, and 5. parent-caregiver supports. In my five-year tenure as a professional sexuality educator, I found that STEP was met with enthusiasm from consumers of BCBMRDD services and their parents; however, the majority of caregivers and residential providers were wary, unsure, and not participating. Caregivers, specifically paid staff, experience challenges that other support services roles do not necessarily encounter. Staff often face the negative outcomes of the sexual challenges, frustrations, and concerns of individuals with disabilities. Paid staff are not trained to work from a person-centered lens and often shift personal values onto the individual with whom they are supporting. Because people feel that they are sexperts, I frequently found myself explaining to staff my credentials, defending the curriculum, and dealing with denial and refusal to support the individual's values, behaviors, and choices.

The priority of STEP is to be person-centered and maintain the individual's rights to sexual health and well-being. Those rights were often questioned by staff with other agendas and priorities. I and the professional staff supporting individuals with disabilities worked diligently to have a provider's contracts terminated because of staff's unwillingness to yield from their personal values typically informed by religious ideology. The struggle in the 1990s was to empower and create access for individuals with disabilities with regard to sexual identity, expression, and behaviors that were legal, consensual, and healthy. Afterall, it is within one's rights to do such.

2000

President George W. Bush furthered the abstinence-only agenda in 2000 by mandating and further defining abstinence-only until marriage verbiage to federal funding. Disallowing the teaching of anything but sex after marriage became the focus of national discourse. Because of the overt moralization of prioritizing marriage, many educators providing sexuality education services to the disabled just continued the work where able with private funding. Although understanding that the intellectually disabled are more typical in their sexuality expression and desires than not, marriage in this population was not prevalent or the norm. The struggle for providing quality sexuality education to the developmentally disabled shifted from prevention and inclusion to working with providers (support staff). Efforts focus on training staff to not impose their personal values on to the people with whom they provide services. Focus in sexuality education efforts center on rights of the disabled and how those facilitating services must ensure access while upholding the individual's beliefs. For consenting adults, relationship status should not preclude choices for sex and sexual expression. Increasing knowledge, comfort level, and resources for staff to uphold the disabled individual's values and choices is preeminent.

In spite of this short-sighted, noninclusive, and shame-based agenda of abstinence only until marriage, the STEP program flourished. STEP added a therapeutic services component as well for a very underserved population: intellectually disabled sex offenders "on paper" and those who had committed offenses, but had not yet been adjudicated, began receiving Sex Ed services. STEP, although the name has been changed, continues to thrive today under the reigns of a professional sexuality educator and clinician.

2010

Sexuality education, with President Obama's administration, was championed and replaced abstinence only until marriage programs. *The Washington Post* (2010) reported:

> Over the past decade, politicians have battled about how to reduce the teen pregnancy rate: safe-sex vs. abstinence-only sex education programs. . . . Now, the Obama administration has entered the politically sensitive debate, promising to put scientific evidence before political ideology. . . . The initiative exemplifies the administration's oft-repeated quest to find new strategies to defuse some of the nation's most divisive issues . . . officials are hoping to appease advocates of teaching teens about condoms and other forms of birth control as well as those who oppose sex outside marriage.
>
> (www.washingtonpost.com, section A)

This fiscally supported strategy is needed for sexuality professionals to do the work. After a long history of counterintuitive mandates from the federal government that disallowed for evidence-based, research-sustained, and medically accurate programs, sexuality education professionals anticipated many more opportunities to dig deeper into the interdisciplinary approaches of best practices, pedagogy, and praxis. From the same *Washington Post* article, colleague Michael Resnick from the University of Minnesota nailed the sentiment,

What's exciting and innovative about that is not only the full-fledged return of science to the field of teenage pregnancy prevention but also the opportunity to adapt these approaches to the needs of individual communities.

(2010, www.washingtonpost.com)

Indeed, Ohio county boards of developmental disabilities, began accessing professionally informed sexuality education services with a fervor.

In 2011, I began a long-term relationship with several county boards through the effort of the Clearwater Council of Governments. Much staff training occurred, parents and caregivers sought supports, and individuals with disabilities formed self-advocate groups that explored relevant issues such as relationships, online sexuality resource access, and effective communication strategies for sexual health and wellness. Based on a nine-county partnership in northwest Ohio, I developed a comprehensive sexuality education program including curriculum and training for staff to implement it in whatever capacity worked best for their particular county board. The following is excerpted from, "Invested in being ME!: A sexual health and wellness curriculum for folks with developmental disabilities" (Frabotta et al., 2013), and is an example of contemporary best practices in sexuality education:

Hello and Welcome

. . . to a quality Sexuality Education program written by professional Sexuality Educators for County Board of DD staff who have been specifically trained in best teaching practices and methods, and ethical foundations to deliver this curriculum to adults with developmental disabilities.

. . . to this curriculum as it aims to educate and empower both the teacher and the student in a reality-based, personally affirming, and community valuing manner. Each lesson plan is structured to practice skill building, assist with gaining a greater comfort level, and stresses personal choice along with accountability.

. . . to a labor of love rooted in long-term experience and assembled by a group of caring, compassionate and concerned folks who value sexual health and wellness and see prevention education as a foundation for actuating one's life goals.

Invested in Being ME! is . . .

. . . *experience and expertise in action.* Jacque, Kathleen and Richelle are AASECT Certified Sexuality Educators who have a combined 65+ years of experience providing reality-based, student-centered, culturally aware, medically accurate and research supported

Sexuality Education specifically in southern Ohio and central Indiana, as well as nationally. Our programs are designed around and taught with actionable principles:

practicing critical thinking
valuing human diversity and experience
raising awareness for personal reflection
stressing interpersonal communication skills
accepting responsibility for personal choices

. . . quality and sound pedagogy. All Sexuality Education services provided by Jacque, Kathleen and Richelle are grounded in and incorporate contemporary standards of excellence, best practices and ethics. We have cited the National Sexuality Education Standards in each lesson plan and have wrapped activity-based learning around those identified Standards.

. . . aware that Individuals are integral members of their respective communities. This curriculum actively promotes dialogue and discussion about all the facets that make us uniquely human! Individuals will be supported, via skill-building lesson plans and HOMEWORK tasks, to engage self, others within the family, personal acquaintances, peer groups and identified professionals/sites in the community with queries and statements regarding the information that they are learning. This inclusive dialogue approach helps to dispel myths, relay accurate information with values attached, support quality folks with whom personal sharing can occur and adds to a developing identity as a sexually healthy person.

. . . one of many Sexuality Education services available. SOSECS goal is to meet the County Boards of DD's needs (as identified by the CCOG) to provide accurate sexual health and wellness information to Individuals, as delivered directly by trained Board staff. Through education, exploration and establishing on-going resources, staff will progress Individuals' sexuality knowledge and comfort level; therefore, encouraging an agenda of personally defined sexual health and wellness. This includes engaging parents, caregivers, providers and the community at large so that all are as enamored with the philosophy and practice of sexual health and wellness as we are!

"The Clearwater Council of Governments (CCOG, n.d.) is committed to collaborating with our partners to enhance people's lives one system, one community and one person at a time" reads the mission statement on their website. They certainly have included sexual rights and access to quality sexuality education in their enhancement of people's lives.

2015 and Beyond . . .

Already Doing It: Intellectual Disability and Sexual Agency, by Michael Gill, unabashedly and unequivocally calls for sexual and reproductive justice for the intellectually disabled on the grounds that sexuality, sexual expression, and choices about such are indeed human experiences. "When we assume to know what is best for others, this knowledge can often actively hide or deny individual sexual self-determinism" (Gill, 2015, p. 194).

Gills' contemporary assertions are not rights oriented, but justice centered. He contends that, "sexual ableism is the system of imbuing with determinations of qualification to be sexual based on criteria of ability, intellect, morality, physicality, appearance, age, race, social acceptability, and gender conformity" (Gill, 2015, p. 2). From this critical lens, Gill explores a historically ignored, denied, condemned, and pathologized concept too dangerous to utter, let alone embrace: to be human is to be sexual and to be sexual is to be human. He removes what is considered a most progressive "rights" argument and simply contends that the "artfulness of disability" is reason enough for accepting the sexuality of disabled individuals. Drawing on Siebers' work, Gill demonstrates that disabled individuals have consistently pushed through obstacles constructed by medicine, rehabilitative processes, parental authority, popular culture, and those who provide residence and residential supports to be creatively sexual and to express an "artfulness of disability."

Gill references a discourse of protectionism that also (most insultingly) denies an innate expression of human desire by the intellectually disabled. Looking to feminist theorists, disability studies, and queer theory to critically dismantle the overt protections of the disabled's sexual expression, Gill (2015) "envisioned a future where disabled individuals and their sexual and reproductive lives are not constructed as 'special' or in need of regulation" (p. 192). He states that, "The challenge is to continue to forward sexual pleasure and desire in sex education materials, to continue partnerships with disability justice and reproductive justice, to advocate for and believe in coalitions that enable equitable and accessible futures."

Great consideration has been given to the specific challenges that intellectually disabled experience "growing into" and identifying their unique sense of sexuality. With these selected references, one can note that language has evolved, however, conceptually, not much changed until the 1990s. Expectations of and for the intellectually disabled have also progressed: but consistent, wide-spread, and holistic sexuality education services supporting such, not so much. As pro-active and inclusive educators, how do we assist, advocate, and support the intellectually disabled person's learning journey? The short answer: as directed by people within the disability's community.

The goal is to consistently create and deliver the most effective learning opportunities for all students. Learning about specific disabilities and learning styles found in any classroom establishes a foundation upon which inclusive praxis can be built. Honing skill sets to be able to modify teaching methods and learning activities allows for greater impact for all learners. Maintaining networking systems and credible, accessible resources are essential for continuing to progress as effective and relevant sexuality educators.

Gill's work is cutting edge and forefronts equity. In fact, many trained and certified sexuality educators approach the work of teaching sex/ual/ity from a social justice perspective. Certification by The American Association of Sexuality Educators, Counselors, and Therapists supports this approach. All populations, and especially the marginalized who have been left out of formal opportunities for sex/ual/ity education for longer than most, deserve an informed educator who subscribes to and practices ethics. Having an academic preparation rooted in critical theories and a social justice paradigm espousing that human sex/ual/ity and expression is unique to the individual is also best practices. Sexual health, wellness, and pleasure education is not a simple right, but simply right. It is imperative that contemporary society join with credentialed sexuality educators and reach the reasonable conclusion: All people, including and especially people with disabilities, should have access to and be provided a quality curriculum of sexuality information throughout the lifespan.

I long for futures not where disability is rendered legible or absent, but rather where disability and impairment are perceived to enhance, not spoil life, including conceptions of sexuality and reproduction.
(Gil, 2015, p. 194)

Process Questions and Considerations

1. "Accruing information about one's sexuality is a lived experience." Given your life experiences, can you identify three areas or topics about sex/ual/ity where you perceive that you are most educated? Least educated? Where are you situating your predominate sources of learning?
2. "Ultimately, the enduring understanding is about sexual health and well-being." Please consider and list a minimum of five topics that you believe should be included in a sexual health and well-being curriculum. How does that list change (or does it) for persons with developmental disabilities/the intellectually disabled?
3. "The invisibility and dismissal of people with disabilities as sexual beings is perhaps the most problematic of the abuses as it completely denies the basis of being human." What might be some

the assumptions that you hold about sexuality education and people with developmental disabilities/the intellectually disabled?

4. "Gills' contemporary assertions are not rights oriented, but justice centered." What are concrete or specific differences between "rights oriented" vs. "justice centered"? If you were explaining these two paradigms or ways of thinking to someone from Mars, what would be your two main points?

5. "Sexual health, wellness, and pleasure education is not a simple right, but simply right." What does sexual health, wellness, and pleasure look like? In a perfect world, how would we know when people with disabilities/the disabled are embodying, demonstrating, actuating, practicing sexual health? Wellness? Pleasure?

References

The ARC. (November, 1990). Sexuality.

Bass, M. S. (1974). Sex education for the handicapped. *The Family Coordinator,* 23(1), 27–33.

Chapman, J. W., & Pitceathly, A. S. (1985). Sexuality and mentally handicapped people: Issues of sex education, marriage, parenthood, and care staff attitudes. *Australia and New Zealand Journal of Developmental Disabilities,* 10(4), 227–235.

Clearwater Council of Governments. (n.d.). *Mission statement.* Retrieved from https://clearwatercog.org/who-we-are/

Couwenhoven, T. (2007). *Teaching children with down syndrome about their bodies, boundaries, and sexuality.* Bethesda, MD: Woodbine House.

Crocker, A. C. (1992). Data collection for the evaluation of mental retardation prevention activities: The fateful forty-three. *Mental Retardation,* 30(6), 303–317.

Edmonson, B., McCombs, K., & Wish, J. (1979). What retarded adults believe about sex. *American Journal of Mental Deficiency,* 84(1), 11–18.

Foxx, R. M., McMorrow, M. J., Storey, K., & Rogers, B. M. (1984). Teaching social/sexual skills to mentally retarded adults. *American Journal of Mental Deficiency,* 89(1), 9–15.

Frabotta, R., Baldwin, K., & Daugherty, J. (2013). *Invested in being ME!: A sexual health and wellness curriculum for folks with developmental disabilities.* Tiffin, OH: Clearwater Council of Governments on Behalf of 9 County Boards of Developmental Disabilities in Northwest Ohio.

Gill, M. (2015). *Already doing it: Intellectual disability and sexual agency.* Minneapolis, MN: University of Minnesota Press.

Hingsburger, D. (1992). *I witness: History and a person with developmental disability.* Mountville, PA: VIDA Publishing.

Kempton, W. (1988). *Sex education for persons with disabilities that hinder learning: A teacher's guide.* Santa Barbara, CA: James Stanfield Company, Inc.

24   *Richelle Frabotta*

Kempton, W. (1993). *Socialization and sexuality: A comprehensive training guide for professionals helping people with disabilities that hinder learning.* Santa Barbara, CA: James Stanfield Company.

Kempton, W. (2010). *Obituary.* Retrieved from: www.stretchfuneralhome.com/obituary/WINIFRED-KOB-KEMPTON/Haverford-PA/812878#sthash.s3SEC bm4.dpuf

McCabe, M. P. (1993). Sex education programs for people with mental retardation. *Mental Retardation, 31*(6), 377–387.

McCabe, M. P., & Schreck, A. (1992). Before sex education: An evaluation of the sexual knowledge, experience, feelings and needs of people with mild intellectual disabilities. *Australia and New Zealand Journal of Developmental Disabilities, 18*(2), 75–82.

Sex Information and Education Council of the United States. (August 2018). *A brief history of AOUM funding.* SIECUS.org. Retrieved from https://siecus.org/wp-content/uploads/2018/07/4-A-Brief-History-of-AOUM-Funding.pdf

Stein, R. (2010). Obama administration launches a sex ed program. *Washington Post.* Retrieved Thursday, October 28, 2010, from www.washingtonpost.com/wpdyn/content/article/2010/10/27/AR2010102707471.html?noredirect=on

2 Seven Leadership Skills for Sexuality Educators

Kirsten deFur

Introduction

Sexuality educators embody the role of *leader* – someone who sets an example of attitudes and behaviors for a group of people and guides the implementation of strategies that get positive results. Leaders influence and inspire. Leaders dedicate themselves to the betterment and growth of others. No matter whether sexuality educators' role or responsibilities say they are a leader, they serve as leaders for the people who learn from them. However, just because a sexuality educator serves as a leader, it does not mean they automatically have leadership skills – those skills need to be cultivated.

Sexuality educators need to learn about a variety of leadership skills in order to support their mission and goals and act as effective leaders. Sexuality educators who are in management positions *especially* need to learn these skills. Incredible work is happening in the field, such as innovative programming, engaging vulnerable populations, and promoting forward-thinking policy, but because leaders often lack strong leadership skills, progress can be stymied or even halted.

Within the field of sexuality education, leadership skills are not traditionally included in professional development – often the focus is on content, theory, values clarification, curriculum writing, facilitation, program planning, research, and evaluation. All of this information is critical for sexuality educators. However, topics related to leadership need to be added to that list. While sexuality educators may look to other affiliated fields for guidance on leadership, there are very few, if any, leadership development resources designed specifically for sexuality educators, thus the need for this chapter (and this book!).

To inform this chapter, a survey, "Leadership Development in Sexuality Education," about experiences that sexuality educators have had learning about specific leaderships skills (see Figure 2.1) was distributed to professionals who participate in several listservs and social media platforms, such as the Advanced Sexuality Educators and Trainers (ASET) listserv, Teaching College Sexuality listserv, Our Whole Lives Trainers

% Respondents Reported "Yes" to Having Learned About the Leadership Topic

Topic	% reported "yes"
Leadership Styles	82.35
Employee Motivation	51.92
Organizational Culture	76.47
Leading Teams/Collaborative Leadership	53.85
Managing Conflict	78.00
Diversity & Inclusion	96.15
Feedback/Performance Reviews	65.38

Figure 2.1 "Leadership Development in Sexuality Education" Survey Responses

listserv and Facebook group, and the Sex Educator's Union #69 Facebook group. The survey was available for a three-week time period, from September 10, 2018 through October 2, 2018. Fifty-two self-identified sexuality educators completed the survey with eight questions about experiences learning about leadership skills, at what point their career they learned about that skill, and how helpful it was. Throughout this chapter, results from the survey will be discussed.

This chapter introduces readers to seven fundamental topics related to leadership development and helps readers self-reflect, identify topics to learn more about, and determine how they can integrate leadership skills into their day-to-day work. The following leadership topics will be explored:

- Styles of Leadership
- Motivation
- Organizational Culture
- Leading Teams
- Managing Conflict
- Diversity and Inclusion
- Feedback/Performance Reviews

Throughout this chapter, recommendations are provided for further development, and a checklist allows readers to assess their own level of knowledge about a topic and set a course for further education. As it is impossible to cover all areas of leadership development, this chapter also lists additional key topics and areas for readers to explore in order to continue their education on leadership.

This chapter, much like this book, encourages self-reflection. Being an effective, and impactful leader requires that people give careful thought as to who they are, and who they want to be. Throughout this chapter, keep the following questions in mind:

- How would I describe my leadership style?
- How would others describe my leadership style?
- How much do I know about this leadership skill?
- How can this leadership skill help me grow as a leader?

Leadership, Defined

The field of "Leadership Studies" dates to the 1940s when Ohio State Leadership Studies sent a questionnaire to leaders and subordinates to examine how "leaders could satisfy common group needs" and concluded that the most important attributes for leaders were "initiating structure" and "consideration" ("History of Leadership as a Field of Study", n.d.). The Michigan Leadership Studies emerged in the 1950s and determined that effective leaders had three main qualities: "task oriented behavior, relationship-oriented behavior, and participative leadership" ("History of Leadership as a Field of Study", n.d.). In the 1960s, Douglas McGregor, at the MIT Sloan School of Management, identified Theory X and Theory Y, which describes employee motivation (Robbins & Judge, 2016).

From that point on, a long catalog of leadership theories emerged, including the following:

- Trait theory – that individuals need to have inherent traits in order to be a good leader (Zaccaro, 2007)
- Behavioral theory – focuses on the actions of leaders and that individuals can learn and develop the skills needed to lead effectively (Yukl, 1971)
- Contingency and situational theories – suggest that no one style of leadership is correct, that leaders need to shift their style according to the environment or situation (Ayman, 2004)
- Transactional theory – focus on a system of rewards and punishments, taking into consideration roles and responsibilities within an organization (McCleskey, 2014)
- Relationship theories – center around the connections between leaders and followers (Graen & Uhl-Bien, 1995; Uhl-Bien, 2006)

As demonstrated here, there are a wide range of theories related to leadership, and there seems to be only one thing that can be agreed on – there is no one theory or style that will work for every individual or setting.

In the field of sexuality education, leadership theories and skills are not typically introduced as a proactive learning opportunity, rather sexuality educators receive training on these topics as either a corrective action if a leader is not performing well or because an individual decides to pursue the opportunity of their own volition. Of the respondents to the "Leadership Development in Sexuality Education" survey, only one of the topics – diversity and inclusion – was listed by nearly all (96.15%) the respondents as a topic they had learned about. In addition, many respondents indicated they could have benefited from learning about the respective topic earlier in their career. One respondent shared this in response to the question about leadership styles and at what point in their career they learned about the topic: "I could have used it about 5 years earlier – at the point I was moving from direct service to a supervisory role."

Leadership encompasses a wide range of theories and topics, each of which can apply to different settings and different people. It is up to individuals to determine their own style, reflect on their strengths and weaknesses, and define their own leadership mission – what impact might one want to have as a leader and how will they accomplish that mission?

Leadership Skill #1: Styles of Leadership

Within the literature, there are countless descriptions of different styles of leadership and ways of characterizing those styles. Is a leader more authoritative or collaborative? Is a leader more relationship-oriented or task-oriented? Is a leader more big-picture or detail-oriented? Is a leader more situational or transformative? And so on.

Of the respondents to the "Leadership Development in Sexuality Education" survey, 82.35% reported having learned about styles of leadership. One respondent shared,

> I didn't get a chance to learn about leadership styles until much later in my career. I had already been a supervisor for several years and had wished I'd learned about different leadership styles much earlier. It was helpful to identify what type of style I had, the strengths and weaknesses that come with each style, and ways to improve.

Learning about different styles of leadership can give insight into one's own predispositions and help leaders flex their style as needed. Since sexuality education happens in a wide range of settings and engages a variety of stakeholders that may warrant a particular style of leadership, it can be very valuable to know about the various styles.

One of the most well-known thinkers in the field of leadership is Daniel Goleman, who describes six specific styles of leadership in his article, *Leadership That Gets Results* (see Table 2.1) (Goleman, 2000).

Table 2.1 Applying Goleman's Leadership Styles to Sexuality Education (Goleman, 2000)

Style	Approach	Relevant Application to Sexuality Education
Directive (coercive)	"Do what I say"	Responding to difficult staff who have not responded to feedback; policy enforcement. Use sparingly
Visionary (authoritative)	"Come with me"	Gaining buy-in for sexuality education; developing a rapport with a group
Affiliative	"People come first"	Building team harmony and increasing morale; responding to push back or challenges implementing a program because of differing values
Participative (democratic)	"Decide together"	Generating new ideas; giving voice in decisions; building organizational flexibility
Pacesetting	"Do as I do"	Meeting tight project deadlines; engaging staff who are highly skilled and motivated – use along with another style
Coaching	"Let me help you develop"	Developing staff skills and understanding; supporting staff who are new to the field

Goleman's styles of leadership can be seen in other models, and no one style is best – in reality, "being able to switch among [them] as conditions dictate creates the best organizational culture and optimizes business performance" (Goleman, 2000). Goleman's styles are connected to the four capabilities of Emotional Intelligence (another leadership skill that is not covered in depth in this chapter; however, it is worthwhile for leaders to learn about it) – self-awareness, self-management, social awareness, and social skills. These competencies may feel familiar to sexuality educators, as they connect to messages conveyed during lessons on relationships, negotiation, self-esteem, support networks, body image, and likely other topics. These concepts can also be applied to leadership styles that will help sexuality educators be intentional about the approach they are taking, rather than only relying on their go-to style that represents their comfort zone. In reading the descriptions of Goleman's styles, one may see oneself clearly in one or two of the styles, however, a good leader will observe the situation and apply the appropriate style accordingly.

The directive style (also known as coercive) is characterized by top-down decisions with little input from employees and no flexibility – a "do what I say" approach with the drive to control at its core. This style should be used sparingly, as it can negatively impact motivation and a sense of ownership of work. Situations such as a hostile takeover or a low performing employee where nothing else has worked may be appropriate for a directive style, however, it should not be a long-term or prevailing approach.

The visionary leader (also known as authoritative) "charts a new course and sells his people on a fresh long-term vision" (Goleman, 2000). This style gives employees the choice to achieve a goal in their own way, and is characterized by motivation and enthusiasm, and inspires commitment. The visionary style draws upon empathy and self-confidence. Described as one of the most effective styles, the visionary style works well in most settings, but particularly when the organization is adrift or not accomplishing stated goals sufficiently. This style may not be as effective when the leader is working with a team of experts or employees that have more experience. This style also runs the risk of becoming overbearing (they may "see the leader as pompous or out-of-touch") or undermining (they may feel the leader is inhibiting "the egalitarian spirit of an effective team") (Goleman, 2000).

The affiliative style centers around people, placing more value on emotions and relationships than tasks and goals. Drawing upon empathy and communication, an affiliative leader seeks to ensure the satisfaction of their employees and promote harmonious relationships among the team. Affiliative leaders create a bond among their team members, offer plenty of positive feedback, and build a sense of belonging resulting in fierce loyalty. This style is particularly relevant for situations demanding increased morale, improving communication, or repairing broken trust. Drawbacks to this style include overlooking or avoiding correction of poor performance and setting a standard of mediocrity.

The participative (also known as democratic) style is characterized by giving employees a voice and a say in the decision-making and processes, and draws upon collaboration and team leadership. Participative leaders take the time to seek input from their team members and gain buy-in. This can positively influence employees' responsibility, creativity, and realistic goal-setting. Drawbacks to the participative style include overemphasis on meetings and stalling on decision-making. This style has the most positive impact when the leader is unsure of what direction to go in and wants to generate fresh ideas. A participatory approach is not effective when employees are not skilled or capable enough to provide valuable advice or ideas, or in times of crisis.

The pacesetting leader sets very high standards of performance and serves as a role model, focusing on doing things better and faster – expecting the same of others. The pacesetting style draws upon the drive to achieve and initiative. When used consistently, this style can have a negative impact on the climate of an organization because employees often feel overwhelmed and confused by expectations, as pacesetting leaders believe that they should not have to tell an employee what to do – they should just know. Trust becomes very low and commitment decreases.

Pacesetting can work well if the team is highly skilled and self-motivated; however, the style should not be used on its own.

The coaching style focuses on the development of someone, rather than accomplishing project goals/tasks. Coaching leaders help others identify their own strengths and weaknesses, and encourage growth and development of their skills, working towards career goals. Coaching leaders delegate tasks to their team members and give challenging assignments to provide opportunities to learn or improve upon skills and draws upon empathy and self-awareness. Coaching demands constant dialog and constructive feedback and is most effective when the person is willing to be an active participant in that type of approach. The coaching style is least effective when the individual is resistant. Coaching, while used the least often, can have a significant positive impact on an individual and the organization overall.

Of Goleman's six styles, three of the styles that have an overall positive impact – visionary, affiliative, and coaching – draw upon empathy as a capability of emotional intelligence. The ability to recognize and reflect on the emotions of oneself and others can enhance someone's leadership skills significantly, and inform a leader's ability to sense the challenge at hand and determine the most appropriate style to assume.

When facilitating sessions, cofacilitating with another sexuality educator, developing curricula, creating policy, or training others, sexuality educators can draw upon various leadership styles to inform their interactions. If in a school setting, the culture may lend itself to a directive style, however a more affiliative or visionary style may be more effective in gaining critical buy-in for teaching about sexuality and developing a rapport with participants. A democratic style might be effective when generating new ideas for a curriculum, program, or outreach strategy. A coaching style can help when conducting training of trainers, rather than a pacesetting style that can be overly demanding and leave little room for errors – which is one of the ways people learn.

Sexuality educators need to constantly reflect on their own leadership style, the styles of others, and how each style applies to different situations. There are a variety of assessments available to aid professionals in learning about their innate style, ranging from a quick online survey to an in-depth psychometrics analysis with a professional – available for those ready to put in the time, effort, and resources to reflect and understand themselves. Whether that assessment uses Goleman's six styles, or if it's colors, shapes, directions, etc., the critical component is self-reflection. As one survey respondent shared, learning about leadership styles is "a game changer in dealing with self and others."

Leadership Skill #2: Motivation

In the field of sexuality education, the work is often intense and involves challenging conversations with participants, stakeholders, policy-makers, parents, and so on. It can be tempting to assume that sexuality educators are intrinsically self-motivated (and they often are); however, there are a variety of internal and external factors that can impact motivation and overall performance. Motivation can be defined as "the processes that account for an individual's intensity, direction, and persistence of effort toward attaining a goal" (Robbins & Judge, 2016). Motivation can be seen as a combination of individual self-direction and the outside influencing factors, such as leadership, culture, environment, and rewards. Of the topics included in the "Leadership Development in Sexuality Education" survey, only 51.92% of respondents reported they had learned about motivation – the least of all seven topics. However, motivation is particularly important for work that entails discussing sensitive, often difficult subject matter related to sexuality. In order to care about the work itself, sexuality educators need to feel supported, valued, and challenged in a variety of ways (in addition to pay and benefits) so they can sustain the energy needed to do the work and to do it well.

There are a variety of theories related to motivation, which is also one of the most widely researched topics in organizational behavior (Robbins & Judge, 2016). Maslow's Hierarchy of Needs (see Figure 2.2) divides individual needs into five categories: physiological (food, shelter, and other bodily needs), safety (security and protection), social (relationships, affection, belonging), esteem (self-respect, autonomy, recognition, attention), and self-actualization (drive, growth, self-fulfillment). The theory asserts that in order to satisfy the higher needs of esteem and self-actualization, the basic needs (physiological and safety) need to be satisfied. Leaders can consider how it may be challenging to see high levels of motivation from sexuality educators whose basic needs are not met because they are underpaid, do not feel secure in their jobs, or do not have adequate benefits.

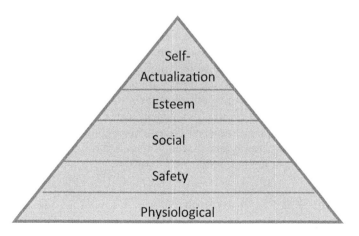

Figure 2.2 Maslow's Hierarchy of Needs

Another theory of motivation relevant for sexuality educators is *goal-setting theory* – that motivation stems from "intentions to work towards a goal" (Robbins & Judge, 2016). Goals drive what needs to be done, and how much effort is needed to accomplish that goal. Performance has been shown to be highest when an individual is given a specific, difficult goal to achieve – beyond the "do your best" directive (Locke & Latham, 2002). Goal-setting affects performance by keeping the focus on goal-relevant activities, energizing an individual, encouraging persistence in the face of setbacks or failure, and engaging existing and new knowledge and skills. In goal-setting theory, achieving goals is impacted by both the *importance* of the goal, and *self-efficacy*. Importance can be enhanced by describing the value that achieving that goal will have for both the individual, and the organization – the "why" behind the goal. Self-efficacy can be increased by providing learning opportunities related to that goal and giving someone encouragement and consistent feedback. In fact, goal-setting theory complements self-efficacy theory – the higher the self-efficacy the more confidence one has in the ability to succeed (Robbins & Judge, 2016). Leaders can develop employee motivation by incorporating goal-setting theory into their work. To do that, set specific, challenging goals, clearly describe the importance of that goal, provide learning opportunities to build on knowledge or skills needed to accomplish the goal, and get/give feedback along the way.

Another widely accepted and evidence-supported theory of motivation is the *expectancy theory*, which asserts that effort (a.k.a. motivation) is connected to how much someone believes there will be a particular outcome or reward, and what that outcome or reward is (Robbins & Judge, 2016). For example, "I will work hard because my hard work will be recognized, and I will then get promoted." Expectancy theory focuses on outcomes, rather than needs, such as Maslow's theory. There are three relationships that drive expectancy theory:

1. *Effort-performance relationship* – the perception that a certain amount of effort will lead to performance
2. *Performance-reward relationship* – the perception that performing at a particular level will lead to achieving a desired outcome
3. *Rewards-personal growth relationship* – the degree to which the rewards satisfy an individual's personal goals/needs and the desirability of those rewards

For example, if sexuality educators believe that their preparation through studying the content, developing a relationship with the host, learning about the audience, and collecting materials in advance will result in a well-received, engaging session that is recognized by leadership, which included in their performance appraisal and contributes to their desirable reward (such as promotion, bonus, assignment of an appealing project, flex time), then they are more likely to put in the effort to be fully prepared. If educators feel the prep work does not have any positive outcome, then they are less likely to go through all the steps to be fully prepared. That reward may also be as straightforward as recognition for both significant successes and "small" everyday wins. The progress principle states that "Of all the things that can boost emotions, motivation, and perceptions during a workday, the single most important is making progress in meaningful work" (Amabile & Kramer, 2011, p. 71). Those "small wins" make a big difference. If someone's work is not recognized or acknowledged by a leader, they will not know what to continue doing, and they won't feel good about doing it.

Other theories of motivation, such as McGregor's Theory X and Theory Y (McGregor, 1957), Herzberg's Two-Factor Theory (Herzberg, 1964), McClellands' Theory of Needs (McClelland, 1961), self-determination theory (Ryan & Deci, 2000), equity/organizational justice theory (Adams, 1963), and employee engagement theory (Kahn, 1990), may feel more relevant for some sexuality educators or settings. Regardless of the theory applied, it's important consider how to both cultivate and sustain motivation among sexuality educators and recognize that it will be different for everyone. One respondent to the "Leadership Development in Sexuality Education" survey shared that learning about motivation was "Helpful – to realize that there are a diversity of forms of motivation – not one size fits all. Must tailor to the individual employee – and not assume that what motivates me also motivates others!" No matter one's role in an organization, integrate conversations about motivation into supervision regularly – a conversation should be had with supervisors informing them about what motivation looks like for them. Mid-management and senior level leadership need to take motivation into consideration when making decisions and setting the tone for the organization.

Leadership Skill #3: Organizational Culture

What is an organization's culture? More than just the "hidden rules" of an organization, it is made up of a variety of conditions, including behavioral regularities (e.g., starting meetings on time, a structured daily schedule, responding to emails within a few hours, having written agendas, etc.), norms that emerge among working relationships (e.g., greeting others at the beginning of the day, giving feedback directly and immediately, decision-making processes, etc.), prevailing values (e.g., developing accessible materials, respecting others, honoring diversity, etc.), the mission driving the work (e.g., reducing the likelihood of unintended pregnancy, educating about consent, promoting healthy relationships, reaching underserved populations, etc.), and the feelings or climate (e.g., positive attitude towards the work, high level of energy and enthusiasm, supportive working relationships, etc.) (Christensen, 2006). Every organization has its own culture, which may shift over time and may influence how people think, act, and perform (Warrick, 2017). Just over three-quarters of respondents (76.47%) to the "Leadership Development in Sexuality Education" survey indicated they had learned about organizational culture. A leader has an immense impact on the culture, as they set the tone and the standards, and team members look to leaders (both formal and informal) for guidance and role modeling.

High performance cultures have skilled and trusted leaders, clear and compelling vision, core values, commitment to excellence and ethics, clear roles/responsibilities, positive attitudes, open and transparent communication, collaboration, emphasis on improvement and growth, and willingness to learn from successes and failures (Warrick, 2017). On paper, these characteristics may seem like common sense and easy to achieve; however, in practice, they are quite difficult to accomplish and maintain.

To establish organizational culture that is both positive and promote high performance, leaders need to commit to making culture an integral part of the organizational strategy and a high priority. To do that, leaders need to take a close, honest look at the current culture – maybe using an anonymous questionnaire or third-party involvement in order to account for fear of retaliation. Leaders also need to involve all team members in the process of both identifying and living out organizational cultural ideals – culture doesn't exist in a vacuum. Culture is about how people interact and work together, so it's critical not to omit them from the process. Leaders also need to model the desired behaviors – the age-old aphorism, "actions speak louder than words" applies. If starting meetings on time and having established agendas is a cultural ideal, the leader needs to start meetings on time and always have an agenda. Leaders also need to consider cultural fit as they hire and onboard new employees. Having an onboarding buddy – someone from the organization that is on a parallel or adjacent team that can share the ins and outs of what it's like to work there – can help acclimate a new person into the organization. Lastly, leaders need to acknowledge behaviors and attitudes that contribute to positive organizational culture. Positive culture has been shown to stem from the following:

- "Caring for, being interested in, and maintaining responsibility for colleagues as friends.
- Providing support for one another, including offering kindness and compassion when others are struggling.
- Avoiding blame and forgive mistakes.
- Inspiring one another at work.
- Emphasizing the meaningfulness of the work.
- Treating one another with respect, gratitude, trust, and integrity."
(Seppala & Cameron, 2015, p. 3)

To accomplish those behaviors, leaders need to foster social connectedness, show empathy, go out of their way to help, and encourage dialog with others, especially about any issues or problems.

An organization's culture can either positively or negatively impact performance and achievement. A culture defined by support, compassion, open dialog, positivity, and celebration will ultimately result in higher performance, retention of employees, attracting talent, and successfully accomplishing goals. A culture defined by urgency, stress, negative feedback, and lack of accountability will ultimately result in poor performance, a toxic work environment, retention issues, inability to attract talent, and mission derailment. Leaders need to be mindful, intentional, and diligent in paying attention to organizational culture and working towards a culture that is productive and positive. As one survey respondent shared, "I learned that culture can be a fragile thing, that it takes a skilled individual to identify culture through feedback from the group and buy in to improve that culture with focus around the mission of the organization."

Leadership Skill #4: Leading Teams

Most sexuality education happens because people are working in groups. Sexuality educators may be a part of a facilitation team, they may be part of a planning team, they may be part of a decision-making team, or even a policy-making team. Sexuality educators spend a considerable part of their work leading groups in the form of teaching/facilitating for a group of participants. Therefore, it would behoove sexuality educators to learn about teams early in their careers. However, of the survey respondents, just over half (53.85%) reported participating in learning about leading teams. One respondent commented, "I should've had it far sooner [in my career], it was invaluable." Teamwork and collaboration are about people and process, and having a clear process can help people feel engaged and motivated to do their part.

Leading teams effectively boils down to these tasks: clearly outlining goals/objectives, identifying strengths/weaknesses of the team, defining roles/responsibilities, and knowing how to measure whether goals are accomplished (see Figure 2.3) (Polzer, 2003).

Sexuality educators that commit to these components will not only help educational programs and projects run smoothly, they will also contribute to the overall potential impact of the program by modeling collaborative behaviors.

A team is not always necessary for a particular program/project. Before forming a team, always decide if the task requires, or benefits from, multiple people to be involved. As discussed earlier, nearly all sexuality education exists within some type of team/group setting, therefore a team approach often makes sense; but it should not be assumed. Take the time to examine whether a team is needed to accomplish the goal. Next, an effective team has clearly defined goals and objectives. Is the goal to prevent unintended pregnancy or promote healthy relationships?

Figure 2.3 Key Tasks of Leading Teams

Or both (they often go hand in hand)? Is the goal to engage a certain number of participants or community partners, or is it to successfully implement a specific number of sessions? Is the primary goal to develop the skills of the participants, or help them inform their peers? Each of these goals could potentially point to different tasks or priorities. Without clear goals/objectives, team members may not know why they are doing the work for the team or may do work differently. These are ideally established before a team is launched; however, an idea may be at the development stage, so the purpose of the team would be to develop those goals/objectives. If that is the case, then that needs to be clearly stated so that the members know the goals are under development. Writing out those goals/objectives can provide much-needed opportunity to revisit and reflect on how the work circles back to the goals.

As a team is formed, leaders need to consider the strengths and weaknesses of the individuals that make up the team and how they can effectively work together to accomplish the shared goal. For example, some team members may be more task-oriented and are thus better suited to detail-level work on the team, such as preparing materials. Other team members may be more relationship-oriented and are thus better suited to developing partnerships, such as connecting with parents or higher-level administrators. There are a variety of working style assessments that help individuals identify strengths and weaknesses in themselves (and others), such as Myers Briggs (Myers, 1995), StrengthsFinder (Buckingham, 2001), De Bono's Six Thinking Hats (de Bono, 1985), and DISC (Marston, 1928). Leaders can ask team members to take an assessment and share what they learned about their work style in order to help identify appropriate roles on a team. While leaders may think they know their team members well, an outside assessment can reveal new insights about colleagues that a leader has known for a long time.

Once goals/objectives are clearly outlined and strengths and weaknesses identified, roles/responsibilities need to be stated. Who takes notes and shares with the team? Who reaches out to partners? Who makes budget decisions? Who prepares materials? Who enters and analyzes data? Who holds team members accountable for meeting deadlines? Who ensures that the team stays on track and focused on the stated goals/objectives? Oftentimes there is confusion about who is doing what (and by when), so stating roles/responsibilities mitigates that confusion, and helps team members accomplish goals more effectively. Whether using a sophisticated project management platform or old-fashioned pen and paper, defining roles so everyone has a clear (and consistent) understanding of who is doing what is essential.

It is critical to outline how success will be measured. Is it the number of participants that attend a program? Is it an increase in knowledge, captured before and after a program? Is it based off feedback from the facilitators, or from parents, or from the organization? Is it the completion of a curriculum? Is it the engagement of a particular audience? Is it recruiting certain partners? Determine what "done" looks like – the more detailed, the better. Most importantly though, these measures are clearly defined so team members know what they are working towards, and go hand in hand with the goals/objectives.

In addition to the processes described previously, leaders need to give special attention to the team launch. "The initial meeting is a critical juncture in the life of the team, setting the foundation for all subsequent activities and performance" (Polzer, 2003). A team that launches and does not agree to certain processes and structures, such as frequency of meeting, deadlines, decision-making processes, runs the risk of derailing and facing unnecessary challenges. A team may want to create an agreement or contract that outlines processes. Sexuality educators often do this through "group agreements" or "ground rules," and those principles can apply to teams as well.

While this content helps when forming a new team, working with an existing one can have its challenges. When first joining that team, take steps to assess the team by asking a lot of questions (What are the goals? How are the goals measured? Who is doing what?), describing one's strengths/weakness, meeting one-on-one with the team members, making recommendations, and adjusting one's approach and style to match that of the team's. For teams that are not functioning well, leaders can insert a pause into the work of the team as a way to reassess, and possibly reshape the team. It's better to establish that process too late than not at all.

Overall, leading and participating on teams can be incredibly rewarding, or frustrating. By taking the time to follow the steps outlined here, a leader increases the likelihood of meeting goals/objectives, and having teams be a positive experience for the members. One pitfall to keep in mind, though, is groupthink – the domination of concurrence-seeking tendencies. Groupthink happens when team members "strivings for unanimity override their motivation to appraise the consequences of their actions" (Janis, 1972). Therefore, it is critical to have internal and external checks in place to mitigate against groupthink. Some examples of checks include assigning one team member to purposefully articulate a dissenting opinion or poke holes in a strategy and inviting nonteam members to review decisions or content.

Sexuality educators can benefit significantly from learning about teams and collaborative leadership in order to strategically form a team and to be effective team member. One survey respondent shared, "I should've had it far sooner, it was invaluable. Got it too late, but used what I could of it."

Leadership Skill #5: Managing Conflict

Conflict is an organizational reality that leaders need to prepare for, and see as opportunities for growth and understanding (Ware & Barnes, 1978). Organizations are made up of people, who are bound to have differing opinions, thoughts, and views on how things should happen, and who are the best people to get them done. Therefore, conflict will inevitably arise – and is not necessarily a bad thing (Tjosvold, 2008). Conflict is often considered to be dysfunctional – in fact the traditionalist view of conflict that prevailed in the mid-20th century is associated with violence, destruction, and irrationality, therefore should be avoided (Robbins & Judge, 2016). However, leaders can reframe conflict to be a signal that something needs to change, and then managing conflict can be a productive piece of an organizational puzzle. Leaders can recognize the worth and value of *functional* conflict, which supports the goals of the group and improves its performance (Robbins & Judge, 2016).

The topic of managing conflict is one that many sexuality educators shared learning about in a variety of ways – both formal learning and

40   *Kirsten deFur*

"on the ground": 78% of the "Leadership Development in Sexuality Education" survey respondents reported having participated in learning about managing conflict. One respondent shared this about a group conflict issue: "Knowing how to deal with the emotions and experiences everyone brought to the group was paramount in avoiding unnecessary future conflicts." In addition, three survey respondents mentioned in their comments they would like a "deeper dive" on this topic, indicating that what they have learned so far is not sufficient. While the field of sexuality education is largely made up of altruistic, passionate individuals, that does not exempt them from conflict. Sexuality educators need to take the time and energy to learn about managing conflict in order to shift it to a level of productivity.

In some regards, conflict can actually be a good thing, helping explore various possibilities and make informed decisions. "Management teams whose members challenge one another's thinking develop a more complete understanding of the choices, create a richer range of options, and ultimately make the kinds of effective decisions necessary in today's competitive environments" (Eisenhardt, Kahwajy, & Bourgeois, 1997, p. 78). Rather than shy away from conflict, leaders need to lean in to it with an open mind and coming from a space of inquiry.

Why does conflict happen within an organization? There are two distinctive issues: 1. *substantive issues*, which entail disagreements over policies, procedures, resources, roles, responsibilities and/or other organizational practices; and 2. *emotional issues*, which entail personal perceptions and feelings about each other and the substantive issues (Ware & Barnes, 1978). Another way to break down conflict is using the categories of task conflict, relationship conflict, and process conflict (Robbins & Judge, 2016). Regardless of how a leader categorizes conflict, it is important to consider where the conflict is coming from, because that will help inform helpful ways to manage the conflict. A conflict that arises from emotional issues or relationships may demand different approaches than conflict that is connected to tasks or substantive issues. However, no matter the type of conflict, emotions are likely involved because conflict can feel like a threat (Gallo, 2017). People often avoid conflict out of fear, concern for others' emotions, or because that is the prevailing approach in the environment. Research indicates that while avoiding conflict may be one of the most common responses, avoidance does not have a positive impact on an organization because it undermines relationships and promotes a competitive, rather than collaborative, atmosphere (Tjosvold, 2008).

A critical step to shifting conflict from a traditionalist or negative construct to a functional one is having effective and thoughtful ways to manage conflict – "the kind or source of the conflict is not the culprit. It is how people manage it that determines its course and outcomes" (Tjosvold, 2008). While there are countless models and theories on managing conflict, experts agree there is no perfect approach – it will depend on the situation and the people involved, as well as what is at stake. In her article *The Right Way To Fight*, Amy Gallo describes the following steps for managing conflict:

1. *Prepare* – determine the type of conflict, decipher the positions of all parties, leave emotions out of the conversation as much as possible, and schedule the conversation to take place in person, and with sufficient time allotted.
2. *Identify Common Ground* – agree on a common goal that all parties believe in and check in about that goal.
3. *Hear the other person (people) out* – enter the conversation with an open mind and ask clarifying questions to seek to understand the other party's position (more on asking questions, below).
4. *Propose a resolution* – once all the information has been shared by all parties, recommend a resolution to the conflict based on that information (not the resolution that was determined prior to the conversation); engage in cooperative problem-solving if the resolution does not work for all parties.
5. *If needed, refocus the conversation or take a break* – if the conversation becomes heated or unproductive (which might happen if things get very personal or emotional), refocus on the common goals, and if needed, pause the conversation until all parties can reconvene, and consider changing the process to increase the chances of resolving the conflict.

(Gallo, 2017)

When managing conflict, all parties need to remain respectful and open-minded that their perspective may not be the same as others.

A helpful model to keep in mind when engaging in difficult conversations is seeing the conversation as consisting of the following components:

- *Advocacy* – sharing one party's perspective/story, filling in gaps the other party did not state or discuss
- *Inquiry* – seeking to understand, and approaching the conversation with an open mind and no assumptions about the other party's perspective/feelings
- *Acknowledgement* – recognizing and reflecting back the other party's perspective/feelings showing that they are heard and understood, and stating any defensiveness or feelings that emerge
- *Bridging/Problem-Solving* – building solutions together, especially coming from a place of inquiry about what would work for the other party

(Ringer, n.d.)

In most difficult conversations, people spend the majority of their time engaging in advocacy, defending their position or stance – often from a place of feeling right. However, in order to truly understand someone and the conflict at hand, people need to focus more on inquiry-seeking to understand. Ask questions about their perceptions of the situation, why something took place, and what things they wish would have been different. In addition, be present (by not interrupting), be open (by not making assumptions), and listen more: "We have two ears and one mouth, so we should listen more than we say" (Seppala & Stevenson, 2017). Listening helps demonstrate investment in the relationship and a genuine interest in learning about their perspective, which also cultivates trust.

Not addressing conflict can have disastrous consequences, including decreased motivation, toxic work culture, and bad attitudes about collaboration. Sexuality educators need to equip themselves to have a productive approach to managing conflict and see it as a critical growth opportunity. It also takes a certain amount of bravery and vulnerability to manage conflict. Difficult conversations are called difficult for a reason – it's rarely a task a leader will choose to engage in. By embracing conflict as a component of collaboration and making conflict management a part of organizational culture and effective teamwork, those conversations can be not only easier, they can be productive. One survey respondent shared that they have learned, "About staying IN the conflict. Not fearing [it]. Going towards. Boldly speaking with full permission. Holding my point of view lightly. Deeply inviting and listening to others. Creating safe space for deep honoring of all."

Leadership Skill #6: Diversity and Inclusion

Of the seven topics explored in the "Leadership Development in Sexuality Education" survey, diversity and inclusion was the topic that the most respondents reported having learned about – 96.15%. It practically goes without saying that diversity and inclusion is an essential skill for sexuality educators, as it informs their interactions with others at an organizational level, and their implementation of effective and impactful sexuality education. One survey respondent shared this: "I believe that our ongoing work in sexuality education lives squarely in this land. As we over decades have created space for and voice for and honoring of sexual diversity and inclusion of all people." However, while nearly all the survey respondents indicated they had participated in learning about diversity and inclusion, 23% of respondents made a comment reflecting that the training/learning was only semi-helpful, or not helpful enough, especially on a practical level. One respondent shared, "I have attended many diversity and inclusion meetings and trainings, and even helped to plan and lead some, but I have never found that they seem particularly helpful to those who need them." This indicates that leaders need to be taking a hard look at diversity and inclusion efforts to identify ways to make them both relevant and practically applicable.

What do people mean when they refer to diversity and inclusion? *Diversity* is often thought of as the cultural and ethnic backgrounds of the people who work at an organization, frequently focusing on surface-level demographics (Robbins & Judge, 2016). There are a myriad of benefits of having people from differing backgrounds, perspectives, and expertise work together, as those differences can contribute to overall organizational effectiveness (Thomas & Ely, 1996). However, leaders need to move beyond numbers to also consider how to leverage differences and establish an inclusive working environment. *Inclusion* centers on employees feeling welcome and a central part of the organization. Vernā Myers describes the distinction between diversity and inclusion beautifully: "Diversity is being invited to the party. Inclusion is being asked to dance" (Sherbin & Rashid, 2017).

So what do sexuality educators need to know about diversity and inclusion at a base level? Leaders need to be bought in to the idea that *both* diversity and having an inclusive working environment is beneficial. They need to value diversity, and model inclusive behaviors through their actions and accountability. Leaders need to take steps to hire diverse staff and engage in recruiting strategies that help diverse audiences learn about available positions and what they can do to be hired for those positions. Leaders need to offer training and educational opportunities that cover topics such as power and privilege, gender, race, sexual orientation, and intervention skills (Pruitt, Brinkworth, Young, Abonte, 2018). (Note: Some research indicates that training/education programs that are *mandatory* do not have a positive impact, and may exacerbate interpersonal conflict. However, training/education programs that are voluntary have the opposite effect, building off the inherent buy-in of opting-in to attend [Dobbin & Kalev, 2016].) In addition, leaders need to take an active part in learning about diversity and inclusion and reflect on their own strengths and weaknesses in this area.

Two key concepts help inform strategies for diversity and inclusion: *unconscious bias* and the *integration paradigm*. Unconscious bias refers to the biases that people don't know they have, which then in turn influences their behaviors in ways they don't realize (Ross, 2014). For example, a research study showed that white basketball referees called fouls more often on Black players, and Black referees called fouls more often on white players (Ross, 2014). Unconscious bias can negatively influence diversity efforts, among other organizational behaviors. Examples of unconscious bias in sexuality education include inviting someone with an Anglo-sounding name to an interview because they appear more qualified than another person with similar experience/skills, always depicting male-identified individuals as manipulative or controlling in role-plays or scenarios about relationships, or developing an activity that only provides options for able-bodied participants that requires movement around the room. Leaders may be making assumptions and decisions that unintentionally harm others. Even if that harm is unintentional, impact trumps intention. These biases can influence behavior unknowingly, however, with awareness, their effects can be diminished. For example, having a neutral or third-party player hear out decisions can bring in an outside perspective. Including several people of diverse backgrounds on a hiring committee can help ensure any candidate with the necessary skills is considered. Using tools to remove names or other identifying information can help anonymize the hiring process. Encouraging dissent among groups can help people voice thoughts and opinions that might uncover unconscious bias – practice by having employees disagree with a manager in a constructed environment with a fabricated issue so everyone becomes more comfortable with each others' communication styles regarding disagreement. The key to unconscious bias is remaining aware that it exists and taking the steps needed to bring those biases to the surface so they can be managed accordingly. It takes more than consciousness-raising to change behavior – the individual needs to not only be willing to change, they need to commit to change over time (Noon, 2018). Regardless, training about unconscious bias cannot be a stand-alone strategy, yet can be an important step for leaders to become more aware of their own self and help them not make assumptions about others.

When thinking about diversity and inclusion on a practical level, some people focus solely on ensuring representation from a diverse set of backgrounds, cultures, etc. – essentially, a numbers game. Having people from different cultural, educational, geographic backgrounds can certainly help get different perspectives in the room. However, once a diverse group of people comes together, what are the expectations for 'fitting in' to the organizational culture? In their article *Making Differences Matter: A New Paradigm for Managing Diversity,* Thomas and Ely assert that organizations need to adopt an *integration paradigm*, rather than an *assimilation paradigm*, which encourages uniform behavior, or *differentiation paradigm*, which matches employees with a particular identity with particular audiences/focal areas (Thomas & Ely, 1996). The integration paradigm promotes both equal opportunity and valuing cultural differences. This approach encourages organizations to see diversity "more holistically – as providing fresh and meaningful approaches to work," rather than the way someone looks or where they come from. To implement the integration paradigm, leaders need to create an inclusive and mission-driven culture, where everyone feels valued. Thomas and Ely propose the following preconditions for adopting the integration paradigm:

1.   "The leadership must understand that a diverse workforce will embody different perspectives and approaches to work, and must truly value variety of opinion and insight.

2. The leadership must recognize both the learning opportunities and the challenges that the expression of different perspectives presents for an organization.
3. The organizational culture must create an expectation of high standards of performance from everyone.
4. The organizational culture must stimulate personal development.
5. The organizational culture must encourage openness.
6. The organizational culture must make workers feel valued.
7. The organization must have a well-articulated and widely understood mission.
8. The organization must have a relatively egalitarian, nonbureaucratic structure."

(Thomas & Ely, 1996, p. 9)

All of this is easier said than done and takes long-term commitment. It requires leaders to be vulnerable in order to identify weaknesses and take the time and energy to address them. It also requires leaders to broaden their perspectives to see diversity as more than gender and race – it can also encompass ability, income, education, geographic location, religion, and the list goes on (Johnson, 2017).

As a skill, diversity and inclusion may be the most difficult to both establish and maintain out of the seven described in this chapter. There is a myriad of complex factors that influence diversity and inclusion, both with leaders themselves and the make-up of an organization or group of people. Sexuality educators need to see this as an area integral to their work, and from the survey results alone, more concrete strategies and discussion of inclusion are needed to truly develop this leadership skill. One survey respondent shared the following:

> My earlier diversity and inclusion learning focused on people with different physical capacities and on people who identified as anything other than heterosexual or cisgender. Later learning focused on racial, ethnic and cultural diversity. As a white professional in a field dominated by white people and white power structures, this is inexcusable. Glad we are starting to do more work, but it's pretty damn late, in my career at least.

At the core of teaching about sexuality is the aim to create welcoming, inclusive spaces where participants feel valued and comfortable enough to push their learning edges, and diverse experiences are both acknowledged and represented. It's time for the field to reexamine how this information is being communicated and offer both deeper learning and practical applications. Leaders can take the step of learning on their own, encouraging others, and setting the expectation that diversity and inclusion will be part of the core mission of sexuality education.

Leadership Skill #7: Feedback/Performance Reviews

It's no surprise that people fear feedback (Jackman & Stober, 2003). They often make assumptions about what that feedback will entail, which results in negative behaviors such as "procrastination, denial, brooding, jealousy, and self-sabotage" (Jackman & Stober, 2003, p. 101). While feedback does not always have to be negative, it's often thought of as such. However, feedback – both positive and constructive – is one of the ways that people learn and grow personally and professionally, as difficult as it may be. Of the "Leadership Development in Sexuality Education" survey respondents, 65.38% reported participating in learning about feedback/performance reviews. Sexuality educators should be accustomed to feedback. Part of becoming a good facilitator/teacher is having someone conducting observations and providing professionals with feedback on what's working, what needs to change (e.g., asking closed ended questions when trying illicit discussion). However, feedback needs to be done well – respectfully, empathetically, and from an informed and unbiased perspective, with a balanced approach. It's not easy to give feedback, and do it well, which is why it's critical that leaders take the time to learn about giving feedback. One survey respondent even shared, "I really wish I had something like that when I first started out!"

One model that can help leaders provide feedback is the Four-Step Feedback Loop (Nexient Learning Inc, n.d.). The first step is to discuss the observed behavior. Then discuss what impact that behavior has on the situation or other people. The next step is to address what may be needed or requested in the future. Finally, wrap up by agreeing on what will change. For example:

> Observation: "I heard you use closed-ended questions several times during the workshop when you were trying to illicit discussion."
> Impact: "The closed-ended questions meant that participants gave only one-word responses, instead of discussing their thoughts fully."
> Request: "Next time, I'd like you to change your closed-ended questions to open-ended ones."
> Agreement: "Can we agree that you'll work on using more open-ended questions?"

This example is relatively simple; however, the model works with more complex or personal issues as well. The model also works very well for positive feedback. For example:

> Observation: "I reviewed the lesson plan you wrote and it's very interactive, clearly accomplishes the goals and objectives, and is inclusive of diverse participant experiences."
> Impact: "I think the teachers will be able to interpret the instructions and students will really benefit from this fresh perspective on sexual decision-making."

Request: "I'd like you to work on another lesson plan about sexual pleasure using the same approach you used on this one."
Agreement: "What do you think about continuing to use the format and approach you did?"

Using the Four-Step Feedback loop can help leaders avoid some common pitfalls of giving feedback. One pitfall is not providing the feedback at all – if the feedback is not given, then behavior will not change, and the person will never be aware they did something wrong or problematic. Another pitfall is waiting too long to provide feedback. Feedback is best given as soon as possible after a behavior takes place, as long as there is an appropriate venue and opportunity to speak about it. Note that feedback does not always need to be provided, especially if one is not able to discuss a first-hand observation, the impact, and what change is needed. Think about why that feedback needs to be communicated, what the purpose is, and how the person or working relationship can benefit from that feedback. Also consider what emotions are involved, and how that person will react. Emotions aren't a reason not to provide feedback, but they may affect how that feedback is given/received. Consideration needs to be given to one's tone and nonverbal expressions – feedback given quickly and in passing may not be taken seriously or may not leave room or space for any emotions that emerge and need to be processed.

One formal way feedback is provided is through performance reviews – a structured conversation about performance over a given period of time (often conducted annually) and discussion of goals for the future. Performance reviews are not always part of an organizational structure, however, can be a valuable practice if done well. Each organization often has its own format for a performance review and may include a series of closed-ended questions with a Likert scale, some open-ended questions about performance attributes, and skills to work on. Performance reviews may include suggested trainings, and generally include an overall rating. Some organizations only have performance reviews once per year, some also have a midyear review, and some organizations don't do them at all. A critical element of a review is that it should be just that – a review. Nothing that is covered during a performance review should be a surprise to the person being reviewed – it should be a recap of feedback that has been provided previously (which is one reason why it's so important to give feedback in an ongoing capacity). Another important practice when conducting performance reviews is to consistently document feedback that is given (both positive and constructive), in whatever way that works for professionals – paper, email, electronic document – something that one can look back to once it comes time to conduct a performance review. One pitfall when conducting a review is recollection bias – the reviewer only recalls and incorporates recent events into a review because that's what they remember, rather than including things that happened at the beginning of the time-frame being reviewed.

Feedback is a critical step in personal and professional growth that sexuality educators need to embrace and learn about doing well. It might not always go the way one wants it to (actually, it rarely will), but it's important to be brave, and have the feedback conversation early and often. Feedback is best when it's natural, and often – providing feedback out of the blue when it hasn't been part of a working relationship can be off-putting, and can result in someone not feeling valued, rather than seen as contributing to growth. One survey respondent shared that the learning about feedback was "Helpful. Necessary. How to create energetic developmental growth space. Mutuality. Curiosity. More opportunity-focused. Shared and built upon the individual's strengths and goals – tied to organizational needs and goals. (Thus, looked forward to, not dreaded!) A continuous learning culture of curiosity." Just as sexuality educators encourage open, honest conversations about sexuality, they need to have open, honest conversations about feedback.

Recommendations

This chapter highlights the rationale and some key points describing seven skills of leadership development, which are relevant for sexuality educators at any point in their career. Leadership skills need to be a priority in professional development from the beginning, so those skills can be applied early, and often. Sexuality educators need to commit to developing those skills in an ongoing capacity – just like sexuality, one can't learn about leadership once and be done with it. It requires consistent learning and self-reflection. See Figure 2.4 for a checklist to reflect on one's current level of knowledge and comfort with each skill, and action items to help develop that skill.

For each leadership skill, reflection on one's current level of knowledge about that skill (e.g., beginner, intermediate, advanced, expert), what can be done to build upon that knowledge in the coming months, and how one can integrate that skill into their day-to-day functioning. For increasing knowledge, consider some of the following steps to take:

- Read a book related to that skill
- Attend an in-person professional development or training session
- Participate in an online training or course
- Discuss with a supervisor and/or peer
- Take an assessment
- Watch a video (i.e., TedTalk)
- Read a journal article
- Mentor another sexuality educator on this skill

Leadership Skill	Current Level of Knowledge	What actionable steps can you take to learn more about this skill in the next six months?	What actionable steps can you take to integrate this skill into your day-to-day?
Leadership Styles			
Motivation			
Organizational Culture			
Leading Teams			
Managing Conflict			
Diversity & Inclusion			
Feedback/Performance Reviews			
Other:			

Figure 2.4 Leadership Skills Development Checklist

Completing this checklist regularly can help a sexuality educator remain reflective about their current level of knowledge about leadership skills and encourage them to always be striving to learn more about leadership, and themselves.

In addition to the seven skills explored in this chapter, there are many other skills that sexuality educators can learn about and integrate into their work. Some additional skills to learn more about include the following:

- Emotional intelligence
- Psychological safety
- Communication skills
- Decision-making
- Delegation
- Project management
- Prioritization/time management
- Organizational change
- Entrepreneurship
- Negotiation
- Ethics
- Strategic thinking and planning
- Mentorship
- Trauma-informed leadership – a new concept to introduce to the field

This list could likely go on; however; the most important aspect of developing leadership skills is committing to do so and helping others prioritize leadership development as well. In fact, a common theme throughout the survey was the importance of mentoring relationships and learning leadership skills by observing them in others.

To undertake the task of embarking on the journey of leadership development, consider doing the following: Ask for support from one's supervisor to attend a training or professional development seminar related to one of these leadership skills. For sexuality educators who supervise employees, encourage one's staff to learn more about these skills, bring them up during supervision meetings, and discuss one's own journey learning about leadership. For program directors, make leadership skills a standard professional development step in one's organization, and model that learning by attending seminars, reading books, and engaging with content then bringing it back to one's team. For professors and teachers that are teaching the next cohort of sexuality educators, include leadership skills in one's coursework in some capacity.

Limitations

This chapter has its limitations in terms of drawing on leadership skills specifically related to sexuality education. There is currently little to nothing published about leadership skills development among sexuality educators. Further insight, reflection, and research on leadership skills within the field of sexuality education is needed in order to identify gaps in knowledge, practical application of skills, and new frameworks specifically for sexuality educators. Some questions for consideration in future work include the following:

- What skills are most important for sexuality educators to prioritize?
- What frameworks for leadership are most relevant for sexuality educators?
- What skills do sexuality educators need to learn most early on in their careers?
- What skills do sexuality educators need in order to advance in their careers?
- What is the impact of seasoned sexuality educators mentoring others? How is mentoring done most effectively in order to cultivate leadership skills?

In addition, the survey distributed to gather insight for this chapter only had 52 respondents, out of what can be assumed to be thousands of sexuality educators, and their responses may not correlate to the broader population of professionals in the field. The terms referenced in the survey were not explicitly defined, thus a survey respondent may have had a different understanding of a leadership skill. In addition, demographics such as age, education, and location were not captured in the survey.

Conclusion

Leadership development is not an easy journey to embark upon. One must be vulnerable and truly self-reflect about strengths, weaknesses, personality, and find room and ways to grow. It takes time and diligence, and among all the other priorities, professional development can easily get left by the wayside. However, in order for the field to continue to evolve and succeed, sexuality educators with all levels of experience need to take on the challenge of learning about and implementing critical leadership skills. As one survey respondent shared, "Everything rises or falls on leadership. The more you grow, the better you lead yourself and others."

Process Questions and Considerations

1. What impact do I want to have as a leader?
2. What are my strengths as a leader?
3. What are my weaknesses as a leader?
4. Which of the seven leadership skills discussed in this chapter do I feel strongest in?
5. Which of the seven leadership skills discussed in this chapter do I feel weakest in?
6. How will I learn more about leadership skills?
7. How will I integrate these seven leadership skills into my day-to-day work?

References

Adams, J. (1963). Toward an understanding of inequity. *Journal of Abnormal and Social Psychology, 67*, 422–436.

Amabile, T., & Kramer, S. (2011). The power of small wins. *Harvard Business Review, 89*(5), 70–80.

Ayman, R. (2004). Situational and contingency approaches to leadership. In J. Antonakis, A. T. Cianciolo, & R. J. Sternberg (Eds.), *The nature of leadership* (pp. 148–170). Thousand Oaks, CA: Sage Publications, Inc.

Buckingham, M. (2001). *Now, discover your strengths*. New York: The Free Press.

Christensen, C. (2006). *What is an organization's culture?* HBS No. 9-399-104. Boston, MA: Harvard Business School Publishing.

de Bono, E. (1985). *Six thinking hats: An essential approach to business management*. Little, Brown & Company.

Dobbin, R., & Kalev, A. (2016). Why diversity programs fail: And what works better. *Harvard Business Review, 94*(7–8), 52–60.

Eisenhardt, K., Kahwajy, J., & Bourgeois, L. (1997). How management teams can have a good fight. *Harvard Business Review, 75*(4), 77–86.

Gallo, A. (2017). How to control your emotions during a difficult conversation. *Harvard Business Review*.

Goleman, D. (2000). Leadership that gets results. *Harvard Business Review, 78*(2), 4–17.

Graen, G., & Uhl-Bien, M. (1995). Relationship-based approach to leadership: Development of leader-member exchange (LMX) theory of leadership over 25 years: Applying a multi-level multi-domain perspective. *Management Department Faculty Publications, 57*, 219–247.

Herzberg, F. (1964). The motivation-hygiene concept and problems of manpower. *Personnel Administration, (27)*, 3–7.

History of Leadership as a Field of Study. (n.d.) Retrieved from www.k12academics.com/education-theory/descriptive-theories-education/leadership-studies/history-leadership-field-study

Jackman, J. M., & Stober, M. H. (2003). Fear of feedback. *Harvard Business Review, 81*(4), 101–108.

Janis, I. (1972). Groupthink and group dynamics: A social psychological analysis of defective policy decisions. *Policy Studies Journal, 2*(1), 19–25.

Johnson, S. K. (2017). What 11 CEOS have learned about championing diversity. *Harvard Business Review*.

Kahn, W. (1990). Psychological conditions of personal engagement and disengagement at work. *Academy of Management Journal, 33*(4), 692–724.

Locke, E., & Latham, P. (2002). Building a practically useful theory of goal-setting and task motivation. *American Psychologist, 57*(9), 705–717.

Marston, W. (1928). *Emotions of Normal People*. K. Paul (Ed.), Trench, Trubner & Co. Ltd.

McClelland, D. (1961). *The achieving society*. Princeton, NJ: Van Nostrand.

McCleskey, J. (2014). Situational, transformational, and transactional leadership and leadership development. *Journal of Business Studies Quarterly, 5*(4), 117–130.

McGregor, D. (1957). The human side of enterprise. *Management Review, 46*, 622–628.

Myers, I. (1995). *Gifts differing: Understanding personality type.* Mountain View, CA: Davies-Black Publishing.

Nexient Learning Inc. (n.d.). *Performance management: Staff development & goal setting at Columbia University.* New York, NY: Participant Guide for training session held at Columbia University.

Noon, M. (2018). Pointless diversity training: Unconscious bias, new racism and agency. *Work, Employment and Society, 32*(1), 198–209.

Polzer, J. (2003). *Leading teams.* HBS No. 9-403-094. Boston, MA: Harvard Business School Publishing.

Pruitt, A., Brinkworth, C., Young, J., & Abonte, K. (2018). Five things we learned about creating a successful workplace diversity program. *Harvard Business Review.*

Ringer, J. (n.d.). *We have to have a talk: A step-by-step checklist for difficult conversations.* Retrieved on November 29, 2018 from www.judyringer.com/resources/articles/we-have-to-talk-a-stepbystep-checklist-for-difficult-conversations.php

Robbins, S., & Judge, T. (2016). *Essentials of organizational behaviors* (13th ed.). Boston, MA: Pearson.

Ross, H. (2014). *Everyday bias: Identifying and navigating unconscious judgments in our daily lives.* Lanham, MD: Rowman & Littlefield.

Ryan, R., & Deci, E. (2000). Self-determination theory and the facilitation of intrinsic motivation, social development, and well-being. *American Psychologist, 55,* 68–78.

Seppala, E., & Cameron, K. (2015). Proof that positive work cultures are more productive. *Harvard Business Review, 12*(1), 44–50.

Seppala, E., & Stevenson, J. (2017). In a difficult conversation, listen more than you talk. *Harvard Business Review.*

Sherbin, S., & Rashid, R. (2017). Diversity doesn't stick without inclusion. *Harvard Business Review.*

Thomas, D., & Ely, R. (1996). Making differences matter. *Harvard Business Review,* 1–12.

Tjosvold, D. (2008). The conflict-positive organization: It depends on us. *Journal of Organizational Behavior, 29*(1), 19–28.

Uhl-Bien, M. (2006). Relationship leadership theory: Exploring the social processes of leadership and organizing. *Leadership Institute Faculty Publications, 19.*

Ware, J., & Barnes, L. (1978). *Managing interpersonal conflict.* HBS 9-479-004. Boston, MA: Harvard Business School Publishing.

Warrick, B. (2017). What leaders need to know about organizational culture. *Business Horizons, 60,* 395–404.

Yukl, G. (1971). Toward a behavioral theory of leadership. *Organizational Behavior and Performance, 6*(4), 414–440.

Zaccaro, S. (2007). Trait-based perspectives of leadership. *American Psychologist, 62*(1), 6–16.

3 Sexuality Education for Current and Future Healthcare Providers

Jenna Benyounes

A New Vision for Sexual Health in Healthcare

Sexual health, as defined by the World Health Organization (2006), is as follows:

> A state of physical, emotional, mental and social well-being in relation to sexuality; it is not merely the absence of disease, dysfunction or infirmity. Sexual health requires a positive and respectful approach to sexuality and sexual relationships, as well as the possibility of having pleasurable and safe sexual experiences, free of coercion, discrimination, and violence. For sexual health to be attained and maintained, the sexual rights of all persons must be respected, protected and fulfilled.

Sexual health questions and concerns are some of the most common medical concerns among patients, yet, they tend to be the most overlooked and under addressed. When sexual health concerns are in fact addressed, they are often disease, pathology, and problem focused. Thankfully, recent recommendations have been encouraging a health and wellness perspective rather than a disease-focused one. An article in the *Journal of the American Medical Association* (JAMA) proposed a national shift to a focus on sexual health rather than simply on disease, which has plagued the medical community for years without producing significant changes (Swartzendruber & Zenilman, 2010). In keeping with the article from JAMA and unlike previous Healthy People initiatives, Healthy People 2020 (n.d.) addresses reproductive and sexual health with an emphasis on wellness. This reframing is congruent with the recommendations from experts who believe "we can only meet the sexual health challenges by shifting away from the current focus on diseases and moving towards a perspective that promotes health and wellness" (American Sexual Health Association, n.d.). To further the focus on health, Satcher, Hook, and Coleman (2015) created a framework that emphasizes wellness, focuses on positive and respectful relationships, acknowledges sexual health as an element of overall health, and provides an integrated approach to prevention.

At first glance, initiatives appear to be working. According to the Kaiser Family Foundation, the percentage of women who speak with their healthcare provider about their sexual history has risen from 31% in 2004 to 61% in 2017 (Kaiser Family Foundation, 2018). While this statistic is reassuring, it does not evaluate the whole picture. It fails to address which questions were asked to assist the healthcare provider in stratifying risk, as well as providing appropriate counseling and education. While there have been improvements over the years, there is still more to be done. This chapter will display the current state of healthcare provider's approach to evaluating a patients' sexual health, why sexual health is important, and where improvements can be made to improve the quality of evaluations, treatment plans, and education.

The Gap in Patient Expectations and Healthcare Provider Actions

The topic of sexual health is equally as important to both the patient as well as healthcare providers. Of primary care, obstetrics, and gynecology physicians surveyed, 89% believed that screening for female sexual dysfunction was somewhat or very important (Nusbaum, Gamble, Skinner, & Heiman, 2000). Shifren et al. (2009) reported in their study that 78% of patients expected their healthcare provider to ask them about their sexual health, especially when they were in the care of a gynecologist or primary care physician. In a study by the Association of Reproductive Health Professionals and the National Women's Health Resource Center (2009), they found that 74% of providers relied on their patients to initiate a discussion about their sexual health, yet 73% of patients preferred that their healthcare provider brought up the topic (Association of Reproductive Health Professionals and the National Women's Health Resource Center, 2009). Sixty-eight percent of patients preferred a provider who appeared comfortable evaluating their sexual health and addressing their concerns (Nusbaum et al., 2000). In the office, it was found that 69% of physicians underestimated female sexual dysfunction in their patients (Goldenhar et al., 2005).

In matters regarding the initiation of discussing sexual health, most patients expect their providers to start the conversation. However, healthcare providers often do not initiate the conversation or even know how to properly address a patient's concerns. While there is a plethora of reasons for not evaluating a patient's sexual health, the most common themes include lack of time, lack of education, and lack of knowledge (Kingsberg & Knudson, 2011).

According to Papaharitou et al. (2005), "women are reluctant to seek medical advice on their sexual concerns." When women seek care for their complaints, they most often saw an obstetrician/gynecologist or primary care provider (Shifren et al., 2009). Only 6% of women scheduled an appointment specifically for their sexual health concerns. Of those women, 80% of them initiated the discussion (Shifren et al., 2009). In urogynecology clinics, 37% of women had a sexual complaint, but only 17% initiated the discussion. Therefore, 83% of patients did not bring up their concerns unless asked specifically (Roos et al., 2012).

Between 73% and 78% of patients expect, or rather prefer, that their provider initiate the discussion, and ask them about their sexual health (Association of Reproductive Health Professionals and the National Women's Health Resource Center, 2009; Shifren et al., 2009). However, in the same study by the Association of Reproductive Health Professionals and the National Women's Health Resource Center (2009), 74% of providers relied on their patients to initiate a discussion about sexual health. Sobecki, Curlin, Rasinski, and Lindau (2012) found that approximately 63% of obstetrician/gynecologists routinely asked about patients' sexual activity, and 40% asked about sexual problems. Of their 1,154 physician participants, less than one third, or 28.5%, routinely asked patients about sexual satisfaction, and 27.7% asked about sexual orientation/identity. Only 13.8% asked about pleasure or satisfaction with sexual activity. In a study completed by 491 urogynecologists, Goldenhar et al. (2005) reported that most participants considered asking at least one question about sexual activity as evaluation of sexual health.

Adolescents and older populations of women are the least likely to have their sexual health evaluated by their provider. In a study by Alexander et al. (2014), the researchers reported that during annual visits, no adolescents initiated the conversation about sexual health, and two thirds of physicians did not ask adolescents about sex. For the physicians that did, the average conversation was 36 seconds long. In a literature review, Hinchliff and Gott (2011) reported that the older patient population are less likely to seek out medical help for sexual concerns. Hinchliff and Gott (2011) also reported that physicians were less likely to ask due to embarrassment or their assumption that sex was less important for older people.

To better evaluate patients' sexual health, a variety of questionnaires have been created. The most frequently used and validated questionnaire, the Female Sexual Function Index (FSFI), uses 19 questions to evaluate six different components of female sexual dysfunction (Rosen et al., 2000). Since its creation, the FSFI been cross-validated for use in multiple languages, for women in adolescence through menopause, pregnant or not, with mixed causes for sexual dysfunction, and for women with chronic medical issues (Rehman, Asif Mahmood, Sheikh, Sultan, & Khan, 2015). While these questionnaires can make screening for sexual dysfunction more efficient and make asking about sexual health easier, many providers do not utilize them (Kriston, Günzler, Rohde, & Berner (2010). In an effort to increase screening for sexual dysfunction and to decrease the amount of time patients and providers spent on paperwork, Kriston et al. (2010) created a one-question version as well as a two-question version questionnaire to screen for sexual dysfunction. Their questionnaire had 74% and 93% sensitivity and 76% and 60% specificity, respectively. While this is promising, questionnaires should not replace the patient-clinician interview and obtaining a sexual history (Kingsberg & Althof, 2009). Questionnaires can be used as a screener, as well as a helpful aid, to minimize time spent with each patient while providing comprehensive assessment, and as an introduction for a conversation about sexual health between the patient and the provider (Kingsberg & Althof, 2009).

Why Healthcare Providers Do Not Discuss Sexual Health With Their Patients

There are numerous studies that state the most common reason providers do not routinely evaluate their patients' sexual health and dysfunction is a lack of time (Abdolrasulnia et al., 2010; Garcia & Fisher, 2008; Kingsberg & Knudson, 2011; Roos, Thakar, Sultan, & Scheer, 2009). In addition to lack of time, other reasons for not evaluating is the healthcare providers' lack of knowledge and training on the subject (Dahir, 2009; Kingsberg & Knudson, 2011; Roos, Sultan, & Thakar, 2012; Rosen, Kountz, Post-Zwicker, Leiblum, & Wiegel, 2006; Wittenberg & Gerber, 2009).

Lack of Education

In regard to sexual health, patients expect that their healthcare providers be knowledgeable and approachable, yet all future medical professionals are ill prepared to meet these needs. In medical school, there are no universal standards in regard to sexuality education.

Criniti, Crane, Woodland, Montgomery, and Urdaneta Hartmann (2016) completed a study with 550 medical residents, of all different specialties, to evaluate the amount of sexuality instruction they received in their training as well as the residents' self-perceived readiness to address sexual health concerns with their patients. The researchers reported that while in medical school, 86.3% residents received some sexuality education, 10% of residents received none, and 4% could not recall. After graduating from medical school and training in their residency programs, only 25% of residents reported that they had received courses or lectures specifically on sexuality issues, and an astounding 68% reported no courses or lectures so far, while 6.3% checked "I don't know." The researchers then attempted to quantify the amount of hours of instruction on human sexuality that the residents received. Approximately 61% of residents reported zero hours of human sexuality education, and approximately 23% reported one to three hours. Therefore, 84% of residents received three hours of less of training on human sexuality in their years of training.

The three topics that more than 50% of residents reported "very strong" or "adequate" instruction in dealt mostly with morbidity. These topics included HIV, sexually transmitted infections, and anatomy/physiology. In 18 other critical human sexuality topics, 70% of residents reported receiving "minimal" or "no education." Only 35.9% of the respondents reported that their instruction for child sex abuse was "strongly" or "adequately discussed." Instruction for male and female sexual dysfunction was reported as "minimal" or "no education" by 72.9% and 73.6%, respectively. Sixty-two percent of respondents reported no instruction on orgasm, 57% received no instruction on sexual pleasure, 56.3% received no instruction on the sexual response cycle, 55.6% received no instruction on transgender patients, and 54.7% received no education on variations in sexual practices (Criniti et al., 2016).

In a literature review completed by Dahir (2009), it was noted that not a single nursing school in the study had sexual health listed as part of their curriculum. In medical schools, one half of schools had three to ten hours of coursework and was often taught by a psychiatrist. The only requirement in curriculum for teaching sexual dysfunction was from the American Board of Obstetrics and Gynecology for pelvic medicine and reconstructive surgery specialist (Dahir, 2009). Despite this, the membership of the British Society of Urogynecology and the American Urogynecological Society found that 76% of members thought training in female sexual dysfunction to be unsatisfactory (Roos et al., 2009).

In their review of the literature, Kingsberg and Knudson (2011) reported that the lack of faculty with a focus in sexual health also contributed to the lack of student education regarding sexual health. In a study of medical students, 69% believe that that sexual concerns will be an important part of their practice, yet only 37% felt like they were adequately trained to do so. In that same group of students, 57% felt inadequately trained to take a basic sexual history (Wittenberg & Gerber, 2009). In a study conducted by Rosen et al. (2006), "48% of residents indicated that they were uncomfortable with open discussion of sexual issues and would not feel comfortable addressing the topic with their patients." They cited inadequate training, barriers to communication and personal discomfort as reasons. After participating in a half-day intensive workshop for sexual health, the residents reported more comfort with the topic, and that they would be more likely to address the sexual issues of their patients (Rosen et al., 2006).

After schooling and residencies, knowledge of female sexual dysfunction remains inadequate. In a study of 1,946 physicians, Bachmann (2006) reported that 60% of them rated both their knowledge of female sexual dysfunction and comfort level with female sexual dysfunction as poor or fair. Embarrassment about the topic in general, as well as a lack of knowledge on how to address their own embarrassment deterred physicians from screening for, or evaluating, patients' sexual dysfunction. Bachman (2006) also found that 86% of physicians believed that there was a lack of effective treatment options, which may deter them from initiating a conversation or addressing patient concerns, especially if they believe that nothing can be done. Shifren et al. (2009) also found that most women who presented with a sexual problem did not receive any treatment.

Clearly, while the significance of sexuality is important, there is a clear discrepancy in quantity and quality of the education on sexuality in North America. Most of the education programs that are currently taught have a focus on avoiding unwanted pregnancy and sexually transmitted disease. Any educational material other subjects such as abortion or differing sexual preferences is not present, or exceedingly rare. However, due to the lack of teaching and information, many student-led interventions have been enacted to ameliorate their understanding and training in the realm of sexual health (Shindel & Parish, 2013).

In the 30-page manual "Accreditation Standards for Physician Assistant Education," there is only one mention of human sexuality in the entire curriculum, in section B2.08, which states

> The program curriculum must include instruction in the social and behavioral sciences as well as normal and abnormal development across the life span. Social and behavioral sciences prepare students for primary care practice. Instruction includes . . . human sexuality.
> (Accreditation Review Commission on Education for the Physician Assistant, Inc., 2018)

Lack of Time

In addition to the lack of education, the second most common reason cited for a lack of evaluation of sexual health was too little time (Abdolrasulnia et al., 2010, Garcia & Fisher, 2008, Kingsberg & Knudson, 2011, Roos et al., 2009). According to Sadovsky and Nusbaum (2006) the clinician can "deal with any sexual problem or dysfunction directly, or refer the patient to an appropriately specialized care source." If a provider already does not feel skilled in the topic, it may take them more time to evaluate the patient. Thus, if they already feel as if they have a lack of time, it can decrease the motivation to evaluate sexual health if the physician feels inadequately prepared (Garcia & Fisher, 2008).

In 2018, MedScape surveyed more than 20,000 physicians to produce the Physician Compensation Report. They reported that 62% of physicians spend 13–24 minutes in the room with patients (MedScape, 2018). Specifically, in primary care, it was found that physicians spent

16.5 minutes face to face with patients (Young, Burge, Kumar, Wilson, & Ortiz, 2018). Although that already does not seem as an appropriate amount of time, consider that only 52.9% of the visit is spent face to face, while the other 37.0% of the visit is spent on paperwork (Sinsky et al., 2016). In a typical 16.5-minute visit, this leaves roughly 8 minutes and 44 seconds for the healthcare provider to hear the patient's history, ask questions, complete an exam if needed, think through a differential diagnosis, possible determine a diagnosis, create a plan of care, and provide patient education. However, this is not due to laziness, as for every hour physicians spend with their patients, they spend another two hours completing administrative tasks and most spend another one to two hours per day of personal time completing administrative work after seeing patients all day (Sinsky et al., 2016; Young et al., 2018).

Why Ask About Sexual Health?

According to Satcher et al. (2015) "Sexuality fulfills an array of personal, reproductive, and social needs, which influence behaviors and affect health." Obtaining an understanding of a patient's sexuality provides clinicians the complete representation of biopsychosocial health and the factors that influence it, thus allowing clinicians to provide personalized comprehensive care to patients. Patients expect comprehensive care from competent clinicians. This can be reflected in their desire to see healthcare providers who to ask them about their sexual health and appear comfortable doing so. Skipping over a sexual health assessment would be analogous to skipping any other part of a health assessment. Sexual health is an integral part of overall health and wellness for patients. Sexual health is just as important as general health, and can even give providers a window into the patient's overall health status, motivations, and future health forecast.

Beyond the ability to be a thorough and holistic clinician, another reason to ask patients about their sexual health is the prevalence of concerns. The Prevalence of Female Sexual Problems Associated with Distress and Determinants of Treatment Seeking (PRESIDE) study included 31,581 U.S. women aged 18 to 102 years. They reported that 44% of participants had any sexual problem which included problems with desire, arousal, or orgasm. The most common problem reported by 39% of women was low desire, while 26% and 21% of participants reported low arousal and orgasm problems, respectively (Shifren, Monz, Russo, Segreti, & Johannes, 2008). Ninety percent of women sought formal help for sexual dysfunction from a gynecologist or primary care provider and most of those women did so during a routine exam (Rosen et al., 2009). The most common sexual concern for women is the lack of interest in sex and for men it is early ejaculation and erectile dysfunction (Laumann et al., 2005).

Correlations From Sexual Health to General Health

Sexual dysfunction is a multifactorial phenomenon that involves biology, psychology, relationships, and societal and cultural factors (Clayton & Groth, 2013). Sexual health and general health are not mutually exclusive; they are often intertwined in how patients present with concerns. For example, men with erectile dysfunction often have cardiac health concerns, yet often these concerns are viewed as two separate problems rather than related. Unfortunately, even more common is that the sexual health concern is not discussed because the patient was expecting the provider to initiate the discussion. Many patients do not know about the correlations between sexual health concerns and general health concerns so it is the duty of the clinician to present and frame the discussion. Patients who present with male and female sexual dysfunction may have a higher risk of comorbid conditions such as cardiovascular disease, hypertension, hyperlipidemia, hyper or hypothyroidism, depression, and diabetes (Grover et al., 2006). Medications that can impact sexual health include the following: anticonvulsants, cardiovascular medications, hormonal agents such as spironolactone, gonadotropin-releasing hormone agonists, combined hormonal contraceptives, tamoxifen, aromatase inhibitors, opioids, antipsychotics, benzodiazepines, lithium, selective serotonin reuptake inhibitors, serotonin and norepinephrine reuptake inhibitors, and tricyclic antidepressants (Parish et al., 2019)

Women's sexual function is influenced by many biopsychosocial factors. The best-known risk factors are depression, poor self-assessed health, anxiety, low educational level, partner sexual problems, sexual abuse, marital difficulties, stress, antidepressant drug use, poor health, cancer, urinary incontinence, and chronic disease such as diabetes, neurologic disease, and pain (Parish et al., 2019). Women who suffer from sexual dysfunction are more likely to have hypertension, diabetes, and elevated lipids (Sadovsky & Nusbaum, 2006). Contributing factors for female sexual dysfunction include these: cardiovascular disease, diabetes, thyroid disease, chronic pain, urinary incontinence, medication, spinal cord injury, multiple sclerosis, neuromuscular disorders, prolactinoma, cancer, cancer treatments, gynecologic surgery, colorectal surgery, pelvic radiation, pelvic organ prolapse, endometriosis, fibroids, vulvar dermatoses, vulvodynia/vestibulodynia, and psychiatric disorders (Parish et al., 2019).

There are four categories of female sexual dysfunction, these include disorders of sexual desire, sexual arousal, orgasm, and pain (Bornstein et al., 2016). These disorders are psychological and physiological in origin and often have overlap (Khajehei, Doherty, Tilley, & Sauer, 2015). Often patients who experience pain with sex also experience a decrease in sexual desire. If a patient has concerns over arousal, this can eventually lead to pain, which can then lead to a decrease in desire. There are physiologic origins at play in regard to sexual dysfunction. Approximately 79% of patients with HSDD, 78.4% of patients with anorgasmia, and 50% of patients with sexual pain dysfunction had female androgen insensitivity (Vale, Coimbra, Lopes, & Geber, 2017). This is something that may be easily overlooked if sexual health is not addressed but can have implications for overall physical health as well as psychosocial health in the future.

In a study conducted by Chapman University, Indiana University, and the Kinsey Institute, the researchers explored the orgasm gap between 52,588 participants. They reported that 95% of heterosexual men usually or always had an orgasm when they are sexually intimate. Gay men reported usually or always having an orgasm 89% of the time which was similar to bisexual men at 88%. Lesbian women usually or always had an orgasm 86% of the time. Compare that to bisexual women who had an orgasm 66% of them time and heterosexual women who had an orgasm 65% of the time. The researchers posit that the gap may be produced by the lack of agency that straight women have over their pleasure as well as the awareness about female pleasure that their heterosexual male partner has. Given that lesbian women are having higher rates of orgasm, it can be deduced that heterosexual women could be experiencing more orgasms (Frederick, John, Garcia, & Lloyd, 2018). Frederick et al. (2018) reported that women who received more oral sex, last longer during sex, are satisfied with their relationship, are assertive with what they want in bed, commend their partner for an act performed in bed, adorn sexy lingerie, attempt different sexual positions, incorporate intimate conversations, and express feelings of love during sex have orgasmed more regularly. Knowing this information, after healthcare providers assess for physical causes of orgasm concerns such as adhesions or idiopathic causes, they can address the other psychosocial aspects that contribute to orgasm.

Thinking about sex led to decreased reports of inability to orgasm in women. Women who felt the future of their relationship was in jeopardy reported more concerns with orgasm as well (Laumann et al., 2005). While sexual health is not all about the orgasm, patients who present with these concerns may have concerns over their relationship, may not be obtaining the stimulation they need, have a health issue causing their concern, or need health education. Lack of interest in sex and non-pleasurable sex were associated with the belief that aging reduced sexual desire and activity, thinking infrequently about sex, depression, low expectations about the future of the relationship, and infrequent sex (Laumann et al., 2005). On the surface, hearing a patient have a concern about lack of interest in sex may seem unsubstantial, however there are often other comorbid factors that can contribute to the patient's initial presentation.

Early ejaculation and erectile dysfunction are the most common sexual health concerns of men, however they often are not addressed as healthcare providers do not ask about sexual health (Laumann et al., 2005). While the most common sexual concern of men was early ejaculation, in a study by Laumann (2005), it had the least explanatory power. Infrequent sex was one of the only things globally that contributed to early ejaculation. In the Middle East, having financial problems was associated with early ejaculation. Knowing this could assist the healthcare provider in evaluating why the patient is having infrequent sex and if there are any social, psychological, or physiological concerns to address.

The second most common concern for men was erectile dysfunction. According to Laumann (2005), infrequent sex, relationship difficulties, and financial problems were contributors to erectile dysfunction. Beyond those contributors, erectile dysfunction has vascular, neurologic, psychological, and hormonal causes. It can also be idiopathic from medications or surgery. Contributing factors to erectile dysfunction include the following: alcohol use, anxiety, being overweight, cigarette smoking, use of other tobacco use, depression, prostate problems, drug use, atherosclerosis, elevated blood pressure/hypertension, hyperlipidemia/high cholesterol, hormone imbalance such a low testosterone, relationship concerns, stress, stroke, spine or pelvic injury, Parkinson's, multiple sclerosis, and nerve damage from diabetes or prostate surgery (American Academy of Family Physicians, 2016). Tobacco use, obesity, sedentary lifestyle, and chronic alcohol use can cause a decrease in testosterone and can negatively impact endothelial function, both of which can lead to erectile dysfunction (Sasayama et al., 2003). It can be reasoned that these same behaviors can also cause sexual dysfunction in women given how they impact physiology. Having excess adipose, or fatty, tissue causes testosterone to aromatize, or convert, into estradiol which is one of the major causes of hypogonadism (Vermeulen, Kaufman, Deslypere, & Thomas, 2003). Adipose tissue also generates inflammatory cytokines, which can cause cardiovascular events such as a heart attack, and impaired endothelial function, which contributes to erectile dysfunction (Giugliano et al., 2004; Vlachopoulos et al., 2006).

Sexual health concerns can be a warning to future health concerns. Erectile dysfunction usually presents two to five years prior to coronary artery disease. This advanced notice may give healthcare providers time to work on lifestyle interventions to prevent or delay the development of coronary artery disease (Inman et al., 2009). Men with erectile dysfunction had a threefold increase in osteoporosis as well (Wu et al., 2016). An astounding 10% of men with erectile dysfunction also have undiagnosed diabetes (Skeldon, Detsky, Goldenberg, & Law, 2015). Infrequent sex, financial problems, prostate disease, and vascular disease contribute to erectile dysfunction (Laumann et al., 2005). Knowing this, the healthcare provider can appropriately address the biopsychosocial aspects that could be contributing to erectile dysfunction and overall health.

In regard to men, the lack of interest in sex was associated with increased age, poor health, not frequently thinking about sex, depression, and infrequent sex (Laumann et al., 2005). If a man presents with decreased desire, the healthcare provider would be cued to evaluate overall health, to screen for depression, evaluate possible causes such as medications, and explore the psychosocial constructs at work,

Healthcare Provider Education and Algorithms

From the research presented already, it is clear that most healthcare providers do not evaluate a patient's sexual health because they feel that they do not have either the training to do so or the time. Thankfully, there are ways to increase the patients who are having their sexual health evaluated, without adding significant amounts of time to an already short visit, and without having to make all clinicians experts in sexual health. Screening tools as well as skills for communication are easy to access, yet can significantly improve rates of evaluation without adding time or stress to the healthcare providers' workload.

Tools for Evaluation

Utilizing tools and screeners can improve the rates of sexual health evaluation while not monopolizing a significant amount of time during an office visit. Administrative staff in healthcare offices can provide the necessary forms to patients upon entering the practice, and the clinician can review the forms before the visit with the patient. Another utilization of tools and screeners is to provide forms to patients after an appointment when a sexual health concern was mentioned, but there is not enough time to address the concern that day. Providing patients with a tool or screener gives them something to complete before the next appointment, while providing the healthcare provider with meaningful information on the patient's return. Listed here are tools and screeners that may be utilized in practice.

The Female Sexual Function Index, or FSFI, is a well-validated 19-item self-reported questionnaire to assess female sexual function. It is comprised of six subscales that include desire, arousal, lubrication, orgasm, satisfaction, and pain (Rosen et al., 2000).

When evaluating Hypoactive Sexual Desire Disorder, or HSDD, in women, the Decreased Sexual Desire Screener was created to specifically aid providers who are not trained in female sexual dysfunction. It provides a perfunctory diagnostic exam that assists providers in adequately diagnosing HSDD (Clayton et al., 2009).

The Female Sexual Distress Scale Revised is a 13-item questionnaire that evaluates distress over the last four weeks related to hypoactive sexual desire disorder. The revised scale was validated as an acceptable replacement for the Female Sexual Distress Scale (DeRogatis, Clayton, Lewis-D'Agostino, Wunderlich, & Fu, 2008)

The International Index of Erectile Function (IIEF-5) is a comprehensive questionnaire that assesses the relevant areas of male sexual function with 15 questions. The assessment is psychometrically accurate and has been translated into ten languages thus far. The test can easily be self-administered in a variety of settings, and clearly shows the accuracy in examining treatment related changes in patients with erectile dysfunction issues. It is used for clinical assessment and can be used to evaluate how effective treatment is (Rosen et al., 1997).

The Sexual Health Inventory for Men (SHIM) is a five-item questionnaire designed to evaluate sexual function in men over a time span of six months. This questionnaire is most frequently used in clinical practice not only in the United States, but around the world. Most notably, the SHIM has been accepted as the standard diagnostic tool for office screening of erectile dysfunction (Cappelleri & Rosen, 2005). The Brief Male Sexual Function Inventory is an 11-item self-administered questionnaire that evaluates sexual drive, erectile function and ejaculatory function, problems, and overall satisfaction (O'Leary et al., 1995)

There are two tools that only have one question, the Erection Hardness Score (EHS) and the Single-Question Assessment of Erectile Dysfunction. The EHS is a simple questionnaire that is filled out by the patient himself. Its goal is to evaluate the hardness of a man's erection (Mulhall, Goldstein, Bushmakin, Cappelleri, & Hvidsten, 2007). The Single-Question Assessment of Erectile Dysfunction is another single-question self-report of erectile dysfunction that can be a useful and valid tool in identifying those who experience erectile dysfunction. It can also be used as a referral screening tool in a variety of practice and research settings (O'donnell, Araujo, Goldstein, & McKinlay, 2005).

Starting the Conversation With Patients

Many healthcare providers feel embarrassed to evaluate a patient's sexual health and do not know where to begin. The International Society for the Study of Women's Sexual Health (ISSWSH) created The Process of Care for Identification of Sexual Concerns or Problems in Women to use as a step-by-step guide.

The first step in discussing sexual health with a patient is to normalize the conversation. Normalization conveys to the patient that concerns regarding sexual health are normal, common, and may even be expected by the healthcare provider. Normalization may also make the healthcare provider appear to be more comfortable with the topic as well (Sadovsky et al., 2006). The Center for Disease Control and Prevention (CDC) recommends that clinicians start the conversation by informing the patient that they are going to ask them about their sexual health, to acknowledge that the questions may be personal, but that they are important to their overall health, and that the information will be kept confidential (Center for Disease Control and Prevention, 2015). Something of note to add to the initiation of this discussion is consent from the patient to proceed. It is recommended that rather than following a script, clinicians create their own dialog using the formulas mentioned as a guide. The more comfortable the clinician is with the dialog, the more comfortable the patient will feel as well.

What Is Next?

As already noted, many office appointments are of limited time. One of the easiest and fastest ways to ascertain if a patient has a concern is to ask "do you have sexual health concerns that you would like to discuss today?" (Parish et al., 2019). If the response from the patient is yes, many of the questions from the five Ps of the CDC plus three should be utilized. The four step model created by ISSWSH on how to address a positive screen will also be reviewed.

The Five Ps of the CDC Plus Three

The CDC created "A Guide to Taking a Sexual Health History" to assist clinicians determine sexually transmitted infection (STI) risks for their patients (Center for Disease Control and Prevention, 2015). The five aspects to address include partners, practices protection from STIs, past history of STIs, and prevention of pregnancy. There are three additional aspects added by the author to complete a thorough sexual health assessment. The best approach to completing a sexual health evaluation is to use open-ended questions to elicit a patient-centered discussion and to only ask questions that are clinically actionable. Clinically actionable means that the answer provided by the patient directs the plan of care. An example of a common question that many clinicians think is necessary to ask patients about, but is not actually clinically actionable, is the patient's number of lifetime sexual partners. This is a question that can invoke unnecessary shame in patients regardless of the number, and does not have major significance in clinical care. Even if the patient had a significant number of sexual partners in their past, the clinical care for education and screening is the same. Therefore, it would behoove the clinician to ask a more clinically actionable question, such as partners in the last 12 months, and what other sexual partners those partners had.

Readers may note that the multitude of questions listed by the CDC may not be feasible in a short office appointment. Depending on the patient population, some of the questions may also cause the patient discomfort, which may lead them to not disclose important information. The CDC scripting is included for readers to utilize for patients who need more detailed questions, or who need a guided discussion. For each of the five Ps, the patient-centered version will be presented along with the scripting from the CDC.

Partners

A patient-centered way to ask about partners is "tell me about your sexual partners." The CDC scripting includes this: "Do you have sex with men, women, or both? In the past 2 months, how many partners have you had sex with? In the past 12 months, how many partners have you had sex with? Is it possible that any of your sex partners in the past 12 months had sex with someone else while they were still in a sexual relationship with you?"

Practices

A patient-centered way to ask about practices is "tell me about your sexual practices." CDC scripting includes this: "To understand your risks for STDs, I need to understand the kind of sex you have had recently. Have you had vaginal sex, meaning 'penis in vagina sex? If yes, do you use condoms: never, sometimes, or always? Have you had anal sex, meaning 'penis in rectum/anus sex'? If yes, do you use condoms: never, sometimes, or always?" "Have you had oral sex, meaning 'mouth on penis/vagina'?" For condom answers: If "never": "Why don't you use condoms? If "sometimes": "In what situations (or with whom) do you use condoms?" Readers may note that some of the questions, especially those that begin with the word "why" may make the patient defensive or make them feel as though they are being judged. A more patient-centered approach is to use the phrasing "help me understand" rather than "why."

Pregnancy

CDC scripting includes this: "What are you doing to prevent pregnancy?" This question assumes that the patient desires to prevent pregnancy or that she is even having sex with a sperm-producing partner. A patient-centered approach is to use the One Key Question Model that focuses more on a patient's pregnancy intention without clouding the discussion with provider assumptions. The One Key Question is "would you like to become pregnant in the next year?" Then it is simple. If the patient says yes, then the focus is on preconception and helping the patient be the healthiest and informed she can be to achieve pregnancy. If the patient says no, then the discussion focuses on the prevention of pregnancy. If the patient answers that she is ok either way or is unsure, the clinician would address both topics (Oregan Health Authority, 2016).

Prevention of STIs

CDC scripting includes this: "What do you do to protect yourself from STDs and HIV?" A patient-centered approach is very similar except to use the term *STI* rather than *STD*.

Approximately four in ten women report that they have had a test for HIV (42%) or other STIs (42%) in the past two years; however, roughly half (49%) of these women assumed this test was a routine part of an examination – which is often not the case. Therefore, the actual screening rate is likely lower than the share of women who report being tested. Per the Kaiser Family Foundation, about four in ten women report that they have been tested for HIV and other STIs in the past two years; although half of the women polled presumed that the test was a regular occurrence in the examination process. Consequently, the screening rate may actual be lower than the share of women who are being tested. In a two-year period, 42% of women reported having an STI test. Of those who received testing, 41% asked to be tested, 48% thought the test was a routine part of the exam, and 11% had a healthcare provider recommend the test (Kaiser Family Foundation, (2018).

Past STIs

CDC scripting includes this: "Have you ever had an STD? Have any of your partners had an STD?" Additional questions to identify HIV and viral hepatitis risk include the following: "Have you or any of your partners ever injected drugs? Have your or any of your partners exchanged money or drugs for sex? Is there anything else about your sexual practices that I need to know about?" A patient-centered approach is to ask if the patient or their partners have had an STI. If so, were they treated? Another patient-centered question may include "do you or your partners engage in activities that could expose you to blood?"

Pain

Pain is not addressed in the CDC guidelines yet it is an essential component of a sexual health assessment, especially given the high prevalence of sexual pain. The easiest way to ask about pain is "do you experience pain before, during, or after sexual activity or arousal?"

Pleasure

Pleasure is also not addressed in the CDC guidelines and is probably the most uncomfortable for clinicians to address. While it may appear taboo at first, there is a link between pleasure and consent. Sexuality counselor Andrea Barrica states "how do we teach anyone about giving their enthusiastic 'yes' if they don't understand pleasure?" (Barrica, 2018). One way to ask about pleasure is "do you find pleasure in your sexual activities?" or if the word *pleasure* is too much "do you enjoy sexual activity?" A reminder, this question is not simply asking about orgasm as that is not the same thing as pleasure. It is a means to discuss all aspects of sexual health with your patients. Sometimes this is the question that may elicit further discussion of concerns or health-related problems that need to be addressed.

Past or Present Trauma or Violence

While in the space of discussing sensitive topics with patients, discussion of past or present trauma or violence is not only appropriate but necessary. Avoid asking patients if they feel safe at home as this does not get to the root of the question. Asking direct questions. "Have you ever been or currently being hit, slapped, kicked or otherwise physically or emotionally hurt by someone? Have you ever been touched without your consent? Have you ever been forced to have sex?" (CDC, 2007). Avoid using the words abused or victim. Currently, the most appropriate nomenclature is "a person who experienced <insert act here>."

When There Is a Positive Response

Given the prevalence of sexual health concerns, when clinicians begin asking patients if they have any concerns, they will begin to obtain many positive screens and questions they may not know how to answer. This is not a reason to skip these questions as patients expect and want clinicians to discuss sexual health with them. Sometimes clinicians know how to address these concerns and questions and other times they do not have the knowledge to traverse the topic. Often clinicians will have the knowledge to address the patients concern but will need more time to do so. Each of these instances and how to manage them will be addressed in the following.

ISSWSH created a four-step model for when there is a positive screen, the patient says yes, that they have a sexual health concern. Step 1 is to elicit the story. Allow the patient time to tell their story and to consider how her concern is impacting their life. This provides the ability for the clinician to ask questions, preferably open-ended ones, clarify concepts with the patient, assess the magnitude of distress, and therefore be able to move forward to create a plan of care with the patient. The next step is to name and reframe attention to the sexual problem or concern. The purpose of this step is to validate the importance of the sexual concern rather than have a diagnosis. Often times what patients initially present with is may not their major concern. In the article the authors recommend using the phrasing "it seems to me that in addition to your <initial

complaint>, what you've told me about your <sexual concern> is just as painful, important, and worthy of attention." This allows the patient to see that the clinician understands the importance of their concern. Step 3 is empathetic witnessing. Often times, this is the first step in treatment for patients. To practice empathetic witnessing, the clinician will commend the patient on steps they have taken to cope with the challenges they have experienced.

The last step is two pathways of either referral or assessment and treatment. If the clinician does not have the training of knowledge to address the patient's concern, the recommendation is to refer the patient to a sexual health specialist (Parish et al., 2019). When referring a patient, in order to continue the therapeutic response and appear not to be sending the patient away to another provider who cannot help them, language is important. A formula that can be utilized is to acknowledge the importance of the concern, let the patient know it deserves a specialist, who that specialist is and how you have vetted them. Many patients who experience sexual health concerns have seen multiple providers without help, therefore it is important to provide reassurance that they are not being sent to the next clinician who will not be able to help them. An example of a patient requiring referral, "The painful penetration you are experiencing is real and worthy of a specialist who knows how to treat this. I want you to get the best care so I'd like to refer you to Sally who has treated many of my patients with similar concerns."

Often times clinicians who are able to assess and treat sexual health concerns have a patient flow, policies, and procedures. When a clinician is able to assess and treat the patient but does not have time that day, they can use a similar formula to when referring a patient. Start by acknowledging the importance of the concern, let the patient know it deserves more time, and how they should follow up. An example of this discussion may sound like "I'm so glad you told me about the pain you are experiencing. This discussion deserves more time than we have today so I'd like you to come back Friday for a longer appointment so we have plenty of time to address your concern. In the meantime, please complete the <questionnaires> and bring them with you on Friday."

Creating Change Through Quantum Leadership

What Is Quantum Leadership?

The major tenet of quantum leadership is that leadership should be unstructured and unpredictable in order to be dynamic and adaptive. Leaders will be able to manage change and prepare those they are leading for change as well. Beyond being dynamic, adaptive, flexible, and proactive, quantum leadership also provides the opportunity to delegate and to share power. In doing this, quantum leadership creates an adaptive shared vision and mission for the system (what system) (Erçetin & Kamacı, 2008).

There are four basic assumptions to quantum leadership: Leadership is an interaction field between the leader and followers, leadership cannot be structured and estimated, discontinuity of the leadership is a fact, and the impact of leadership depends on interaction. In regard to the first basic assumption, the relationship of leadership arises from contributions from the leader as well as the follower. A quantum leader welcomes the participation and contribution of followers. The leader does not perceive themselves as more important or elite than the followers, rather that there is a unity in creating a shared future. The second assumption, that leadership cannot be structured and estimated, stands to convey the concept of being adaptable and flexible to the dynamic world. Leaders often employ guides rather than rules and offer followers alternatives to action as a means to take initiative. This creates a system that is always ready for change and uncertainties, therefore creating innovation and the best outcomes possible as all points have been accounted for. Quantum leaders empower their followers to be autonomous, which in turn improves the followers' leadership potential. This aspect, discontinuity of the leadership fact, demonstrates this as it allows for changes in leadership as a natural process of ebb and flow in order to utilize talents of the system when and how they are needed. The last assumption, that the impact of leadership depends on interaction, postulates that interaction creates "the edge of chaos" which produces uncertainty and risk, yet in the chaos also creates space for learning, development, and creativity. With each interaction comes a new interaction style that serves to move the system forward in a shared, respected, and innovative vision (Erçetin & Kamacı, 2008).

Leadership of Individual Scope

Quantum leadership is about the relationship between the leader and the follower being one that is dynamic, and serving the needs of that system. A system, for example, can simply be a clinician, such as healthcare provider or therapist, and their patient. Utilizing quantum leadership, the clinician can utilize the four basic aforementioned assumptions. In a typical sense, the clinician would be the leader and the patient would be the follower. As noted in the third basic assumption, discontinuity of the leadership fact, this relationship can change multiple times throughout an appointment or interaction, and should as the patient should be the leader in their healthcare and disclosure. Being a clinician who partners with the patient in their care rather than imposing one's static view on a situation will produce a shared vision for wellness, thus making the interaction a successful one.

Beyond caring for the patient through quantum leadership, or what may even be viewed as holistic, an individual clinician can make a significant impact in patient care by evaluating a patient's sexual health and providing recommendations as necessary. Being dynamic and continuously learning is a trait of the quantum leader. By utilizing the skills outlined below to complete a sexual health assessment, the clinician can significantly change the trajectory of the patient's care and life.

Because sexual health can be a taboo topic that is poorly addressed, it may be solely one clinician who guides care and advocates for the patient. For example, a sex therapist may be the one to suggest that the patient be evaluated by a healthcare provider and may even need to go so far as to tell the patient what should be evaluated. As noted earlier, sadly, many sexual health concerns go unaddressed in healthcare due to lack of time and more often due to lack of education of healthcare providers. In this example, the sex therapist could empower patients to receive the care they deserve, help guide them through the process, and provide education on certain conditions.

Leadership of Systemic Scope

More often quantum leadership is thought of as occurring in a large system beyond the scope of only the clinician and the patient. These multidimensional systems are always evolving, thus making quantum leadership an excellent approach for creating welcome and innovative change. Two systems that could benefit from quantum leadership in sexual health are the healthcare system and healthcare education. Here is information that should, and can, be utilized to train healthcare providers to address patient's sexual health concerns in ambulatory care settings. This information can be disseminated through medical and nursing school education, resident education, grand rounds, or as part of healthcare provider continuing education.

An Example of Quantum Leadership of Systemic Scope in Education

The educators at the University of Minnesota medical schools strongly encourage the medical school to integrate courses and conversations about sexuality and sexual health throughout the students' entire education and residency training at the medical school. The educators also see a need for the education to be multifaceted and culturally diverse, as most students and residents will be treating a wide range of patients from varying backgrounds, race, and ethnicity. The panel pushed for the existing curriculum to be expanded into a more diverse and expansive syllabus, as it currently focuses on disease and dysfunction. The recommendations include a focus on overall sexual health and well-being, in addition to disease and dysfunction. Their final recommendation was that education on sexuality become a mandatory core focus of the medical licensing exams, as it should be an aspect that residents and students should be evaluated on.

Summary

Sexual health is an integral part of general health. Often times, sexual health concerns will have an underlying physiologic or psychologic pathology that is associated with general health. Patients expect to have health-care providers who will address sexual health and their concerns, yet many healthcare providers do not evaluate patients' sexual health because they feel they do not have the time or the knowledge on how to do so.

Quantum leadership is leadership that is dynamic, evolving, innovative, and teamwork between the leader and followers. Utilizing quantum leadership in an individual sense and in a system can create an environment that is ripe to improve sexual health, and therefore overall health for patients. Individuals can utilize quantum leadership by learning new skills (utilizing screening tools, outlines, and communication skills) and by creating a space of shared vision with the patient to address patient's sexual health concerns. On an individual basis, quantum leaders can advocate for patients to obtain the care they deserve by providing them education, guidance, and empowerment. From a system perspective, quantum leadership lends itself well to improving sexual health for patients. This can be done by improving the education of healthcare providers and by making improvements in the healthcare systems that serve patients. A quantum leader is able to assess a system while realizing that it is ever changing and, alongside their followers, create a vision for the future of sexual health that dovetails into the systems flow, or inherent lack thereof. Each institution is nuanced and different so a recipe of how to implement education, policies, and procedures to improve addressing sexual health will be dependent on the needs and vision of the organization as well as the leadership of the quantum leader. The only things to hold on to in quantum leadership are the four basic assumptions, and even then, do not hold too tightly.

Process Questions and Considerations

1. How might a lack of education tie into healthcare providers serving as leaders?
2. Discuss the role of time management and leadership. Do you find that you demonstrate greater and influential leadership when your time is constricted or if you an abundance of time?
3. Should healthcare professionals be capable and willing to open to facilitating conversations with patients about sexuality? Can

they be good leaders if they cannot lead conversations about sexuality? Why or why not?
4. What may make it difficult for healthcare leaders to talk candidly about pleasure?
5. How might the use of quantum leadership relate to the work that you do?

Acknowledgment

Ms. Leila Benyounes, Research Assistant

References

Abdolrasulnia, M., Shewchuk, R. M., Roepke, N., Granstaff, U. S., Dean, J., Foster, J., . . . Casebeer, L. (2010). Management of female sexual problems: Perceived barriers, practice patterns, and confidence among primary care physicians and gynecologists. *The Journal of Sexual Medicine, 7*(7), 2499–2508.
Accreditation Review Commission on Education for the Physician Assistant, Inc. (2018). *Accreditation standards for physician assistant education [PDF Document]*. Retrieved from www.arc-pa.org/wp-content/uploads/2018/12/Accred Manual-4th-edition.rev5_.18.pdf
Alexander, S. C., Fortenberry, J. D., Pollak, K. I., Bravender, T., Davis, J. K., Østbye, Tulsky, J., Dolor, R., & Shields, C. G. (2014). Sexuality talk during adolescent health maintenance visits. *JAMA Pediatrics, 168*(2), 163–169.
American Academy of Family Physicians. (2016). Erectile dysfunction. *American Family Physician, 94*(10), 820–827.
American Sexual Health Association. (n.d.). *JAMA viewpoint on sexual health in America*. Retrieved from www.ashasexualhealth.org/jama-viewpoint-sexual-health-america/
Association of Reproductive Health Professionals. (2009). *Handbook on female sexual health and wellness*. Retrieved from www.arhp.org/Publications-and-Resources/Clinical-Practice-Tools/Handbook-On-Female-Sexual-Health-And-Wellness/Female-Sexual-Response
Bachmann, G. (2006). Female sexuality and sexual dysfunction: Are we stuck on the learning curve?. *The Journal of Sexual Medicine, 3*(4), 639–645.
Barrica, A. (2018). *How can we teach consent if we don't teach about pleasure?* Retrieved from https://theestablishment.co/how-can-we-teach-consent-without-pleasure-91ec6e451585/index.html
Bornstein, J., Goldstein, A., Stockdale, C., Bergeron, S., Pukall, C., Zolnoun, D., & Coady, D. (2016). 2015 ISSVD, ISSWSH, and IPPS consensus terminology and classification of persistent vulvar pain and vulvodynia. *The Journal of Sexual Medicine, 13*(4), 607–612.
Cappelleri, J. C., & Rosen, R. C. (2005). The Sexual Health Inventory for Men (SHIM): A 5-year review of research and clinical experience. *International Journal of Impotence Research, 17*(4), 307.

Center for Disease Control and Prevention. (2007). *Intimate partner violence and sexual violence victimization assessment instruments for use in healthcare settings.* Retrieved from www.cdc.gov/violenceprevention/pdf/ipv/ipvandsv screening.pdf

Center for Disease Control and Prevention. (2015). *Clinical prevention guidelines.* Retrieved from www.cdc.gov/std/tg2015/clinical.htm

Clayton, A. H., Goldfischer, E. R., Goldstein, I., DeRogatis, L., Lewis-D'Agostino, D. J., & Pyke, R. (2009). Validation of the decreased sexual desire screener (DSDS): A brief diagnostic instrument for generalized acquired female hypoactive sexual desire disorder (HSDD). *The Journal of Sexual Medicine, 6*(3), 730–738.

Clayton, A. H., & Groth, J. (2013). Etiology of female sexual dysfunction. *Women's Health, 9*(2), 135–137.

Criniti, S., Crane, B., Woodland, M. B., Montgomery, O. C., & Urdaneta Hartmann, S. (2016). Perceptions of US medical residents regarding amount and usefulness of sexual health instruction in preparation for clinical practice. *American Journal of Sexuality Education, 11*(3), 161–175.

Dahir, M. (2009). Female sexual dysfunction: Barriers to treatment. *Urologic Nursing, 29*(2), 81.

DeRogatis, L., Clayton, A., Lewis-D'Agostino, D., Wunderlich, G., & Fu, Y. (2008). Outcomes assessment: Validation of the female sexual distress scale-revised for assessing distress in women with hypoactive sexual desire disorder. *The Journal of Sexual Medicine, 5*(2), 357–364.

Erçetin, Ş. Ş., & Kamacı, M. C. (2008). Quantum leadership paradigm. *World Applied Sciences Journal, 3*(6), 865–868.

Frederick, D. A., John, H. K. S., Garcia, J. R., & Lloyd, E. A. (2018). Differences in orgasm frequency among gay, lesbian, bisexual, and heterosexual men and women in a US national sample. *Archives of Sexual Behavior, 47*(1), 273–288.

Garcia, M., & Fisher, W. A. (2008). Obstetrics and gynaecology residents' self-rated knowledge, motivation, skill, and practice patterns in counselling for contraception, STI prevention, sexual dysfunction, and intimate partner violence and sexual coercion. *Journal of Obstetrics and Gynaecology Canada, 30*(1), 59–66.

Giugliano, F., Esposito, K., Di Palo, C., Ciotola, M., Giugliano, G., Marfella, R., . . . & Giugliano, D. (2004). Erectile dysfunction associates with endothelial dysfunction and raised proinflammatory cytokine levels in obese men. *Journal of Endocrinological Investigation, 27*(7), 665–669.

Goldenhar, L., Karram, M., Kleeman, S., Pauls, R., Segal, J., & Silva, W. (2005). Practice patterns of physician members of the American urogynecologic society regarding female sexual dysfunction: Results of a national survey. *International Urogynecology Journal, 16*(6), 460–467

Grover, S. A., Lowensteyn, I., Kaouache, M., Marchand, S., Coupal, L., DeCarolis, E., & Defoy, I. (2006). The prevalence of erectile dysfunction in the primary care setting: Importance of risk factors for diabetes and vascular disease. *Archives of Internal Medicine, 166*(2), 213–219.

Healthy People 2020. (n.d.). *Reproductive and sexual health.* Retrieved from www.healthypeople.gov/2020/leading-health-indicators/2020-lhi-topics/Reproductive-and-Sexual-Health

Hinchliff, S., & Gott, M. (2011). Seeking medical help for sexual concerns in mid-and later life: A review of the literature. *Journal of Sex Research*, 48(2–3), 106–117.

Inman, B. A., Sauver, J. L. S., Jacobson, D. J., McGree, M. E., Nehra, A., Lieber, M. M., & Jacobsen, S. J. (2009, February). A population-based, longitudinal study of erectile dysfunction and future coronary artery disease. *Mayo Clinic Proceedings*, 84(2), 108–113.

Kaiser Family Foundation. (2018). *Women's sexual and reproductive health services: Key findings from the 2017 Kaiser women's health survey*. Retrieved from www.kff.org/womens-health-policy/issue-brief/womens-sexual-and-reproductive-health-services-key-findings-from-the-2017-kaiser-womens-health-survey/

Khajehei, M., Doherty, M., Tilley, P. J., & Sauer, K. (2015). Prevalence and risk factors of sexual dysfunction in postpartum Australian women. *The Journal of Sexual Medicine*, 12(6), 1415–1426.

Kingsberg, S., & Althof, S. E. (2009). Evaluation and treatment of female sexual disorders. *International Urogynecology Journal*, 20(1), 33–43.

Kingsberg, S. A., & Knudson, G. (2011). Female sexual disorders: Assessment, diagnosis, and treatment. *CNS Spectrums*, 16 (2), 49–62.

Kriston, L., Günzler, C., Rohde, A., & Berner, M. M. (2010). Is one question enough to detect female sexual dysfunctions? A diagnostic accuracy study in 6,194 women. *The Journal of Sexual Medicine*, 7(5), 1831–1841.

Laumann, E. O., Nicolosi, A., Glasser, D. B., Paik, A., Gingell, C., Moreira, E., & Wang, T. (2005). Sexual problems among women and men aged 40–80: Prevalence and correlates identified in the global study of sexual attitudes and behaviors. *International Journal of Impotence Research*, 17(1), 39.

MedScape. (2018). *Medscape physician compensation report 2018*. Retrieved from: www.medscape.com/slideshow/2018-compensation-overview-6009667

Mulhall, J. P., Goldstein, I., Bushmakin, A. G., Cappelleri, J. C., & Hvidsten, K. (2007). Outcomes assessment: Validation of the erection hardness score. *The Journal of Sexual Medicine*, 4(6), 1626–1634.

Nusbaum, M. R., Gamble, G., Skinner, B., & Heiman, J. (2000). The high prevalence of sexual concerns among women seeking routine gynecological care. *Journal of Family Practice*, 49(3), 229

O'donnell, A. B., Araujo, A. B., Goldstein, I., & McKinlay, J. B. (2005). The validity of a single-question self-report of erectile dysfunction: Results from the Massachusetts male aging study. *Journal of General Internal Medicine*, 20(6), 515–519.

O'Leary, M. P., Fowler, F. J., Lenderking, W. R., Barber, B., Sagnier, P. P., Guess, H. A., & Barry, M. J. (1995). A brief male sexual function inventory for urology. *Urology*, 46(5), 697–706.

Oregan Health Authority. (2016). *One key question ®: Implementation in public health (focus on clinic setting)*. Retrieved from www.oregon.gov/oha/PH/HEALTHYPEOPLEFAMILIES/DATAREPORTS/MCHTITLEV/Documents/One%20Key%20Question%20Presentation.pdf

Papaharitou, S., Nakopoulou, E., Kirana, P., Iraklidou, M., Athanasiadis, L., & Hatzichristou, D. (2005). Women's sexual concerns: Data analysis from a helpline. *The Journal of Sexual Medicine*, 2(5), 652–657.

Parish, S. J., Hahn, S. R., Goldstein, S. W., Giraldi, A., Kingsberg, S. A., Larkin, L., . . . & Kelly-Jones, A. (2019, April). *The international society for the study of women's sexual health process of care for the identification of sexual concerns and problems in women.* In Mayo Clinic Proceedings. Elsevier.

Rehman, K. U., Asif Mahmood, M., Sheikh, S. S., Sultan, T., & Khan, M. A. (2015). The Female Sexual F unction Index (FSFI): Translation, validation, and cross-cultural adaptation of an Urdu version "FSFI–U". *Sexual Medicine, 3*(4), 244–250.

Roos, A. M., Sultan, A. H., & Thakar, R. (2012). Sexual problems in the gynecology clinic: Are we making a mountain out of a molehill? *International Urogynecology Journal, 23*(2), 145–152.

Roos, A. M., Thakar, R., Sultan, A. H., & Scheer, I. (2009). Female sexual dysfunction: Are urogynecologists ready for it? *International Urogynecology Journal, 20*(1), 89-101.

Rosen, C., Brown, J., Heiman, S., Leiblum, C., Meston, R., Shabsigh, D., Ferguson, R., & D'Agostino, R. (2000). The Female Sexual Function Index (FSFI): A multidimensional self-report instrument for the assessment of female sexual function. *Journal of Sex & Marital Therapy, 26*(2), 191-208.

Rosen, R. C., Riley, A., Wagner, G., Osterloh, I. H., Kirkpatrick, J., & Mishra, A. (1997). The International Index of Erectile Function (IIEF): A multidimensional scale for assessment of erectile dysfunction. *Urology, 49*(6), 822–830.

Rosen, R. C., Shifren, J. L., Monz, B. U., Odom, D. M., Russo, P. A., & Johannes, C. B. (2009). Epidemiology: Correlates of sexually related personal distress in women with low sexual desire. *The Journal of Sexual Medicine, 6*(6), 1549–1560.

Rosen, R., Kountz, D., Post-Zwicker, T., Leiblum, S., & Wiegel, M. (2006). Original research-education: Sexual communication skills in residency training: The robert wood johnson model. *The Journal of Sexual Medicine, 3*(1), 37–46.

Sadovsky, R., Alam, W., Enecilla, M., Cosiquien, R., Tipu, O., & Etheridge-Otey, J. (2006). Epidemiology: Sexual problems among a specific population of minority women aged 40–80 years attending a primary care practice. *The Journal of Sexual Medicine, 3*(5), 795–803.

Sadovsky, R., & Nusbaum, M. (2006). Reviews: Sexual health inquiry and support is a primary care priority. *The Journal of Sexual Medicine, 3*(1), 3–11.

Sasayama, S., Ishii, N., Ishikura, F., Kamijima, G., Ogawa, S., Kanmatsuse, K., . . . & Yamamoto, Y. (2003). Men's health study. *Circulation Journal, 67*(8), 656–659.

Satcher, D., Hook, E. W., & Coleman, E. (2015). Sexual health in America: Improving patient care and public health. *Journal of the American Medical Association (JAMA), 314*(8), 765–766.

Shifren, J. L., Johannes, C. B., Monz, B. U., Russo, P. A., Bennett, L., & Rosen, R. (2009). Help-seeking behavior of women with self-reported distressing sexual problems. *Journal of Women's Health, 18*(4), 461–468.

Shifren, J. L., Monz, B. U., Russo, P. A., Segreti, A., & Johannes, C. B. (2008). Sexual problems and distress in United States women: Prevalence and correlates. *Obstetrics & Gynecology, 112*(5), 970–978.

Shindel, A. W., & Parish, S. J. (2013). CME information: Sexuality education in North American medical schools: Current status and future directions (CME). *The Journal of Sexual Medicine, 10*(1), 3–18.

Sinsky, C., Colligan, L., Li, L., Prgomet, M., Reynolds, S., Goeders, L., . . . & Blike, G. (2016). Allocation of physician time in ambulatory practice: A time and motion study in 4 specialties. *Annals of Internal Medicine, 165*(11), 753–760.

Skeldon, S., Detsky, A., Goldenberg, S., & Law, M. (2015). Erectile dysfunction and undiagnosed diabetes, hypertension, and hypercholesterolemia. *Annals of Family Medicine, 13*(4), 331–335.

Sobecki, J. N., Curlin, F. A., Rasinski, K. A., & Lindau, S. T. (2012). What we don't talk about when we don't talk about sex 1: Results of a National Survey of US Obstetrician/Gynecologists. *The Journal of Sexual Medicine, 9*(5), 1285–1294.

Swartzendruber, A., & Zenilman, J. M. (2010). A national strategy to improve sexual health. *The Journal of the American Medical Association (JAMA), 304*(9), 1005–1006.

Vale, F. B. C., Coimbra, B. B., Lopes, G. P., & Geber, S. (2017). Sexual dysfunction in premenopausal women could be related to hormonal profile. *Gynecological Endocrinology, 33*(2), 145–147.

Vermeulen, A., Kaufman, J. M., Deslypere, J. P., & Thomas, G. (2003). Attenuated Luteinizing Hormone (LH) pulse amplitude but normal LH pulse frequency, and its relation to plasma androgens in hypogonadism of obese men. *Journal of Clinical Endocrinology and Metabolism, 76*(5), 1140–1146.

Vlachopoulos, C., Aznaouridis, K., Ioakeimidis, N., Rokkas, K., Vasiliadou, C., Alexopoulos, N., . . . & Stefanadis, C. (2006). Unfavourable endothelial and inflammatory state in erectile dysfunction patients with or without coronary artery disease. *European Heart Journal, 27*(22), 2640–2648.

Wittenberg, A., & Gerber, J. (2009). Recommendations for improving sexual health curricula in medical schools: Results from a two-arm study collecting data from patients and medical students. *The Journal of Sexual Medicine, 6*(2), 362–368.

World Health Organization. (2006). The world health report 2006–Working together for health. Retrieved from www.who.int/whr/2006/en/

Wu, C., Lu, Y., Chai, C., Su, Y., Tsai, T., Tsai, F., & Lin, C. (2016). Increased risk of osteoporosis in patients with erectile dysfunction: A nationwide population-based cohort study. *Medicine, 95*(26).

Young, R., Burge, S., Kumar, K., Wilson, J., & Ortiz, D. (2018). A time-motion study of primary care physicians' work in the electronic health record era. *Family Medicine, 50*(2), 91–99.

4 Feminist Activist Leadership and the Five Stages for Matching Values With Practice

A Case Study

Katherine Martinez and Sydney Fowler

Feminist activist leadership (FAL) serves to promote collaboration between individuals, communities, and organizations that work toward sex/gender equity and social justice. It falls within the realm of "leadership as practice" (LAP), which focuses on "what people may accomplish together" (Raelin, 2011, p. 196) and promotes collaboration, cooperation, creativity, respect, and reflexivity (Egan et al., 2017). LAP is a perspective that, when utilized within a feminist framework, purposefully challenges masculinist leadership traditions and status-based hierarchies. Whereas status-based hierarchies may be useful for increasing organization performance, research suggests that these hierarchies may also result in lower member motivation, satisfaction, and intergroup coordination (Anderson & Brown, 2010).

In practice, feminist activist leaders work toward social change by facilitating dynamic interactions in the classroom, on the street, at home and at work, and in the office. For instance, feminist leaders in the classroom promote collaboration when they ask students to sit in a circle rather than rows – in the circle, all voices are heard, all eyes are seen, and students learn to empower one another through reflexive participation in discussion. Feminist leaders on the street promote collaboration as they organize against workplace sexism and harassment, joining forces with those seeking economic equality, and educating the masses about the connection between the two. In both examples, feminist activist leadership is the basis for cooperation and respect across and amongst individuals, communities, and organizations.

The purpose of this chapter is to present the collaborative work between two organizations as a case study of how feminist activist leadership evolved within and between organizations with similar goals in gender equity and social justice. The Gender Institute for Teaching and Advocacy (GITA) of Metropolitan State University of Denver and The Gathering Place (TGP), a women's day shelter in the Denver-metro area, began working together in early August 2018. The goal of this collaboration was to assist one another in reaching their social justice-related goals: TGP actively sought transgender inclusivity training from GITA, while GITA actively sought community connections with gender-inclusive organizations.

Both GITA and TGP, as social justice-oriented programs, center gender equity and social justice within their founding missions. Specific to transgender people, both programs seek to be inclusive in their outreach to and servicing of these individuals and their communities. This outreach is particularly important for spaces such as TGP due to the history of transgender exclusion in many institutions and spaces across the country; transgender people face oppression on multiple levels that render them especially vulnerable to homelessness and housing insecurity. According to the 2015 U.S. Transgender Survey, 30% of the 17,715 respondents had experienced homelessness during their lifetime and 12% had been homeless within the year that they took the survey (James et al., 2016).

When broken down by race and gender, the homelessness crisis is even more severe. For instance, 51% of Black trans women reported experiencing homelessness in their lifetimes and 40% had experienced homelessness within the year that they took the survey. These numbers also vary by location. In Colorado, 34% of the respondents had experienced homelessness in their lifetimes ("2015 U.S. Transgender Survey," 2017). The rates of homelessness for transgender people are astronomical when one considers that nationally, 0.17% of the population is actively homeless (Henry, Watt, Rosenthal, Shivji, & Abt Associates, 2017).

Many of the participants in the U.S. Transgender Survey were homeless due to the housing and job discrimination they had experienced for their transgender identities. Additionally, compounding oppression across identities often creates housing environments that are unsafe for transgender people. Unfortunately, discrimination frequently continues when transgender people seek services. In the U.S., most shelters are gender (often sex) segregated (Mottet & Ohle, 2006). If trans people are welcome in the space at all, it is not uncommon for them to be forced to present outside of their identities or comfort so that they may stay in these spaces. In Colorado, 24% of those who were homeless within a year of taking the U.S. Transgender Survey said that they avoided staying in shelters because they feared mistreatment for their identity. Indeed, of those who did access a shelter within a year of taking the survey, 70% reported mistreatment around their transgender identity (National Center for Transgender Equality, 2017).

For these reasons and many more, the work that The Gathering Place does to actively include transgender members is incredibly important. Further, their decision to reach out to another institution (in this case, GITA) for help strengthening their commitment to transgender people is an excellent example of putting organizational values into practice. This example of feminist activist leadership models humility, reflexivity, and vulnerability. These ideas are further elaborated upon after a brief description of the theorization around feminist activist leadership, along with some of the studies that highlight the main ideas behind activist leadership as feminist praxis.

Activist Leadership as Feminist Praxis

Storberg-Walker and Haber-Curran (2017) suggest that theories influence, mold, and shape the future and that theorists engage in processes of visualization which take into consideration the theorists' values, beliefs, and ideas as they look to impact future actions and behaviors. To these authors, theorists serve as change-agents when theories impact practice. Specific to feminist theorists, Storberg-Walker and Haber-Curran note that "alternative ways of knowing" (i.e., embodied experience, indigenous knowledge, intuition, and imagining) influence the theorists' values, beliefs, and ideas and therefore would reasonably influence future actions and behaviors in more holistic ways from those who do not have these alternative ways of knowing. In other words, people who theorize utilizing bodily sensations, emotions, and intuition typically engage in collaborative meaning-making, theorizing, and action – Storber-Walker and Haber-Curran describe this as praxis.

Feminist praxis as collaboration "requires an acknowledgement of difference; legitimation of different ways of knowing; and space for different leadership goals, objectives, and intentions" (Storber-Walker & Haber-Curran, p. 13). However, it is not enough to acknowledge difference without also understanding that difference exists within various hierarchies (i.e., women and men are treated as different *and* unequal in the United States), and these hierarchies differ across various communities (i.e., women are valued differently across racial/ethnic communities). It is especially important, then, to incorporate inclusivity and reflexivity into feminist praxis.

Reflexivity involves reflecting upon one's own intersecting identities and positionalities in the theory-building and action process. In her research on social justice leadership development, Venegas-García (2017) claims that her participants developed social justice leadership "concurrently with an activist identity over time and in response to injustice and inequality" (p. 205). To understand this form of activist leadership, however, participants needed to engage in a critical self-reflection of their own discrimination and disenfranchisement experiences – she describes this as "activism motivated by a reflective understanding of social location" (p. 207). For many participants, their disenfranchisement and thus activism in leadership involved several key themes, including the following: family influence in social justice ideals; significant life events, often concerning education and politics; and feelings of social responsibility, which evolved into theories of action. Importantly, Venegas-García found that leadership development is "shaped by circumstances and encounters from lived experiences in gendered, ethnic/racial, and class positions" (p. 219).

For instance, women of color often feel an added sense of responsibility to the most marginalized people in their communities, having been influenced by their activist parents or other family members.

Inclusivity, on the other hand, involves understanding one's own positionality (i.e., privileges/oppressions) in relation to others and consciously working to include a variety of these others, and especially those who are most marginalized. Inclusive women's leadership, more specifically, "necessitate[s] an attention to inclusivity across disciplines and views that [challenge] normative approaches to thinking about and developing leadership that are typically leader centric" (Stead et al., 2017, p. 40). Stead et al. describe inclusive leadership as being dynamic, shifting as one learns more about others and more about the "responsible leadership" process which incorporates social responsibility into leadership practice. In their eyes, social responsibility is about creating space for dialog with the suspension of assumptions, evaluation, and judgement.

Responsible leadership, social justice leadership, and feminist activist leadership align in their vision of collaboration toward common goals. While Stead et al. (2017) clarify that no specific goals need to be outlined within the collaborative process, it is nonetheless clear that each form of leadership requires inclusive and reflexive processes in order to positively impact future actions and behaviors. Each leadership model sees leadership as a nonhierarchical practice that is dynamic, allowing for change and growth. Important to this project, then, the authors of this chapter offer brief histories of the Gender Institute for Teaching and Advocacy (GITA) and The Gathering Place (TGP) next, as these histories help explain the growth process that each has followed as separate organizations, and that each continue to follow as organizations in collaboration.

Histories (Where, How, and Why)

The Gender Institute for Teaching and Advocacy (GITA) began as the Institute for Women's Studies and Services (IWSS) at Metropolitan State College of Denver (now Metropolitan State University, MSU Denver) over 30 years ago. It emerged from the efforts of Dr. Jodi Wetzel, Professor of History, who served as its Director from 1985 to 2005 and who also started the Front Range Feminist Scholars Forum in an effort to bring feminist scholars from the Denver-metro area together in community. With the help of Dr. Tara Tull, Professor of Human Services and IWSS Associate Director, Dr. Wetzel created a two-pronged approach to addressing the academic needs of women on campus and within the Denver community: through feminist-based academic programming and student-centered services. The two created a Women's Studies major, an active internship program, and the first Outstanding Women Awards, which honored women faculty, staff, students, alumni, and community members for their work in gender and social justice. Further, Dr. Wetzel worked with students to create the alpha chapter Iota Iota Iota (Triota) women's honor society at MSU Denver, which promotes feminist values (i.e., diversity, egalitarianism, and empowerment) and academic support across 108 chapters nationwide.

Drs. Wetzel and Tull's emphasis on feminist values have had a major impact on faculty and students to this day. Although the Institute has gone through various transitions in leadership and programming (including a name change from IWSS to GITA and from Women's Studies to Gender, Women, and Sexualities Studies), it continues to serve as a feminist hub for transformative education at MSU Denver. Indeed, the faculty and staff at GITA specifically value critical and engaged dialog, social justice, and collaboration. In more recent efforts to commit to these values, GITA faculty and staff have worked to take more active roles in their communities through service-oriented projects and community collaborations, including collaboration with the Denver Transformative Justice Collective to promote "community-centered solutions to violence in queer/trans* communities" (Denver Transformative Justice Collective, n.d.). Further, students regularly engage in social justice-oriented internships and service-learning projects, such as the volunteer work students did with the GLBT Community Center of Colorado to gather and assess historical data for the Colorado LGBTQ History Project. GITA also offers one-credit career and personal development courses that teach students valuable skills such as time and stress management and assertiveness, as well as courses on sexual harassment and women's leadership.

On the services side of the Institute, programming involves collaborations with various on- and off-campus organizations such as Brother to Brother (a male-of-color mentorship program), Stand Up Colorado (a community collaboration to end relationship violence), and more recently The Gathering Place (a drop-in center for cisgender and transgender women and their children to access resources, such as food, showers, clothing, laundry, and physical/mental health between the hours of 8:00 AM and 5:00 PM, Monday through Friday).

The Gathering Place (TGP) serves all transgender individuals and cisgender women who may be experiencing poverty and/or homelessness. Like GITA, TGP first opened its doors in the mid-1980s. It began as a collaborative effort between two University of Denver Social Work students, Toni Schmid and Kathy Carfrae, who wanted to create a safe space for women and children during the daytime. In the beginning, TGP assisted about 30 "members" daily and has since grown to serving approximately 270 members with shelter and meals daily. They provide programs and services that include job readiness education and physical/mental health wellness. They also center their services around member empowerment, such that members are called to participate in hiring committees and other decision-making roles at TGP through a Member Engagement Steering Committee. In this way, members' voices directly influence the environment as they collaborate with staff to make important changes to TGP. Further, TGP staff are trained in Trauma-Informed Care practices to help promote empowered decision-making in day-to-day interactions.

On May 1, 2018, Family Program Manager at TGP and Chair of the TGP Team Inclusion Committee, Matt Wallington, contacted Dr. Kat Martinez, Interim Director/Chair of GITA to request a presentation on gender identity and sexuality. Because TGP is one of the few transgender-serving day-shelters and resources, Matt was concerned about whether all TGP staff had adequate knowledge and tools to combat transphobia and homophobia in the environment. Kat expressed interest in the project and asked for an initial consultation with Matt at TGP to explore their options. Kat, along with training facilitator Sydney Fowler from GITA, met with Matt on May 17, 2018 to see the site and to discuss how best to approach transphobia and homophobia in the workspace. The three agreed that a transgender inclusivity training facilitated by Sydney and Eneri Rodriguez, Associate Director of GITA, and geared toward TGP staff and volunteers would be the best option. Further, Matt and two former leaders at GITA, Dr. Tull and Dr. Sgoutas, were asked to reflect on their thoughts about leadership and the importance of feminism in their activist agendas. In the following section, the authors of this chapter review what each leader had to say.

Leadership in Activism

Matt Wallington began working at The Gathering Place (TGP) nearly four years ago, although has been involved in social justice activism for over 25 years. Having worked with homeless populations since the late 1990s, Matt noted during conversation that despite the changes in politics and environments (i.e., Denver growing by 100,000 inhabitants in just seven years and experiencing high levels of gentrification in most neighborhoods), not a lot has changed for the homeless population in Denver. Indeed, there are still crises around affordable housing, livable wages, and equal access to healthcare and food – the basic human needs and rights. In his experience, Matt sees the margins being pushed further and further out, meaning that community members needing the services offered by TGP are greater than before. Ultimately, Matt explained that Denver's ten-year plan to end homelessness has been an abject failure, and that feminist activist leadership is more important than ever (Matt Wallington, personal communication, October 2018). As such, Matt described leadership within TGP and his own values and beliefs related to this leadership and to his ultimate desire to collaborate with GITA.

According to Matt, Leslie Foster, the CEO of TGP, has been one of the biggest advocates for women and transgender folks in the Denver-metro area. She, like Matt, values momentum toward social justice, which for TGP means being inclusive in who they serve and pushing back against the status quo. For instance, when people feared that TGP may lose their funding base by promoting transgender inclusivity, Leslie fought back, clarifying that providing for those in need was more important than these fears. Matt and Leslie, thus, present a type of leadership that requires action. Indeed, Matt explained that his goal as a leader is to put ideas into action, which is one of the main reasons he reached out to GITA for feedback on TGP's transgender inclusive practices. He had already considered that working with marginalized people and that providing a space for and services to marginalized groups is a political act. Given his years of experience in the field, he knew that the homeless are criminalized and marginalized to the point of not having a voice in matters that directly and indirectly impact them (i.e., Denver's Unauthorized Camping ordinance, or "Urban Camping Ban" targets homeless populations by criminalizing their very presence in public spaces). In his outreach to GITA, Matt sought feedback on how to be a better leader in transgender inclusivity (Matt Wallington, personal communication, October 2018). His actions suggest that feminist activist leadership involves the willingness to change and grow, the ability to collaborate, the sharing of power, and the use of one's own privileges to make spaces more accessible and welcoming for the marginalized.

Similarly, Drs. Tull and Sgoutas explained their values around leadership at the Gender Institute for Teaching and Advocacy (GITA). While Dr. Tull and Dr. Sgoutas had been leaders at GITA several years apart, they shared the sense that the Institute served a very important role on the Metropolitan State University of Denver campus and in the broader Denver community, namely to provide a space for student and community organization and activism. As part student services and part academics, GITA by its very nature is collaborative: Faculty collaborate with staff on campus and community events, staff collaborate with others around campus on justice-oriented workshops and trainings, and faculty/staff collaborate with students in campus and community social justice activities, such as internships, service-learning opportunities, and student organization work. Dr. Tull noted that, despite this synergetic effect, collaboration in the early history of GITA often derived out of the reality that GITA had to fight for its existence in a university that did not see the need for woman-focused programming and curriculum and therefore was given few financial resources (Tara Tull, personal communication, November 2018). And yet, the feminist values that each of the leaders at GITA had brought to the Institute allowed them to reimagine and enact collaboration beyond a needs-based model.

One of the most interesting ideas that Dr. Tull presented as important to leadership at GITA was the recognition that the Institute has changed and shifted with each new Director/Chair it has seen, therefore all leaders need to be flexible with their goals; and, despite similarities in programmatic vision (i.e., gender equity and social justice), all leaders bring their own personalities and practices to GITA and their own visions for change. Dr. Sgoutas, the most recent Director/Chair shared what she believed to be the core principles of feminist activist leadership. Having experienced a difficult transition between Associate Directors in her sixth year of leading, she recognized the need for flexibility, collaboration, trust, and accountability. Without these, it would be very difficult to problem solve as a team. Dr. Sgoutas also noted that it is important to consider various ways of addressing the seemingly inherent power differences within the academy. For instance, feminist activist leaders must ask themselves two questions: 1. How might they develop strategies for empowering people to utilize their strengths? 2. How might they begin seeing one another as coleaders in the fight for social justice? Finally, feminist activist leaders must "tend to their own wounds" as well as those of their peers and communities (Arlene Sgoutas, personal communication, November 2018). Healing oneself requires critical self-reflective thinking (i.e., who we are, where we come from, what privileges and oppressions we bring with us) and self-care, while tending to the wounds of others requires open ears, eyes, and hearts – to make space for the less privileged.

Some common themes that run through the leadership work at GITA and TGP include these: collaboration, reflexivity, growth, inclusivity, and the sharing of power. As each of the leaders spoke to their capabilities and practices, they elucidated the importance of empowering those who have experienced oppression in their lives but doing so in a way that allows these folks to come forward in the manner they see most fit for themselves. This requires being attentive to the power dynamics that exist within ideological, institutional, interpersonal, and intrapsychic realms. Feminist activist leadership, thus, requires consistent (re)education in inclusive practices. In an effort to make TGP more transgender inclusive and GITA more community-needs focused, the leaders of each set out to reeducate themselves through collaboration. The following section outlines the five stages of collaboration between GITA and TGP, especially as they relate to the connection between their feminist activist leadership values and their practices.

Activism as Leadership

The idea of this chapter section is to provide insight into the various lessons the authors learned from their activist engagements with one another. It is here that they make recommendations for how to effectively engage in feminist activist leadership in the support of gender equity and social justice. Using the collaboration between The Gathering Place and The Gender Institute for Teaching and Advocacy as an example, the authors suggest a five-stage model for matching feminist activist leadership to practice, using humility, reflexivity, and vulnerability.

Stage One: Privilege Awareness

The first stage is privilege awareness. According to Venegas-García (2017), leadership rooted in social justice requires participants to critically reflect on their experiences with oppression. As with gender, privilege is a false binary. All people have a network of privilege and oppression, meaning they are not solely privileged nor oppressed. However, feminist activism as leadership requires that one reflect on the ways in which they experience unearned benefit for the identities they hold. Through understanding the ways that certain identities are considered default or normative, such as being white or a Christian in the United States, people can start to look for the ways that their identities narrow their perspectives. They may learn to consider how those with different life experiences see things that they cannot. This is a key thought to revisit when troubleshooting decisions that affect an organization and the people they serve. A good leader is thus someone who works to see outside of their own experiences; this step should not be skipped, nor does it have a clear end. Instead, these steps are an ongoing process which demand consistent maintenance.

One of the challenges that Matt brought to GITA was one that Sydney and Eneri talked about seeing in most of the inclusion trainings they had facilitated up to that point. Specifically, people attend trainings at widely varying expertise levels and certainly varying levels of privilege and identity. This is why the authors highlight the point that all social justice leaders have work to do around their privileges. For instance, Sydney identifies as transgender non-binary, but they are also white, able-bodied (for now), and middle class. As a facilitator, which is a position of power, it is important that they are mindful of the space that they take up, the ways that their more privileged identities create biases in what they present on, and how they interact with the people in the room who have their own levels of expertise and lived experiences with intersections of oppression. This example demonstrates that the collaboration between TGP and GITA required all participants to engage with privilege awareness as activists and as leaders.

Stage Two: Identifying Areas for Growth

Growth is an important part of leadership. Particularly in the ever-evolving social and cultural context, it is important to evaluate gaps in knowledge between oneself, the supporting organization, and the communities served. At GITA, staff serve a diverse population of students experiencing sexism and other intersections of oppression. Before they changed their curriculum and name to become more inclusive of the MSU Denver student body, they had to reflect on the limitations of their previous model. Growth is a vulnerable process that requires humility. Fresh needles on a pine are tender and at risk to their environment, however, unless the tree risks growth, it becomes weaker and ultimately cannot compete with the other trees in the race for sunlight, water, and other resources. Similarly, when The Gathering Place reached out to GITA leaders, it was a moment of vulnerability. It is not easy to admit that there are challenges in how one's mission is put into practice. With that said, it is completely healthy for an organization to be honest about its desire to grow and reach its full potential.

Humility involves putting impact before ego. Recognizing the ways in which the impact and the intent of an organization may not always align is a fruitful step towards getting on track. Caldwell, Ichiho, and Anderson (2017) explain that a combination of humility and fierce resolve are characteristics shared by highly effective leadership. Level 5 leaders "channel their ego needs away from themselves and into the larger goal of building a great company" (Caldwell et al., 2017, referencing Collins, 2001, p. 725). In this case, putting TGP values and mission before ego allowed them to access resources without being restricted by a fear of showing weakness.

Additionally, when organizations serve a community, they need to get information about how to serve that community from the source. In this case, the best people to improve the services for transgender people at TGP are transgender people themselves. One thing to be aware of, however, is that marginalized communities are often expected to educate those with more privilege for free and in many cases at their own financial, emotional, or physical expense. TGP could have put the onus on their transgender members or even their transgender staff and/or volunteers, but instead they contacted a third party. GITA employs people to do facilitation work and who are trained in intersectional feminism – a framework and orientation which considers the way multiple marginalized identities interplay to create a nuanced spectrum of privilege and oppression. This collaboration, then, did not put the facilitators in a place of personal risk in the same way as it would have if they were presenting to their own bosses or the people who provide services for their survival. For this reason, GITA leaders discussed with Matt (who strongly agreed) that transgender people affiliated with TPG would not be an appropriate resource for an initial training or evaluation. It is a tricky thing when recruiting help for organizational growth not to exploit the population served. Therefore, it is necessary to be conscientious and privilege awareness in order avoid a coercive dynamic. At the same time, this raises a question for GITA leaders around the hierarchical relationship that exists between both organizations and the members of TGP. GITA's work will continue as leaders ask themselves how they are going to incorporate the voices of transgender members, who are the true experts on homelessness and transgender inclusion, into this process.

Stage Three: Problem-solving Through Collaboration

Collaboration was a foundational value for GITA's work with TGP. Both organizations worked together, but there was also a focus on collaboration within the groups. To build on the previous stage, "humility includes a broader awareness of the overall perspective. It understands context, the nature of relationships, and the importance of treating others as valued partners" (Caldwell et al., 2017, referencing Collins, 2001, p. 727). Next, the authors briefly outline the nuts and bolts of this process and reflect on the ways that collaboration framed their efforts. This includes reflective thinking about their positionality as academics and the value of cocreating knowledge.

GITA leaders began with an interview between Matt, Kat, and Sydney. The goal was to identify the challenges TGP was having with transgender inclusion and to brainstorm potential solutions. In the end, the group decided on an inclusivity training with pre- and post-training surveys for staff and volunteers, which would measure the attitudes and inclusive behaviors of their team towards transgender people. The group further discussed a few known conflicts that were arising at The Gathering Place and decided to build a curriculum around the pre-survey results and these known issues. It was important to GITA leaders that the training was tailored to the specific needs of the organization. In order to increase impact, they exercised feminist activist leadership through listening closely to their needs, values, and history. Because of TGP's honesty about their goals and challenges, GITA team members were able to understand the reality for transgender members and create a training that addressed real needs.

Within the GITA team, collaboration occurred in the development of curriculum for the training. Each part of the team brought unique background and skills into this process. The team met as a group and worked outside of their title hierarchies to decide on the components of the curriculum that have been most impactful in previous training experiences and which met the TGP requirements. These meetings were particularly helpful for problem solving. When the group thought about the challenges at TGP, it was great to be able to draw on one other's perspectives. The team incorporated into the curriculum their varying lived experiences with homelessness, transgender identity, being people of color, and even what motivated them in trainings they had previously taken. Sharing in this work helped them develop a training that was rooted in TGP's goals while feeling well-rounded and innovative.

Additionally, this nonhierarchical design made GITA team members consider the ways that they, as academics, need to be considerate of their own privileges in this dynamic. It is not uncommon for researchers to present themselves as the sole knowledge producers, "here to save the day" by gracing activists on the ground with their theories. This underscores the importance of keeping TGP's needs and unique environment at the forefront of the process. This kind of a collaboration requires humility in order to be genuine in intent. In fact, humility is something that was necessary to carry forward into the training itself.

Part of activism as leadership is the recognition that participants have their own expertise. Similar to the practice of students circling up to engage in a discussion in the classroom, it was GITA's goal to cocreate the facilitation space with TGP staff and volunteers. Participants entered the room with various levels of knowledge and expertise about transgender identity, TGP's practices and history, other intersecting identities, and social systems surrounding homelessness and poverty. Some views of leadership suggest that there are passive and active roles in a training setting. It was GITA's goal to disrupt this false binary and to include participant voice as a crucial element of the knowledge in the room. Together, GITA and TGP were able to dig into some of the ongoing challenges TGP is facing and create relationships for troubleshooting beyond the training.

Stage Four: Putting Values Into Action

It is not enough to put an organization's intention in their mission, the intention must *become* their actions. Arguably, the crux of activism as leadership is putting values into practice and Stage Four is all about the synthesis of theory and action. After the training on transgender inclusion, staff and volunteers at TGP completed a post-survey including providing additional feedback for the GITA team. The team combined all the information they had received from the initial interview, the training, and the post-survey feedback and compiled their reflections into a summary and recommendations report for TGP. TGP and GITA leadership have also organized a meeting to discuss options for continuing the relationship. Likely, this will include follow-up conversations regarding specific challenges that were not fully resolved in the training and exchanging feedback about this collaboration.

One of the most challenging parts about leading is knowing that you cannot please everyone, yet your decisions affect everyone. Implementing values from an equitable framework is not always the easiest thing to do, but it preserves the integrity of the organization. Stages One and Two are relevant again here. Combining privilege awareness and identification of areas for growth takes a high level of humility. Matt and TGP demonstrated their commitment to addressing what is and is not working for their transgender members from the beginning of this process. Further, their eagerness to continue working with GITA in order to iron out nuanced challenges with transgender inclusivity demonstrates that they are willing to be flexible with their policy and procedures in the name of an equitable outcome.

Stage Five: Self-reflection, Change, and Growth

When getting into the fifth stage of the activism as leadership model, it is necessary to remember that this process is nonlinear and ongoing. Work towards equity is never done and requires continuous maintenance and perspective in order to do well. Consider self-reflection, change, and growth as part of the recipe for this maintenance. "Where are we now and where are we going?" This question broadens the "self" in self-reflection beyond an individual leader. It encompasses an identity in organization and in community. In other words, it is important to invite community to work alongside the organization. Let community voices be heard and their wisdom incorporated into the DNA of the organization. As the community evolves, evolve with it through ongoing discussions and shared feedback.

Conclusion

Activism as leadership requires reflexivity, humility, and vulnerability in order to succeed. As feminist activist leaders, individuals need to show a willingness to collaborate, to share power equitably, and to make space for those at the margins. TGP demonstrated each of these characteristics, as did their leaders, by soliciting help from GITA to build a more inclusive space for transgender members and throughout the collaborative work together. At GITA, team members have sought to mirror these traits through the intentional cocreation of the curriculum, training, and a follow-up conversations and reports. GITA's team has stepped outside of their restrictive academic environment to embrace a community partnership with TGP. They have seen a lot of changes in the organization of the past several years, from leadership, to mission, to academic program, to name, and even the demographics of students who come through our doors. As such, they are excited to carry forward the lessons they have learned in this collaboration and to see where feminist activist leadership carries them next.

Process Questions and Considerations

1. How do your individual and/or organizational privileges impact the services that you provide and/or the individuals that your serve? What actionable steps could you or your organization take to de-center your own privileges?
2. Are there areas of growth that your or your organization could take to put policy into practice? How might this growth look different if you were to engage in feminist activist leadership,

which promotes the sharing of power and making of space for the marginalized?

3. In which ways can you or your organization work to expand collaborative opportunities within and outside your personal, social, and institutional networks? In other words, who could you call into conversation and how could you share resources across public and private spheres?

4. What does it mean for you or your organization to put your values into action? Are you currently doing all that you can to do so? Are there areas for improvement? If so, how might you address these areas?

5. What excites you and/or your organization about change and growth? What fears do you or your organization have around change and growth? How might you utilize your excitement to address these fears?

References

2015 U.S. transgender survey: Colorado state report. (2017). Washington, DC: National Center for Transgender Equality.

Anderson, C., & Brown, C. E. (2010). The functions and dysfunctions of hierarchy. *Research in Organizational Behavior, 30*, 55–89. Retrieved from https://doi.org/10.1016/j.riob.2010.08.002

Caldwell, C., Ichiho, R., & Anderson, V. (2017). Understanding level 5 leaders: The ethical perspectives of leadership humility. *Journal of Management Development, 36*(5), 724–732. Retrieved from https://doi.org/10.1108/JMD–09–2016–0184

Collins, J. C. (2001). *Good to great: Why some companies make the leap—And others don't* (1st ed.). New York, NY: Harper Business.

Denver Transformative Justice Collective (Denver TJC). (n.d.). Retrieved February 15, 2019, from http://denvertjc.strikingly.com/

Egan, C., Shollen, S. L., Campbell, C., Longman, K. A., Fisher, K., Fox-Kirk, W., & Neilson, B. G. (2017). Capacious model of leadership identities construction. In *Theorizing women and leadership: New insights and contributions from multiple perspectives* (pp. 121–140). Charlotte, NC: Information Age Publishing.

Henry, M., Watt, R., Rosenthal, L., Shivji, A., & Abt Associates. (2017). *Annual homeless assessment report*. Washington, DC: U.S. Department of Housing and Urban Development.

James, S. E., Herman, J. L., Rankin, S., Keisling, M., Mottet, L., & Anafi, M. (2016). *The report of the 2015 U.S. transgender survey*. Washington, DC: National Center for Transgender Equality.

Mottet, L., & Ohle, J. (2006). Transitioning our shelters: Making homeless shelters safe for transgender people. *Journal of Poverty, 10*(2), 77–101. Retrieved from https://doi.org/10.1300/J134v10n02_05

Raelin, J. (2011). From leadership-as-practice to leaderful practice. *Leadership*, 7(2), 195–211. Retrieved from https://doi.org/10.1177/1742715010394808

Sgoutas, A. (2018, November). Later Leadership at GITA.

Stead, V., Elliott, C., Blevins-Knabe, B., Chan, E., Grove, K. S., Hanold, M., & Smith, A. E. (2017). Collaborative theory building on women's leadership: An exercise toward responsible leadership. In *Theorizing women and leadership: New insights and contributions from multiple perspectives* (pp. 37–50). Charlotte, NC: Information Age Publishing.

Storberg-Walker, J., & Haber-Curran, P. (2017). *Theorizing women and leadership: New insights and contributions from multiple perspectives*. Charlotte, NC: Information Age Publishing. Retrieved from http://ebookcentral.proquest.com/lib/cudenver/detail.action?docID=4789294

Tull, T. (2018, November). Early Leadership at GITA.

Venegas-García, M. (2017). Social justice leadership: Theorizing the relationship between leadership and activism for Latina/Chicana educators. In *Theorizing women and leadership: New insights and contributions from multiple perspectives* (pp. 205–224). Charlotte, NC: Information Age Publishing.

Wallington, M. (2018, October). Leadership at TGP.

Section II

Leadership in Sexuality Activism, Counseling/ Therapy

5 Marginality, Transformational Leadership, and Sexuality Work as a Psychologist

Traversing a Tough Terrain With Multiple Intersecting Identities

Kamilah Marie Woodson

Debebe and Reinert (2014) ask the question, "How does identity influence and shape leadership development?" (p. 271). They assert that to answer this question, one must be thoughtful about how identity is defined. They ultimately posit that although our larger society has the tendency to view identity in singular terms, it is more accurately conceived in multiple terms. This author is a Christian, Black, cis woman, psychologist. Much of the leadership literature on women of color suggests that Black women exist at the intersection of two primarily underrepresented social identity groups; thus intersectionality is an essential framework through which Black women emerge as unhidden figures (Ireland et al., 2018). Consequently, it is through these convergent lenses that some women experience the world. When issues of diversity like ability status, SES, and sexual orientation are factored in, the exercise of leadership becomes even more complex. For example, African American women throughout history have been able to be effective leaders despite living in an oppressive environment and dealing with power structures that do not always include their voices. This may be disempowering and incensing, and it creates circumstances for African American women leaders to use anger as an ally to help speak the truth, even when it is unpopular. They may also tend to use more direct communication styles (Eagly & Karau, 2002). Unfortunately, this has the potential to impact their credibility, effectiveness, and ascension. While current leadership theories favor transformational and servant leadership styles in general, organizational cultures often mirror social constructions of gender and ethnicity norms in society (Eagly & Johnson, 1990) that create tensions between hierarchical and collaborative forms of leadership. This may impact many women, African American women in particular, as they often subscribe to feminist leadership styles when the goal is to transform organizational cultures that mirror social biases against women as leaders. Historical theories of leadership may have professionals subscribe to the notion that gender and ethnicity are inconsequential; however, the current literature suggests that cultural worldviews, the socialization of gender roles, and different life experiences do contribute to ones' paradigm and leadership style. Further, women leaders may find it challenging to be authentic when negotiating multiple intersecting identities (Avolio, Gardner, Walumbwa, Luthans & May, 2004).

Women have increasingly moved toward greater equality at home and in the workplace (Chin 2011). Yet, some women are still underrepresented in leadership roles, still considered an anomaly compared to men when in high positions of leadership, especially within institutions of higher education, and contend with stereotypic gender role expectations that tend to constrain leadership behaviors (Eagly & Karau, 2002). White males are typically the prototype for effective leadership. That is, evaluations of leader effectiveness often favor the white male trope (tall, dark, handsome, and masculine). Consequently, the context of masculinized norms and the expectations about "what a leader looks like" introduce conditions of bias against women and racial/ethnic minority leaders. It raises challenges not faced by males, white males in particular. Literature suggests that there is bias against women leaders in appraisals of their effectiveness and expectations of their leadership behaviors (Chin, 2011); thus, women often find themselves in a "double bind" where they feel compelled to conform to differing role expectations associated with gender and leadership (Rankin, Mack & Woodson 2013). For example women have to decide if they will be "feminine" and perceived as weak or more "masculine" and perceived as too domineering. According to the Pet to Threat Phenomenon (Thomas, Johnson-Bailey, Phelps, Tran & Johnson, 2013), there are a set common experiences of women (especially minority women) who have been treated as "pets" early in their careers, as efforts to diversify traditionally male dominated fields. The "pet" term refers to the endearing affection that has been shown toward young women as they enter these fields – provided in the form of extra professional development resources, special grants and funding opportunities, and a generous chorus of "we believe in you" from older male colleagues who know that young women are the ticket to economic stability (Thomas et al., 2013). While this may be considered a good practice, according to Thomas et al. (2013), it seems that these efforts – although chivalrous and well-meaning – do not survive the entirety of a woman's career. These same young women who were encouraged to succeed are reporting that their male colleagues are surprised when they actually do. This surprise, unfortunately, paves the way for the "threat" portion of this phenomenon. Further, as women transition from acquiescent novice to competent professional, their male predecessors become threatened by a marked increase in competition. Thus, women are reporting that the same colleagues who once lauded them and told them to reach for the stars, are now accusing them of being difficult to work with, insensitive, and competitive (Thomas et al., 2013). Although this phenomenon is relative to some male colleagues having power, it may be argued that female colleagues who have internalized sexism could also function similarly, giving rise to a "same gendered" Pet to Threat Phenomenon. For the present author, being perceived as a threat in my professional environments, by both male and/or females, gets further exasperated when one of my substantive areas of interest and work is contextually controversial.

The 21st century has a new understanding and appreciation of LGBT-QIA identities, gender variance, relationship freedom/fluidity, and freedom to discuss the complexities of sex. The roles some African American Christian women who are leaders in the areas of sexuality and sexology can be arduous. Given that some women who benefit on some level from the hegemonic suppositions of the heterosexist dominant society (Shelton, 2018), they find themselves having to work to legitimize their voices, while creating brave spaces for others. Capturing the role of these multiple identities in leadership development, in this subfield, is a more complex undertaking, but not to do so risks oversimplifying the inherently multiple character of identity, not fully understanding leadership effectiveness (Debebe & Reinert, 2014), and subverts what the presumed role of being a licensed Black psychologist. Therefore, a major focus of the present author's career has been to combat the ways in which the dominant heteronormative beliefs regarding biological sex, gender, and androcentrism have neglected to include and thereby subsequently marginalize racial-ethnic group and sexual minority group members in the gender discourse (Ferguson, Carr & Snitman, 2014). For example, according to Jones and Hill (1996), African American lesbians, gay men, and bisexual individuals stand painfully juxtaposed between the fear of cultural estrangement from the African American community and the fear of racial and ethnic alienation from the gay and lesbian community. The push to "take a side" is clear and psychologically consequential for constituents in all communities. According to Debebe and Reinert (2014), leadership development involves the process of becoming an integrated leader engaged in a struggle to shed internalized messages that constrain them from pursing a passion and expressing their talents fully. For decades, the field of psychology has attempted to understand human behavior and development from a single myopic cultural lens, perpetuating the belief that all behavior is universal (Ferguson et al., 2014). Further, Western psychology is rooted in a Eurocentric sociopolitical ideology and worldview (i.e., white, heterosexual, male, Christian able bodied, middle/high SES, educated, verbal, individualistic). Thus, being a leader with a transformational leadership style, having intersecting identities, while working to support and edify marginalized people who do not ascribe to or align with dominant discourse (Ferguson et al., 2014) can be taxing, yet rewarding. This chapter addresses the intersections of multiple identities, a transformational leadership style, and experiences while conducting the ever-so-needed sexuality/sexology work in the various contexts.

Intersection of Gender, Sexuality, and Psychology Leadership

The field of psychology is one that is charged with preexisting notions and feelings about sexuality. As was mentioned earlier, the field of psychology is rooted in heteronormative, hegemonic, dualistic, sexist, and racist ideologies. For example, in the 1960s, just 50 or so years ago, there were distinct and harsh barriers to African American participating in psychology, including restricted training opportunities, extremely limited occupational opportunities, and widely held assumptions among European American psychologists of the intellectual and social deficits of African Americans, which promoted a disciplinary consensus of the impossibility, difficulty, or lack of necessity of identifying "qualified" African American graduate students and professionals (Holliday, 2009). Fortunately, in the 1970s and 1980s, institutions began to seek students of color, African Americans in particular, however, the underlying assumptions of the discipline remained unaffirming of and pathologizing to individuals who were not middle- to upper-class Caucasians. Therefore, those trained as psychologists have had to learn "decode" information and work to not only make it relevant to people of color, but to ensure that it "does no harm." Psychologists, on some level, have been trained to be tools of oppression which has been inherent to the field; thus, having this identity can produce dissonance especially when the ultimate goal is to be an advocate, facilitate inclusivity, and to promote social justice. Leadership in this context truly requires malleability and self-determination. This flexibility is required when dealing with basic psychological principles; however, when sexuality becomes a part of the discourse, work as a psychologist (as a clinician, researcher, and professor) becomes more challenging and difficult. Combatting structures that maintain the muting and dismissal of sexuality work becomes the major goal, while the additional goals are to create sensitive solutions to those suffering in silence, often in plain sight. With regard to research, many of our colleagues in the discipline of psychology, in the academy, do not find the utility in sexuality and or sexology research. There are likely all kinds of reasons for this; however, from an HBCU perspective, given that HBCU's are largely rooted in Christianity, there is less support for researchers who exist in, conduct research on, or have scholarly conversation regarding the "margins" where the discourse on sexuality resides. Consequently, there is often the need to create safe spaces, even for academicians to come together to facilitate scholarly discourse, or the need to create opportunities for scholarship on sexuality or sexology. Also, often, one of the requirements of being a successful academician is procuring funding for research and program development. Unfortunately, many of the extramural funding opportunities are interested in the concepts of sexuality and/or sexology when it is coupled with some mental/physical health or environmental problem, further pathologizing, marginalizing, and villainizing groups of people. Similarly, in professional organizations, leaders walk a fine line in attempts to be advocates, while maintaining the appearance of neutrality to insure the objectivity of the organization.

Intersection of Gender, Sexuality, and Christian Church Leadership

Serving as a leader and an advocate for sexual minorities in a Christian church can also be incendiary. Even a cursory examination of our country's history reveals hundreds of years of religious and political actions sanctioning racism and homophobia. In this country, Africans were bought and sold and inundated with rigid views about white supremacy and heteronormativity. Though most Blacks would later challenge claims about "racial inferiority," religious dogmas about sexuality remained unchallenged (Griffin, 2006). Religious and political institutions dictated the limits of sexual practice. Patterns of religious messages, social scripts, and family teaching enable individuals to understand when they ought to have sex and how sex ought to be expressed. These patterns construct sexual mores and lay the foundation for sexual morality. Sexual morality, however, like morality in general, has not remained a constant throughout this country's history. Sexual morality exists as an evolving system based on the sexual experiences and moral reasoning of each generation (Griffin, 2006). According to Griffin (2006), Black heterosexuals are more homophobic than their white counterparts especially in terms of morality, and it cannot simply be chalked up to white racism. In light of historical racism and the indoctrination of rigid gender and sexual attitudes through the Christian church, African Americans generally possess a large degree of sexual shame and a limited range with regard to sexual morality. Moreover, when Black ministers and church leaders speak of issues of sexuality, they almost always present a restricted vision of sexual morality as possible only within the confines of heterosexual marriage. Seemingly, this stunted approach to sexuality prevents African Americans from progressing toward a healthier and fuller sexuality both in attitude and practice.

Gomes (1996) suggests that it is virtually impossible to alter the understanding of scripture relative to the issues of sexuality among most African American Christians. As a transformational leader seeking to promote growth and tolerance, it is important to acknowledge the fact that the source of conviction that allows some Christians to be prejudicial is their interpretation of the Bible, while highlighting their belief that "if we are to be faithful to the clear teachings of scripture, we too must condemn homosexuality." Simultaneously, theologians underscore the fact that in spite of misleading English translations which may imply the contrary, the word *homosexual* does not occur in the Bible, it does not appear in any extant text or manuscript, and that Hebrew, Greek, Syrian, or Aramaic contains no such a word. Theologians further posit that none of these languages ever contained a word corresponding to the English homosexual term, nor did any language have such a term before the late nineteenth century. Thus, one could argue that the issue of homosexuality is rooted in our own sense of identity and morals, not necessarily in the Bible. That statement alone could "seat" someone in the leadership of the church. Moreover, as a leader in the church, it can be difficult to transform the environment when salvation is inextricably linked to the maintenance of the status quo. Further, while examining the use and misuse of scripture in Black churches, most would be stunned by the fact that may Pastors continue to adhere to outdated models of understanding of sexuality and gender when they have been trained about the dangers of doing so and they know new models and have new insights!

Interestingly however, when queried about the fact that Pastors ignore truths and continue to espouse misinformation, theologians posit that there are a number of reasons why this is occurring. They suggest, by and large, that this tendency could be about survival. As one could imagine, the survival of the church is contingent upon church membership and participation, thus church goers typically want to hear messages that are in line with (*oppressive*) traditional messages, and the Pastors are afraid of being ostracized by their congregations. Seemingly this concern of careerism keeps many Pastors in a less courageous position and they live a bifurcated existence, while the same phobic and denigrating messages persist. Understanding that this is disheartening and needs remediation, this leader seeks to create shifts in consciousness and tolerance and to speak "truths" even when they are not popular.

According to Boswell (2015), discrimination against persons of homosexual orientation is a special instance of the general problem of intolerance. Boswell (2015), however, made a strong plea to the reader to be sure to differentiate between conscientious application of religious ethics and the use of religious precepts as justification for personal animosity or prejudice. Moreover, religious beliefs may cloak or incorporate intolerance, but it is most often "popular" discrimination that fuels the discrimination. Further, there are several scriptures in the Bible that are typically used to bolster discrimination against homosexuality. The idea that homosexual behavior is condemned lies in the Old Testament, while the word *homosexual* is never mentioned in scripture. The most influential and most well-known scripture relative to this issue is the account of Sodom in Genesis 19. Which is often misunderstood, misinterpreted, and misappropriated (Boswell, 2015).

Being a member of the sexual majority provides privilege, particularly in a religious context, while being a woman often does not. Having both privileged and oppressed statuses simultaneously can be quite a quagmire. Receiving affirmation about heteronormative sexuality while being disavowed as a woman and relegated to bearing children and being the objects of our male counterparts can be disconcerting, particularly when one is visibly in a leadership position. Also, with regard to sexuality, serving in an "Ally status" may not be legitimizing enough to facilitate trusting relationships with sexual minorities or even evoke change in sexual majorities, particularly in the church.

A female transformational leader in the church, with a sex-positive agenda, operating within this oppressive paradigm, may find it difficult to create change or inspire growth, and may find it difficult to serve. To better navigate this space, it may be important to understand what undergirds such radical beliefs. Understanding sexuality historically involves making connections between the social control and of the of women (Ellison & Brown Douglas, 2010). Not only in Christian history but moreover in Western history (in which social control has been dominated by the church), the connection between women and sex has been so close as to be synonymous. Further, the place of women in this chaotic world is one of toil and trouble, scapegoating and violence, hatred and trivialization, poverty and despair. Women's bodies are kept in the service of heterosexist patriarchy – as wives, whores, fantasy objects, and as a vast, deep pool of cheap labor (Ellison & Brown Douglas, 2010). Consequently, the role of women in leadership in many Christian Black churches can be limited and at times nonexistent. Christianity can best be described from a patriarchal perspective. Again, women historically in Christianity are undervalued, are rendered invisible, and are often abused or brutalized. Interestingly, Christianity may indirectly support the "rape" culture as evidence of this can be found in many scriptures. For example, St. Paul's advice in 1 Timothy 2:12, in which the saint says: "I do not permit a woman to teach or to have authority over a man, she must be silent." Unfortunately, the passage is often used to justify opposition to women priests and clergy. In addition to the spiritual silencing of women, Women have been totally disavowed; therefore, serving in church leadership in a society that continues to not only perpetuate the abuse, but edify it, is extremely challenging and at times literally sickening. For example, in the Book of Judges, there is a story about a man who is trapped in a house by a hostile crowd and sends out his concubine to placate them. The tale is a follows

> So the man took his concubine and sent her outside to them, and they raped her and abused her throughout the night, and at dawn they let her go. At daybreak the woman went back to the house where her master was staying, fell down at the door and lay there until daylight. When her master got up in the morning and opened the door of the house and stepped out to continue on his way, there lay his concubine, fallen in the doorway of the house, with her hands on the

threshold. He said to her, "Get up; let's go." But there was no answer. Then the man put her on his donkey and set out for home.

(Judges 19:25–28)NKJV

The sociohistorical basis for Black attitudes toward the body is relative to the oppressive and longstanding psychological consequences of the enslavement of African people (Brown-Douglass, 1999). These consequences can be observed on many levels. For example, Hopson (2019) cites the denial of "the body and the promotion of life in the spirit," suggesting that, from a theological perspective, the masses are taught that the body is bad! This in part stems from Augustine, as Christians have learned that in order to have salvation, we must have control of our bodies, the flesh. Hopson (2019) provocatively states that according to "the Word" God took a body, body is bad, and his body had to die through crucifixion. On another level, as a result of Black and white relations in this country, Black is considered undesirable and all things bad, while white is considered good and "pure as the driven snow." Further, the white body is considered pristine and virginal, while the Black body is to be disregarded, disrespected, and abused. In sum, it can be best described by the following three statements: 1. Body is bad, 2. Blacks are as body (embodied), and 3. Black body is bad. Unfortunately, this gets exercised in white culture and Black culture as well. Again, with this being the context for church leadership, being a transformational leader can be tenuous, if the underlying supposition is denigrating of "the flesh."

Conclusion

Although the previous sections highlight the difficulties in leadership and sexuality, it is important to recognize that change, often incremental, can be truly observed over time. With that, there are some prescriptive things that can be done in the meantime. Clinicians, academicians, and scholars in psychology must be willing to utilize their voices and platforms to promote understanding, advocacy, and healing with regard to sexuality work. They must be willing to speak the unspeakable, and address the injustices that they encounter. They should inspire their students and colleagues, and challenge oppressive institutional postures and/or policies even when their positions are not appreciated. Further, they should lead by example and ensure that their discourse and behaviors work to edify sexuality work and those who benefit from its propagation. Accordingly, religious sex-positive transformational leaders may want to espouse the notion that the Bible is the church's Book, and that in essence refers to the notion that the Bible is to the Church, what the Constitution is to the United States (without the ability to amend) (Gomes, 1996). Given that, it is important for leaders to approach the Bible with intentionality, open-mindedness, and with the understanding of the best uses of it. According to Gomes (1996), the Bible is not one book, but a collection of books, in fact a library. As we know, the Bible is comprised of 66 separate books that have been collected and brought together over a period of centuries to form the book that we know. Theologians suggest that we are not to examine the Bible as a historical account, but as a series of metaphorical allegorical stories that can be used to help us understand the challenges of life. Specifically, leaders must do the following: 1. Understand that the Bible is a "document" with a history and context, 2. assume that we do not understand it, and 3. have hermeneutic humility when working with it. Ultimately, leaders are not to lead people to be deceived and work against their own interests, but we are to help facilitate liberation and healing (Hopson, 2019)!

Process Questions and Considerations

1. How might we combat the religious precepts that serve as justification for prejudice and discrimination while serving as leaders in sexuality pursuits?
2. How does one negotiate the "pet" to "threat" phenomenon successfully?
3. When conducting sexuality work, is a transformational leadership style the best? If not, what is?
4. How does the intersection of various identities impact leadership while working in the discipline of sexuality?
5. What are ways that leaders can effectively utilize their voices as platforms to promote the discipline of sexuality?

References

Avolio, B. J., Gardner, W. L., Walumbwa, F. O, Luthans, F., & May, D. R. (2004). Unlocking the mask: A look at the process by which authentic leaders impact follower attitudes and behavior. *The Leadership Quarterly*, *15*, 801–823.

Boswell, J. (2015). *Christianity, social tolerance and homosexuality*. Chicago, IL: The University of Chicago Press.

Brown Douglass, K. (1999). *Sexuality and the Black church: A womanist perspective*. Maryknoll, NY; Orbis Books.

Chin, J. L. (2011). Women and leadership: Transforming visions and current contexts. *Forum on Public Policy*, *2011*(2).

Debebe, G., & Reinert, K. A. (2014). Leading with our whole selves: A multiple identity approach to leadership development. In M. L. Miville & A. D. Ferguson (Eds.), *Handbook of race-ethnicity and gender in psychology* (pp. 271–294). New York, NY: Springer.

Eagly, A., & Johnson, B. (1990). Gender and leadership style: A meta-analysis. *Psychology Bulletin*, *108*, 233–256.

Eagly, A., & Karau, S. J. (2002). Role congruity theory of prejudice toward female leaders. *Psychological Review*, 109(3), 573–598.

Ellison, M. M., & Brown Douglas, K. (2010). *Sexuality and the sacred* (2nd ed.). Louisville, KY; Westminster John Knox Press.

Ferguson, A. D., Carr, G., & Snitman, A. (2014). Intersection of race-ethnicity and gender and sexual minority communities. In M. L. Miville & A. D. Ferguson (Eds.), *Handbook of race-ethnicity and gender in psychology* (pp. 271–294). New York, NY: Springer.

Gomes, P. J. (1996). *The good book. reading the bible with mind and heart.* San Francisco, CA; HarperOne Publisher.

Griffin, H. L. (2006). *Their won receive them not.* Eugene, OR: Pilgrim Press.

Holliday, B. G. (2009). The history and visions of African American psychology: Multiple pathways to place, space, and authority *Cultural Diversity and Ethnic Minority Psychology*, 15(4), 317–337. Doi:10.1037/a0016971

Hopson, R. L. (2019). *Black bodies and the black church.* Unpublished manuscript

Ireland, D., Freeman, K. E., Winston-Proctor, C. E., DeLaine, K., McDonald-Lowe, S., & Woodson, K. M. (2018). Unhidden figures: A synthesis of research examining the intersectional experiences of black women and girls in STEM education. *Review of Research in Education*, 42, 226–254. Doi:10.3102/0091732X18759072

Jones, B. E., & Hill, M. J. (1996). African American lesbians, gay men, and bisexuals. In R. P. Cabaj & T. S. Stein (Eds.), *Textbook of homosexuality and mental health* (pp. 549–561). Arlington, VA: American Psychiatric Association.

Rankins, C., Mack, K., & Woodson, K. M. (2013). From graduate school to the STEM workforce: An entropic approach to career identity development among stem women of color. *New directions for higher education* (Vol. 163, pp. 23–34). San Francisco, CA: Jossey Bass Publishers.

Shelton, P. L. (2018). (Re) Conceptualizing Femme: Centering trans* femme counterculture. *Journal of Black Sexuality and Relationships* (in press)

Thomas, K. M., Johnson-Bailey, J., Phelps, R. E., Tran, N. M., & Johnson, L. (2013). Moving from pet to threat: Narratives of professional black women. In L. Comas-Diaz & B. Green (Eds.), *The psychological health of women of color: Intersections, challenges, and opportunities* (pp. 275–286). Westport, CT: Praeger.

6 The Sex Therapist as Leader
Existential/Humanistic Reflections From the Therapist's Chair

Dr. Daniel N. Watter

Introduction

Leadership, like much of life, is a bit of a puzzle. Are leaders born or made? Do leaders seek out positions of influence, or do roles of high impact find them? Are effective leaders visionaries, or do they take their cues from those whom they serve? Is there a particular type of leadership style that works best? Do all great leaders have certain traits in common? There are so many questions to ponder when considering what makes the best leaders, not the least of which is this: *Does great leadership depend most on skill or character?*

The present author has had the great privilege of serving many professional associations in positions of leadership for many years. In addition, this author has chaired dozens of committees, task forces, and meetings. Moreover, he has been honored by his peers with elected offices in The Society for Sex Therapy and Research (SSTAR), and the American Association of Sexuality Educators, Counselors, and Therapists (AASECT). Also, he has written several book chapters, articles in peer-reviewed journals, and have given hundreds of professional talks, lectures, and workshops. Each of these opportunities has allowed for an increased sense of satisfaction and pride. While leadership positions have not been actively sought, there is a recognition of the importance of being ambitious and accessible to invitations to participate in organizational leadership. *Without doubt, it seems as if the best, and most impactful leadership expeditions have been the numerous journeys taken with patients through the course of psychotherapy in search of resolution to their sexual difficulties and the soothing of their sexual distress.*

The focus of this chapter examines, through an existential/humanistic lens, the leadership provided by the sex therapist while working with individuals and couples in the office. It is postulated that even though sex therapists do not create the agenda for patient change, they guide their patients through the oftentimes-murky waters of living. At first glance, it may seem odd to consider the process of sex therapy as a form of "leadership," yet therapists have an expertise that allows them to identify obstacles to growth, and assist their patients in navigating the vagaries of their existence. *Leadership is most often sought during times of crisis or trauma.* So too, is when individuals and couples are most likely to seek out sex therapy services. While sex therapists may not think of themselves as "leaders," per se, they are exactly that to their patients. Therapists guide patients and stand with them during times of crisis and in the aftermath of significant trauma. Patients often look for the strength and leadership of their therapist as they work to process the impacts of trauma, and assume responsibility for creating the rest of their lives. Frequently, sex therapists see those who are stuck in repeating self-defeating, dysfunctional patterns that often manifest in a disruption in their sexual/relational lives. Much as Alice Miller (1997) points out:

> Without realizing that the past is constantly determining their present actions, they avoid learning anything about their history. They continue to live in their repressed childhood situation, ignoring the fact this it no longer exists. They are continuing to fear and avoid dangers that, although once real, have not been real for a long time. They are driven by unconscious memories and by repressed feelings and needs that determine nearly everything they do or fail to do.
>
> (p. 2)

It is the strength, skill, and leadership of the well-trained sex therapist that will enlighten patients and empower them to begin recognizing the impact of their past trauma(s) and move forward in discovering the meaning in their lives. Recognizing this reality will serve to enrich professionals' appreciation of the vitally important role they play in their clients' lives.

Attributes of Great Leaders

There is little agreement on exactly what it is that makes for great leaders. Presidential historian Doris Kearns Goodwin (2018) suggests that scholars who have studied leadership and its development have identified resilience, and the ability to sustain ambition in the face of frustration as key commonalities of some of society's greatest leaders. She reports that many of those she has studied have faced great adversity and have been able to rebound and effectively respond to the challenges of misfortune. In discussing the life of Abraham Lincoln, Goodwin emphasizes that Lincoln's experiences of poverty, illness, and episodes of significant depression converged to create in him a profound sense of empathy that allowed him to put himself in the shoes of others. In addition, Lincoln's many defeats shaped an acute sense of humility that led him to a willingness to acknowledge his errors, learn from his mistakes, and take corrective action.

Others who understand great leadership echo many of Goodwin's thoughts and observations. University of Alabama football coach, Nick Saban is widely considered one of the greatest college football coaches. His leadership on and off the field is often credited with helping his student-athletes achieve prodigious levels of success in football and in life. In discussing leadership, Saban (2005) states:

> Leaders are people who are willing to follow when it is called for. They are courageous and steadfast in their beliefs. They do what is right all the time, regardless of the consequences. They make difficult decisions that are best for the masses, not for themselves, even if those decisions prove to be unpopular. They present a vision that their followers buy into and allow those same followers to control their destinies.
>
> (p. 126)

Saban, much like Goodwin, recognizes that great leaders rebound in the face of adversity. They lead, but also know how to follow and give those they serve an opportunity to have a substantial say in, and assume responsibility for, the direction of the organization. They are not intimidated nor swayed by failure. Indeed, both Goodwin and Saban are of the belief that great leaders are resilient and are energized and motivated by setbacks and defeat. Defeat, frustration, failure, and adversity are often regarded as meaningful learning experiences that not only sharpen one's focus and commitment, but also remind one to be humble and self-effacing. Both Lincoln and Saban shared a conviction that great leaders create other great leaders, and most effective leaders surround themselves with good people who challenge them, push them, and share their values of hard work, long hours, discipline, execution, dependability, flexibility, responsibility, compassion, and a striving for excellence.

Noted author and psychotherapist Brene Brown (2018) endorses and reaffirms much of this, and also adds that great leaders create "cultures of courage." She identifies in great leaders an unwillingness to get bogged down in fear, setbacks, disappointments, shame, blame, panic, and perfectionism. She believes that great leaders are courageous and willing to take calculated risks. They don't get caught up in managing problem after problem, but rather are visionary and have the skill, foresight, and fortitude to push their visions to fruition. She stresses the importance of leaders being willing to "show up and lead through discomfort." Brown's final point, most particularly, is echoed in the words and philosophies of Saban and Goodwin. Namely, that genuine, effective leaders are not deterred by that which is uncomfortable. They have all suggested that great leaders are willing to confront the complex, and find a way to muster the courage to face the oftentimes frightening feelings that come with uncertainty. This is no less true about the work of great therapists. They, too, model for their patients the patience and value in learning to sit with feelings of anxiety and discomfort. Great therapists stand with their patients and provide support and necessary guidance as they struggle to tolerate the dysphoric emotions that often accompany the dilemmas of their existence.

Attributes of Great Therapists

Many of the traits mentioned previously also are applicable to the most influential and effective psychotherapists. Typically, however, when consideration is given to the process of therapy, professionals rarely think to describe the therapist as a "leader." It is more likely to suggest that the therapist is someone who actively abdicates or avoids the leadership role. Strategic therapists learn to emphasize the importance of "following" the patient's lead, or "beginning" where the patient is. While these skills are certainly of paramount importance in working with patients, an exclusive focus on them obscures some of the less often identified, yet no less important, aspects of the therapeutic relationship.

For example, it is important to think about the important roles that therapists play in the lives of patients. Some therapists may neglect to adequately appreciate that while they have many patients, most patients usually have only one therapist (Yalom, 2002). As a result, therapists' attention to, and interest in, the people they work with have tremendous bearing on successful treatment outcomes.

Some people are most likely to seek out sex therapy services when they are in a state of crisis or great distress. They are often feeling extremely vulnerable and in need of some stabilizing guidance. They look to professionals for hope, reassurance, strength, and professional expertise. In other words, they look to therapists to guide them through times of great adversity, and the pursuit of resilience. In these days of "patient centered" treatments, and an emphasis on patient autonomy, some therapists often forget that they are not dealing with people on an even playing field. Most patients may feel exposed, afraid, confused, worried, anxious, depressed, and a host of other possible dysphoric emotions. In addition, they often feel stymied in their attempts to find a solution to their presenting problem(s). While therapists certainly do not want to impose an agenda on their patients, there are times when they need therapists to take the lead in order to assist them in finding the road to healing and good sexual health. In essence, good psychotherapy is a fluid process, with both patient and therapist sometimes taking the lead. However, there are times when therapists need to be mindful of not abdicating the appropriate role of leader.

In the book, *Malignant: Medical Ethicists Confront Cancer* (Dresser, 2012), several prominent bioethicists discuss their personal experiences with cancer. Each of them were strong advocates for patient autonomy and shared decision-making between doctor and patient. Indeed, several were among the primary architects of the patient-centered, informed-consent movement. Yet each of them received a cancer diagnosis and felt wholly unprepared and ill-equipped to deal with the emotional sequelae of such a pronouncement. Even such highly educated, medically sophisticated, and well-connected individuals felt vulnerable and unprotected in the face of serious illness and emotional distress. They each concluded that their ideas about patient autonomy were too abstract, too academic, and too cerebral. They realized that they had miscalculated the emotional toll of illness and uncertainty, and were surprised to find just how much they needed to lean on their physicians for advice, reassurance, and guidance in managing their infirmity and making treatment decisions. In essence, while they very much wanted to be part of their treatment and the decision-making process, they found themselves remarkably in need of the leadership provided by their physicians. They came to poignantly realize that illness left them at a considerable disadvantage, and they expected (rightly so) that their physicians would have information, expertise, and skill to provide direction and a steadying influence. They also came to understand and appreciate that it is reasonable and rational to look to their healthcare team to provide leadership in navigating the pathway through their difficulties. The craving for, and acceptance of, such guidance and leadership is not a sign of weakness nor is it an abdication of personal responsibility.

If therapists review and examine the previously mentioned attributes of great leaders, we see how many of these same skills and philosophies can be extended to the skill set of effective sex therapists and the helping relationship. For example, Brene Brown (2018) suggests that great leaders are willing to "show up and lead through discomfort." This is a great description of a therapist as a leader! While sex therapists avoid setting the patient's agenda, they display a willingness to travel with the patient through their difficult journey and stand by them during times of distress, doubt, and frustration. Therapists model the courage to withstand adversity and face the difficult and complex realities of existence. They provide support, encouragement, and strength when patients are at their most vulnerable. In essence, sex therapists provide the *leadership* necessary to assist their patients in navigating the intricacies and vagaries of being human and the uncertainties of being able to relate to the self and others in meaningful ways.

Great therapists also work with their patients to be able to deal with adversity and rebound from the challenges of misfortune. Therapists lead their patients in recovery from trauma and tragedy, making difficult life decisions, finding the courage to be vulnerable in relationships, harnessing the strength required to make personal changes, venturing forward to be bold and take risks, and to be humble in lovingly accepting themselves for who they are with all of their flaws, foibles, and imperfections.

Therapists' ability to stand with their patients through such trying and difficult times requires the competencies and proficiencies of strong leadership. They may mistakenly assume that leadership is about taking charge, setting agendas, and forcefully pushing through obstacles in order to achieve one's goals. While that is certainly one style of leadership, the ability to gently, yet knowledgeably, guide people to find the answers they seek is also a legitimate style of leadership. It may be quieter, subtler, and less obvious, but it is robust leadership nonetheless. The stories in Dresser's (2012) book about cancer reminds professionals that patients seek them out for their expertise during times of great vulnerability, anxiety, and anguish. They are in need of therapeutic direction and guidance. If therapists are to be effective in their work, how could they be anything if not leaders? It then leads the sex therapist to the question of what type of leader do they want to be? Psychotherapists practice sex therapy through a variety of theoretical lens and approaches. While all this can allow for effective therapeutic leadership, the existential/humanistic lens is particularly well suited to a compassionate, supportive, courageous, and mutually engaging therapeutic experience.

The Existential/Humanistic Lens

Existential/humanistic therapy is a deeply life-affirming and dynamic approach to psychotherapy that focuses on the meaning of existence. Existential/humanistic psychotherapy is rooted in the works of the great philosophers, and views problems of living as a type of puzzle that the patient and therapist jointly work toward piecing together. From the perspective of the existential/humanistic sex therapist, therapy is focused more on the relationship between the sex therapist and the patient than on the direct targeting of presenting symptoms. In other words, the therapeutic relationship is seen as the primary vehicle for healing and effective treatment. As Yalom (2002) suggests, the therapist and the patient are "fellow travelers." There is the belief and understanding that when it comes to navigating the vagaries and dilemmas of human existence, most professionals have similar experiences.

Historically, existential/humanistic psychotherapy and sex therapy have rarely referenced each other. This has begun to change as several current sex therapists are adapting the principles of existential/humanistic psychotherapy to sex therapy, and are creating an approach to working with sexual difficulties known as existential/humanistic sex therapy (Barker, 2011; Kleinplatz, 2017; Watter, 2017). Specifically, we have often seen in the practice of sex therapy situations in which the symptom may have been resolved, yet patients continue to report disappointment due to the fact that their sexual and relational lives have not become more satisfying or fulfilling. Existential/humanistic sex therapists posit that such unsatisfying outcomes are likely the result of the treatment having neglected to address the often-concealed meaning(s) that sexuality and sexual functioning might hold for any given patient(s). Given that existential/humanistic psychotherapy is a very relational form of therapy, and one of its core beliefs is that relationships and the way we live them are defining of who we are and what we become, the existential/humanistic lens is an apt fit with much of sex therapy, and a more than suitable fit for an effective style of leadership.

Yalom (1980) identifies four primary existential concerns that plague human existence: freedom, isolation, meaninglessness, and death. Uncertainties related to any of these can result in sexual and/or relational difficulties (Watter, 2017). For example, Yalom (2002, 2015), Becker (1973), and Watter (2017) have noted that death anxiety, or more specifically death terror, can result in an uncharacteristic acceleration of uncontrolled sexual behavior. Rarely are some patients aware of these underlying existential crises and their impact on behavior. Some sex therapists spend much of their time and energy assisting individuals and couples dealing with these issues as they may manifest themselves in disruptions in their sexual/relational lives. In a sense sex therapists provide a type of leadership as they work with their patients to identify and remove the obstacles that prevent them from living the lives they desire to live. As mentioned previously, both Abraham Lincoln and Nick Saban are of the belief that great leaders create other great leaders. While some professionals may not see themselves as creating "great leaders" per se, their therapeutic leadership helps those they serve to create a more satisfying existence, and become more fully developed human beings. An existential/humanistic style of leadership endeavors to empower people or groups. It strives to assist people in making the decisions that will define their lives, and assume responsibility for the consequences of those choices. For an illustration of an existential/humanistic approach to leadership in sex therapy, consider the fictionalized case here excerpted from Watter (in press).

Harold was an 82-year-old widowed man who presented for treatment after being referred by his urologist. Harold's primary complaint was that he was noticing decreased penile sensitivity that resulted in a less pleasurable orgasm. In addition, Harold complained that it would sometimes take up to an hour of masturbation to reach climax. At the time of referral, Harold had no partnered sexual activity. His wife of almost 50 years, Jocelyn, had passed away the year before, but they had not had any partnered sexual activity for the last 40 years of their marriage. According to Harold, neither seemed to enjoy partnered sex, and he derived a great deal of pleasure from solitary masturbation. His enjoyment and interest in solitary masturbation continued until this past year.

At first glance, I found Harold's presentation surprising. It seemed obvious that an 82-year-old man should, indeed, be experiencing reduced penile sensation and a longer time to reach orgasm. I had expected he probably had some difficulty with erections as well, but Harold said that erections were not problematic. I assumed that much of our work would consist of some basic sex education about the normal sexual changes that an aging body will experience, and/or some unresolved grief about the death of Jocelyn, but something told me to hold my tongue and ask him more about his life.

Harold recalled always being an "odd" person. He was never very socially comfortable, and believed he always struggled to pick up social cues. His childhood was traumatic, and he feared both his mother and father. His parents divorced when he was 11 years old, and he recalls he was a "neglected" and lonely child. He did have an older brother, but his brother was quite cruel and abusive. Harold felt like much of his life had been a disappointment. He was Ivy League educated, including a doctoral degree in English Literature. Harold hungered for a university faculty appointment, but positions in English Literature were few and far between. With a poor job market and his inadequate social skills, Harold was unable to obtain the employment he desperately wanted. He settled for a job in a library that allowed him to surround himself with books he loved, but considered the position far below what he had envisioned for himself. Harold met Jocelyn in graduate school and they married after two years of dating. He reported enjoying married life very much. Although the relationship was minimally sexual, he enjoyed pleasing his wife in non-sexual areas, and she seemed to appreciate him as well. The couple enjoyed reading, visiting museums, and attending chamber music concerts. These are activities Harold had enjoyed doing solo before meeting Jocelyn, and continued to delight in them even after her death. During Jocelyn's extended illness, Harold took great pleasure in being her caretaker, and felt as if he had little to occupy his time since Jocelyn's death. Indeed, Harold reported becoming increasingly distressed about the prospect of his own mortality following the death of Jocelyn. The couple had two children, both now grown, and both live several states away from Harold. He reported having a positive relationship with each of the children, but neither required much of Harold. They would not see each other often, but would speak by telephone on a weekly basis.

At our second session, Harold revealed his infatuation with a 15-year-old girl, who was the daughter of a family friend. Harold spoke of her in very romanticized, loving, yet non-sexual terms. He loved sending her poems, music, and books he imagined she would be interested in. She would voice appreciation for these gifts, but Harold was frustrated by her seeming lack of enthusiasm for his guidance in life matters. This was not the first time Harold had experienced such frustration. He often found himself enamored by older adolescent/young adult females, and would excitedly try to interest them in his cultural pursuits. Unfortunately, for Harold, while most of the girls were polite and gracious, none ever reciprocated his attentiveness.

Harold spent an entire session showing me pictures of his family of origin. His narratives were filled with stories of loneliness, neglect, parental fighting, and a general sense that the world was experienced as an unsafe place. He recalled a life of restraint, fear, tentativeness, loss, and isolation. Harold found his relationship with his mother particularly confusing, as her behavior toward him was very inconsistent. One moment she would be telling him that he was her best friend, and the next she would be humiliating him with insults about his looks and mannerisms. As a result, he both feared his mother, and longed for her love, attention, and approval. As he progressed through life, every rebuff reawakened his fears of not being good enough and made him acutely aware of the loneliness and isolation he endured.

Though Harold's stories were painful for him to tell, and for me to listen to, he began to report an improvement in his sexual functioning and enjoyment. Orgasm was becoming easier to achieve, and he was experiencing sex as increasingly more pleasurable. This trend appeared to continue as our sessions progressed. Harold began to reach out to friends and family he had not communicated with for several years. He still enjoyed his solitary time, but reported experiencing a newfound enjoyment in social interactions. He joined a hiking group and decided to try on-line dating. One afternoon, while picking up his dry cleaning, he began a conversation with a 31-year-old woman, Sami, who was working behind the counter at the drycleaners. Harold found Sami to be extremely attractive and friendly, and he began making frequent trips to the drycleaners. One day, Harold decided to ask Sami out for lunch. To his great surprise, she accepted. Harold was very, very excited and began looking forward to seeing Sami socially. Sami was a recently divorced, mother of a young girl, who had recently moved to New Jersey from Oregon. She knew few people in the area, and was also a bit of a loner. She and Harold began seeing each other frequently, but the relationship remained platonic. Apparently, Sami saw Harold as a mentor and supportive friend. For his part, Harold had more romantic feelings toward Sami, but much as in his marriage, he did not crave partnered sex. Rather, he discovered a feeling of "aliveness" in his relationship with Sami and he relished her appreciation of his cultural sophistication, and her enthusiasm for accompanying him to museums, films, and concerts. Harold reported a significantly enriched sexual enjoyment through masturbation, as well as a generally enhanced overall life satisfaction. Harold's relationship with Sami flourished for approximately 8 months, after which Sami relocated back to the West Coast to be closer to her sister and her sister's family. While disappointed at not being to see Sami regularly, Harold recognized that his relationship with Sami "brought him back to life," and provided him with a renewed sense of "meaning." Harold reported feeling like a "wet blanket" was lifted from covering him, and he found much greater enjoyment in his days. He felt much less lonely, and his fear of his own death substantially diminished. Harold and Sami maintained regular contact via Face Time, and Harold continued pursue limited social opportunities with verve. Sexually, Harold was also quite content.

The story of Harold illustrates several aspects of the sex therapist as leader paradigm. Harold came into therapy lost. He was struggling with the existential crises of death, meaninglessness, and isolation. However, as is often the case with those entering psychotherapy, Harold was unsure as to the cause of his distress, nor did he have any inkling of the direction to take in order to relieve his suffering. Harold presented with a symptom (decreased penile sensation and difficulty achieving orgasm), but had no awareness of its meaning, message, or path toward resolution. He was in need of someone to lead him through the bumpy terrain of sexual decline and human existence. It was not the sex therapist's role or objective to set the agenda for Harold, nor was it the sex therapist's role to push him towards acceptance of the therapist's understanding of the problem. Indeed, it may have been tempting for some sex therapists to exhort Harold to accept that what he was experiencing was the result of aging and nothing more, and unintentionally impose on Harold a vision of his sexuality that was based on symptom presentation alone. However, listening through an existential/humanistic lens may have allowed the therapist to delve more deeply into the crux of Harold's angst, take him by the hand, and guide him to discover the existential meaning behind his difficulties, and uncover a path that would lead him to a life of greater meaning, happiness, fulfillment, and satisfaction. It should be noted that the existential/humanistic lens is a lens that can be applied to almost any model of psychotherapy. One need not be an existential/humanistic sex therapist in order to utilize many of the principles typically identified with existential/humanistic psychotherapy. Yalom (1980) and Watter (in press) have both pointed out that the existential/humanistic approach is as much a philosophy as it is a style of psychotherapy.

Abraham Lincoln was of the opinion that in a democracy the leader's strength ultimately depends on the strength of his bond with the people. Such is also the case in considering leadership in existential/humanistic sex therapy. Existential/humanistic sex therapy believes that the healing, therapeutic outcome is firmly rooted in the potency of the therapeutic relationship. Yalom (2002) asserts that the therapist has no more powerful method to heal than to model relational engagement with his/her patient. In existential/humanistic sex therapy leadership, it is the process of engagement, as opposed to any specific suggestion or advice the sex therapist may give, that facilitates exploration and change. In the case of Harold, the therapist took great care to engage with Harold and nurture the therapeutic relationship. This allowed Harold to find the courage required to take more risks in his own life, and thus assume more responsibility for his own emotional well-being. The result was a substantial improvement in his overall happiness, life satisfaction, and sexual enjoyment.

The leadership, or therapeutic relationship, began with a practice familiar to most good leaders and therapists – the ability and the willingness to listen. It seemed clear that Harold was looking for more than just symptom relief. He was feeling increasingly isolated, lonely, and adrift. The death of his wife was more traumatic than he had realized, and his sense of loneliness following her death had reawakened the trauma of neglect and abuse from his family of origin. It is noteworthy that just the retelling of the narrative of his life to an engaged listener was therapeutic for Harold. Even at its early stages, the therapeutic connection began to bring about positive changes in his sexual experience. Harold longed for connection with others, and hoped that such bonds would give meaning to his life. He wanted to mentor the young, and rediscover his own lost aliveness, vitality, and vigor. His relationship with Sami brought an end to his sense of isolation, loss, and meaninglessness and reminded him of what it felt like to be truly alive and engaged with the world around him.

Harold's sexuality mirrored the way in which he experienced his life. The existential/humanistic lens allowed him to develop a better understanding of what it was that he was seeking, and to discover a path that would lead him where he ached to go. However, without strong leadership Harold would have struggled mightily to find the avenue that was essential to the resolution of his sorrow and suffering. Harold was exceedingly grateful for his experiences in therapy, and valued the professional leadership and strength he was able to lean on and learn from.

The Existential Life of the Sex Therapist

How often do sex therapists reflect on their reasons for going into the field of sex therapy? Certainly, there are many reasons given for a choice of profession. For some, it may be the desire to be helpers to those looking for more satisfying and fulfilling sexual and relational lives. But on a deeper level, some therapists may choose this field for more existentially based reasons. Providing sex therapy and leadership for patients may satisfy some therapists regarding their own existential concerns of freedom, isolation, meaninglessness, and death. While the existential/humanistic lens may provide a profound therapeutic experience for patients, it offers a deeply reflective, rewarding, and gratifying encounter for the sex therapist as well. As being among the few that is privileged with entry into a patient's most intimate life, therapists' lives may achieve a sense of meaning that is exceedingly life affirming and imbued with meaning. The therapeutic benefits that patients take from their guidance and leadership help us cement a legacy of purpose, inspiration, and influence. Existential/humanistic sex therapists encourage people to explore their regrets and strive for a life that is as free from regret as possible. Being a leader for those who are struggling is a most powerful antidote for precluding regrets in the life of the therapist. Yalom (2008) discusses the concept of "rippling." Rippling refers to the notion that professionals create concentric circles of influence that may affect others for years. The effect therapists have on patients may be passed on to others, much like the ripples in a pond. In his recent autobiography, Yalom (2017) once again revisits the concept of rippling. Now, however, as Yalom reflects on his life and influence, he is cognizant of the fact that he has, through his writing and therapy practice, rippled into the lives of his students, patients, and family. What greater legacy could a leader (or therapist) wish for?

Conclusion

Leadership is a privilege. What greater honor could there be than to be allowed access to the private life and personal struggles of another human being? What greater compliment could there be than being relied upon to guide and lead someone who is feeling vulnerable and distressed through the vicissitudes of life and its myriad dilemmas?

Leadership comes in many forms. While many often think of leaders as having a commanding presence, some of history's greatest leaders have led with a quiet dignity. An aura of strength, competence, and trustworthiness need not be achieved through an obvious demonstration of power and force. This awareness allows professionals to view the sex therapist as a leader of sorts in that we are often called upon to gently, yet skillfully, lead patients through difficult and confusing times. An existential/humanistic approach to leadership in therapy is suggested as many of the sexual difficulties faced by patients are related to unconscious conflicts regarding the existential dilemmas of existence. Assisting patients in dealing with the existential quandaries and predicaments that often result in a disruption in sexual functioning and satisfaction calls for a competent, trustworthy, and skillful leader to stand with the patient as he/she/they navigate the impasses and imperfections of their lives.

As noted at the outset of this chapter, leadership, like much of life, is a puzzle. So much of living cannot be known, yet professionals must strive to assume responsibility for their lives and to make the best decisions they can in order to live a life that is meaningful. Such is the case with sex therapy as well. Applying an existential/humanistic lens to sex therapy facilitates the ability to guide and travel with patients as they seek to traverse the uneven terrain of existence. Much of what drives human behavior is not easily accessible to the conscious mind. Individuals and couples are most likely to seek therapy when they are feeling the most confused, frustrated, and vulnerable. Competent, compassionate, and skillful leadership is necessary in order to provide a pathway toward healing and the restoration of healthy, satisfying sexual and/or relational functioning.

Early in this chapter, the question was posed, *Does great leadership depend most on skill or character?* The answer is probably, "both." Great leaders, and great therapists, are highly skilled, professionally competent individuals. In addition, they are of the highest character in that their motivation is to help their patients discover the ability to assume personal responsibility for the direction and meaning of their life. Therefore, it is reasonable to suggest that while a sex therapist may not be the most obvious or noticeable of leaders, the sex therapist may, indeed, be the most important and influential leader in the life of a patient.

Process Questions and Considerations

1. How does the "therapist as leader" sit with you? Do you see these roles as consistent or conflicted?
2. Does the existential/humanistic lens fit with your view of leadership or the practice of sex therapy?
3. Do you think that great leadership is about skill, character, or both?
4. The field of sex therapy, and our understanding of human sexual behavior, is in a time of substantial flux and transition.

What type of leader(s) does the field need most at this time in our evolution?
5. Do you think that providing leadership in sex therapy is an effective way of confronting the existential concerns of the sex therapist? That is, does the providing of sex therapy help to create and/or cement a legacy of meaning for the therapist?

References

Barker, M. J. (2011). Existential sex therapy. *Journal of Sexual and Relationship Therapy*, (26), 33–47.
Becker, E. (1973). *The denial of death*. New York: Simon and Schuster.
Brown, B. (2018). *Dare to lead: Brave work. Tough conversations. Whole hearts.* New York: Random House.
Dresser, R. (Ed). (2012). *Malignant: Medical ethicists confront cancer.* New York: Oxford University Press.
Goodwin, D. K. (2018). *Leadership in turbulent times*. New York: Simon and Schuster.
Kleinplatz, P. J. (2017). An existential-experiential approach to sex therapy. In Z. D. Peterson (Ed.), *The Wiley handbook of sex therapy* (pp. 218–230). Hoboken, NJ: Wiley Blackwell.
Miller, A. (1997). *The drama of the gifted child: The search for the true self.* New York: Basic Books.
Saban, N. (2005). *How good do you want to be? A champion's tips on how to lead and succeed at work and in life.* New York: Ballantine Books.
Watter, D. N. (2017). Existential issues in sexual medicine: The relation between death-anxiety and hypersexuality. *Journal of Sexual Medicine*, 6, 3–10.
Watter, D. N. (in press). Sexuality and aging: Navigating the sexual challenges of aging bodies. In Y. M. Binik & K. S. K. Hall (Eds.), *Principles and practice of sex therapy* (6th ed.). New York: Guildford Press.
Yalom, I. D. (1980). *Existential psychotherapy*. New York: Basic Books.
Yalom, I. D. (2002). *The gift of therapy: An open letter to a new generation of therapists and their patients.* New York: Harper Collins.
Yalom, I. D. (2008). *Staring at the sun: Overcoming the terror of death.* San Francisco, CA: Jossey-Bass.
Yalom, I. D. (2015). *Creatures of a day and other tales of psychotherapy.* New York: Basic Books.
Yalom, I. D. (2017). *Becoming myself: A psychiatrist's memoir.* New York: Basic Books.

Section III
Sexuality Leadership and Mentoring

7 The Unit

Considerations and Challenges for Developing Leaders in the Field of Sexology

Shadeen Francis

Introduction

Educational leadership has a unique position in the larger landscape of sexology. There is a necessity for leaders in education to balance skill in group dynamics, maintain an understanding of the larger political landscape of the institution and region, and preserve an awareness of the possibilities of their teaching position (for example, a lecturer or an instructor, an adjunct or a full-time professor may have different opportunities). As leaders in education will undoubtedly be responsible for teaching material that reflects the values of the field, an active engagement with ideas around advocacy, justice, and service is also inherent in the role. The field of sexuality has an expressed commitment to diversity and inclusivity. Teaching, regardless of the discipline, is a realm in which these larger lessons are not just described, but modeled. The nature of the educator's relationship with the students serves as a powerful vehicle for their growth where learning occurs within relationships.

Consideration of how these apply to affective content, namely sex, adds a layer of complexity to the work of education. How can educators address this subject matter with sensitivity to issues around privilege, multicultural competence, and intersectionality with students who vary in their understandings of these topics? When selecting teaching methodologies, what is an educator's responsibility to reach across barriers of difference to empower students who have been underserved, or face barriers of prejudice and marginalization? What are some strategies that educators can compassionately respond to students' resistance to challenging material while maintaining accountability for the course objective? This chapter will not only cover considerations, challenges, and success strategies for emergent leaders in the field of sexology, but will also discuss the significance of educators in their critical role in the development of future generations of sexological leadership. In addition to these discussions, this chapter will pose critical questions of the leadership process and offer suggestions about how to promote leadership potential through difficult circumstances.

Challenge One: Course Design in an Ever-Changing Field

The development of leaders in a field ensures its long-term success. At the collegiate level, the first order of business for an educator of future leaders in sexology, is to define the objectives for the course. While this is a standard part of the educational process, it has been argued that the most effective educators focus their attention on course design as a primary way to develop learners (Whetten, 2007). Creating course objectives is of greater influence on the students' development than teacher skill (Whetten, 2007). Despite these facts, very few educators are given guidance on the process of course design; most have had little or no training in how to design courses (Fink, 2005). The strength of an educators' ability to design courses is usually the most limiting factor in their professional efficacy. This segment will not cover the full breadth of course design instruction, but it will highlight the considerations that are most relevant in the field of sexological education.

Sexology is an ever-growing field with reaches in a number of platforms, including medicine, education, policy-making, and mental health. With such vast applications of sexological expertise, it is understandable that there are a number of challenges in not only developing basic proficiency in sexology, but in cultivating leadership in aspiring sexologists. As the field broadens, there is increased cross-talk between disciplines. The borderlines between the subspecialties of sexology can be unclear. What does it mean to be a sexologist? Who are sexologists and what do they do? Defining the field is important to establishing important positioning questions, such as who will be the students' community of peers who are they hoping to serve? How will their respective communities and what might be some of the implications? What are the ethical obligations and what are their professional goals? What are their limitations of practice? In leading with these questions, the process of clarifying the necessary outcomes of the course follows more organically and can provide an organizing focus from which to find a center amidst the potential distractions and rebuttals that may occur over the semester.

What degree program does the course fit within? What department or specialty track does it belong to? What licensing or credentialing are students most likely to pursue upon graduation? Given the multiplicity of the field, it cannot be taken for granted that those interested in developing future leaders are teaching within well-defined or distinct degree programs, such as a Master's of Science in either counseling or social work. Many programs are broad enough to capture students with a wide array of professional goals and interests. These programs may act as a prerequisite or foundational training site for students that intend to pursue further, more specialized, sexuality training. Educators teaching sexuality-related material in academic institutions can provide meaningful career guidance as part of their curricula, as they will undoubtedly be contending with students' confusion and misinformation about sexology and sexuality work.

It must be acknowledged that there may be a difference between what the students' or institution's expectations are for course objectives versus what material actually has real-world application. It would be a failure on the part of the college or university to graduate students without equipping them with the practical tools that would allow them to navigate the full landscape of the field with ease and success. For example, not all programs offer business information related to marketing oneself or teach financial principles like setting fees in clinical practice. Whether people work in agencies, in private practices, in classrooms, or elsewhere in the community, business-related skills are integral to the practice of sexology. This is most obviously true for those ending up in domains like sales of sexuality-related goods and services or in private practice. Each sexologist must be able to pitch, promote, and understand the value of their labor to appropriately bill for their services. It would be advantageous for those designing courses to not only consider the theoretical course requirements, but also the professional information that can be integrated into the course. Students will have the opportunity to learn professional practices and develop their skills when working in the field, however students' employability after graduation is measured by whether or not they are able to use the skills, knowledge, and understanding gained through their degree studies in a graduate-level job (Poole & Sewell, 2007). Employers are looking to hire students with subject knowledge, emotional intelligence, life experience, and career skills (Poole & Sewell, 2007). Therefore, educators are not only expected to teach their students the material that they will need to be successful in the program, they will also be expected to be building students' professional expertise

How does a leader come to recognize what the necessary objectives are as they set the parameters for courses they teach? Who decides what is necessary or relevant information? Is it according to the instructor, according to the profession (perhaps through the mandates of the appropriate licensing board), according to the institution, or according to the needs and desires the students express upon enrollment in the course or program? Having competing stakeholders poses a challenge for classroom-based leaders as they seek to create clear, actionable course objectives that will orient the trajectory of the course. They are tasked with negotiating and reconciling whatever discrepancies exist between these perspectives. For the best outcomes, educators must be sure to check in at multiple levels using posted materials from national boards, comparing their courses to the those offered by similarly positioned institutions, having conversations with their department heads to gain insight on how the course fits into the larger educational ecosystem, and to take into serious account the evaluations of current students and alumnae who can share what information did or did not prepare them for the workforce.

There are many concurrent shifts in every discipline. As credential and licensing requirements evolve and change, the landscape of the field changes, along with the skill requirements of practice. The resulting impact is that educational requirements need to be continuously reviewed for programs to be competitive and prepare students for the positions they will pursue. Leaders need to be in touch with the larger community. If the goal is to develop sexological leaders through their educational experiences, course material needs to be reflective of the changes. Much of these standards are regulated by national accreditation boards, but, of course, not all programs are interested or able to meet the often stringent criteria and labor intensive application processes. Educators should consider themselves accountable for bringing the most current information to their courses and advocating for the changes needed to keep the course in alignment with the larger field.

Challenge Two: Selecting Appropriate Teaching Methodologies

As education moves to a consumer model, student disengagement is not uncommon. Over 50% of the American workforce is not engaged at work (Gallup, 2017). It would be fair to expect that professional habits are built on the foundations learned in training institutions. If more than half of the larger population is not engaged in their professional responsibilities, it can be expected that as students they were not active participants in their education and development as leaders. How can educators get students engaged in an academic process? Once course objectives are defined and clarified, educators must carefully consider the best vehicles through which to deliver the message to developing sexological leaders.

The way people learn has changed over time. Traditionally, materials were presented in oral or written formats, favoring auditory and visual learners. Classrooms were predominantly didactic, with the occasional group exercise. Research on learning modalities makes it clear that these methodologies are not universally effective for student development. The diversity of learning styles means that not all students will respond to the method by which material is presented. Working to accommodate students with different learning styles, especially those who are not didactic or auditory learners, can provide a challenge. Those in institutions that are preparing clinicians for the field might have challenges in finding learning opportunities that allow students to practice clinical, research, or policy development skills beyond memorizing and reciting theory.

An established trend is that students overwhelmingly prefer hands-on, experiential activities (Gomez, 2018). Educators must adapt their teaching methodologies to include experiential learning activities, such as roleplays and class discussions, to increase engagement and meaningful skill development. Models like experiential learning theory (ELT) have been developed to help guide this process. ELT states that learning is best conceived as a process and as a set of measurable outcomes (Kolb & Kolb, 2005). To enhance learning in higher education, the primary focus should be on engaging students using processes that include feedback on the effectiveness of their learning efforts. Some key components include ensuring teacher-student contact, communicating high expectations, encouraging student cooperation, and respecting diverse talents and ways of learning (Whetten, 2007). This has informed techniques like the flipped classroom model, in which didactic learning happens outside the classroom as "homework," and engagement in active learning occurs in the classroom using case studies, labs, games, simulations, or experiments (Herreid & Schiller, 2013). The "flipped" approach has become attractive in part because of the availability of technological resources and the increasing demand for experiential learning opportunities. Other strategies gaining popularity include online education (Koehler, Mishra, Hershey, & Peruski, 2004), learning by design (Bryson, 2016), and peer-to-peer learning. These practices can be well integrated into a sexological course; however educators need to select whatever educational practices best fit their abilities and intended audience. As general best practice, educators' teaching methodologies should consider three key components of the course's design: the desired learning outcomes, the experiential learning activities meant to move students towards these outcomes, and the intended learning assessments that would communicate the effectiveness of the strategies used (Whetten, 2007). A thorough curriculum design begins with clarity on what the students must learn by the end of the course. Educators then create their lectures and assignments to facilitate this learning. In choosing assessments, educators must be aware of how to measure knowledge development, as well as how to best access the type of learning achieved (e.g. conceptual knowledge versus practical knowledge) and create evaluations accordingly. These considerations can help rule in or out the appropriateness of different teaching approaches.

The style of leadership of the educator also matters. Not all leadership models fit well into a classroom setting. Every institution has its own culture and tone around the provision of education and it is up to educators to be sure they are not out of sync with the educational practices of their institutions. Even those hired for their innovative ideas and practices still need to fit within the operational norms and values of their institution.

Challenge Three: Navigating the Political

Sexuality, as with all things, is political. Any person involved in sex education, sexuality work, or the instructing of sexology is inherently connected to the political policies and practices of the time. Therefore, the development of sexuality leadership is also a practice of navigating political positioning.

First, it is necessary to consider what the dominant and local ideas of sexuality are. When guiding leaders into a field, both the educator and the students must be aware of the landscape they are entering. Despite individuals holding a diversity of perspectives, sex has been framed in particular ways and is influenced by political narratives and ideologies. Sex is an object of political focus. Collective understanding about sexuality has been shaped by various discourses, such as that of science (e.g., biology and psychoanalysis), philosophy (e.g., purpose and ontology), religion (e.g., spirituality and morality), and political structures like regulations, laws, and rules (Bacchi, 2012). These perspectives come to inform the knowledge and ethics of sex, and also shape the content of information transmitted intergenerationally and from peer to peer through media platforms, social discourse, and, of course, in educational institutions. From this lens, it can be more clearly understood that sexuality is contextual, as each region has its own epistemologies that inform its policies around sexuality. Therefore, in positioning the classroom politically, it is necessary to have an understanding of the political position of the institution, the local community, as well as the state that the institution is in.

To demonstrate this, consider that sexologists are often called upon to offer their expertise in resolving sexual problems and dysfunctions. How a problem is defined is a reflection of the ideologies and beliefs of the referring party. What are the perceived problems? What issues are considered within the scope of work the students are being trained for? What are considered viable and appropriate means of addressing the problem? All of this is informed by sexual politics.

Politics can, and often does, incite controversy. In 2018, the introduction of new anti-trafficking laws in the United States had significant impact sex work discourse and provided tangible evidence for the necessity of political awareness of those employed in the field of sexuality (United States Senate, 2017). The topic of sex work is relevant to sexuality educators in several ways: from analyzing sex education trends, exploring norms and taboos around sexual behavior, tracking historical trends, or training clinicians on how to work with marginalized populations. Is sex work criminalized in the state? How is sex work seen as distinct or related to sex trafficking? Does the academic institution recognize sex work as legitimate employment or as an outcome of systemic or familial dysfunction? These inform the educator's instructional position on the topic. Despite one's personal beliefs, the educator's role is to instruct their students according to the expectations of the larger professional landscape.

Those in positions of instruction must consider not only how to orient their students and trainees, but also become aware of their own positionality. Whatever the values the educators hold are expressed through their political orientation. Whatever is taught will speak to their own politics, but also inform the learners' perspective of the larger political landscape. As such, it is important for educators to be aware of their own values. Educators should ask themselves how their critical analysis and sexological lens communicates a personal set of values. What biases could follow from this personal perspective and inform how material is presented? How can they hold themselves accountable to keeping personal beliefs separate from politically charged messages? Sexuality work will likely never be value-neutral given the affective nature of the content. Nevertheless, students will need a fair presentation of the varying ways issues can be understood.

Social identity is also political. Given the widely documented and vast histories of systemic oppression across the globe, the identity of the educator is relevant to the material that they teach. Is the educator reflected in the material provided? If so, in what way or ways? How does their identity inform the message the students receive? A simple demonstration of the relevance of identity could appear in the context of gender. It is expected that, in any course around sexuality, orientation and gender will be a part of the curriculum, or at least a part of the conversation. In teaching this material, it may matter whether the instructor identifies as a cisgender person (a person whose assigned sex at birth aligns with their gender identity), a transgender person (a person whose assigned sex at birth does not align with their gender identity), or as a non-binary person (a person who does not subscribe to gender binaries). These identities may be known to the students and have a bearing on their engagement with the instructor as well as the material itself. How comfortable will the students be to ask questions? What sorts of questions might they have about presented material, as a result of the educator's identity? Will they question whether the content is reflecting the position of the field at large, the position of a select few, or the educator's individual perspective? The influence of privilege is salient here, as structural social hierarchies color our daily experiences. For example, what is the impact on the message when a white educator is teaching a course on multiculturalism? How is the material received when a person of color teaches the same course? Identities like physical ability and age also can play an influential role in the process of sexuality leadership development. Younger instructors may face challenges around credibility, or fail to command the respect that is often given to older instructors based on age hierarchies.

This level of self-reflection can be challenging, but represents a depth of social awareness that is significant to the educator-student relationship. When students learn about their instructors, it increases their trust in their instructor's leadership. In particular, appropriate and content-relevant personal disclosures actually improve students' perception of the educator's credibility (Schrodt, 2013). For that reason, it is important for educators to ask themselves this: What identities matter in their understanding of self? Are these identities relevant or useful to the course material or the relationship with the students? How comfortable do they feel acknowledging or disclosing these identities with the students, knowing that such identities impact the material taught through their positionality in the classroom? Furthermore, all identities must be considered in context. Educators must also consider how their identity mirrors or contrasts the identities of their students. What are the similarities and differences? Which of these similarities and differences are relevant to the teaching relationship and to the content being described? How do students identify themselves, and which of these identities are being activated or subjugated through their time in the program, or in this course specifically? Who is being taught should be considered as the educator is determining what will be taught, because the means and method of instruction should be tailored to fit the population according to their experiences. It is argued that learning is a process of creating knowledge by transforming personal experiences (Kolb & Kolb, 2005). Without this key piece of information, educators miss the opportunity to ground the learning in a way that students can integrate and own. Identity consciousness can be a way of building a bridge to connect with students across lines of difference.

Teaching is a process of engaging with learners who also have their own convictions about the material that is taught. The students have beliefs that inform everything from why they chose the program to what they want to do in the field. An educator is expected to teach them what to see and how to think about critical issues, knowing that all of this is impacted by their affective response to the content. Research on student engagement and classroom success find that student learning is best facilitated by processes that make the students' beliefs and ideas about a topic known so that they can be examined, tested, and integrated with new, more sophisticate ideas (Kolb & Kolb, 2005). Kolb and Kolb (2005) go on to assert that "conflict, differences, and disagreement are what drive the learning process." Understanding the intersecting identities of the students gives deeper perspective on the values underlying their expressed and covert beliefs.

A popular pop culture saying goes, "everything in the world is about sex except sex. Sex is about power." (Lisicky, 1995). There is no way to talk about power without it being political. As a result, if educators are intending to teach about sex and develop leaders in the field of sexology, they are doing an experiment in politics. It would be unwise to do this without knowing the political consciousness or praxis of their student body, of their colleagues, of their department's administration, and of their community. Upon discovery of this information, can instructors teach without pushing a political agenda or narrative? It is a delicate balance to orient the students to the stance of the field while doing so with enough neutrality or objectivity to be non-defensive. Despite living in a heavily politicized world, the goal is not to change students' beliefs but to provide success-giving field information.

Challenge Four: Lack of Resources

Many educators will take positions in institutions whose surrounding school districts have historically suffered through marginalization. Poverty, isolated geography, and inadequate staffing can greatly influence how a school district performs in its ability, or inability, to meet national educational standards. Even in schools that are well-reputed or have recognized legacies, funding streams do not always follow. Many colleges and universities are underfunded, and given the unequal distribution of resources, individual programs and departments can struggle even within well-endowed institutions. This can be true for sexuality-related programs and departments – despite being popular among students, sexology may not have the benefit of government grants, donor funding, or other external sources of financial support.

When schools are under-resourced, the shortcomings are expected to be filled by personnel, despite being impacted themselves. Educators in these institutions are overworked, undercompensated, and may lack the support necessary to do their jobs to their full potential. Lack of resources from an educator perspective could be a lack of appropriate teaching materials (like videos, curricula, or physical models), a lack of educational support (as in teacher-mentors, supervisors, or accessible peers), a lack of job security (through absence of full-time positions or strict performance outcomes), a lack of adequate physical space (as in reasonable class-sizes or personal offices), or a lack of job satisfaction (as a result of feeling creatively stifled, tense, or disillusioned by their work environment). Educators in these systemic circumstances are strong candidates for burnout.

Of course, students are also negatively impacted by this. Marginalization and lack of access can greatly impede their leadership development. In addition to the psychological consequences of systemic stress and neglect, another deleterious effect of a school's lack of resources is that students are often pushed through these systems without having met the full scholastic criteria for what is need to be successful at the next level (Karp, O'Gara, & Hughes, 2008). A subset of these students will arrive at college and, by little fault of their own, not be equipped with the skills and tools required to complete tasks like independent learning, study habits, and critical thinking. Many will struggle to achieve the standard of academic rigor expected of students at their level. This can be seen even in graduate school, where although students may have graduated from undergraduate programs and may have some lived experience in the field, many still may not be well-equipped for masters-level work. Part of educators' role is to push their students to match national performance averages and program requirements. If educators hope to develop leaders, they must be able to challenge their students to new levels of insight and competence. This can be difficult to accomplish when the students are starting off in deficit, lacking the knowledge or competencies expected upon entry to the course or program. In these cases, the dilemma is either to continue meet the students where they are and modify expectations, or to hold the students to a higher standard (at minimum, the national average) knowing that historically under-resourced students may struggle to meet this benchmark. On one hand, it may feel like educators would be betraying their own academic standards or the integrity of academic institutions, and, on the other, risk appearing cruel, unsupportive, or ineffective. From this lens, educators' attempts to promote students facing barriers may not actually encourage access and social mobility, but instead preserve stratification and reproduce inequalities (Karp et al., 2008). Conversely, educators that fail to promote students may legitimatize these inequalities by making personal attributions for structural failures to adequately resource students.

These issues will show up most for students coming from school districts that are poorly rated and under resourced. Certain categories of schools might disproportionately fit this description, such as rural programs, historically black colleges and universities (HBCUs), and liberal arts schools. This may also represent smaller state schools and community colleges, whose students are likely to pursue acceptance at their local schools that allow them to be close to support networks like their families or employment, provide the stability of familiarity of region, and limit the financial burdens associated with relocating and out-of-state tuition (Karp et al., 2008). Notice that the burden of lack of resources rests most heavily on marginalized students: students of color, first-generation students, and students belonging to lower socioeconomic statuses. The students of these groups that demonstrate the academic ability or have the financial opportunity to go to schools that are bigger, are more reputable, or have high standards of academic rigor may have bigger hurdles to jump than their counterparts that attend local schools, as more is expected from the students.

Regardless of their program's specific criteria, educators need to fill in the gap of where the students are expected to be at entry and where they are expected to be at the end of the course. Educators typically will only have the length of the semester or trimester, roughly 10–15 weeks, to figure out where the students are in their scholastic development, address the key issues or obstacles in their progress, and usher them towards the objectives of the course and the larger degree track. In this process of meeting the students where they are, it must be acknowledged that remedial or corrective work takes time and may result in the course falling behind on the intended content timeline. For programs tight on resources, opportunities for support outside of the classroom may be limited: Adjunct heavy programs struggle to offer office hours for students and educators to meet, there may not be funding to have on-campus writing centers or academic development labs, and supplementary lessons or tutoring may have to be paid out-of-pocket by the students themselves. These further limitations to student improvement can perpetuate cycles of underachievement for these schools.

It can feel like walking a tightrope for educators caught between what underserved populations have been told is enough and what they are actually expected to achieve. How can educators help students address deficits and achieve the programmatic requirements without them feeling less than in the process? If they have the right support, they can rise to challenges and overcome them successfully; however, it would not be unusual for these students to struggle in those programs. Educators hoping to effect positive change should hold themselves accountable to intervening when they notice there are students who are falling behind or are displaying symptoms of stress as they try to navigate their academic journeys.

Challenge Five: Dealing With Student Resistance and Consumerism

Student entitlement is a growing phenomenon in academia (Greenberger, Lessard, Chen, & Farruggia, 2008). Historically, education was an opportunity, a benefit for the select few that could afford to participate in the institution. Due to numerous social shifts, including increasing credential requirements for entry-level positions, higher tuition costs, greater access to loans and credit, students enter higher education not only because of a love of learning or a desire to be a part of the academic academy, but also out of necessity to participate in the competitive employment market. This shift has several implications on how educators can work with them to build leadership potential.

Academic entitlement is often referred to as student consumerism (Cain, Romanelli, & Smith, 2012). By the time students enter postsecondary education, they have internalized a consumerist mindset. Rather than seeing education as a process, many see education as a product. If students are consumers, what are they paying for? Are they paying for the degree, or are they paying for the opportunity to learn? Are they purchasing the academic experience, the professional network, or the access to a specialized line of work? A consumer orientation informs a particular lens in Western world: positions such as "You get what you pay for," and "The customer is always right." These are some of the subtext underlying financial exchanges, even in the case of education. Students, from a consumer model framework, may feel that the educator's role is to provide them a "service" and feel entitled to certain academic outcomes. A consumer model suggests reciprocity, those who are spending money expect to get what they pay for. If what they are "buying" is a degree, their ongoing deposits will be made to earn the grades that will eventually add up to the degree of their choosing. Research into students' service mindset confirmed that the majority agreed that they care more about earning a high grade than learning, and would take a course in which they would learn nothing if they would receive an A (Delucchi & Korgen, 2002). Students also believed academic success was their right, feeling entitled to a degree if they are paying tuition (Delucchi & Korgen, 2002). Consistently, students with this perspective demonstrate a lack of responsibility for their learning and a resistance to engaging in education as a process rather than a product to be purchased (Ranjani, 2008); student entitlement goes as far as to hold educators responsible for holding student attention (Delucchi & Korgen, 2002).

In addition to accountability, effort suffers in a culture of student consumerism. However, what they fail to invest in effort, the students pay in tuition. Rising tuition costs increases the pressure for students to achieve a positive return on investment (Cain et al., 2012). Education is purchased at great cost, and in the United States the majority students embark on their post-secondary journeys with immense anxiety and even greater personal debt. Therefore, when students are engaging in the classroom, they may expect their grades to be reflective of their economic or time investment, despite educators being positioned to grant what is earned. Student perspectives of earning can be very discrepant from the educator's perspective of earning; despite consumer mantras or the premise of a global meritocracy, achievement is not a natural byproduct of effort. It is entirely possible for someone to work hard and not be successful at grasping content, communicating clearly, integrating and applying their learning, or following instructions. Students often erroneously believe that working hard should factor into the grade received. For many students, up until this academic level, the demonstration of their effort was "good enough." Effort is often used as a way to promote self-esteem and rebalance other challenges and hurdles, however this mythology at primary levels fuels academic entitlements seen in colleges and universities. Educators in higher education contend with these beliefs, and must find ways to address and counter them in a way that doesn't undermine student esteem. Low self-esteem actually fuels academic entitlement, thus cementing these problematic views and blocking authentic student progress (Cain et al., 2012; Greenberger et al., 2008).

If education is a product, who is selling? As much as the students get to school and experience themselves as consumers, many schools are now operating as businesses. Both publicly owned and private institutions are marketplaces of the global knowledge economy. Many decisions are based first on financial considerations, such as how much money does the institution need to make through student tuition contributions to be able to run. Courses are designed not just for what would be best for the students' learning or for the opportunities available in the field, but based on what amount of tuition incoming will allow the program to be fully funded. Therefore, not only is it the sense of consumerism driving student resistance, but it is supported by their institutions. Increased reliance on tuition as a primary source of revenue influences institutional behavior toward students, such as approaching them as customers in order to attract and keep them (Cain et al., 2012). Education is a competitive market – very few schools offer degrees or programs that are one-of-a-kind, and even top institutions need consumer awareness and recognition to inspire students to attend there as opposed to another institution. Institutions must market their degree programs and maintain student satisfaction, knowing that the student who is unhappy with instructors or student services can simply choose to receive an education elsewhere (Cain et al., 2012). It would be a difficult sell for a university to exchange high tuition cost for the opportunity to learn rather than a guaranteed degree that will result in a higher paying job and an economically sound lifestyle post-graduation: to say opportunity sounds more like a gamble than a purchase. As a result, students are awarded a lot of power: the power to purchase, the power to choose, and the power to say no.

What is often overlooked or unknown to aspiring educators is that, at the collegiate level, the students hold a lot of power. Job security for educators is largely dependent on the evaluations of their students. The traditional professional culture of open intellectual inquiry has been replaced with institutional stress on performativity, as evidenced by the emphasis on subjective evaluations and academic audits (Olssen & Peters, 2007). Quality-testing seeks to improve the product, and by strongly valuing student evaluations, institutions seek to strengthen the hand of consumers (Ranjani, 2008). This means that, while participating as learners, students are encouraged to evaluate teaching and learning. From this lens, in the landscape of student consumerism, educators have a new manager: their students. This leads to highly commodified faculty-student relations (Rhoades & Slaughter, 1997). Education becomes a commercial transaction, with the educator as the commodity producer and the student as the consumer (Ranjani, 2008). Over time, previously valued relationships between educators and students are likely to erode due to the high stakes of student financial investment and educators' professional vulnerability to the judgment of the students. Risk aversion and the erosion of trust do not make leadership development an easy task. In fact, it leads to student resistance.

Resistance falls under a broad category of classroom incivility, demonstrated through unprofessional behaviors including loud sarcastic remarks, arguing with a faculty member, conversing loudly with other students, arriving late to class, and other actions that signal disrespect of the educator or the educational process. However, students understand their behavior in the context of distributive justice, which here refers to the perception of fairness in academic outcomes (Chory-Assad & Paulsel, 2004). Note that this sense of justice arises in interactions that are experienced as transactional. When students assess the fairness of their grades, they compare the grade they achieved to grade they expected based the grade they felt they deserved, and to the grades received by others. Mismatches between the expected outcomes of their efforts and the actual grade received are related to aggressive, hostile, and resistant student behaviors, as well as low satisfaction and poorer ratings of the educator (Chory-Assad & Paulsel, 2004). Perceived injustice also is associated with lower motivation, lower compliance with classroom rules, and decreased affective learning. Again, from a perspective informed by the customer is always right and a person gets what he/she pays for, complaints are an expected consequence of customer dissatisfaction. Student resistance can often be judged to be an issue at the level of the individual, however there is a global system of capitalism that drives it. The privatization of education and the reimaging of academic institutions as fuel for a global system of knowledge production seriously undermines the value of higher education. Students with a greater sense of entitlement feel more empowered to make demands rather than engaging in meaningful dialog with their instructors (Cain et al., 2012). This impedes their ability to develop professional skills like emotional composure, diplomacy, and negotiation, all of which are critical to professional success. And, in turn, it also creates cultures of grade inflation, where educators work to appease their students rather than challenge them, which perpetuates cycles of underperformance and low achievement (Cain et al., 2012).

Why discuss consumerism, marketing, and expectations in this conversation about student resistance and sexological leadership development? It is largely used as a vehicle to demonstrate the larger impact of social context on the education process. Student consumerism causes instructors to fear the students, fear their administrators, and, most unsettling, creates the fear of losing their jobs. Students enter college and university with the promise of successful outcomes but may exit underprepared for a high skills society. To disrupt this constant churning of the economic machine, educators must consider their position and to whom they are primarily accountable. Educators must decide who is their primary stakeholder, what is their primary objective as an instructor, and whose desires they must prioritize to fulfill their role with competence, effectiveness, and integrity. Despite being beholden to student evaluations and critiques, the educator's goal is to develop leadership, which must involve student discomfort and an investment in creating an environment within their classroom that inspires faith, respect, and accountability.

General Strategies for Success: A Toolkit

The instruction and development of future sexological leaders is no easy task. In the face of systemic barriers, student anxieties, and confusion about the field, it can be difficult to remain focused on course objectives and address issues with sensitivity and competence. Regardless of the unique experiences of each educator, there are some general strategies for success that can be added to one's professional toolkit to remain ground face of these challenges and considerations:

Obtain Buy-In: Long-standing structures can be resistant to change and innovation, but development requires it. In addressing challenges, educators will be disrupting the status quo. Gaining buy-in from the stakeholders of identified institutions makes it more possible to successfully implement change. To gain executive buy-in, educators should first consider the key goals of the department or program and communicate how their position helps achieve the intended outcomes (Oesch, 2018). Also communicate why or how the selected course of action impacts them – why are they being asked to participate in this student development process? Demonstrating positive impact using metrics and person stakes helps individuals feel a part of a collective experience, making them more likely to offer support, or at least make clear the hard barriers to execution. Educators should not leave out the students in this process! Create a sense of belonging in the classroom by offering students choice where possible, creating clear course policies, and acknowledging their personhood (Quay & Quaglia, 2004). Feelings of agency, trust, and recognition help address issues of resistance and increase motivation (Quay & Quaglia, 2004) and personal accountability (Delucchi & Smith, 1997).

Leverage Technology: When looking to overcome resource barriers in personnel, in time limits, in supports for differences in student ability (such as learning differences or physical differences in ability), or in material resources, educators can look to technology. Courses can be supplemented with digital content to improve learning, classroom engagement, and access: videos, audio recordings, games, and digital tools all provide supplements to in-class processes. Educators are cautioned against using technology for technology's sake; despite living in a technocracy, there is still value in face-to-face and analog strategies. Technology can be expensive, confusing to implement or understand, and can magnify class barriers for those who do not have easy access. It also may not be helpful in applying material or the development of emotional intelligence and soft skills (Oesch, 2018). At its best technology can create the opportunity for tailored self-paced learning and can be a modality for exposure and practice that may bridge resource barriers educators face.

Seek Mentorship: The field of sexology can be an isolating field. Sexuality educators may be the only people on staff covering content that addresses identity, relationships, communication, power, etc. Some educators report feeling under-supported in their fields in regards to emotional challenges like anxiety and burnout, and professional process skills like course development and classroom management (Whetten, 2007). Even when colleagues are available, courses can become silos with few opportunities to connect with others during the semester (Cain et al., 2012).

This can especially be true for adjunct-heavy institutions where educators may not feel like a cohesive unit and there is no agreement for long-term affiliation with the organization. Although structural supports may not exist, educators can assume responsibility for their professional development through seeking mentorship. Mentors can assist in identifying career goals, selecting effective coursework, engaging in professional networks, and participating in formal research or other scholarly activities (Cain et al., 2012). Intentional mentorship can be especially helpful for educators who hold marginalized, oppressed, or minority identities (Yager & Parker, 2007). Peer-to-peer mentorship is also valuable as support does not only exist in a hierarchy. Collaboration fuels creativity, fosters community, and makes it possible to access information outside one's own individual experiences. Upon entry to an institution, educators should identify their organization's core competencies to understand what they can do themselves and where they would benefit from support (Oesch, 2018). Visiting faculty listings at their alma mater, professional licensing boards, organizational listservs, and online forums may be ways to find peers and colleagues that may be available for support. There's an abundance of knowledge to be gained from developing a professional network, and through connection to others it can be possible to create strategies to approaching challenges while pooling resources to accomplish more than could be done individually.

Get Feedback: Feedback is an important part of a change process; we cannot rely on our individual knowledge alone as it is biased and incomplete. Accessing the perspectives of stakeholders, administration, colleagues, and students allows for educators to get a fuller view of their work developing sexological leaders. Therefore, instructor and course evaluations are an integral and necessary component of any professional development plan. The first step in being able to measure the impact of leadership development is to identify relevant short- and long-term goals, and select the appropriate metrics for that (Oesch, 2018). Student evaluations provide educators with data regarding the quality and the effectiveness of their instruction and the course at large. In addition to student evaluations, a holistic approach to educator feedback could include the following: teaching portfolios, professional development in the area of pedagogy, and peer evaluations of teaching (Cain et al., 2012). Implementing measures that track progress, milestones, skills development (all defined broadly) help educators integrate their learning over time and across courses. In conducting various polls and assessments in the hopes of constructive feedback, educators should clearly communicate with their reviewees the exact purposes of data collection and provide them with realistic expectations regarding their input. How will their feedback be used? Additionally, they should be oriented in some regard to the process of providing sound and constructive comments, including clarity around ideal and nonideal feedback (Cain et al., 2012). If asking for feedback, educators must be prepared to receive reflections that may feel critical. Consider seeking those within their network whose feedback would be valuable, trustworthy, direct, and compassionate. Educators should keep those invested in their development informed about the changes made as it shows accountability and commitment (Chertok, n.d.). It will also reassure people that their input was well received and encourage them to continue to be open and provide useful contributions in the future (Chertok, n.d.). Professional communities that can support one another with honesty have a greater opportunity to thrive.

Process Questions and Considerations

1. Identify the competing stakeholders for your current course. What specific processes would you undertake to reconcile their differing expectations?
2. What experiential learning activities would enhance your current curricula? How could its effectiveness be equitably assessed?
3. What identities do you bring into the classroom? Which are you uncomfortable with sharing, and why?
4. How would you address a student who expresses that the course was a waste of money because they didn't learn anything?
5. Who are your trusted professional colleagues? When was the last time you connected with them?

References

Bacchi, C. (2012). Why study problematization? Making politics visible. *Open Journal of Political Science*, 2(1), 1–8.
Bryson, C. (2016). Engagement through partnership: Students as partners in learning and teaching in higher education. *International Journal for Academic Development*, 21(1), 84–86.
Cain, J. Romanelli, F., & Smith, K. M. (2012). Academic entitlement in pharmacy education. *American Journal of Pharmaceutical Education*, 76(10), 1–8.
Chertok, Z. (n.d.). *Developing leadership skills: Top challenges and solutions*. Retrieved from https://blog.impraise.com/360-feedback/common-leadership-challenges-and-how-to-overcome-them-performance-review.
Chory-Assad, R. M., & Paulsel, M. L. (2004). Classroom justice: Student aggression and resistance as reactions to perceived unfairness. *Communication Education*, 53(3), 253–273.
Delucchi, M., & Korgen, K. (2002). We're the customer—We pay the tuition: Student consumerism among undergraduate sociology majors. *Teaching Sociology*, 30(1), 100–107.
Delucchi, M., & Smith, W. L. (1997). Satisfied customers versus pedagogic responsibility: Further thoughts on student consumerism. *Teaching Sociology*, 25(1), 336–337.

Fink, L. D. (2005). *Self-directed guide to designing courses for significant learning*, p. 1. Retrieved from www.ou.edu/idp/significant/Self-DirectedGuideto CourseDesignAug%2005.doc

Gallup. (2017). State of the American workplace.

Gomez, E. (2018). *The top three challenges impacting leadership development programs*. Retrieved from www.capsim.com/blog/the-top-three-challenges-impacting-leadership-development-programs/

Greenberger, E., Lessard, J., Chen, C., & Farruggia, S. (2008). Self-Entitled college students: Contributions of personality, parenting, and motivational factors. *Journal of Youth and Adolescents*, 37(10), 1193–1204.

Herreid, C. F., & Schiller, N. A. (2013). Case studies and the flipped classroom. *Journal of College Science Teaching*, 42(5), 62–66.

Karp, M. M., O'Gara, L., & Hughes, K. L. (2008). Do support services at community colleges encourage success or reproduce disadvantage? *Columbia University*, 1–24.

Koehler, M. J., Mishra, P. A., Hershey, K., & Peruski, L. (2004). With a little help from your students: A new model for faculty development and online course design. *Journal of Information Technology for Teacher Education*, 12(1), 25–55.

Kolb, A. Y., & Kolb, D. A. (2005). Learning styles and learning spaces: Enhancing experiential learning in higher education. *Academy of Management Learning and Education*, 4(2), 193–212.

Lisicky, P. (1995, August 5). A talk with Michael Cunningham. *Provincetown Arts*, 11, 36–42.

Oesch, T. (2018). *7 common leadership training challenges and their solutions*. Retrieved from https://trainingindustry.com/articles/leadership/7-common-leadership-training-challenges-and-their-solutions/

Olssen, M., & Peters, M. A. (2007). Neoliberalism, higher education and the knowledge economy: From the free market to knowledge capitalism. *Journal of Education Policy*, 20(3), 313–345.

Poole, L. D., & Sewell, P. (2007). The key to employability: Developing a practical model of graduate employability. *Education and Training*, 49(4), 277–289.

Quay, S. E., & Quaglia, R. J. (2004). Creating a classroom culture that inspires student learning. *The Teaching Professor*, 18(2), 1.

Ranjani, N. (2008). Building of eroding intellectual capital? Student consumerism as a cultural force in the context of knowledge economy. In J. Välimaa & O. H. Ylijoki (Eds.), *Cultural perspectives on higher education* (pp. 43–58). Finland: Springer.

Rhoades, G., & Slaughter, S. (1997). Academic capitalism, managed professionals, and supply-side higher education. *Social Text*, 51, 15(1), 9–38.

Schrodt, P. (2013). Content relevance and student's comfort with disclosure as moderators of instructor disclosure and credibility in the college classroom. *Communication Education*, 62(4), 352–375.

United States Senate. (2017). *S.1693: Report No. 115–199* (115th Congress 2nd Session, Calendar No.292). Washington, DC: U.S. Government Printing Office.

Whetten, D. A. (2007). Principles of effective course design: What I wish I had known about learning-centered teaching 30 years ago. *Journal of Management Education*, 31(1), 339–357.

Yager, J., & Parker, T. (2007). Educating, training and mentoring minority faculty and other trainees in mental health services research. *Academic Psychiatry*, 31(2), 146–151.

8 Networking, Mentoring, Collaborating, and Risk-Taking

A Four-Strand Approach to Sexuality Leadership

Melanie Davis and Katherine Glick

Social media proficiency makes personal branding easy in an era when anyone can hang out a virtual shingle and call themselves a sexuality expert, or "sexpert" (Albury, 1999). However, true leadership as a sexuality professional requires more than amassing followers: It takes relationship building through networking and mentoring; in addition, it requires innovation through collaboration and culture change through risk taking. The interpersonal relationships involved can be initiated through social media, but that level of communication generally remains shallow. In-person interaction enables people to form deeper relationships with more meaningful outcomes. They also may be more effective at generating the spirit of altruism that fosters a leader's commitment to others' success and to the health of the profession.

This chapter begins with an exploration of the characteristics of leadership and the hurdles faced by marginalized people, particularly women and especially women of color, when attempting to interact with some leaders or be perceived as leaders. The authors then present networking, mentoring, and collaboration as practices for sex therapists, sexuality educators, sex researchers, and others in the sexuality field. The chapter explores how these professionals can use connective strategies to build their careers and to contribute to the growth of the sexuality profession. These practices are explored through an anti-oppression lens that exposes common weaknesses and presents techniques of leading that not only respectfully acknowledge difference but also maximize it to improve interactions and outcomes. Risk taking is presented as an individual and community effort necessary to decrease oppression in the sexuality field and to make leadership accessible to a range of professionals. The chapter concludes with a series of processing questions designed to foster personal reflection and new concepts for leadership.

Leadership in Sexuality

In 1999, graduate student Kath Albury was branded an "expert sex researcher" and "sexpert" based on a few papers she had written and a comedy persona she developed three years earlier to explore cultural representations of female heterosexuality (Albury, 1999). She had neither given herself that label nor earned it by virtue of being published in peer-reviewed sexology journals or presenting at prestigious conferences. She writes,

> Media exposure results from an academic's ability to perform their own scholarship. Those who appear in front of the camera or microphone are referred to in media jargon as "the talent." Good talent, in media terms, is spirited, passionate/humorous, open to direction and, above all, able to present unqualified statements in short, simple sentences.
>
> (Albury, 1999, p. 60)

Albury describes her unsuccessful efforts to clarify her status as a student, researcher, and performer to reporters and producers who promoted her as an expert. This story may be helpful for sexuality professionals seeking to affiliate with people more advanced in their careers and who are recognized as leaders. This is not to dismiss the value of education and advice provided by popular culture sexuality educators; rather, it is to encourage emerging and established professionals to emulate not only people spotlighted as experts but also those whose actions and contributions led to their leadership status. Likewise, the authors encourage leaders to be open-minded about with whom they network, mentor, and collaborate.

Leaders in the field of sexuality have ascended to their positions through multiple modalities of professional training, entertainment, art, public speaking, social media presence, and human service experience. Many of these individuals have transcended the traditional lines of leadership that privilege formal education and standardized training. The nuances of the field allow for diverse individuals to embody a leadership or mentor role based on the merit of their creativity, lived experience, or personal story. The social justice arm of the field of sexuality requires that the door to leadership be opened for individuals who reach and serve populations in diverse ways.

Holding a position of authority does not automatically equate to leadership. Monique Howard, executive director of the Philadelphia Center Against Sexual Violence and adjunct professor of Public Health Leadership and Management for the La Salle University Master of Public Health Program, holds and has held leadership positions in nonprofit organizations. She defines leaders as those with expertise and the ability to communicate it in addition to a willingness to guide others:

> A leader's expertise lifts the field, makes it more credible. With leadership comes a large responsibility of always acting a certain way – responsibly, carefully. You utilize the information that you know to your advantage and share it to the best of your ability.
>
> (M. Howard, personal communication, November 12, 2018)

Impact of Gender/Gender Norms Within Leadership

Intuitive and preconceived notions of what leadership entails are the hallmarks of implicit leadership theory (Forsyth & Nye, 2008; Kenney, Schwartz-Kenney, & Blasocovich, 1996; Lord & Maher, 1991, as cited in Hoyt & Murphy, 2016). Working professionals develop schemas and arrive at unconscious conclusions of the most (and least) ideal characteristics of a leader, with particular attention to identity characteristics such as gender and race. These implicit theories often reflect dominant social identities associated with traditional leaders, (i.e., white, male, able bodied, etc.); indeed, numerous studies highlight prejudice toward female leaders (Heilman, 1983, 2001; Eagly & Karau 2002 as cited in Hoyt & Murphy, 2016). Gendered expectations of women in professional spaces include the view that they are complicit, easygoing, and flexible, which are associated with more communal characteristics that highlight a concern for others; whereas men are viewed as possessing characteristics that emphasize confidence, self-reliance, and dominance (i.e., traits often associated with good leadership, particularly in white professional spaces) (Hoyt & Murphy, 2016). The notion that men are better and stronger leaders is based on stereotypes originating from male-dominated structures and systems steeped in patriarchy and is not reflective of reality, particularly that of the evolving field of sexology. Without awareness of implicit schemas of leadership, leaders and those they lead may unconsciously contribute to a dominant system that puts nondominant identified professionals at a disadvantage within an oppressive system.

Impact of Race Within Leadership

Implicit notions of racial identity factors align with dominant leadership models, as candidates who are racial minorities are often perceived as less suitable for management positions than white candidates (Sy et al., 2010). Members of marginalized groups are at an automatic disadvantage concerning their likelihood of attaining leadership in the field.

Women of color (WOC) in particular face intersecting challenges of gender and minority differences, including how these sources of identity influence their struggle to achieve success and feel comfortable in majority-dominated organizations (Bell & Nkomo, 2001; Blake, 1999; Sanchez-Hucles & Sanchez, 2007 cited in Sanchez-Hucles & Davis, 2010). Carrying the burden of both racism and sexism, WOC have a slower progress toward leadership, a process that includes combating negative stereotypes, overt or covert discrimination, and lack of advancement potential in a majority-dominated organization. The general gender bias in leadership tends to result in women being perceived as less apt to be leaders because they do not possess the typical "masculine" traits that connote leadership, such as dominance. Women instead are seen as more communal and cooperative, which are less-desirable traits for individuals in a position of power. Sanchez-Hucles & Davis (2010) noted that the stereotypes that WOC face are more complex than that of white women, and that WOC face not only gender discrimination but also negative stereotypes related to race and ethnicity. "A woman [of color] who feels she is experiencing discrimination must decide if this prejudice is due to race, ethnicity, gender, or some other dimension to her identity" (Sanchez-Hucles & Davis, 2010, p. 173).

In a study of academic leaders, Turner (2002) highlighted special challenges faced by WOC in leadership positions. They reported feeling "socially invisible" despite the visibility of their position, and they have difficulty being perceived as credible while facing their colleagues' misperceptions of their identities and roles (Sanchez-Hucles & Davis, 2010). An examples of this would include a woman in management being treated like an assistant. Sy et al. (2010) reviewed the literature on race-occupation fit with Asian Americans to demonstrate the presence of contextual factors such as gender, identity, and culture that influence leadership perceptions. They provide evidence for a direct linkage between race and perceptions about an individual's presumed fitness for leadership. Individuals develop schemas of leadership prototypes as well as the identity factors that make good leaders. An individual who encounters a leader who does not fit into one of those prototypes may put up silent and unconscious defenses and resistance, and may express microaggressions and/or lack of readiness to receive the mentoring and guidance necessary to advance. For people represented by dominant culture in the field, it is easy to find mentors and leaders who feel comfortable and familiar; however, much can be gained by learning from people with new perspectives, new skills, new knowledge, and different ways of leading. The ultimate beneficiaries are clients who will gain access to more culturally sensitive practitioners.

Impact of Bad Examples

It behooves sexuality professionals to take an anti-oppressive perspective on professional relationships so that they can network, mentor, and collaborate with professionals offering perspectives that differ from their own – at times very different. John Hadley, a principal in Leadership Growth Strategies, posits that professionals can learn as much from leaders they do not admire as from those they seek to emulate, noting, "Anyone who's read Steve Jobs' biography would be hard pressed to conclude that he was either a nice person or a benevolent leader" (Hadley, 2012, p. 2), and yet, the Apple, Inc. chairman, chief executive officer, and cofounder led the company to soaring heights of success. Early in his career, Hadley found himself observing what other supposed leaders were doing that he did not want to emulate. He writes:

> I experienced a repertoire of tactics, strategies and skills that were either not effective in leading groups or were effective in achieving

the wrong aims. I found as much that I knew I wanted to do differently as that I wanted to repeat. Don't just ignore "leaders" because you don't want to be like them . . . act like a sponge in soaking up both the good and the bad. Carefully distinguish between what you want to be like in the future and what you do not want to emulate.

(Hadley, 2012, p. 2)

In addition to carefully observing leaders in action, sexologists seeking to advance their careers can engage in networking, mentoring, and collaboration. These practices can build the knowledge, contacts, and recognition that may position them for leadership and changemaking in the sexuality field. Sexuality leaders can use these practices to challenge institutional barriers facing emerging and marginalized professionals. Leaders have a responsibility to use the privilege they have earned – or inherently have, due to racial, academic, economic, or other status – to eliminate oppression and marginalization that hampers others from achieving similar success. This is not to imply that leaders owe it to anyone to share their time and expertise with anyone who requests it, since doing so would put them at risk of burnout and may prevent them from providing effective, focused attention where it is most needed. Each individual must weigh how, where, and when they can use their leadership position to effect positive change.

Networking

Networking refers to goal-directed behavior aimed at creating, cultivating, and utilizing interpersonal contacts (Gibson, Hardy, & Buckley, 2014), as well as information exchange for mutual benefit (Mashek, 2015; Himmelman, 2002). The process can foster relationships that help individuals enter the sexuality field (e.g., graduate students may network strategically to identify research and publishing opportunities, internships, and job opportunities). Networking also helps established professionals move into leadership by fostering relationships that lead to referrals, create mentoring and collaboration opportunities, identify advisors for problem solving, and provide career-advancing guidance.

Networking is positively associated with short-term effects including career optimism and satisfaction and long-term effects related to salaries and promotions (Volmer & Wolff, 2018). It builds on the social capital that exists in interpersonal relationships, and its potency "is realized in its capacity (just like physical and human capital) to facilitate productive activity" (O'Brien & Ó Fathaigh, 2004, p. 3). Networking has led to career advancement and goal attainment for Howard, who stated:

Networking is key – the getting out, the meeting, the ability to discuss what you do and make it of interest to other people without talking about it directly. People who network well will always have a gig. It's extremely important to be connected.

(Monique Howard, personal communication, November 12, 2018)

Networking builds social capital through social relationships nurtured over time, and it allows individuals to achieve interests and goals they could not achieve on their own. The four forms of social capital as outlined by O'Brien and Ó Fathaigh (2004, citing Coleman, 1988) are as follows:

- Obligations and expectations (e.g., doing favors and receiving favors from others)
- Informational potential (e.g., sharing useful information)
- Norms and effective sanctions (e.g., establishing community values and shared standards of behavior)
- Authority relations (e.g., skillful leadership that informs others' actions) (p. 3)

Coleman detailed *obligations, expectations* thusly:

If *A* does something for *B* and trusts *B* to reciprocate in the future, this establishes an expectation in *A* and an obligation on the part of *B*. This obligation can be conceived as a credit slip held by *A* for performance by *B*.

(S102)

This type of exchange is a hallmark of effective networking and may lead to deeper relationships if the participants approach it with a spirit of generosity and maintain a balance of favors given and received.

Informational potential has significant networking benefits, as no single individual can access all of the information that might be useful to them for decision making and taking action. Coleman describes information as the basis for action (S104) – a catalyst, in other words. He notes that its acquisition can be costly. Therein lies the value of networking partners who can fill that void.

Norms and effective sanctions refers to a prescriptive norm within a collectivity that one should forgo self-interest and act in the interests of the collectivity. Coleman lists many benefits of this norm, such as nation building and family strengthening (S104). A similar norm benefits networking partners within the sexuality field when one person refers another to a client, or for a position on a professional organization's board.

Authority relations refers to the give and take between people with a power differential. This happens frequently in the sexuality field as emerging professionals interact with established professionals. This differential does not imply that the emerging professional has less to offer; on the contrary, they may bring a wealth of new perspectives and information to the networking table.

Diane Johnson, founder of MMAPEU Consulting, reports that she developed networks and increased her social capital to gain access to interesting projects and to be involved in research. She said that when she entered the organizational consulting field, she wasn't a leader but her participation let her develop stronger relationships and network with leaders. "It creates centrifugal force around networking. Now, 30 years later, I have increased the mentoring I do and the partner relationships I have with people" (D. Johnson, personal communication, November 8, 2018).

Networking to build social capital differs greatly from the type of networking promoted strictly as a way to boost one's career. Consider the book, *Networking: Work Your Contacts to Supercharge Your Career*, which promises to teach readers how to cultivate existing contacts, turn new friends into assets, and ensure their address book is "worth its weight in gold" (King, 2008). Effective networking is not about how much you can get from others but rather how quickly you can identify how you can be of service to them. Eli R. Green, founder of the Transgender Training Institute, describes it thusly:

> I try to be generous with what I have and not expect anything in return. Be somebody people want to work with. One bad interaction won't hurt you, but multiple ones will.
> (E.R. Green, personal communication, August 29, 2018)

Green's approach is especially important for professionals seeking to increase access to and advancement within the sexuality field. Networking that consists only of handshakes and exchanging business cards is a numbers game played in hopes that someone may eventually need the other's services or products. When practiced as relationship building through mutual generosity, networking allows sexuality professionals to nurture each other's growth and knowledge while also addressing each other's concrete needs. Howard recommends setting a networking goal for each professional event such as identifying three people to meet, why meeting them is important, and who can provide a personal introduction to them. She explains,

> I write notes on a person's card while talking to them, noting where the initial meeting took place and what was discussed. . . . It's like dating. I'll write in my date book that I'll send a follow-up in two weeks. If they don't answer, I figure out how to get back in their face. It is particularly important in a field where we work as consultants: I'm 100% reliant on individual and corporate donations.
> (M. Howard, personal communication, November 12, 2018)

Mentoring

Mentoring can be an effective way to grow in one's specialty and to help emerging professionals learn from the shared wisdom of more experienced sexology professionals. Like coaching, mentoring is a process of setting goals, examining needs, and creating a learning environment with a trusted source of expertise. Hadley notes that both coaching and mentoring are collaborations in which the coach or mentor helps the direct report or mentee to find the answers that are right for them. Said Hadley,

> You do this in a way that increases their awareness and their sense of responsibility and ownership because a transfer of knowledge does not translate into changed behavior. . . . Mentoring is a process of staying in relationship, of empowering, of raising awareness, of keeping concepts and ideas alive long enough that they take root in the individual. It's the medium in which growth and change occur.
>
> (J.A. Hadley, personal communication,
> December 12, 2018)

The GROW model (Whitmore, 2017) is an executive coaching framework that mentors can use to help clients focus on both short- and long-term goals. The model encourages learning, action, and growth and is flexible in how users translate the acronym into action. When Hadley uses it for mentoring, he describes it as follows: G stands for *goals* for a mentoring session and for the length of a mentoring relationship; R stands for *reality*, in terms of asking objective questions that will not put the mentee on the defensive; O stands for *options*, or new ways to approach a challenging issue; W stands for "*What will you do?*" in terms of specific steps a mentee can take (Hadley, 2009). It should be noted that in Whitmore's original interpretation, the W stands for *way forward*, in terms of tasks needing completion and appropriate delegation of those tasks.

Power Dynamics in Mentor-Mentee Relationships

Leaders in the sexuality field can embody simultaneous roles of supervisor, mentor, and coach. While a supervisor role inherently implies being responsible for a supervisee, the mentor role is often embodied by someone who has worked in and knows the field and provides guidance and coaching. Mentoring can be an element of supervision, but mentoring does not typically involve supervision. Because the role of mentor can include authority, even in terms of the mentee respecting the mentor at a higher level than a typical colleague, the power dynamics within the mentor-mentee relationship may impact how that relationship grows and functions. These dynamics are often unspoken, yet they can affect how safe and open the mentee feels with bringing challenges to the attention of their mentor, which can ultimately impact the quality of the mentee's work and their openness to feedback and coaching. Sexuality professionals often advocate for social justice, breaking down structural and systemic barriers to access and equity within domains of sexuality, and this work can begin within one-on-one professional relationships, including the mentoring experience. Mentors who open the door for honest discussion about power structures and dynamics also empower the mentee within the mentoring relationship. This discussion of power dynamics within mentorship necessitates a discussion of privilege and intersectionality. Each individual in the relationship brings to it elements of privilege as well as oppression. Whether they exhibit racism, sexism, ageism, ethnocentrism, ableism, or any of the other silent and pervasive systems of oppression, both mentor and mentee bring to bear personal identity factors that have influenced how they have moved through and interacted with the world. Discussions about these topics can empower the mentee, allowing them to feel seen and to appreciate that their unique identity factors are inherent and integral to professional growth. White mentors must acknowledge their racialized privilege; likewise, mentors who are heterosexual and/or gender conforming must openly acknowledge the advantages that come with adhering to the gender and sexuality norms of their society and culture. Mentors who are members of marginalized groups can highlight not only advantages denied to them based on their identity status, but also the privileges they may receive based on other elements of their identity. Once a mentor breaks the ice by discussing their own privileges and direct implications of systems of injustice, the mentee will likely be more comfortable opening up about their own experiences and advantages or disadvantages (Wise & Case [of Pedagogy for the Privileged: Addressing Inequality and Injustice without Shame or Blame], 2013). The conversation can be a significant step toward deconstructing these systems of oppression within the field, enabling mentors to create an inclusive and anti-oppressive environment that fosters their mentee's and others' professional enhancement, growth, and advancement.

Johnson emphasizes the importance of mentors and mentees examining the potential power dynamics present in the relationship, as well as the chance to reframe mentoring as an opportunity for co-learning (D. Johnson, personal communication, November 8, 2018). Recognizing and eliciting the skills and resources that each individual brings to the table, no matter the titles held by those people, helps to form and cultivate an egalitarian relationship that empowers each individual to take equal responsibility for leadership and professional evolution. A transformational leadership approach such as this, i.e., one that is steeped in individualism, helps mentors create communication spaces where decisions can be collaborative and each individual feels their voice is heard. This dynamic encourages idea sharing and validates individual perspectives. It is the foundation upon which the Women of Color Sexual Health Education Network (WOCSHN) was formed by Mariotta Gary-Smith, Bianca I. Laureano, and Trina Scott, who sought to include and retain people of

color–with a focus on women and gender expansive people of color–
in the professions of sexuality, sexual science, and sexology. As Gary-
Smith said, "We work in more hierarchical organizations but [within
WOCSHN] wanted to honor all the voices present in the decision-making
discussions. We wanted everyone to feel validated at the end of the decision-making [because] their thoughts and feelings were heard" (M. Gary-
Smith, personal communication, December 12, 2018).

Altruism

Altruism is a characteristic that enables sexuality leaders to offer professional guidance to others without expecting anything in return except,
perhaps, appreciation and potential allies and collaborators. Mentors can
provide important guidance and moral support in an often-controversial
field of work. As Maxwell (2008) noted, "One of the greatest values
of mentors is the ability to see ahead what others cannot see and to
help them navigate a course to their destination" (p. 212). Mentors can
employ their knowledge of potential challenges and roadblocks related
to everything from the need for professional development and interpersonal skills to the importance of realistic goal setting, timelines for goal
attainment, certification, and contributions to the field. This notion is
particularly true within the helping professions where white privilege is
dominant and people of color find it hard to succeed without facing significant institutional barriers and boundaries. Green noted,

> A lot of the success I have had is because I am White and showed up
> at the right time. For others who came before me, there have been
> some tough moments. That's not lost on me: I've tried to pay it for-
> ward and be as generous as I can be.
> (E.R. Green, personal communication, August 29, 2018)

Leaders in sexuality can use the privilege of their position to identify
or create opportunities to those entering the field. This is particularly
important and impactful for those individuals whose identities are marginalized and who face institutionalized and structural barriers to equal
and fair advancement. Johnson emphasizes the altruistic foundation of
collaboration, mentoring, and giving back, saying, "It's not what I can
get out of it, but how can I contribute to the field I am working in. It's
what I can do for you, not what I can get from you. There's a generosity
of spirit" (D. Johnson, personal communication, November 8, 2019).

That is not to say that one must only be altruistic in one's mentoring
and networking efforts: Giving back to the sexuality field can also be a
stepping stone to leadership that mentors may recommend to mentees.
Despite their expertise and accomplishments, many leaders are only recognized once they commit to doing significant volunteer work, by joining

the board of an organization, or by participating on panels that highlight their knowledge, innovation, or vision (D. Johnson, personal communication, November 8, 2018).

Collaborating

Collaboration can be an important part of moving into and maintaining leadership within the sexuality field, as well as the advancement of sexuality specialties. Himmelman defines collaborating in relationship to three other strategies for working together, networking, coordinating, and cooperating, that build upon each other along a developmental continuum (Himmelman, 2002). Johnson describes how she employs the model in her professional relationships:

> *Networking* is only about information sharing; there is no need for trust or relationship. Once you know what people do, you might want to begin *coordinating* efforts (e.g., "I'm running a soup kitchen on Monday, Wednesday and Friday, and it's the same population you serve, so how about you run the kitchen on Tuesday, Thursday, and Saturday?" You're still working separately. When you are cooperating, you begin to start working together (e.g., "There's a proposal to submit, so why don't you do your part and I'll do mine and we'll put it together"). Once you begin collaborating, you're robustly working together and co-designing. As you go down the continuum, you invest more time and energy; the model is incredibly helpful.
>
> (D. Johnson, personal communication,
> November 8, 2018)

Mashek's adaptation of Himmelman's model can serve as a guide to the types of support needed for effective collaboration. The model adds several layers of interaction and identifies the necessary capacities and inter-institutional support needed at each level. Mashek's continuum consists of the following attributes, in order of the interpersonal investment required:

- Immuring: Conducting activities without input from or exchange with other institutions
- Networking: Exchanging information for mutual benefit
- Coordinating: In addition [to earlier activities] Altering activities to achieve a common purpose
- Cooperating: In addition, sharing resources (e.g., staff, finances, space, instrumentation)
- Collaboration: In addition, learning from each other to enhance each other's capacity
- Integrating: Completely merging operations, administrative structures, and budgets. The constituent parts are no longer discernable.

(Mashek, 2015)

By using Himmelman's model or Mashek's adaption, sexuality professionals can clarify the types of interactions in which they seek to engage, based on their needs. They also can use the model to identify where their interpersonal interactions or organizational structures are at fault because assumptions, decisions, and systems perpetuate oppression. Once these fault lines are identified, sexuality leaders can focus on the risky business of creating change.

Risk Taking

Sexuality leaders who are willing to take the risk to advocate for significant change can break down barriers that keep marginalized professionals from either envisioning themselves as leaders or becoming recognized as leaders. The field is rife with opportunities to deconstruct the organizational aspects of white supremacy culture, which include perfectionism, a sense of urgency, defensiveness, quantity over quality, worship of the written word, paternalism, either/or thinking, power hoarding, fear of open conflict, individualism, progress is bigger/more, objectivity, and the right to comfort (Jones and Okun, 2001). These ways of thinking and performing marginalize minority individuals and create barriers to success at each juncture of their careers. All of the aspects cause harm, but power hoarding has direct application to leadership in the sexuality field. Jones and Okun identified five characteristics of power hoarding:

- Little, if any, value around sharing power
- Power seen as limited, only so much to go around
- Those with power feel threatened when anyone suggests changes in how things should be done in the organization, feel suggestions for change are a reflection on their leadership
- Those with power do not see themselves as hoarding power or as feeling threatened
- Those with power assume they have the best interests of the organization at heart and assume those wanting change are ill-informed (stupid), emotional, inexperienced

The rationale for highlighting power hoarding within the sexuality leadership context is to point out that sexuality professionals and organizations may advertently/inadvertently employ these characteristics as norms and standards or practice that make it difficult, if not impossible, to open the door to professionals with other cultural norms and standards. This myopic view of professionalism can affect choices made regarding with whom one networks, who will be considered a potential mentee or worthwhile mentor, and who will be considered as a collaboration partner. Predominantly white professionals in the field may claim a desire to practice in an anti-oppressive, multicultural manner while still expecting others to adapt or conform to existing cultural norms. In reality, such a great need exists for sexologists' expertise and services that there is ample room for professionals of all backgrounds and identities. For change to happen, leaders would do well to review the antidotes proposed by Jones and Okun, which include adding power sharing to an organization's values statement; discussing what good leadership looks like and making sure people understand that a good leader fosters others' development of power and acquisition of skills. Leaders understand that change is inevitable and challenges to leadership can be healthy and productive; in addition, they make sure that the organization is focused on its mission (2001). Another way leaders can support their organization's future and mission is to advocate for fair and consistent renumeration for services that professionals provide.

Risk Taking and Remuneration

Risks on a microscale involve the specific practices we maintain within our organization, particularly as they relate to our staff, mentees, and other colleagues. Some organizations perpetuate silent expectations that staff will be committed and available for events outside of work hours without additional compensation. Creation of equity and equality within sexuality practices and in the field starts with ensuring that people are compensated fairly and consistently for their regular work, expenses, and required training and professional development. Johnson noted that one aspect of white supremacy culture is the notion that people should be willing to participate and not be remunerated for providing information and/or other resources or for presenting at conferences that will not pay their speakers (D. Johnson, personal communication, November 8, 2019). To engage in progressive risk-taking, sexuality leaders can ensure fair, consistent, and commensurate compensation for students and professionals who contribute their services and resources to enhance the field.

Another risk sexuality leaders can take is to create an intentional professional space steeped in collaboration and open communication, giving voice to all individuals in the decision-making process. Collaboration is emphasized in transformational leadership models and contributes to a collective participation and investment of all staff members. WOCSHN is a prime example of this type of leadership, as the foundresses challenged the white supremacy culture upon which sexuality professions were established and by which they are maintained. The foundresses' solution was to create an organization that is both welcoming and supportive of sexologists of color.

Gary-Smith said her commitment to a transformational leadership was inspired by her mother, who was a leader in the Black Women's Health project in the 1980s. She witnessed a collaborative leadership style that embraced mutual understanding of how and why decisions were made (M. Gary-Smith, personal communication, December 12, 2018). WOCSHN's leadership employs that method as well as diverse cultural practices around decision-making. The collectivist approach in sexology leadership allows for individual voices to be heard, validated, and included in the decision-making process. According to Gary-Smith, "The way we organize and do our work is that we all do our part for the collective whole. This network was born out of a collective desire to collaborate" (M. Gary-Smith, personal communication, December 12, 2018).

In other professional spaces, a dominant narrative exists that conflates success with innate brilliance, not taking into account systemic factors that directly impact marginalized individuals' access to educational and advancement opportunities. Hoyt and Murphy (2016) stated, "Organizational structures, particularly those permeated by a competitive ethos and the belief that success stems from innate brilliance, have the potential to be threatening, especially as women move further up the hierarchy in leadership roles" (p. 11). In organizational cultures that extol the virtues of competition or innate brilliance as paths to success, individuals of marginalized and nondominant identities (i.e., women, people of color, sexual minorities) are at a significant disadvantage when it comes to advancement and leadership potential. To correct this injustice, sexology leaders who are white have a responsibility to create professional spaces that elicit the many types of skills and abilities their staff and peers have, recognizing multiple intelligences and the unique success variables that each person brings to the collective professional table. Gary-Smith considers it imperative for leaders to be anti-oppressive in their work, which may mean creating space for others to lead, noting:

> Be willing to be an accomplice in the movement for equity and justice. You need to know when this may not be a space where you can engage, and be willing to give that up. It's going to take that in all the places where people hold privilege and power.
> (M. Gary-Smith, personal communication, December 12, 2018)

Sexuality leaders can also take the risk of setting aside personal or organizational success goals to prioritize social advocacy and social justice work. As Green noted, "In the future, I don't think people will find it good enough to be a brilliant sex educator if you aren't also doing anti-racism and anti-oppression work" (E.R. Green, personal communication, August 29, 2019).

Transformational Leadership and Queering Leadership Space

On a larger scale, sexology leaders should risk letting go of their own privilege to create an anti-oppressive and inclusive professional environment for their staff, mentees, and colleagues. Open discussions about privilege, marginalization, discrimination, and systemic/structural oppression begin that process. In order to do this successfully, sexuality leaders must understand and anticipate barriers and obstacles that may be present in the teaching/learning process, including staff defensiveness and feelings of personal judgment (Wise & Case, 2013). When discussing privilege such as white or heterosexual privilege, some individuals may feel it is presumed that they are deliberately seeking to harm others or are guilty of passively accepting advantages they have not earned. Privileged individuals may experience feelings of shame, guilt, and hopelessness associated with the taboo prohibiting the acknowledgment of one's unearned advantages. In response to these feelings, some professionals who associate with majority groups (heterosexual, gender conforming, white) may create barriers to their own learning and professional growth. To effectively navigate these situations, sexuality leaders and mentors must anticipate potential reactions and create a safe and supportive environment that permits people to process and navigate feelings successfully. Leaders can insist that separate times and spaces be set aside for both the privileged and the marginalized to discuss themes of identity, privilege, and oppression; otherwise, marginalized individuals may feel burdened with the responsibility for educating the privileged while investing emotional labor to maintain harmony in professional spaces.

When taking a transformational leadership approach, sexuality leaders can create a motivating and supportive mentoring environment in which other professionals can connect their sense of identity and of self to the mission and vision of their organizations and/or of their sexuality specialties. This allows professionals to connect more deeply to their ownership of their work and to enhance overall performance (Bromley & Kirschner-Bromley, 2007). Through individualized consideration and open communication, leaders and mentors can tune in to their mentees' needs and skills required for professional growth and development. Mentors can also attend to personal identity factors that impact how the mentee moves through the world. Empowering mentees with shared power and responsibility within the professional space helps to motivate them and increase their confidence (Bromley & Kirschner-Bromley, 2007) while counteracting harmful power dynamics.

Threats Based on Orientation Stereotypes

In order to maintain good relationships with their professional peers and supervisors, individuals who present and/or identify as female tend to live up to the expectation that they will be less confrontational and more open and accommodating to the dominant norms within the professional space. For professionals facing structural and systemic (and often silent) oppression based on marginalized identity factors, maintaining low levels of conflict (and thus, enhancing one's potential for advancement) means downplaying elements of their identity that may conflict with the status quo as they maintain silence about their marginalized status in the workplace. The act of hiding one's identity can also lead to stereotype threat (Steele & Aronson, 1995), which is the risk of confirming, as a self-characteristic, a negative stereotype about one's social group. The effects of stereotype threat have been substantiated by many social psychology studies (Steele, 1997; Steele et al., 2002, as cited in Hoyt & Murphy, 2016) and can lead individuals to underachieve as result of their response to being assessed according to negative stereotypes.

Sexuality leaders can actively counteract stereotype threats by deconstructing stereotypes in the workplace. Having discussions of power and privilege and prioritizing social advocacy and justice within the professional workspace helps to counteract negative stereotypes, and provides visibility to those of marginalized identities. Fostering a professional environment of inclusion, diversity, and collaboration deconstructs power systems that would otherwise perpetuate negative stereotypes. In their article on affirmative LGBT leadership paradigms, Fassinger, Shullman, and Stevenson (2010) reviewed the literature and noted that identity dimensions, particularly those arising from marginalized status, are significant in understanding leader and follower behavior, however, research is lacking on the effect on how a leader's gay, bisexual, or transgender identity might "influence the enactment of the leadership role, including the response of the group being led" (p. 202). They also noted that marginalized groups may more quickly and comprehensively prefer and implement transformational approaches to leadership, thus reflecting the need to create professional environments that embody an emphasis on inclusion, power sharing, collaboration, two-way communication, inspiration, meaning-making, and fostering collective identity (Fassinger et al., 2010). With increasing diversity in professional spaces in both leadership and non-leadership positions, newer notions of leadership create room for individuals with diverse styles, needs, and perspectives. Further research and examination is required to understand identity status dimensions in leadership, including the effects of marginalization on the way leadership is enacted (Fassinger et al., 2010, p. 203).

WOCSHN can be used as a case study of transformation leadership. The network's origins dated to the 2009 annual meeting of the American Association of Sexuality Educators, Counselors, and Therapists (AASECT) at which WOCSHN foundresses sought to create a space for themselves within a conference and organization steeped in dominant whiteness. Founded as a collective of women of many ethnic and cultural identities and color, WOCSHN was initially a casual meeting space for women of color who felt, at a white-dominant, international sexuality conference, invisible, ignored, and unwelcomed. Within the course of the conference, Gary-Smith, Scott, and Laureano had committed to remain connected so as to honor and maintain the space they had created for themselves. They initiated a WOCSHN Yahoo listserv that was transitioned to a website, online directory of members, and a private Facebook group that provides space women of color in the sexuality field "to share their experiences; a place to gain support when they are shut out, pushed aside, silenced, erased, and otherwise considered nonexistent" (Women of Color Sexual Health Network [WOCSHN], 2013, para. 4).

WOCHSN's membership has grown as women seek a place to connect, share experiences, and challenge each other to grow. The network's mission is to "create opportunities for inclusion and retention of people of color – with a focus on women and gender expansive people of color – in the fields of sexuality, sexual science, and sexology and challenges the white supremacy these fields were built upon" (para. 7). As listed on the WOCSHN website (www.wocshn.org/about/), the network's goals are to

- Create and nurture spaces where people of color are centered
- Mentor emerging sexuality professionals and public intellectuals of color
- Provide access to resources (publishing, presentations, public speaking)
- Extend partnerships, collaborations, and networks to ensure greater equity and inclusion of people of color in the sexuality field
- Provide technical assistance, evaluation, and critical commentary through expertise of the Foundresses and Leadership Collective (2013)

WOCSHN is a prime example of effective collaboration and risk-taking combined, wherein Women of Color came together to create their own space within an organization that neither recognized their identity nor created space for them. They did not accept the invisibility that had been perpetrated by the white-dominant culture of their professional organization; rather, they created an organization that would ensure their visibility. Sexuality leaders, particularly those who are white, would do well to look at WOCSHN as an exemplar of the power of disrupting and dismantling white-dominant professional workplace cultures and structures in order to give voice and visibility to *all* professionals in the space. Purposeful integration can create organizations that reflect the rich diversity of the public they serve. People of color also deserve to have their own spaces and organizations, particularly within professional fields that are white-dominant. No need exists to create white-dominate spaces because they already exist and flourish.

Conclusion

Professional relationships that are built and maintained have a powerful influence on developing sexologists. These relationships are created through varying levels of networking and collaboration amongst peers and offer shared resources, support, and a sense of community.

Simultaneously, nuanced mentoring and supervisory relationships help professionals shape their individual career path. Mentors may provide education and training, consciousness-raising opportunities, skills development, second opinions, problem-solving assistance, and support in the establishment of a professional values system that aligns with the mentee's ethics and priorities. Sexuality leaders are in a position to champion professional environments that holistically support individual sexologists and their career trajectory, while also anticipating and breaking down barriers to that person's success. It cannot be argued that marginalized and minority individuals face constant, pervasive systemic oppression that precludes an equal playing field, particularly for those attempting to ascend into leadership in the sexuality field. Leaders must take the risk to dismantle systems of oppression that exist in their own workspaces and in the field itself. Decreasing oppression accomplishes far more than diversity; indeed, it maximizes the presence of talented individuals and welcomes their identities, bringing increased depth to the field.

Process Questions and Considerations

Sexuality professionals may continue to learn about these issues by processing the following questions alone or with others.

1. What was your most rewarding networking story, and how can you continue to prioritize the engagement in proactive and intentional networking opportunities?
2. What can you do to ensure that your professional interactions, research, and relationships are anti-oppressive?
3. When mentoring someone whose identities, abilities, academic background, or professional standing differ from your own, how can you ensure that both of you feel seen, heard, and respected? How would you have that conversation?
4. What two risks are you willing to take to help yourself attain, maintain, or strengthen your leadership skills?
5. How will you leverage your leadership standing to dismantle white supremacy culture and systems of oppression in the sexuality field?

References

Albury, K. (1999). Instant sexpert: Academic experts and media experience. *Media International Australia*, *92*(1), pp. 55–63.
Bromley, H. R., & Kirschner-Bromley, V. A. (2007). Are You a Transformational Leader? *Physician Executive*, *33*(6), 54–57. Retrieved from http://0-search.

ebscohost.com.libcat.widener.edu/login.aspx?direct=true&db=bsh&AN=278 80805&site=eds-live

Coleman, J. S. (1988). Social capital in the creation of human capital. *American Journal of Sociology*, 94(Issue Supplement), pp. 95–120.

Fassinger, R. E., Shullman, S. L., & Stevenson, M. R. (2010). Toward an affirmative lesbian, gay, bisexual, and transgender leadership paradigm. *American Psychologist*, 65(3), 201.

Forsyth, D. R., & Nye, J. L. (2008). Seeing and being a leader: The perceptual, cognitive, and interpersonal roots of conferred influence. In C. L. Hoyt, G. R. Goethals, & D. R. Forsyth (Eds.), *Leadership at the crossroads: Leadership and Psychology* (Vol. 1, pp. 116–131). Westport, CT: Praeger.

Gibson, C. Hardy III, J., & Buckley, R. (2014). Understanding the role of networking in organizations. *Career Development International*, 19(2), pp. 146–161 [Findings]. Retrieved from www.emeraldinsight.com/doi/full/10.1108/CDI-09-2013-0111

Hadley, J. W. (2009). Dear stepping stone: The GROW model for coaching. *Career Tips Newsletter*, 34.

Hadley, J. W. (2012). Choose role models wisely. *Career Tips Newsletter*, 46.

Himmelman, A. T. (2002). *Collaboration for a change: Definitions, decision making models, roles, and collaboration process guide*. Minneapolis, MN: Himmelman Consulting.

Hoyt, C. L., & Murphy, S. E. (2016). Managing to clear the air: Stereotype threat, women, and leadership. *The Leadership Quarterly*, 27(3), 387–399.

Jones, K., & Okun, T. (2001). *Dismantling racism: A workbook for social change groups* ChangeWork. Retrieved from www.cwsworkshop.org/PARC_site_B/dr-culture.html

King, N. (2008). Networking: Work your contacts to supercharge your career. Oxford: Infinite Ideas, promotional copy Retrieved from https://bit.ly/2Dusv2C

Mashek, D. (2015, June). *Capacities and institutional support needed along the collaboration continuum*. A presentation to the Academic Deans Committee of the Claremont Colleges, Claremont, CA.

Maxwell, J. C. (2008). Mentoring moment. *The leadership handbook: 26 critical lessons every leader needs* (p. 121). Nashville, TN: Nelson Books.

O'Brien, S., & Ó Fathaigh, M. (2004). *Bringing in Bourdieu's theory of social capital: Renewing learning partnership approaches to social inclusion*. Paper presented at the ESAI Annual Conference, NUI Maynooth.

Sanchez-Hucles, J. V., & Davis, D. D. (2010). Women and Women of Color in Leadership: Complexity, Identity, and Intersectionality. *American Psychologist*, 65(3), 171–181. Retrieved from http://0search.ebscohost.com.libcat.widener.edu/login.aspx?direct=true&db=eric&AN=EJ878744&site=eds-live

Steele, C. M., & Aronson, J. (1995). Stereotype threat and the intellectual test performance of African-Americans. *Journal of Personality and Social Psychology*, 69, 797–811.

Sy, T., Shore, L. M., Strauss, J., Shore, T. H., Tram, S., Whiteley, P., & Ikeda-Muromachi, K. (2010). Leadership Perceptions as a function of race-occupation fit: The case of Asian Americans. *Journal of Applied Psychology*, 95(5), 902–919. Retrieved from http://0-search.ebscohost.com.libcat.widener.edu/login.aspx?direct=true&db=eric&AN=EJ931586&site=eds-live

Turner, C. S. V. (2002). Women of color in academe: Living with multiple marginality. *The Journal of Higher Education, 73*, 74–93.

Volmer, J., & Wolff, H.-G. (2018). A daily diary study on the consequences of networking on employees' career-related outcomes: The mediating role of positive affect. *Frontiers in Psychology, 9*(2179).

Whitmore, J. (2017). *Coaching for performance: The principles and practice of coaching and leadership* (5th ed). Boston, MA: Nicholas Brealey Publishing.

Wise, T., & Case, K. A. (2013). Pedagogy for the privileged: Addressing inequality and injustice without shame or blame. In K. Case (Ed.), *Deconstructing privilege: Teaching and learning as allies in the classroom* (pp. 17–33). New York, NY: Routledge.

Women of Color Sexual Health Network. (2013). *How it all began*. Retrieved from www.wocshn.org

9   Clearing the Path

Queer Faculty of Color Navigating Tenure and Promotion

Dr. Jayleen Galarza

Within academia, obtaining tenure and promotion is often considered the pinnacle of achievement. However, in recent years, there have been increased discussions regarding the challenges associated with achieving such an important goal, as well as lack of representation within higher education itself, among more marginalized, underrepresented communities (Nadal, 2018; Stanley, 2006; Williams, 2015). Although not a new phenomenon, it is becoming clearer that some queer faculty of color cannot easily access the academic pinnacle that is tenure and promotion. Several scholars have explored the various dynamics that contribute to this issue among faculty of color, including the following: focus of research agendas and service commitments, lack of clarity of tenure and promotion processes, limited mentoring; added pressure of mentoring/advising others, lack of departmental and university support, and experiences of discrimination (Griffin, Pifer, Humphrey, & Hazelwood, 2011; Patton & Catching, 2009; Stanley, 2006; Sue et al., 2011; Williams, 2015; Zambrana et al., 2014). Social media campaigns such as the one initiated by Kevin Nadal (2018), #Thisiswhataprofessorlookslike, are significant in drawing further attention to the existing disparities in academia. The fact remains there are too few faculty of color, especially queer faculty of color, represented in academia.

Contributing to these barriers is the overall lack of representation of faculty of color within higher education. According to the National Center for Education Statistics (NCES, 2017),

> Of all full-time faculty in degree-granting postsecondary institutions in fall 2016, 41 percent were White males; 35 percent were White females; 6 percent were Asian/Pacific Islander males; 4 percent were Asian/Pacific Islander females; 3 percent each were Black males, Black females, and Hispanic males; and 2 percent were Hispanic females.
>
> (para. 5)

This data does not track or include other aspects of identity such as diverse sexual orientations/identities and gender identities. In essence, queer Latinx faculty are not fully represented in these statistics (Latinx is used here as a more gender-inclusive term to allow for more diverse genders beyond the traditional Latina/o). These statistics highlight the fact that the proverbial ivory tower of academia is still just that – majority white, and a case could be made it is also built upon the foundations of heteronormativity.

Stanley's (2006) autoethnographic, qualitative study affirms what this author has observed firsthand – the silencing of faculty of color at predominantly white universities and colleges, the risk associated with using their voices, and the collusion of white faculty members and/or administrators in perpetuating such silence. Specifically, Stanley writes,

> When members of the dominant group speak up, it has tremendous impact because the dynamics of power, positionality, and authority are attributes that can only serve to deepen dialogues and influence policy and decision making on diversity and social justice in our colleges and universities. Conversely, when members of the targeted group speak up, the cost for us is enormous because these same dynamics are not yet equitable. We become at risk for a number of reasons, but a reason that often undergirds the silence is the lack of a critical mass of faculty of color in higher education.
>
> (p. 702)

Upon further reflection of the statistics provided by the NCES (2017), it is dismaying to know the author falls within the 2% of full-time faculty lumped into the category of "Hispanic females." Although not surprising, it is difficult to grasp and accept there are not more; Latinas haven't even reached the boundaries of what could be considered critical mass. Such data also affirms the wave of emotions the author felt when submitting her dossier and being granted tenure and promotion. When examining the data further based on rank, it becomes evident the pool of "Hispanic females" keeps getting smaller as one's rank moves to the next tier. Couple this experience with the embodiment of queer Latina identities and there is a deepening of emotions in processing the impact of what was accomplished. Although the path was not always clear, the author is compelled, if not obligated, to share the insights gained in order to assist other queer faculty of color in their journeys and breakdown the doors of predominantly white, heteronormative institutions.

Overview of the Chapter

This chapter will provide an overview of the relevant literature, deepening the comprehension of what it means to navigate the tenure and promotion process as a faculty member who manages the intersections of marginalized identities within a predominantly white and rural academic institution. Rooted in an intersectional, critical race theoretical framework, this chapter emphasizes the significance of intersectionality as practice and critical inquiry in challenging systemic, institutional processes that are often barriers to academic advancement and leadership for queer people of color (Hill-Collins & Bilge, 2016; Solorzano & Yosso, 2001). Furthermore, this discussion extends the concept of sexuality social justice (Galarza & Anthony, 2015) as it applies to leadership within college and university settings. Ultimately, in sharing this journey, this chapter contributes to the existing literature on sexuality leadership and expands current understandings of the impact of institutional processes on queer women of color in academia.

This chapter explores the following:

• Existing literature on queer faculty of color navigating tenure and promotion in higher education
• Insights gained from traversing this process
• What contributes to meaningful allyship in achieving tenure and promotion
• Using spaces of marginalization and privilege to resist and challenge systems

Queer Faculty of Color

While there is a growing body of literature aimed at better understanding the experience of faculty of color in higher education (Griffin et al., 2011; Patton & Catching, 2009; Stanley, 2006; Sue et al., 2011), the unfortunate reality is there is limited research focused on exploring the lived experiences of queer faculty of color (Delgado-Romero, Manlove, Manlove, & Hernandez, 2007; LaSala, Jenkins, & Fredriksen-Goldsen, 2008). Furthermore, there is even less specifically focused on the intersectional experiences of queer Latinx faculty, especially in traversing the realities of tenure and promotion processes (Delgado-Romero et al., 2007). In examining the current literature, there are common themes inherent in faculty of color navigating higher education, including the following: The impact of campus climate, experience of racism and microaggressions within the classroom; increased isolation; pressure to engage in diversity-related service; and limited access to mentorship (Delgado-Romero et al., 2007; Griffin et al., 2011; Patton & Catching, 2009; Stanley, 2006; Sue et al., 2011). Central to understanding these experiences is the reality of racial microaggressions, which are defined as "brief and commonplace daily verbal, nonverbal, and environmental slights, insults, invalidations, and indignities, whether they are intentional or unintentional, which are directed toward people of color" (Sue et al., 2007 as cited in Sue et al., 2011). Campus climate is experienced both at the interpersonal level and the structural level and, at times, microaggressions are woven into the fabric of campus life and these interactions. These microaggressions can be as subtle as commenting on (or complimenting) a queer Latinx person's ability to pass (lack of accent, speaking "good English," being visibly aligned with expected cultural/gender/sexual stereotypes, i.e., you're not like others I've met). However, the message of invalidation can also be conveyed at the institutional level via the limited efforts or focus on retention of faculty of color (Delgado-Romero et al., 2007).

Given what could be extracted from the existing literature, it is clear queer faculty of color contend with multiple minority stress within academia – absorbing the impacts of racially based as well as sexual identity/gender based microaggressions. In validating the LGBT People of Color Microaggressions Scale, Balsam, Molina, Beadnell, Simoni, and Walters (2011) found there are unique stressors that contribute to the health and wellness of LGBT people of color as they navigate their communities as well as larger society. Themes highlighted within their results resulted in three domains of microaggressions: "racism within LGBT communities, heterosexism within racial/ethnic communities, and racial/ethnic discrimination in dating and close relationships" (Balsam et al., 2011, p. 171). Of particular significance to higher education is the unique reality of occupying multiple marginal spaces and the potential impact on meeting the traditional expectations of service, scholarship, and teaching. For example, there may be a perceived bias against producing and presenting intersectional scholarship, which may inhibit queer faculty of color from pursuing desired research agendas or service opportunities.

In applying the multiple minority stress model to the experiences of LGBTQ faculty of color while crossing the academic terrain, it is evident that the decision to come out or not, essentially the decision to disclose about sexual and/or gender identities, has several impacts (Delgado-Romero et al., 2007; LaSala et al., 2008). Some LGBTQ faculty of color may contend with increased pressures to succeed as well as isolation (LaSala et al., 2008).

As Delgado-Romero et al. (2007) noted in their article focused on recruitment and retention of Latinx faculty,

> Heterosexism and homophobia may be present on a personal or institutional level. For the faculty member, these aversive concepts may cause emotional and physical harm, feelings of isolation and alienation, fears of rejection or judgment, or loss of opportunity for tenure and promotion.

(p. 43)

In understanding the impact of outing oneself when on the academic market or upon achieving a tenure-track line, it is important to grasp the significance of microaggressions and potential influence on experiences within various levels of institutional processes. As Balsam et al. (2011)

discuss, regardless of the type of microaggression, overt or unintentional, there is significant impact. Comments about research (e.g., "probably not a good idea to research that" or "that kind of research will never get funded"), or service ("be mindful of the type of service engaged in" or "might not want to be too social/racial justice oriented"), or level of outness ("don't be too out" or "don't out yourself in the classroom"), does not translate as helpful guidance, but, in fact, communicates the message that queer faculty of color are undoubtedly vulnerable if not playing by the more implicit rules. A queer person of color's own research agenda, service contributions, and teaching could make them a target, posing clear barriers to tenure and promotion.

Theory

As previously mentioned, intersectionality, critical race theory, and sexuality social justice are important to the lens of this chapter (Galarza & Anthony, 2015; Hill-Collins & Bilge, 2016; Solorzano & Yosso, 2001). According to Solorzano and Yosso (2001), there are five themes that form the foundation of critical race theory: "The centrality of race and racism and their intersectionality with other forms of subordination"; "the challenge to dominant ideology"; "the commitment to social justice"; "the centrality of experiential knowledge"; and "the transdisciplinary perspective" (pp. 472–473). In unpacking this discussion, understanding the worldviews of people of color requires valuing their lived experience as a form of critical knowledge as well as acknowledgment of the influences of oppression, including racism, sexism, and heterosexism on those worldviews.

This work is also grounded in social justice. Solorzano and Yosso (2001) write, "We envision social justice education as the curricular and pedagogical work that leads toward: (1) the elimination of racism, sexism, and poverty; and (2) the empowerment of underrepresented minority groups" (p. 473). Furthermore, sexuality social justice (Galarza & Anthony, 2015) entails a comprehensive understanding of the challenges to achieving equity – access to opportunities, representation, and fair treatment – as it relates to the sexual identities, behaviors, and experiences of various communities. In examining how individuals reach leadership opportunities within academic institutions, there needs to be insight into the ways in which a person's sexual/gender identities play a role in either barring or permitting access.

These theories form the foundation for a more comprehensive understanding of the complex journeys of queer people of color in not only accessing tenure-track positions in higher education but surviving and thriving once in these institutions. As such, there are clear barriers to queer Latinx faculty achieving tenure and promotion at predominantly White and heteronormative institutions. In the author's experience, the largest of these is the increased isolation, vulnerability, and the residual impact.

Clearing the Path

The sparse literature on the unique experiences of queer women of color faculty, let alone queer Latinx faculty, emphasized the need for further understanding. For this reason, the author shares her experience to illustrate how, although resiliency exists, the journey to achieving tenure and promotion is often marked by experiences of microaggressions, isolation, and pressure. Furthermore, the author offers insights into how she was able to continue this path, settle into meaningful leadership opportunities, and ultimately achieve tenure and promotion.

In exploring the experiences of faculty of color or LGBTQ faculty, isolation is a common theme within the literature (Delgado-Romero et al., 2007; Griffin et al., 2011; LaSala et al., 2008; Patton & Catching, 2009; Stanley, 2006; Sue et al., 2011). This was evident in the author's experience as well. After securing a tenure-track position within a midsized, rural, and predominantly white institution, self-doubt quickly set in. Surveying the campus landscape revealed very few people who maintained the same strongly held identities and communities, which are further embodied through the author's research and service. Although the author was excited about the prospect of contributing a queer, Latina lens to the department and larger campus, the challenge was certainly daunting. There were both self-imposed and external pressures to succeed. Not only was the author fully aware of the weight of other queer Latinas on her shoulders given the few Latinas encountered along the way, but there was an immediate sense that tenure and promotion was the not-so-easy grand prize to be achieved.

Adding to a wide range of emotions, the keys to institutional tenure and promotion processes often felt guarded and unclear, and such vagueness about the quantity and quality of materials considered sufficient compounded the existing hurdles toward advancement, as well as internalized societal messages of not being enough. Breaking the barrier and clearing the path for future generations of queer women of color faculty also means shattering years of internalized messaging of what it means to be a queer, Latina woman in the United States: invisibility and not quite making the grade (e.g., not Latinx enough or not queer enough) and expectations of not succeeding or pressures to settle (e.g., higher education isn't for you, especially not in a position of authority).

Given the author's professional training and work as a social worker, she immediately jumped into service – where were the gaps and how could she contribute to improving campus knowledge of and climate for LGBTQ communities, as well as the intersections? However, there was always a sense of vulnerability. Although the author was tenure-track, she was not tenured, and an internal, persistent voice emerged cautioning against being too loud or too passionate on particular advocacy efforts. The author would argue these are also remnants of internalized messaging rooted in larger oppressive structures and residual stereotypes (i.e., Latinas are too loud and dramatic) perpetuated by some of the major societal institutions – media, school, peer groups. Some of these messages also came directly from external sources, warning that particular leadership positions could in fact hinder the ability to achieve tenure. There was also the issue of contending with invalidation – would academics and administrators take the author's work, both in research and service, seriously?

These pressures were not absent from the classroom. As indicated in the literature, classrooms are often a microcosm of broader, societal structures and when it comes to discussing race, racism, and related intersections, faculty of color must contend with particular dynamics given their own identities (Patton & Catching, 2009; Sotello Viernes Turner, Gonzalez, & Wood, 2008; Sue et al., 2011). Coupled with a faculty member's decision to come out or not to students and colleagues, these conversations can be even more challenging (Delgado-Romero et al., 2007; LaSala et al., 2008). Teaching is intrinsically tied to obtainment of tenure and promotion, especially at institutions that prioritize teaching in their mission. The author experienced first-hand how the introduction of traditionally taboo and contentious topics, which is the foundation of her work and training as a clinical social worker specializing in sexuality social justice, plays out during class discussions as well as student evaluations. The author can recount early in her career receiving comments from students in evaluations insisting she focused "too much on LGBT stuff" within a course specifically designed to tackle gender and sexuality-related issues in the helping professions.

Given these realities, the author was able to navigate the path to tenure and promotion. What contributed to the author's success in academia? In reflecting on these experiences, there were factors that provided some relief to internal and external pressures, including recognizing privilege, building interdisciplinary collaborations, developing community connections, and finding quality mentorship and departmental support. The following discussion will provide further elaboration on each of these points.

Recognizing Privilege

When traveling the road to tenure and promotion, more senior faculty will often encourage junior faculty to think about how they will craft their story when the time comes to create and submit their materials. In reflecting on this, it is important to acknowledge the author's points of privilege. She identifies as a light skinned, Puerto Rican cisgender woman who was born in the United States. There are a few inherent privileges attached to several of these identities. Although not minimizing feelings of isolation within this area, it is important not to discount the impact of colorism and disproportionate level of burden on darker skinned faculty of color. Additionally, the author's citizenship status is a protective factor against xenophobic-based acts or related barriers to navigating the academic process. This is not to say there are not assumptions made upon learning the author's last name or when she discloses her ethnic identity, but the reality is that faculty of color who have different levels of citizenship status are more vulnerable and face more risks in achieving a tenure-track line as well as remaining at an institution, let alone advancing into leadership positions. Recognizing privileged identities is important; however, it is even more valuable to leverage these identities to make space for others who may not have as much power or privilege.

Building Interdisciplinary Collaborations

A key aspect of this story is fostering interdisciplinary collaborations, which can help sustain the energy needed to follow through on projects or advocacy efforts. They also contribute to more community building at the college level and create space for more underrepresented faculty to be heard. Therefore, although there were not as many queer faculty or queer faculty of color in the author's own department, her capacity to build relationships across disciplines and even at other universities resulted in several sustainable partnerships at local and national levels.

Furthermore, in deciding on what service activities to participate in or building a research agenda, the author weighed the potential risks and benefits of utilizing her voice and energy. Centering social justice within an academic career can increase exposure to possible roadblocks or experiences of microaggressions; however, in acknowledging privileges, it is possible to comprehend actions contributing to larger goals and purpose that address the structural roots of oppression in higher education. For the author, it was important to understand that campus climate could not shift without her speaking up, and her narrative was not authentic if it did not center around social justice. Although the author's identities as a queer Latina woman put her in vulnerable positions at times, being a leader meant making space for other underrepresented voices. This commitment to an overarching social justice vision allowed for such interdisciplinary relationships to thrive and ultimately support the author's ability to meaningfully contribute to local and national service opportunities.

Community Connections and Support

Remaining genuine and authentic while working toward tenure and promotion can be difficult, especially in trying to achieve expectations that at times feel more tailored to dominant identities and narratives. Throughout this process, the author gained a deeper appreciation for the communities that kept her grounded and offered inspiration. Cultivating networks comprised of other faculty of color, queer faculty, women faculty, and queer people of color beyond academia was instrumental in achieving this goal. Not only were they sources of support, but they offered formal and informal mentorship and guidance, sharing insights and best practices. As demonstrated in the literature, effective and institutionalized mentorship is at times limited for or not as easily accessible by underrepresented faculty (Delgado-Romero et al., 2007; Patton & Catching, 2009; Sotello Viernes Turner et al., 2008; Zambrana et al., 2014). Some of this is due to the lack of available mentors who fully comprehend the racial and gendered nuance of traversing the academy as underrepresented faculty and can provide insights or guidance about this particular aspect of navigating academia (Zambrana et al., 2014). As Zambrana et al. (2014) found in their study on mentorship of underrepresented minority faculty, not only are mentors essential to instilling hope and providing inspiration, but they also offer insights into social inequality. Zambrana, Ray, Espino, Castro, Cohen, and Eliason further highlighted with the following, "The ability to identify inequality, understand systems of oppression, and recognize how inequality influenced their lives and communities protected participants from internalizing discrimination and helped them develop a resiliency that bolstered them in the academy" (pp. 52–53).

The author is fortunate to reside in a department that values mentorship and although faculty members could not always fully comprehend the experience of being a queer person of color at a predominantly white, heteronormative institution, they were mindful in trying to understand the particular dynamics that might occur in teaching, service, and research. They would also encourage networking outside the department and offer connections to senior faculty who could provide a deeper level of guidance. This type of quality mentorship was a demonstration of more meaningful allyship occurring at the departmental level.

Meaningful Allyship

Clearing the path toward tenure and promotion does not necessarily mean the path is completely cleared. In order to undo the larger systemic issues at hand, it is vital that academic institutions play a more active role. Recommendations based on findings from the few existing studies focused on faculty of color highlight the need for more meaningful allyship in academia at all levels but in particular recruitment and retention (Delgado-Romero et al., 2007; Sotello Viernes Turner et al., 2008). For queer faculty of color, the same argument can be made (Lasala et al., 2008).

An essential demonstration of allyship at the university level is the establishment of mentoring programs at departmental, university, and national levels specifically designed for faculty of color and related intersections, such as queer faculty of color, and based on their feedback (Sotello Viernes Turner et al., 2008; Zambrana et al., 2014). Zambrana et al. (2014) found that often more generic formal types of mentorship, such as those assigned via routine university policy, are less meaningful and can sometimes pose a barrier if they are not attuned to the impact of social identities and related dynamics on the experiences of minority faculty. Participants highlighted the need for mentors to provide connections to other senior faculty as well as access to scholarly opportunities, encouragement, and respect for autonomy; however, they also emphasized the importance of guidance related to navigating the more implicit, political landscape in academia. Zambrana et al. (2014) also uncovered the following in their qualitative findings:

> In addition to the role of race and power relations, political guidance explicates the unique social location of URMs [underrepresented minorities] and helps URM faculty understand the informal rules, norms, and values that are part of the power exchange among actors in the academy. Knowledge of these rules – how they are created, maintained, interpreted, and enforced – reflect a consciousness on the part of a mentor that intersecting racialized identities and the accumulation of disadvantage over the life course influence their experiences in the academy. The reality that the culture of academic institutions is opaque and has unwritten rules is apparent to URM faculty.
>
> (p. 6)

With this said, another important aspect to increasing the representation of underrepresented faculty who are tenured and promoted is providing more clarity to the tenure and promotion processes. Although the basics of tenure and promotion are often outlined and accessible to faculty, the more implicit expectations are often not. For queer faculty of color, such lack of clarity adds to the layers of isolation and vulnerability. Again, this further reflects larger forms of oppression and reinforcing a message that underrepresented faculty are not meant to advance through the academic pipeline.

Resistance

Representation matters, especially in leadership, because it gives voice to the most marginalized but also provides a source of inspiration. Within academia, representation can truly be achieved once tenure and promotion are secured – offering the faculty member freedom of fuller expression of self and minimizing vulnerabilities in order to contribute to systemic change. As Anzaldua (1999) noted, marginalization can be a space of pain and loneliness; however, it also has the potential for resistance and opportunities for challenging systemic oppressive structures. So, although there are few queer women of color represented among tenured, promoted ranks, those who are able to successfully navigate academia can open the doors wide for future generations and remove the secrecy so often clouding these processes.

Process Questions and Considerations

1. How do the intersections of racism, sexism, and heterosexism impact queer faculty of color navigating the path toward tenure and promotion?
2. What contributes to the successful achievement of tenure and promotion at predominantly white and heteronormative institutions?
3. How does community building play a role in leadership development?
4. How can academic institutions demonstrate meaningful allyship to queer faculty of color?
5. How can queer faculty of color operationalize marginalization as a space for resistance within higher education?

References

Anzaldua, G. (1999). *Borderlands: La Frontera, the new mestiza.* San Francisco, CA: Aunt Lute Books.

Balsam, K. F., Molina, Y., Beadnell, B., Simoni, J., & Walters, K. (2011). Measuring multiple minority stress: The LGBT people of color macroaggressions scale. *Cultural Diversity and Ethnic Minority Psychology, 17*(2), 163–174. Doi:10.1037/a0023244

Delgado-Romero, E. A., Manlove, A. N., Manlove, J. D., & Hernandez, C. A. (2007). Controversial issues in the recruitment and retention of Latino/a faculty. *Journal of Hispanic Higher Education, 6*(1), 34–51. Doi:10.1177/1538192 706294903

Galarza, J., & Anthony, B. (2015). Sexuality social justice and social work: Implications for social work education. *Journal of Baccalaureate Social Work, 20*(1), 27–41.

Griffin, K. A., Pifer, M. J., Humphrey, J. R., & Hazelwood, A. M. (2011). (Re) Defining departure: Exploring Black professors' experiences with and responses to racism and racial climate. *American Journal of Education, 117*, 495–526. Doi:0195–6744/2011/11704–0003

Hill-Collins, P., & Bilge, S. (2016). *Intersectionality.* Malden, MA: Polity Press

Lasala, M. C., Jenkins, D., & Fredriksen-Goldsen, K. (2008). LGBT faculty, research, and researchers: Risks and rewards. *Journal of Gay & Lesbian Social Services, 20*(3), 253–267. Doi:10.1080/10538720802235351

Nadal, K. (2018). What does a professor look like? *Psychology benefits. https:// psychologybenefits.org/2018/03/09/what-does-a-professor-look-like/*

Patton, L. D., & Catching, C. (2009). 'Teaching while Black': Narratives of African American student affairs faculty. *International Journal of Qualitative Studies in Education*, 22(6), 713–728. Doi:10.1080/09518390903333897

Solorzano, D. G., & Yosso, T. J. (2001). Critical race and LatCrit theory and method: Counter-storytelling: Chicana and Chicano graduate school experiences. *Qualitative Studies in Education*, 14(4), 471–495. Doi:10.1080/09518390 110063365

Sotello Viernes Turner, C., Gonzalez, J. C., & Wood, J. L. (2008). Faculty of color in academe: What 20 years of literature tells us. *Journal of Diversity in Higher Education*, 1(3), 139–168. Doi:10.1037/a0012837

Stanley, C. A. (2006). Coloring the academic landscape: Faculty of color breaking the silence in predominantly White colleges and universities. *American Educational Research Journal* 43(4), 701–736.

Sue, D. W., Rivera, D. P., Watkins, N. L., Kim, R. H., Kim, S., & Williams, C. D. (2011). Racial dialogues: Challenges faculty of color face in the classroom. *Cultural Diversity and Ethnic Minority Psychology* 17(3), 331–340. Doi:10.1037/a0024190

U.S. Department of Education, National Center for Education Statistics. (2017). *The condition of education 2017* (NCES 2017–144), Characteristics of Postsecondary. Faculty.

Williams, A. (2015). The invisible labor of minority professors. *The Chronicle of Higher Education*. Retrieved from www.chronicle.com/article/The-Invisible-Labor-of/234098

Zambrana, R. E., Ray, R., Espino, M. M., Castro, C., Cohen, B. D., & Eliason, J. (2014). "Don't leave us behind": The importance of mentoring for underrepresented minority faculty. *American Educational Research Journal*, 52(1), 40–72, Doi:10.3102/0002831214563063

10 Sexuality Leadership

The Next Generation

Tanya M. Bass and Bill Taverner

I remember my first visit to SIECUS in New York. I had read about the organization [in my textbook] in the late 1980s, and decided it was a place I must visit. Unfortunately, my copy of *Sexual Interactions* had one piece of outdated information in it – SIECUS's old street address on West 4th Street in Manhattan. Probably, [the authors] never anticipated that a crazy college student would use that address to go knocking on SIECUS's door to ask for a job (or at least an internship), but that is exactly what I did. The former SIECUS headquarters had since been converted into an apartment complex, and there I was demanding entry of the doorman. The poor fellow did not know what to say as I repeatedly insisted that there was a "sex organization" upstairs. I was convinced he was concealing their identity, and did everything I could to explain I was pro sexuality education. When he would not yield, I waited in Washington Square Park until his shift was over, and then tried my luck with the next doorman. I did not know, until months later, that SIECUS had moved to midtown.

Bill Taverner, The Center for Sex Education

There is no instructor's manual for developing a career in sexuality. The pathways are extraordinarily varied and often unpredictable, as described in anthologies of sexuality professionals such as *How I Got Into Sex* (Bullough, Bullough, Fithian, Hartman, & Klein, 1997) and *How I Got Into Sex . . . Ed* (Rayne, Dukes, & Taverner, 2014). Other disciplines have clear guideposts for success in their fields. Want to be a nurse? Go to nursing school and to become a registered nurse (RN) or become a licensed practical nurse (LPN). Want to get into business? There are hundreds of schools that offer a Master of Business Administration (MBA) degree. Police officer? Engineer? Lawyer? Pharmacist? Teacher? Truck driver? Each career outlines tests that must be taken, steps that must be followed, and a litany of places to apply. To enter the field of sexology, there may be fewer formal options but a multitude of paths that can be taken.

Without clearly established guideposts and benchmarks for success in the field of sexology, many aspiring future leaders may find themselves much like that passionate but clueless person in the epigraph. Yet it is difficult to imagine leadership in sexuality without envisioning *future* leadership. Like all professions, sexology very much needs to replenish its next generation of leaders. This chapter utilizes and updates recommendations for carving a professional career in sexology primarily from Taverner (2006), and incorporates personal anecdotes from *How I Got Into Sex . . . Ed*, as well as quotes from interviews with colleagues in the field.

Accidental Careers

> I was born into sex education in a way. My dad was an adult film actor in the 1970s and my mom was a sex therapist. I was raised in a pleasure affirming, inclusive household, and I am so grateful. Teachers and artists, the best ones, have a way of making space for students to become fuller versions of themselves. That's what I aspire to in both of those fields, and by mixing them together. I believe that making art is a really powerful way to put young people in the driver's seat of their own sex education and so I think of myself as a teaching artist in the field of sex education, always learning, and always growing.
>
> Robert "Bobby" Gordon, AMP!/SexEd Squad, UCLA

Not everyone is "born into" this work, selecting the career path of sex educator, counselor, or therapist requires courage, tenacity, and creativity especially with such few entry points into the profession. While sexuality professionals may obtain degrees in complementary areas including public health, health education, or social work, others may emerge into the profession with little intention. In addition to academic preparation, sexuality professions fortuitously arise because of required job responsibilities or volunteerism.

> I initially did not intend to become a sexuality educator. My mother served as a mentor for teen moms through a local nonprofit organization. From that experience, I became interested in maternal and child health and upon graduating college, I applied for a job at a local non-profit as a case manager for teen moms. Soon after I was hired, they received a pregnancy prevention program grant and I became the program coordinator. After being trained to facilitate three evidence-based curricula, I knew that I had found my passion. This experience ignited a long-term fire in me to focus on the sexual health of adolescents in my Masters and Doctoral program and led me to start my own business.
>
> Shemeka Thorpe, https://theminoritysexreport.com, Minority Sex Report

In an episode of *The Wonder Years*, a popular television show from the late 1980s, physical education Coach Cutlip finds himself assigned to teach sex education, which he does reluctantly, and without a great deal of comfort or competence, drawing the female reproductive anatomy in comically stick figure style (Black & Marlens, 1988). Since the United States government does not provide funding for sexuality education in the schools, physical education and health education teachers nationwide find themselves in similar predicaments: asked to teach a topic without proper training, certification, or subject matter expertise. Teachers interested in the well-being of young people make the best of these circumstances.

One fateful day in the fall of 1986, my life changed dramatically. I was sitting in my cubicle with my physical education consultant colleague who turned to me and asked what I knew about AIDS. I responded, "Not much," although I had just read a fascinating article in *Time* magazine about this emerging disease. He asked if I would be interested in attending an important meeting at the Ministry of Education to represent the Health and Physical Education consultants and supervisors in the province of Ontario. They were going to try to develop and implement a curriculum for all middle and high school students in the province, in record time.

Al Craven, Adrian College

With no true aspiration to become a sexologist, some professionals stumble across this fascinating career and find lifelong careers.

I started out with intentions to be an Ob/Gyn and changed to Nursing. Through my volunteer work I came to realize I was an effective and engaging educator but did not desire to teach in a classroom, as I was still very passionate about health issues, so I narrowed my focus on community health. When deciding on a focus area, it became important to me to figure out ways to help folk in rural poor communities overcome many health challenges. I grew up in a small town and all I observed were teen pregnancies, diabetes, kidney disease and heart disease. Teen pregnancies were so real to me as most of my peers became pregnant and never went to college. Today, the evidence of my perseverance to gain an education is apparent in my life versus those who became paralyzed [with] their life choices. In reflecting on my upbringing and the experiences of my friends and family throughout life and career, sexual health became an unplanned passion that has been with me and sustained my career for over 20 years.

Michelle Reese, SHIFT NC

For me, I never realized being a sexuality professional was an actual thing. . . . It just happened. Beginning in my undergraduate career

I just began to sign-up to participate in programs focused on sexuality education. As a high school health teacher for nearly two decades, human sexuality was always my focus and favorite part of teaching. I remember when I began at a new school district, we had a new teacher orientation day. One of the administrators said, "be careful of people who enjoy teaching about sexuality – they are a red flag." It's interesting because teaching is a very isolating profession as it is, but this comment further isolated me – and I was afraid of being "found-out." As I further developed into my career – and became more confident and more educated – I began to further stress the importance of sexuality education. When I found the Ph.D. program at Widener, I was so happy to finally be among like-minded individuals. Nothing has impacted my career or professional development more than being a part of that program, I only wish I would have found it sooner.

Rachael Gibson, Widener University

Sexology extends into disciplines and areas related to human growth and development and human services. Sexual maturation is a lifelong process and intersects with other areas of human growth, development, and behavioral studies. The intersection of sexology with another subject areas can create a meaningful niche and fill a service area gap. Kat Pheysey notes that there are gaps in the profession of sexuality services that need to be filled in other disciplines.

I have always worked with people with intellectual and developmental disabilities (IDD) and have worked in several different service settings with a diverse group of clients. I only began working in the field of sexuality after I noticed that people with IDD were not being thought of as sexual beings. If a sexually related question was asked the response was often that it wasn't an appropriate time to discuss whether they were at school, work, camp, or in their homes. I became a sexuality educator to help fill that gap and provide access to information and services to people with IDD.

Kat Pheysey, https://www.inclusivesexology.com,
Inclusive Sexology

Even with an alternate chosen profession, just one experience, one conversation, conference, or one class can pique interest or create the spark to pursue a career in sexuality. No matter how one might end up in the profession, most sexuality professionals tend to make this a part of their life's work.

Academic Programs

Many seeking a career as a sexuality professional want the grounding that comes with an academic degree. There is a growing number of undergraduate programs in sexuality studies, often combined with gender and women's studies majors and minors. A list of graduate and postgraduate programs in sexuality can be found in the Appendix at the end of the book.

Enrollment in formal programs and, sometimes, individual courses can have a profound impact on a person's career track.

> When I started college, I wandered between majors for a short time. . . . I took a class called International Women's Health. . . . During that class, a couple of graduate students made a presentation on their research on Asian-Americans and sexual behavior. I have no recollection what the results were but I was stunned. "You can study sex?" I practically ran up to my professor after the class asking, "How can I study THAT? How can I study sex?"
>
> Catherine Dukes, Planned Parenthood of Delaware

> [I took a course in] Human Sexuality at the University of Denver for my Master of Social Work. The course stressed the importance of recognizing how sexuality is interwoven into all aspects of life, even when clients are not discussing sexuality. I also realized the importance of communicating about sexuality and how empowering it can be for couples and individuals to express their needs and desires.
>
> Shanna M. Dusablon Drone, High Desert
> Juvenile Court School

In addition to the rich content of academic programs in sexuality, these programs can also provide unique networking opportunities. Consider the experience of Lauren Barineau as a case study.

> As an Emory graduate student, I volunteered with the Pipeline Program run by Emory's Center for Science Education in Atlanta, GA. This innovative program connected medical students, pre-med undergraduates, and high school students through teaching and mentorship. The high school students had an opportunity to learn about all aspects of health and the human body from Emory-based mentors and build relationships with these mentors to support them throughout their college and medical school admissions process. My role was to coordinate a health fair with the high school seniors, which served as a culminating experience through which they could share their knowledge with others. It was refreshing and inspiring to watch teens identify and explore public health concepts around which to design health fair booths, and to see them excitedly create interactive ways to disseminate health information to their peers.
>
> Lauren Barineau, Georgia Campaign for
> Adolescent Power and Potential

It is worth noting that while formal programs in sexuality studies exist, many sexuality leaders pursued academic programs that were not directly related to sexuality, or were only peripherally related to the subject.

In my first year of graduate school, I took History of Public Health at the Rollins School of Public Health. This survey course for public health students traced the history of our field through some of its most critical and defining moments including germ theory, smallpox eradication, the vaccination debate, and breast cancer screening. It left me with a deep appreciation for the rapid development of our field, the unique constraints related to ensuring the health of the public, and the importance of context and community in our work.

> Lauren Barineau, Georgia Campaign for Adolescent Power and Potential

Two undergrad courses, Journalism 101 and Independent Study Creative Writing, both of which honed the writing skills I use today.

> Melanie Davis, Unitarian Universalist Association

Honestly? Children/Adolescent Literature, undergrad in Education at the University of Pittsburgh, 1971. It opened my eyes to youth culture.

> Mary Jo Podgurski, Academy for Adolescent Health

Students [in my Introduction to Intellectual Disabilities class] were asked to design a behavior change program with motivators and personal supports. I actually stopped smoking that way (at last!) and became a big fan of using positive reinforcement to change personal behavior.

> Leslie Walker Hirsch, Moonstone Consultancy in Sexuality and Intellectual Disability

Some leaders commented on independent lecture series as being vital to their professional growth. Rebecca Chalker, author of *The Clitoral Truth*, describes independent learning as her favorite source of studies:

[My favorite courses were] numerous videotaped lectures from the Institute for the Advanced Study of Human Sexuality, including those by Erwin Haberle, Wardell Pomeroy, William Masters, Gayle Rubin, Alan Ginsberg, Karla Jay, and numerous others.

> Rebecca Chalker, Pace University

International studies programs can be life-changing.

[At NYU study abroad programs], we spent the summers in places like Sweden, Denmark, Japan, Kenya, and Thailand studying sexuality that always challenged our U.S. perspective.

> Konnie McCaffree, Sexuality Education Consultant

I took a cross-cultural course in human sexuality and had the opportunity to spend three weeks in Copenhagen, Denmark. Sixteen classmates and I had the learning adventure of a lifetime. It was in Copenhagen where I met and befriended Dr. Robert T. (Bob) Francoeur, who would become one of my mentors. Bob was one of three professors who helped us explore the world of sexuality beyond our limited spheres.

Bill Taverner, The Center for Sex Education

Conferences

Professional conferences in sexuality can provide vital networking opportunities for emerging leaders to schmooze with students, colleagues, and established leaders, all while keeping up with current developments and learning best practices.

I . . . went to every conference that was offered in sex education, and began to develop skills to utilize interactive learning, which had always worked well as my own personal learning style as well.

Konnie McCaffree, Sexuality Education Consultant

I have attended ETR Conferences; The Guelph Sexuality Conference; The World Sexuality Conference; American School Health Association; American Alliance for Health, PE, Recreation & Dance; AASECT Regional HIV/AIDS and Sexuality Conference . . .; and now the National Sex Ed Conference.

Su Nottingham, Central Michigan University

I was also professionally involved with various state health education associations and attended many of their conferences. I always attended the sessions on human sexuality education to expand my understanding and also my teaching techniques.

Darrel Lang, Health Endeavors Consulting and Training

In 1991, I attended the first (and as it turned out, last) International Conference on Orgasm, in New Delhi, and continued going to World Congresses on Sexology and SSSS meetings.

Rebecca Chalker, Pace University

In recent years, the . . . National Sex Ed Conference has given me a chance to both explore some cutting-edge ideas in sexuality education and also meet some inspirational leaders in the field.

Kirsten de Fur, Urban Resource Institute

The ability to attend conferences has expanded my knowledge in the field. Most recently, conferences such as NCSexCon and Healthy

Teen Network Conference have created space for people of color and other groups that aren't part of the majority to have a voice. The opportunity to see other educators "at work" provides new strategies and ideas for future program implementation.

Carla Mena, Duke University

I attended AASECT conferences, gave "State of Sexuality Education" presentations at Eastern Region SSSS meetings, and became devoted to SIECUS, writing for the *SIECUS Report* and eventually becoming chair of the board of directors.

Peggy Brick, Sexuality Educator and Trainer, 1928–2018

We attended and had a poster session at the World AIDS Conference in Montreal. I traveled to a one-week sexuality conference in Baltimore sponsored by ETR Associates. It was a fabulous week with Sol Gordon, Michael Carrera, Debra Haffner, and many more magnificent sexuality educators. Perhaps most importantly, I met my future wife, Su Nottingham.

Al Craven, Adrian College

Attending conferences is a great way to develop or add to your professional network. These are the people you can email or call for professional guidance. Attending conferences has provided opportunities for continued education and further exploration of subtopics within the field. Additionally, the networking and information about other jobs in the field shared at conferences has been invaluable.

Kevin Harrell, North Carolina Central University

Barbara Huscher Cohen notes that there are important opportunities for learning even when the program is poor.

I honestly believe you can even learn from a horrible class, as you can learn what not to do when you teach.

Barbara Huscher Cohen, Sexuality Education Consultant

Be Realistic, Expand Your Skills

There are limited paid opportunities in sexology and thus some wise professionals explore academic tracks that are not focused exclusively in sexual studies. One student explained that when reading *How I Got Into Sex . . . Ed*, she took note of all of the different degrees listed at the beginning of each chapter, to help guide her own thinking on which degree she might pursue for herself.[1]

Figure 10.1 is a word cloud representation of advanced degrees mentioned listed next to the names of authors who contributed to *How I Got Into Sex . . . Ed*. The larger the degree, the more frequently it appeared

Figure 10.1 Word cloud representation of author degrees in *How I Got Into Sex . . . Ed.*

next to authors' names. Note "no advanced degree" in the word cloud, indicating there are professionals and leaders in the field of sexology who are making significant contributions without having an advanced degree.

> To expand my skills and increase my knowledge I have obtained my certification as a health education specialist (CHES) and I am furthering my education by seeking my masters and doctorate in the field of human sexuality. We must be lifelong learners because information is always updating, new technology is always being created, and we must be prepared so that our communities do not suffer from our lack of knowledge and understanding. My hope is to leave a community or a classroom better than when I came in, so putting in the groundwork is very necessary. If I could give one piece of advice to someone about expanding their skills it would be to gain as much experience, skill and advice as you can so they can never say you weren't prepared but that you exceeded their expectations!
>
> Ashley Edwards, Johns Hopkins University

Pursuing a degree in health education, nursing, public health, social work, or other broad-based areas of study gives people many more avenues for potential career growth that may not exist with a specialized degree in sexual studies. People can shift gears if they become frustrated with their career pursuits in sexology or use this training to diversify their career pursuits. Further, few programs in sexual studies require courses in business or financial management, and these skills are essential for success in establishing one's practice as a sex therapist or working in a nonprofit, particularly if one wishes to ascend to better-paying leadership roles within their organizations. Leaders will need to be able to discern a budget or apply for a grant. Running a practice in sex therapy will require financial planning and billing skills.

> I've built my department from a department of one with no funding, to a team of six, and then finally a team of four with enough grant and contract money for our department to be essentially self-sufficient. Together we've successfully implemented a federal Personal Responsibility Education Program (PREP) grant statewide and formed positive collaborative relationships with our Department of Education, the Division of Public Health, and many local teacher and community service providers reaching more than 5,000 people per year.
>
> Catherine Dukes, Planned Parenthood of Delaware

> People used to tell me their business all time when I was younger. I guess I have a face that says "tell me everything." I figured I should be better equipped to do so and I thought I would be a therapist. In watching *Meet The Fockers*, and my subsequent research I realized that being a sex therapist was a real thing that I could do. So I went with my research and applied for only one grad school, Widener University and now I have my own practice.
>
> Donna Oriowo, https://www.annodright.com, AnnodRight

Become Well-Read

There are a number of benefits to being an avid reader of sexuality books. Doing so allows emerging professionals to keep up with new research and developments in the field, enables fluency and depth when dialoguing with peers and experts, permits the exploration of the sociocultural context of the work being done, and allows one to make recommendations. Where to start? The Center for Sex Education publishes a free bibliography of sexuality books for parents and children at http://bit.ly/ResourceListSignUp. Using a bibliography such as this one allows emerging professionals to discover the many angles through which the subject is addressed, and, as they become better versed with the genre, they may make recommendations when asked. Other organizations such as SIECUS and Unhushed periodically publish bibliographies. Professionals trying to keep up may also set their Google alerts to "sex education," "sex therapy," or particular subset areas of interest in order to have the latest news available to them. Table 10.1 shows the books that impacted contributors to *How I Got Into Sex . . . Ed*. Note how several of them are not directly about sex or sexuality, but rather give context for the work that is done in the field.

Action Theater: The Improvisation of Presence
A General Theory of Love
A Kid's First Book about Sex
America's War on Sex
And the Band Played On
An Insider's View on Sexual Science Since Kinsey
Arousal: The Secret Logic of Sexual Fantasies
As Nature Made Him: The Boy Who Was Raised as a Girl
Assisted Loving
Because It Feels Good: A Woman's Guide to Sexual Pleasure
But How'd I Get There in the First Place?
Contraceptive Technology
Demystifying Love: Plain Talk for the Mental Health Professional
Does God Belong in the Bedroom?
Feminist Porn Book
For Women Only
Gay, Straight, and In-Between
However Long the Night
How Girls Thrive
I Heart Female Orgasm
Intimate Matters: A History of Sexuality in America
It's Complicated: The Social Lives of Networked Teens
It's Perfectly Normal
Lesbian Woman
Lessons for Lifeguards
Love and Sex in Plain Language
Male Sexuality
Not In Front of the Children
Older, Wiser, Sexually Smarter
Our Bodies, Ourselves
Prime
Promiscuities
Raising a Child Responsibly in a Sexually Permissive World
Real Live Nude Girl: Chronicles of Sex-Positive Culture
Rekindling Desire
S.E.X.: The All-You-Need-to-Know Progressive Sexuality Guide to Get You
   through High School and College
Sex and Sensibility
Sex Tips for Straight Women from a Gay Man
Sexual Behavior in the Human Female
Sexual Behavior in the Human Male
Sexuality Today
Solving America's Sexual Crisis
Speaking Sex to Power: The Politics of Queer Sex
Teaching about Sexuality and HIV: Principles and Methods for Effective
   Education
Tess of the D'Urbervilles
The Dynamics of Relations
The Goldfinch
The Guide to Getting It On
The History of Sex

(*Continued*)

Table 10.1 (Continued)

The Joy of Sex
The Parent Guide to Our Whole Lives K–1 and 4–6
The Period Book
The Reign of the Phallus
The Spiritual Life of Children
They Said What?!: Exploring Self-Disclosure as Sexuality Educators
Unhooked: How Young Women Pursue Sex, Delay Love, and Lose at Both
War Against the Weak: Eugenics and America's Campaign to Create a Master Race
What Your Mother Never Told You About Sex
Yes Means Yes!: Visions of Female Sexual Power and a World Without Rape

---

Network, Network, Network!

Networking can be an intentional or an organic process that occurs in many ways to foster the exchange of information and ideas among individuals or groups that share a common interest, like sexuality education. "Sexuality educator" or "sexologist" as a profession is fairly small in comparison to other professions. For a point of comparison, "Human Resources" includes more than 5.6 million professionals working in that field (Miller-Merrell, 2013), whereas those who have AASECT or CHES certification may run in the thousands. There is a fair amount of sexuality professionals that a person might know already by name, may have met once, maybe even stay in close contact, or maintain a connection on social media, and a few that a person might meet by chance. Routine connections with such professionals can help maintain and expand one's networking circles and keep them abreast of developments and opportunities within the field. The best way to do that is to use platforms such as LinkedIn, Instagram, and word of mouth, in addition to professional meetings and conferences, as described earlier.

Professionals trying to establish themselves as the next generation of leaders in sexuality may benefit from networking effectively, immersing themselves in workshops, plenaries, and keynotes, by becoming a familiar face, asking memorable questions, and generally being a teachable participant in unfamiliar subject matter.

> Networking in this profession is super impactful because everyone has their own style and their own hustle. Learning from others' mistakes gives me the opportunity to make new mistakes and having people available that I can ask questions to makes exploring this field less overwhelming.
>
> Shanae Adams, https://www.honestlynae.com,
> HonestlyNae

I met people. Networking is what really inspired me. I had finally found a career; I was on the right path. I continue to marvel at my fellow sex educators' level of talent, imagination, knowledge, and willingness to share.

Carole Adamsbaum, *How I Got Into Sex . . . Ed*, p. 11.

Networking is extremely important in any professional sector, especially in sexuality. Becoming acquainted with researchers, educators, clinicians, sex workers, etc., allows you to connect with others to expand your knowledge, services or resources. If there are events or programs that other professionals need help organizing or co-facilitating, I can support them which in turn allows me to use my skills and increase my professional net worth – just by networking!

Alicia Andrews, NCSEXCON

I honestly do not recall how I met Bobby Gordon from the UCLA Sex Squad. I saw some of his work with college students, and he presented at NCSEXCON and just knew I wanted to work with him at my alma mater to be a part of creating sexual health videos for youth and young adults that were relevant and impactful. We co-facilitated a human sexuality course to create three awesome sexual health videos on intimacy, prevention and Black sexuality. We continue to collaborate and support each other through genuine friendship!

Tanya M. Bass, Southern Sexologist

Finding connections with people who have different worldviews and passions can be as important as linking with those who do. To become a well-rounded professional, it can be useful to know professionals that may have a contrasting viewpoints. Moreso, networking can lead to long term partnerships or one time impactful opportunities.

A few years ago, Christian Thrasher convened an advisory board for the Satcher Health Leadership Institute that included professionals all over the ideological spectrum. Christian challenged us not to focus on the areas in which we disagreed – that would have been too easy – but rather to find the areas of consensus. Sharing meals and having authentic conversations that went beyond the realm of sexuality resulted in friendships and professional connections I would have never expected.

Bill Taverner, The Center for Sex Education

Use Today's Technology

When it comes to sex ed, the Internet and other online tools aren't just second choices, or ways to supplement other, more traditional, kinds of sex education. They may actually be one of the best ways to provide sex and sexuality information and education.

Heather Corinna, Scarleteen

The use of technology makes it easier to connect with other professionals or provide information to a large, captive audience. In addition to general internet access, social media platforms such as YouTube, Facebook, Instagram, and Twitter give the sexuality professional limitless, real time, prescheduled, and tailored access to individuals at any given time. Social media as a form of sexuality education can be useful and challenging. The source of the information must be trusted and valid, this make take time for a professional to gain a reputation as a source. More so than that, the use of technology can become an invaluable resource in the teaching environment. YouTube videos and other media can reinforce information and allow learning to continue outside the learning environment. These resources can also service as a source of learning and professional growth for professionals.

> Sometimes students will assume that I know everything about sex, and I chuckle, because sexuality information and the way we communicate information is constantly evolving. Applying new research, technology, and educational methodology in sexuality education is a daily and welcome challenge for me, one that I look forward to for years to come.
>
> Melissa Keyes DiGioia, http://www.findingyour individuality.com, Finding Your Individuality

Both professionals and learners have access to information on the internet and through social medial. Professionals can not only identity professional development workshops and conferences, they can also market and share their offerings locally and worldwide as well. Often to gain an audience and meet a need, organizations and individuals will offer workshops, webinars, and podcast for no cost. With the use of technology learning can occur at any time for any length of time.

> One of the things I've learned about being a sex educator is that there's no one structure that will work for everybody. Some people prefer individual work, some people enjoy workshops, some people like to read my blog or other articles that I post on social media. There's no one way to have sex, and there's no one way to be a sex educator. It does get a little bit tricky sometimes, juggling all of these different pieces of my life and career. But that's also what makes it exciting. We're only just beginning to discover how to integrate social media and new technologies in sex education, and who knows what new opportunities will develop?
>
> Charlie Glickman, http://www.makesexeasy.com, Make Sex Easy – Sex & Relationship Coaching

The use of technology can serve as a mechanism to find employment. There are several ways to find employment opportunities including joining email listings, Facebook group postings, searching agency websites, and LinkedIn.

I would sometimes do Internet searches on reproductive organizations. Luckily, there was an opening at the Hyannis, MA, Family Planning Clinic so I applied. I got the job as Reproductive Health Counselor, and they had health insurance!

Erin Livensparger, Planned Parenthood
of Southern New England

Link With Key Leaders

Knowing the leaders in sexuality is an important step in building any career. Leaders serve as models in different ways and can serve as mentors and advisors. While joining professional organizations or attending conferences can be costly, it is an investment worth making when possible. Many leaders in sexuality keynote or have workshops at professional conferences. Meeting leaders face to face to discuss their career trajectory can be useful in one's own professional planning.

I stumbled upon the sexuality profession through Public Health. As I learned more of sexual health and sexuality, I desired to go deeper by seeking an advanced degree of Human Sexuality. During this time, I have met several leaders in sexology. Linking with other leaders in sexuality has impacted my career greatly. I have gained mentors, and friends that I am able to call upon, whenever, I am in need of assistance, guidance and even a shoulder to cry on from time to time.

Bernard Davis, California Institute of Integral Studies

Using technology to follow them on social media or signing up for their email listings can also be a useful way to connect. This is a great opportunity to learn or inquire about what they may be doing or ask their recommendations of books, websites, conferences, or perhaps meet them for lunch or coffee if they live nearby. Eva Goldfarb shared the experience of linking with Konnie McCaffree, a leader in sexuality:

Konnie is the person who would become my lifelong mentor and who would have the greatest impact on me throughout my professional career, on how I think about, create, plan, prepare, teach, discuss, defend, and evaluate my work and how I see myself as a sexuality educator.

Eva Goldfarb, Montclair State University

Be Patient and Work Your Way In

The importance of attending conferences and other professional development events was described earlier. While these can be expensive, time consuming, and difficult getting through the abstract process, it's a valuable part of working one's way into the profession. A good idea on working through the patience of becoming established and grounded is through volunteering for these events. By volunteering, an emerging leader will learn about the challenging process of planning events, serve as a resource for conference participants, and get to meet other colleagues.

> I volunteered during the National Sex Education Conference one year and then subsequently served as co-chair and volunteer coordinator for two years. I met some amazing colleagues and mentors. While I felt somewhat established in my career locally, this national opportunity allowed me to learn from others.
>
> Tanya M. Bass, Southern Sexologist

When employers are unable to support professional development or other career enhancing opportunities, it's wise to consider sharing the expenses with others when possible. It is helpful to take advantage of as many of these networking opportunities. The same is true for students as they work toward completion of their studies. This is the perfect time for them to find part-time work, or internships, while completing their academic studies toward fulfilling their dream. It can often take years before one obtains the ideal position, gains clientele, or lands a keynote invitation for a conference.

> Later, when I decided to re-enter the field of teaching, I worked as a short-term and long-term substitute teacher while waiting on an opening for an elementary PE teacher. I would always get called to sub at a particular middle school, and it always happened to be when the sex education unit was being taught! I then took a position as a regional public health educator.
>
> Lynn Hammond, South Carolina Department of Health

Bill Taverner waited patiently seven years and then one day he received a call from Peggy Brick seeking him out to serve in her soon to be vacated position.

> No luck, every year, until seven years later, she called back to say she was retiring, and she invited me in to interview for *her* position. Today, I run the wonderful Center . . . that Peggy created.
>
> Bill Taverner, The Center for Sex Education

Become a Presenter

There are many ways to present information on sexuality. Most often it can occur during professional development events such as conferences, symposiums, summits, and trainings. Presenting at these events for other sexuality professionals or others can be useful in disseminating information, honing speaking skills and networking. One may become skilled at presenting a one- or two-hour workshop on a topic with which they are comfortable and have a depth of knowledge to share with others.

> I found that presenting at conferences have contributed a lot to my success in the field. Through presenting at a local conference in Philadelphia, I met the co-author of my book: *Pocket Guide For Young Men Without Fathers; Important Life Lessons.* I believe it is important to leave our offices and meet other professionals in the field. You never know what doors will open because you stepped out of your comfort zone.
>
> John Taylor, Widener University

Emerging professionals may submit a workshop proposal to a professional development event as listed earlier or create a standalone workshop, perhaps on a specific niche that is not currently being addressed. Students can use this opportunity to also present their research and topics of interest.

> Presenting at conferences gave me the opportunity to show the work that I am doing with my organization on a larger scale. I also was able to get valuable feedback on that work from others in the field. The process for getting your proposal approved is more daunting then actually presenting. Also, please recognize that presenting and attending conferences is a very expensive endeavor, but it's an investment in your career.
>
> Brittany Mitchell, Intimacy Firm

A benefit of presenting is that it gives voice to one's work and passions, sharing with others potentially life affirming or life changing information.

Get Published

Getting published is no easy feat, especially when conducting research, but there is one tip that may be the most useful of any: Write a review! It may be useful to identify a book, film, website, etc. to share one's critical thoughts, praise, or substantial insights. A book or resource review may be the start of one's publications list, and it can be submitted to an academic journal, such as the *American Journal of Sexuality Education*, or another journal relevant to the topic. The writer's perspective, whether in a review or otherwise can improve your writing and lead to more publications and opportunities.

> My feminist perspective was articulated in an article entitled "Sex Education is a Feminist Issue" in the groundbreaking journal, *New*

> *Directions for Women*, and for nine years, its editor, Phyllis Kriegal, and I provided professional development workshops through our agency, Affirmative Teaching Associates.
>
> Peggy Brick, Sexuality Educator and Trainer, 1928–2018

In addition, whether or not the review is accepted for publication, a submission to a peer reviewed journal will give the writer copious feedback so they can further develop their writing skills.

Don't Be Afraid of Feedback

Giving and receiving feedback can be challenging, rewarding, and useful. Author, speaker, management expert, and business consultant Ken Blanchard is recognized to have stated that "feedback is the breakfast of champions" (Blanchard, 2009). Feedback is a gift, according to Bill Gates "We all need people who will give us feedback. That's how we improve" (Kasperkevic, 2013). Feedback can be just the thing needed at moment, or the gift that is one day realized as useful because it came in handy later in life, or perhaps even the gift to pass on or share with another.

> Meanwhile, I continued to try to find a job in sex ed, and interviewed with Peggy Brick, my predecessor at [The Center for Sex Education]. . . . Peggy candidly told me I was too inexperienced for the job, and so I did all that I could to secure more credentials.
>
> Bill Taverner, The Center for Sex Education

Requesting feedback from peers and colleagues can be valuable at any stage of one's career, serving as a mechanism to improve the quality of one's work. This relates to all aspects of sexuality education including presentation, delivery, and writing. Networking is a beneficial byproduct of asking for feedback through connection with other experienced professionals.

Passing the Torch

Like most professions, there are veterans, midcareer professionals, and those new to the work. All can learn from one another, but it is important that those with a long history and experience support those following in their footsteps. This may occur naturally or through intentional mentorship. Unfortunately, those in the profession face some of the challenges that existed 30 years ago, and, with technological advances, may face even more barriers. It is critical that the torch is passed to the up and coming scholars, educators, researchers, and activists.

> I fell in love with the Human Sexuality field when I took an Intro to Human Sexuality class as an undergraduate student at Kean University

with Dr. Conseulo Bonillas. Not only did I admire her as a professor but as a woman of color. She was the first Latinx professor I ever had, which goes to show the importance of representation. She offered me a position as an undergraduate research assistant for her grant and to positions later, I was promoted to Assistant Director of NJPREP. I am currently pursuing my Doctorate Degree at Widener University where Dr. Consuelo Bonillas is a Ph.D. alumnus. She has passed the torch on to me, and now I do the same with all of my undergraduate and graduate research assistants.

Omara Cardoza, Kean University

For the past 15 years, I've served as an adjunct instructor at my alma mater, North Carolina Central University, teaching personal health and behavioral health courses. I longed to teach the human sexuality course but our beloved sexuality educator for over 20 years, was the mainstay for that course. I had been a guest lecturer in the course a few times and to my surprise as she retired in 2012, I was offered the position to teach this course. I was so nervous, I called and met with her several times to preserve the integrity of the course. She met with me each time but warmly encouraged me to make the course my own and I have been doing just that by being innovative in my pedagogical approach to the course. I am growing and at the same time, I have been inviting other sexuality educators to teach the course with me as a guest lecturer to bring their point of views and offer them teaching experience. The way the torch had been passed to me is the same way I'd like to pass it on to others. This happens when we can share spaces with those new to the profession or those needing a new opportunity within their current work. Collectively we can continue to make sexuality education a profession that fosters the growth and development of those we work with as well as those we teach. Passing the torch can arise in many other ways. I served as a volunteer at the National Sex Education Conference one year, conference co-chair, then as the Volunteer Coordinator two years successively. Later, I served a volunteer for the American Association of Sex Educators, Counselors and Therapists (AASECT) annual conference, then two years later I served on the planning team and coordinated the volunteers. While serving as a point of contact for scores of volunteers at these conferences, I met other professionals with leadership skills and encouraged them to volunteer or serve on conference planning committees. Through this volunteer work, I gained insight from the conference organizers and as I plan the North Carolina Sexual Health Conference (NCSEXCON), with a team of awesome colleagues, I seek to fill the workshop spots not only with the same old names, but also with the brand new names with an eye toward diversity.

Tanya M. Bass, Southern Sexologist

Process Questions and Considerations

1. Which recommendations are the most important to consider when developing a career in sexuality?
2. Which anecdotes resonated with you most? Explain.
3. What themes did you identify regarding personal characteristics of people telling their stories of their career paths?
4. What themes did you identify regarding professional attributes of people developing careers in sexuality?
5. What are some examples in the anecdotes where a person displayed emotional intelligence? How can emotional intelligence help someone forge a career in sexuality?
6. How can the experience of colleagues shape the choices you might make in your professional endeavors?
7. What are the merits of pursuing an academic course of study and sexuality?
8. Why might a person choose to become or not to become certified?
9. How does this chapter relate to leadership in sexuality? What other ideas do have regarding sexuality, leadership, and mentorship?

Note

1. Special thanks to undergraduate student Michelle Stage for sharing this suggestion at the 2019 meeting of The Society for the Scientific Study of Sexuality, Montreal.

References

Black. C., & Marlens, N. (1988). Swingers. In B. Brush (Ed.), *The wonder years.* Los Angeles, CA: ABC.

Blanchard, K. (2009, August 17). *Feedback is the breakfast of champions.* Retrieved December 31, 2018, from www.kenblanchardbooks.com/feedback-is-the-breakfast-of-champions/

Bullough, B., Bullough, V. L., Fithian, M. A., Hartman, W. E., & Klein, R. S. (Eds.) (1997). *How I got into sex.* Amherst, NY: Prometheus Books.

Kasperkevic, J. (2013, May 17). *Bill Gates: Good feedback is the key to improvement.* Retrieved December 31, 2018, from www.inc.com/jana-kasperkevic/bill-gates-proper-feedback-is-key-to-improvement.html

Miller-Merrell, J. (2013, October 15). *Who are the 5.6 million who work in HR & recruiting?* Retrieved December 31, 2018, from https://workology.com/because-lead-generation-funnels-are-people-too/

Rayne, K., Dukes, C., & Taverner, B. (Eds.) (2014). *How I got into sex . . . ed.* Morristown, NJ: The Center for Sex Education.

Taverner, W. J. (2006). Tips for emerging sexology professionals: Networking and nurturing. *Contemporary Sexuality, 40*(2), 1–8.

11 The Color of Change

A Case Study of Student-Powered LGTBQAI Campus Engagement in Historically Black Educational Spaces

Melina McConatha and Denise Ford Brown

Historically Black educational places have played a critical role in social justice leadership throughout time. Notable change makers such as Thurgood Marshall, Dr. Martin Luther King Jr, Langston Hughes, Jesse Jackson, Bayard Rustin, W.E.B. DuBois, Diane Nash, Ida Wells, and Kamala Harris have all gained leadership skills in advocating for peace and inclusivity for marginalized populations at Historically Black Colleges and Universities (HBCUs) around the United States. For the purpose of this chapter the authors share a student-driven project as a case study from the nation's first degree-granting HBCU. The project illustrates student efforts to lead and establish an inclusive campus policy for a growing number of self-identified lesbian, gay, transgender, bisexual, queer, and intersected (LGTBQI) students.

An increasing number of researchers and educational leaders have published studies calling for more supportive and inclusive learning spaces (Walls, Kane, & Wisneski, 2010). In order for students to effectively develop diverse skills and competencies needed to face the challenges of a diverse world, it is important for educational institutions to develop safe and supportive learning environments that meet the needs of all students, including those of various gender or sexual identities (Walls, Kane, & Wisneski, 2010). Rankin, Weber, Blumenfeld, and Frazer (2010) suggest that over half of lesbian, gay, trans, bisexual, queer, asexual, and intersect (LGTBQAI) students report being victimized by discrimination and violence on college campuses (Walls et al., 2010). Bullying, harassment, and violence against individuals with LGTBQAI identities have become strategies for isolating those individuals (Kimmel, 2008). This chapter explores the challenges facing LGTBQAI students as well exploring student-driven efforts to engage and mobilize LGTBQAI communities in order to find inclusive strategies to replace those that currently exist which appear to isolate certain students.

An analysis of higher education programs indicates that university and college leaders, administrators, and program planners are beginning to address violence, abuse, and discrimination based on gender and sexual identity; however, it appears that LGTBQAI students in HBCUs are still finding unreceptive, and at times even hostile, environments on campuses (Gasman, Nguyen, & Kalamazoo, 2013; Squire, 2015; Strayhorn & Scott, 2012). Studies have found that LGTBQAI people of color report higher rates of depression and suicidal ideation as a result of unsupportive and hostile campus climates (Wilton et al., 2018, Evans & Chapman, 2014). These findings call for immediate action and underscore the need for more research highlighting unique challenges and strengths in educational systems serving communities of color.

This chapter explores a student-centered approach to an LGTBQAI community engagement and policy reform at the nation's first degree-granting HBCU, Lincoln University. This project, named the Color of Change, is a student-driven theoretically rich collection of digital stories of LGTBQAI people of color. The goals of the project are to develop informed policy proposals leading to changes in campus climate and to engage students in LGTBQAI activism and social change. The chapter discusses the historical context of LGTBQAI movements at HBCUs, the guiding theoretical frameworks to such movements, and, as mentioned previously, present a case study of the digital media collections and policy proposals. The program incorporates student faculty partnerships as well as identified themes that have been found to be helpful in student leadership focusing on LGTBQAI community engagement.

LGTBQAI Community Engagement in Historically Black Educational Spaces

The information presented in this chapter provides a much-needed visibility to the unique challenges and strengths that historically black institutions have in negotiating campus climate as it relates to LGTBQAI community mobilization in the context of a campus historically rich in activism and social change. Spelman College, for example, one of the nation's leading HBCUs, founded the Audre Lorde Project. In an effort to center the contributions, work, and resources of LGTBQAI communities in historically black educational spaces, the project was named after the activist and social justice leader self-identified as a "black feminist lesbian poet" (Threatt, Kulii, Reuman, & Trapas, 1997).

The first of its kind at an HBCU institution, this important program was student driven and included the digital arches of the life and work of Audre Lorde and writings on race, gender, and sexuality. The Audre Lorde Project lead the way to

> increase public awareness and understanding about African American LGBTQ experiences; to explore the marginalization of racial issues in the LGBTQ movement and in gay and lesbian studies; and to create climates that acknowledge, value, and respect difference,

especially within HBCUs, where profound silences continue to exist around gender and sexuality,

(Williams, 2013, p. 520)

In conjunction with the digital resources

participants from eleven partnering HBCUs and other colleges and universities gathered at Spelman to engage in dialogue about LGBTQ issues on other campuses. Leading experts presented research findings and offered recommendations about how HBCUs might establish more transparent and inclusive environments for their LGBTQ constituents.

(Guy-Shefall, 2012)

Work in historically black academic spaces that consider social justice, activism, and student mobilization is by no means new. The Audre Lorde Protect illustrates how student-driven projects and digital media function as community engagement. The Color of Change Project at Lincoln University involved students collecting digital stories of LGTBQAI people of color on social media. The students collected the stories shared by LGTBQAI identified people of color on social media. Each story was then studied for specific interactions between family, friends, peers, campus organizations, and larger LGTBQ organizations within the changing cultural and political climate. The collection of comments, connections, and shares were framed in a socioecological thematic framework (see later) and used to create a campus policy proposal to support LGTBQAI students of color. For the purpose of this work, community engagement was defined as "a community-level effort to address an issue or concern through organized action" (Fawcett et al., 2000, p. 264). The intention of the Color of Change was to organize and mobilize students to create a more inclusive historically black educational space for students identifying as LGTBQAI. This work also empowered students to take leadership roles in policy development and reform. In order to maintain the nature and history of historically black spaces, the majority of resources came from and are accessible through predominantly black spaces. Theoretical standpoints that center on race, gender, and communities that decentralize power were also applied in an effort to maintain work rooted in communities of color.

Theoretical Framework

By incorporating a feminist critical race perspective, this project did not position faculty or administration as "the expert." By utilizing digital social media, students were able to participate in knowledge-sharing activities from peers. Classroom activities were incorporated to provide students an opportunity to find and collect online resources. The digital work that they turned in positioned students as both "learners and knowledge-producers" (Bondy, Light, & Nicholas, 2015). Breaking away from traditional means of teacher-student educational models provided spaces for student-powered learning.

This project examined experiences of gender and sexual identity as a result of social constructions shaped by culture, history, social expectations, and shared experiences. Applying critical race feminist theory to the exploration of the constructed nature of gender and sexual binaries helped shape the understanding of the digital storytelling and sensemaking of human experiences online in the project. As Beggan and Allison (2017) assert, "from a social constructionist point of view, the importance and nature of sexuality is derived from how we, as a collective culture, choose to see it." Feminist theory has furthered an understanding of the complications associated with the identities individuals are given instead of those chosen or claimed; as well as those that social norms and values embrace or disregard in order to reinforce cisgendered or gender-conforming heteronormativity (Butler, 1990).

A study of the nuanced experience of discrimination toward students of color based on gender and sexual identity requires a broad feminist framework that can help question, discuss, and explore shared experiences of people of color in the context of intersecting identities. In the project, participating students studied critical race feminism prior to the collection and analysis of social media data in order to understand the nuances of intersecting injustices (Rogers, 2017; Patton & Ward, 2016). By centering race, gender, and sexual identity in this work, the project takes significant steps to ending oppression by making use of both social media and scholarship as a catalyst for social change.

A Student Engagement Project: Applications in Socioecological Systems Theory

Urie Bronfenbrenner's (1979) in his classic "Ecological Systems Theory" highlights the importance of the interconnections of the larger social and cultural context in people's experiences and gives way for a better understanding of how relationships create community change. Ecological Systems theory also provides a framework for understanding specific systemic intersections. By exploring interacting systems one can gain a better understanding of the unique strengths and needs of marginalized communities like LGTBQAI students of color.

Bronfenbrenner developed the theory to highlight the dynamic interactions between people and their unique environment. Furman and Gruenewalk (2004) have expanded on this theory in order to understand how individuals can create social change through an analysis and understanding of existing systems. By using ecological systems as a foundation, socioecological systems work looks specifically at social justice movements and supporting community engagement through an existing individual context. This more contemporary application of socioecological systems is a useful framework for students to study and collect representative perspectives of LGTBQAI people of color online and on campus and, in turn, promote community engagement and social change.

As shown in the Audre Lorde Project, by sharing the stories and work of LGTBQAI people of color online, others can easily access, relate to, connect with, share, and support each other. The Systems of Color of Change Project used socioecological theory in its application to organize the digital stories of LGTBQAI people of color. Students chose stories shared by people who inspired them and examined the systems that played a role in the stories they were sharing relating to gender and sexual identity. For example, one student chose a black transgender woman struggling with professors not using her appropriate pronouns in class at another, conservative HBCU campus. One simple social media page shared her friends, peers, family, school, and LGTBQAI support organizations comments and support on her story. Not only were all these connections documented, but shared easily by others helping people in similar situations from the safety of their computer screen or smart phone. A once isolated student can now have a space to share, connect, and take a leadership role in creating change on campuses with a simple post or shares (Brown & Thomas, 2014). A digital story can call for social action, connect with peers, faculty, administration, and communities through a social media post. Most importantly, students can seek out other LGTBQAI people of color who may not be as visible or "out" on campus and, in turn, connect and mobilize to create change. Digital stories not only have the potential to link the needs of the individual to larger communities, but also to make changes in educational systems. An analysis from a socioecological systems theory was used by students in the Color of Change to identify ways a campus can support an LGTBQAI person in different systems of relations. Systems of relationships were studied on LGTBQAI people of color's digital stories shared on social media to helped students better understand their lived experience. Socioecological theories frame these systems of relationships in the context of microsystems, mesosystems, exosystems, macrosystems, ecosystems, and chronosystems. This analysis studied the community connections of LGTBQAI people of color in the context of a socioecological framework. This theoretical analysis was then used to propose a policy that was informed by those it aims to support.

In the Systems of Color of Change project, participating students explored the LGTBQAI person of color's closest community (*microsystem*) and supports and challenges coming from family, friends, peers, and college campuses. Students examined how microsystems interacted with each other on social media (*mesosystem*), in which many examined how posts by schools, friends, family, and peers connected online following posts and shares. In order to better understand the context of these posts, students looked at how the media (*exosystem*) portrayed LGTBQAI people of color and how that, in turn, shaped the visibility or nature of the post. Each of these aforementioned systems exist within the larger cultural and ideological framework of today's world. In an effort to better understand this context, students looked at the current social and political climate (*macrosystem*), while identifying shifts in time and history (*chronosystem*).

In the Color of Change project, students identified ways that the experiences of LGTBQAI people of color were validated, supported, and shared online. Studies show that interactions in social media can reflect relationships and community engagement in physical spaces (Wolff, Allen, Himes, Fish, & Losardo, 2014). In other words, an analysis of systems of support for people for LGTBQAI people of color on social media is an opportunity for students to engage with larger communities; apply a theoretical framework to identify opportunities for systematic change centering around racial, sexual, and gender identities; give visibility and learn from the lived experiences of LGTBQAI people of color; and develop and lead policy reform for and by people of color.

Community Engagement Through Policy Reform

Through the careful collection of digital data, including the aforementioned brief summary of the digital collection work on LGTBQAI people of color, the students developed a theory-informed educational policy for the campus community. As noted, the majority of available online LGTBQAI resources were developed by predominantly white institutions. Our position is that in order to best serve students and to maintain the culture and mission of historically black educational spaces, policies and resources provided to LGTBQAI students must be predominantly created and shared by people of color. Here is a brief summary of the five elements that students developed in the Color of Change Project:

1. Student-Powered: Students must have agency in the development and implementation of all LGTBQAI programs in order to maintain a contemporary cultural context in the black community
2. Policy: It is essential to have specific policies stating that LGTBQAI students, staff, and faculty are protected. These policies must include access to gender-neutral bathrooms, required trainings for existing and new university members, and a code of conduct regarding LGTBQAI student support on campus
3. Student Services in Education: Opportunities for faculty, staff, and students to attend and learn more about how to best support LGTBQAI campus members

4. Administrative Accountability: The campus community must be held accountable for any behavior, discourse, or neglect of people in the LGTBQAI campus community

5. Legacy: Program Development relating to visibility as it relates to the history of leaders in the black community who are lesbian, gay, transgender, bisexual, queer, asexual, and intersexed through a digital LGTBQAI resource page and ongoing LGTBQAI student-lead educational opportunities

Students also wrote personal letters to campus administration in small groups sharing their experiences, identities, and reflections on the project. Here is an example of one letter:

> We are a collective of students from the Department of Human Services working on a project we named The Color of Change. We have been researching the experiences of LGTBQAI people of color online in order to best understand the needs of the community on our campus. Being that we are the first HBCU – we must be leaders in a social justice movement that has already begun without us. Attending a historically black institution is an honor- we look to learn from and support people like ourselves to create a better world. We have been leaders of change since our college doors opened; however, we have some work to do. Many HBCUs have a policy to declare and maintain support and inclusivity for LGTBQAI students. However, our campus community is silent in policy and action as it related to our gender and sexual identity diversity. As one of us wrote in reflection, "If you see me, I look just like any other person and that is exactly what I am – a person – here, at this campus, waiting for someone to hear my voice and stand by my side. We are not different, we are here because we are the same." As students, we look to you to implement a policy here on our campus. Through our project and studies we have learned that so many LGTBQAI people of color live lives filled with violence and discrimination based on who they are. If "Black Lives Matter" then don't LGTBQAI black lives matter just as much? Shouldn't we have a policy that states that we support our students regardless of sexual or gender identity? Our university should welcome and protect our LGTBQAI students, staff, and faculty instead of silencing them. Please consider a policy that declares our inclusivity and engages students in order to see our diversity as a strength instead of a weakness. As one of our mentors Alice Walker wrote "no person is your friend who demands your silence, or denies your right to grow." Please help us share our voice, learn, and grow.
>
> ~A Selection of Students from the Department
> of Human Services, Lincoln University

Navigating Privileges and Partnerships through Positionality in LGTBQAI Campus Leadership

As noted, this chapter explores applications of critical race feminist perspectives in LGTBQAI community engagement at historically black educational spaces. In doing so, the authors must participate in the reflexive practice of positionality (Patton & Ward, 2016; Rogers, 2017). This chapter reflects the perspectives of a collection of students, however, the work was documented, collected, and summarized by a non-tenured, heterosexual, African American woman and a non-tenured, white, queer, cisgendered woman. A short summary of the reflexive process essential to this feminist work is included in this chapter to maintain transparency in leadership roles, power, and privilege in LGTBQAI community engagement:

The Consortium of Higher Education (2016) called for the following points of considerations for faculty in support of LGTBQAI Students of Color on college campuses: 1. Visibility: Do resources for LGTBQAI students primarily include the faces of people of color? 2. Include LGTBQAI people of color when discussing historical and current social justice movements. 3. Consider collaborations and intentionally partner with LGTBQAI people of color. 4. Consider your own positionality to this topic, show up authentically, and practice self-work to examine how we show up in LGBTQAI spaces in historically black spaces. 5. Acknowledge that campus LGTBQAI campus centers have been founded with the "white founding movement narrative" and make spaces and room to challenge these narratives with students leaders of color.

The following is a narrative of the positionality process as it relates to the earlier recommendations:

As an African American straight woman born and raised in Philadelphia, I have the experience of being a product of inner-city struggles which include periods of poverty, discrimination, and injustices. Like many African American women, I was indoctrinated in the church, which was predominately black, and most of my community was African American as well. In terms of sexuality I find that homosexuality is targeted and held to a more severe level of "sinful" behavior within the church. My perception of sexuality in general is that it is far more complex than labels and difficult for the black community to understand that concept due to being restricted by labels. However, seeing sexuality as an experience of personality, feelings, emotions, self-identity and physical evolutions is not a popular thought in many circles regardless of color, human nature gravitates towards labels! As a black woman within the black community I would be accepted and welcomed as a straight woman, however, if I were gay then I would only be welcomed by certain circles outside of the church environment. As a black woman I would also experience rejection and discrimination outside of the black community for just being a black woman. Therefore, it is my understanding that leadership means to support those who are both minority and identify with LGBTQAI because the discrimination they experience is double what I have experienced.

(Brown, 2018)

As a white woman in the queer community working in educational spaces supporting LGTBQAI communities of color, I am constantly questioning my positionality and how it shapes my work and relationship to students. In my research I look to primarily listen, advocate and share the work my students find most important, and work to better understand how to pass on power and privileges provided to be because of the color of my skin. I attempt to stand in solidarity with my students and understand their strengths and challenges. While my "whiteness" had provided me with certain privileges, my queerness has also, at times, created circumstances that have not been safe or easy. However, my whiteness and my gender also provide certain freedoms. These privileges have led to opportunities to write this chapter- allowing me a space to reflect, access to the internet, a working computer, colleagues to comfortably share my thoughts on gender and sexuality safely, and a safe space to develop relationships with people in the LGTBQAI community. At the same time, I have had the resources to take the time to share my students' thoughts and the opportunity to learn a "language" and have a conversation in academia that will be published in my name; however, unfortunately not that of my students. I often struggle with knowing "what to do" with these privileges. Sharing this work is a privilege and falls dangerously close to "white voice" and a framework which develops narratives in LGTBQAI movements. Ultimately, the efforts in this chapter look to center and share the work of students from a historically black educational space, rich in a history of social justice, that will one day be future leaders of the LGTBQAI community.

(McConatha, 2018)

Mobilizing Student Leaders at HBCUs

Ongoing efforts that promote campus LGTBQAI inclusivity must include partnerships with the larger community (Rankin et al., 2010). These connections begin with student leaders. Traditional literature in higher education leadership suggests a more hierarchical model that positions administration and "hero" positions (Eddy and VanDerLinden, 2006). However, by centering students as leaders, the campus climate can shift through peer relationships, student mentorship, and student learning. Liefwood, Seashore-Louis, Anderson, and Wahlstrom (2004) advocate a leadership framework that shares decision-making regardless of power and privilege. As discussed, opportunities for leadership are presented in formats students are already comfortable with, like a simple social media page. Marginalized populations can become visible through safer spaces.

As noted, historically black places have played a critical role in social justice leadership throughout time. The Color of Change depicts the journey of students from a historically black educational spaces in learning community engagement and policy specific to their identity as students of color. These student leaders fought for safer spaces for LGTBQAI students, mobilized campus communities, negotiated power and privilege, and advocated for educational reform. The work represents unique and dedicated student activism in engagement and justice illustrating that much social change is – and has always been – lead by people of color.

Discussion Questions for Future Leaders

People of color continue to be underrepresented in leadership positions. In addition, people in the LGTBQAI community continue to be underrepresented in these same key roles. While centering intersections of race, gender, and sex the following discussion questions may provide critical thinking for future leaders in LGTBQAI community engagement in campus communities of color:

Process Questions and Considerations

1. Where can you find spaces of voices for leadership relating to gender and sexual identity that may be underrepresented?
2. How can student leadership help inform sex ed curriculum?
3. In what ways can a campus provide opportunities for student-driven LGTBQAI policy reform and development?
4. How can someone be an informed Ally for LGTBQAI People of Color?
5. What are other educational spaces where communities of color are the majority, yet underrepresented in the discourse of gender and sexual identities?

References

Beggan, J., & Allison, S. (2017). *Leadership and sexuality*. Bepress. Retrieved from https://works.bepress.com/scott_allison/49

Bondy, R., Light, T. P., & Nicholas, J., (2015). Feminist pedagogy in higher education: Review. *Academic Journal, 86*(3), 180–182.

Brown, A., & Thomas, M. E. (2014). "I just like knowing they can look at it and realize who I really am": Recognition and the limits of girlhood agency on myspace. *Signs*, 39(4), 949–972. Retrieved from http://dx.doi.org/10.1086/675544

Butler, J. (1990). *Gender Trouble: Feminism and subversion of identity*. London: Routledge.

Bronfenbrenner, U. (1979). *The ecology of human development: Experiments by nature and design*. Cambridge, MA: Harvard University Press.

Eddy, P. L., & VanDerLinden, K. E. (2006). Emerging definitions of leadership in higher education: New visions of leadership or same old "Hero" leader? *Community College Review*, 34(1), 5–26. Doi:10.1177/0091552106289703

Evans, C. B. R., & Chapman, M. V. (2014). Bullied youth: The impact of bullying through lesbian, gay, and bisexual name calling. *The American Journal of Orthopsychiatry*, 84(6), 644–652. Retrieved from http://dx.doi.org/10.1037/ort0000031

Fawcett, S. B., Francisco, V. T., & Hyra, D. et al. (2000). Building healthy communities. In A. R. Tarlov & R. F. St Peter (Eds.), The society and population health reader: A state and community perspective, 2, 75–93.

Furman, G., & Gruenewalk, D. A. (2004). Expanding the landscape of social justice: A critical ecological analysis. *Educational Administration Quarterly*, 40(1), 47–76.

Gasman, M., Nguyen, T. H., & Kalamazoo (2013). *The changing faces of historically black colleges*. The graduate School of Education Penn GSE.

Guy-Shetfall, B. (2012). *Transformation of consciousness: The national women's studies association*. Retrieved from www.nwsa.org/files/TransformationofConsciousnessMsFall2017.pdf

Kimmel, A. P., (2008). Title IX: An imperfect but vital tool to stop bullying of LGBT students. *Yale Law Journal*, 125(7), article 4.

Leithwood, K., Seashore Louis, K., Anderson, S., & Wahlstrom, K. (2004). Review of research: How leadership influences student learning. *Center for Applied Research*, 17.

Patton, L. D., & Ward, L. W. (2016). Missing black undergraduate women and politics of disposability: A critical race feminist perspective. *The Journal of Negro Education*, 85(3), 330–349.

Rankin, S., Weber, G., Blumenfeld, W., & Frazer, S. (2010). *State of higher education for lesbian, gay, bisexual, and transgender people*. Charlotte, NC: Campus Pride.

Rogers, S. T. (2017). Womanism and Afrocentricity: Understanding the intersection. *Journal of Human Behavior in the Social Environment*, 27(1/2), 36–47, Doi:10.1080/10911359.2016.1259927

Squire, D. D. (2015). Negotiating race and sexual orientation in the college choice process of black gay males. *Issues and Ideas in Public Education*, 47(3), 466–491.

Strayhorn, T. L., & Scott, J. (2012). Coming out of the dark: Black gay men's experiences at historically black colleges and universities. In R. T. Palmer & J. L. Wood (Eds.), *Black men in college: Implications for HBCUs and beyond*, pp. 26–41.

Threatt Kulii, B., Reuman, A. E., & Trapas, A. (1997). *Audre Lorde's life and career*. Retrieved from www.english.illinois.edu/maps/poets/g_l/lorde/life.htm

The Consortium of Higher Education (2016). *LGBT resource professionals.* Retrieved from https://issuu.com/lgbtcampus/docs/board_report_2016_ver4_final

Walls, N. E., Kane, S. B., & Wisneski, H. (2010). Gay–straight alliances and school experiences of sexual minority youth. *Youth & Society, 41*(3), 307–332.

Williams, E. L. (2013). Women's studies and sexuality studies at HBCUs: The Audre Lorde project at Spelman college. *Feminist Studies, 39*, 520–525.

Wolff, J. R., Kenneth, D. A., Himes, H. L., Fish, A. E., & Losardo, J. R. (2014) A retrospective examination of completed sexual and gender minority youth suicides in the United States: What can be learned from written online media? *Journal of Gay & Lesbian Mental Health, 18*(1), 3–30, DOI: 10.1080/19359705.2013.827607

Leadership in Sexuality Consultation and Special Issues

12 Money Talks . . . Misogynists Walk

A Complex Conversation on Sexual Harassment, Race, and Equal Pay

Leah Hollis

In 2018, the Philadelphia Pennsylvania community and the world witnessed the retrial of America's Dad – Bill Cosby. His first trial, in 2016 for sexual assault, resulted in a mistrial, although over 60 women came forward accusing Cosby of sexual assault, stretching back into the 1960s (Roig-Franzia, 2018). However, in early 2018, the "#MeToo" movement was well under way; the jury swung against this entertainment icon with a guilty verdict. By the fall of 2018, the 81-year-old Cosby was sentenced to 3–10 years in prison without bail (Roig-Franzia, 2018). Many Americans grew up watching *The Cosby Show*. Youngsters in the 1970s relished Saturday morning memories of the Fat Albert cartoon. On a noteworthy historical note, he funded the March on Washington in 1963 with Martin Luther King, Jr. Cosby had a phenomenal footprint and yet, in his prominence, people knew of his exploits and said nothing. His predatory behavior with women was an open secret, yet only in the twilight of his life is he held accountable with the strength of the #Me Too Movement (Day, 2017).

This watershed moment of "#Me Too" is long overdue. The public is collectively witnessing what several have known for years about the frequent predatory experience that some women endure in any employment sector. Within this movement, some women find the one-two punch with a financial inequity in pay: The first punch is the harassment; the second punch is the financial inability to finance a legal battle. Through research on workplace bullying in higher education, this researcher receives several emails and calls from academics, mostly women, asking how to fight bullies and harassers. In the last semester, questions came from Arizona, Texas, New York, California, and Wisconsin. Eventually, someone considers "how" to fight. Strategies are contemplated; colleagues are gathered for support and advice. Government agencies such as state-level human rights organizations and federal equal opportunity institutions present some options, yet those investigations are protracted and cumbersome. Further, even for the Equal Opportunity Commission (United States), the Office of Civil Rights (United States), and the Equality and Human Rights Commission (United Kingdom), a potential complainant must present a proper and precise argument for intake personnel to engage the problem rather than dismiss the issue before it is even investigated. After contemplating these options, often a woman comes to terms with the fact that "I can't afford an attorney." The female violations in the #MeToo are classified as criminal, but often not fought because of a civil rights violation. What remains is unequal pay between males and females.

In the winter of 2017, the *Chronicle of Higher Education* published an article about a female mathematician at Haverford College (Singer, 2017). This faculty appointment was her first job. In her small department, she found that her research interests coincided with those of the department harasser, and everyone knew who he was. The newly appointed professor had learned of several other women who had silently suffered. She spoke up to complain about sexual harassment where others were not in the position to do such.

This story of the female mathematician documents a very real dynamic that occurs daily in higher education, but it also points to the historical problem about women needing the financial security to fight harassment. In discussing her story, the female mathematician also mentioned her safety net: She was married with financial support. She was not only brave but in a social and financial position for self-advocacy. In contrast, so many women are the breadwinners, single mothers, and/or the caregivers of elder parents. They cannot afford the right to speak up or risk unemployment.

The "#MeToo" movement is a fight against misogynist sexual harassment and has evolved in a fight to be inclusive of the range of discriminations against women. Holley (2017) notes that 80% of those seeking legal assistance to fight bias crimes cannot find or afford legal assistance. Further, women only make 80% of men. For Black women, the number is 63% of what men make, and for Latinx women the number is 54% of what men make (Bibler, 2015). Consequently, silence breakers often are not just brave, but also in a position with the resources to mount a legal fight. In higher education, those who speak up typically have the means or safety to speak out either because they have earned tenure or hold an administrative position that affords resources to engage in a viable complaint.

Money: Root of Evil Inequity?

The money issue is complex because money in many cultures signifies worth and value (Smith, 1937). For example, a luxury sedan costs more money than a simple hatchback because the perception is that the sedan is worth the expense. When an organization pays men more money than women for the same duties, the message is that men's work is valued more than women's work. Further, the disparity in pay means that women have fewer resources to even fight for their worth. Organizations compensate employees in the higher ranks of the organizational structure, confirming the worth of those employees, compared to the worth of those toiling in the entry and middle levels. These differences, which illustrate the organizational power, coincide with the economic power assigned to the higher echelon employees (Hauge, Skogstad, & Einarsen, 2009; Hutchinson, Vickers, Jackson, & Wilkes, 2010; Merton, 1968). In turn, the salary establishes a competitive benchmark, confirming organizational worth and recognition of achievement (Nnedum, Egwu, Obinna, Ntomchukwu, & Chukwukeluo, 2011).

When an organization loves money to the point of devaluing one gender for another, that love of money, instead of love for the ethical and legal compliance for equal pay, signals a propensity to engage in other unethical behavior (Singhapakdi, Vitell, Lee, Nisius, & Yu, 2013; Tang et al., 2012). In fact, Srivastava, Locke, and Bartol (2001) suggested that those who love money, instead of ethical management (Brown & Mitchell, 2010), use money to enhance their standing and to acquire and maintain power in order to overcome their intrinsic self-doubts. Such machinations regarding money emerge from their own insecurity and low self-esteem, while in contrast ethical and confident leaders would avoid illegal pay disparities.

For those who love money at the expense of others, they insert money as an artificial equalizer to soothe a potentially lower self-esteem by diminishing the value of others by paying them less. Further, money and power to have and possess things overrides humanity (Freire, 1970). The "haves" and their possessions remain dominant and in control as an oppressor. The oppressed are left disenfranchised and without proper resources to fight for their own humanity (Freire, 1970). Women are twice dehumanized as sexualized automatons, and second with diminished means to resist such objectification. In other words, often women are reduced to sexual objects while their inequitable financial situations often prohibit them from transcending these objectified spaces.

Funding the Fight

A British study considered the type of job as a major contributor to unequal pay. Part-time employment often is assigned to women who are mothers; these employees are often constrained in potential upward mobility or in the location given their considerations of child care (Booth, Francesconi, & Frank, 2003; Manning, 1996; Manning, 2003; Neuburger, 2010). A common finding was reported in a Canadian study, stating that women are more likely than men to step out of their careers or to accept lower-paying part-time positions. Such part-time contingent adjunct assignments underpay talented employees, and an employee typically accepts a series of part-time jobs to make a living (Hollis, 2015). The social expectation that the woman is the caregiver also restricts her career path and earning power. While women may not necessarily subscribe to this social prescription, the dominant culture constrains women's self-determination when imposing such domestic expectation on them.

As reported by the American Council on Education (ACE), women comprise only 26% of higher education presidents (ACE Convenes Discussion on Women in Higher Education Leadership, July 16, 2012). Further, women only serve as 31% of the full professorships and only 38% of the chief academic officers; though, in the last decade, women have exceeded men in the number of doctorates (Johnston, 2016). Power for women in the academy, in the form of organizational power and financial power, is evasive. This contributes to the dynamics that women must consider in their fight against harassment.

In a meta-analysis of studies, Tippet and Wolke (2014) show that those from lower socioeconomic status are more likely to endure bullying. Hence, they are in an inferior position from which to fight. Bullying is an attempt to use social strategies to maintain acceptance, achievement, and access to resources (p. 56). In the higher education context, workplace bullying is also used to maintain the dominance of the powerful (Hollis, 2016). When women attempt to ascend the career ladder through promotion, tenure, supervision, or advanced degrees, they become a more likely target of workplace bullying (Hollis, 2016a). When women attempt to gain organization power, through these aforementioned avenues that also bring additional financial reward, women are often stifled, even harassed, and often remain confined to lower-paying positions. Those staff members with lower rank or less power are more likely to face bullying. Given their entry-level and middle management status, they are also more likely to earn less. Thus, the disenfranchised position for women often leaves women in a diminished position for protest.

Enlightenment and Equity?

University systems presumably hire, promote, and compensate employees and faculty based on merit. Managers and supervisors who evaluate individual performance are expected to do such with objectivity and within the bounds of clarified policies and procedures. In turn, gender bias should not be calculated into the equation, yet unfortunately, ubiquitous gender bias often compromises the compensation decisions. Logically, merit preferences should prevail in systems that espouse enlightened thought (Doucet, 2011).

Nonetheless, people execute these policies and procedures based upon their own experiences that are related to how they construct gender-based social prescriptions. Fallible people with myopic gender-based assumptions do not recognize their shortcomings and unintentionally perpetuate these gender-related biases. Sometimes, these biases and counternormative ideologies are woven into the application of policy/

tenure and promotions are accolades initiated at the department level, which then progress to the college level. The academy harbors a host of idiosyncrasies and predilections that have an impact on the tenure and promotion cycle. Despite national or state policies to eradicate inequity, individual decisions within the organization cast the die for gender inequity in pay. "Inequality at work does not just happen; it occurs through the acts and the failures to act by people who run and work for organizations" (Reskin, 2000, p. 717).

Further, when a woman faces harassment and also struggles against an organization that quietly allows for this harassment, the woman endures the one-two punch of inequity. First, she has to fathom how to respond to sexual harassment without jeopardizing her career; and second, she then has to cultivate the necessary resources to advocate for her rights.

Noteworthy Examples

A federal investigation occurred at the University of California at Berkeley regarding its response to sexual assault. The Office of Civil Rights conducted a four-year review and determined that California-Berkeley was out of compliance in handling sexual assault complaints. While faculty rights remained at the center of the protracted investigation, the target was a female graduate student (Brown, 2018).

The saga of the University of Rochester sexual harassment case documents how four women over several years were sexually involved with a male faculty member. In this case, the male professor pursued female students and had several sexual exploits (Mangan, 2018). The issue came to the forefront when tenured faculty spoke out after years of the campus community knowing of this behavior.

A recent *Guardian* investigation documented how many UK universities are failing to address sexual misconduct: 132 universities reported a total of over 1,900 reports of sexual misconduct in the last seven years (Batty & Cherubini, 2018). Cambridge University had the most incidents with 215 reported cases; Durham University reported 88 cases in the same time frame. Some reports from UK universities are unclear about whether the assailants are students or staff.

In this last example, an article documented that sexual harassment at UK universities occurred in epidemic proportions. Professor Nicole Westmarland of Durham University stated: "Managers failed to recognize that the way the senior lecturer acted towards them as male managers were not necessarily the way that he interacted with those with less power, including students, early career academics, and some administrators" (Batty, 2017, para. 8).

These examples are just a few narratives of how higher education remains rife with inequities for women, inequities that continue to sprout from the power differentials between men and women. A typical theme in these cases is that the women had less power organizationally and financially. They contemplated the adverse effect on their careers if they complained. Comparatively, the men were typically in more powerful positions and had more money. The power differential is a mammoth component of harassment and is partly caused by a woman's financial inability to formally combat the abuse.

Deciding to Fight

Money is not the only element informing a woman's propensity to fight sexual harassment. The historical construct from which women emerge also informs their inclination to fight and consider if their plea for justice will be heard. These dynamics relate to the privileging of middle-class white women's voices, while prejudicial stereotypes such as Mammy, Jezebel, Sapphire, and Strong Black Woman have rendered black women invisible or lacking credibility to defend their virtue (Harris-Perry, 2011).

The patriarchal culture, which often fails to recognize and appreciate women's worth, can have a negative impact on women and their self-perception to engage in nontraditional tasks, such as resisting sexism. McMahan (1982) and Dickerson and Taylor (2000) pose the idea that internalized negative perceptions can stifle someone's inclination to engage in a situation if that person lacks the confidence to proceed. Consequently, that person would avoid the task and settle with something he/she perceives as easier to accomplish (Bandura, 1977). Fighting against discrimination, against sexual harassment, or discriminatory gender-based pay inequity is far from easy. The complainant regardless of race would need a positive self-perception, strong self-esteem, and potentially strong intragroup support to resist sexist and racist normalcy (Spencer-Rodgers, Major, Forster, & Peng, 2016). In short, a woman has to strongly believe first that she is worth the fight. This concept alone can be difficult to cultivate given the subtle yet constant messages from the dominant culture about women being the weaker sex. From that decision, she needs to muster the time and resources to engage the fight; yet these subsequent elements only follow the initial decision regarding self-worth.

Historical Denial of Resources

Historical gender pay inequity originates from ideas that women should be apolitical, domestic, and support their husbands. Women seeking work at the onset of the industrial age were primarily relegated to textiles, cooking, or cleaning. Black women's unequal pay has a deeper inception born of slavery; therefore, they were expected to perform domestic duties but also to perform heavy fieldwork alongside the men. Black women's work while necessary was seldom celebrated or appreciated (Parker, 2004).

Once the Thirteenth Amendment was passed, freedom meant continuing drudgery for Black women as sharecroppers and maids. Though theoretically "free," Black women often experienced problems securing fair pay from white landowners. Jones (1985) documented instances where Black women filed grievances about unfair pay. They "were routinely and ruthlessly defrauded of the small amounts they had earned and then 'run off the place' " (Parker, 2004, p. 54).

Black and white working women in the 19th and 20th centuries were subjected to male supremacy in managing money as men legally controlled wages (Davis, 2011). Even in cottage industries, women reported: "we women work secretly in the seclusion of our bed chambers because all society was built on the theory that men, not women earned money" (Baxandall, Baxandall, Gordon, & Reverby, 1976, p. 46). Black women who migrated north in the 1890s typically were relegated to agricultural or domestic work. Even if Black women were hired into industrial jobs, they were assigned the lowest-paying jobs (Davis, 2011). Into the 1940s, a system emerged analogous to slave auctions; Black women crowded street corners every morning begging to be chosen for work. Once Black women completed the work, white patrons often altered the terms by extending hours, extending the duties, and often paying with clothes or trinkets instead of cash (Davis, 2011). A 1938 article from *The Nation* documented that Black women domestics worked 72 hours a week, "receiving the lowest wages of all occupations" (Lerner, 1977, p. 269). Many live-in Black women domestics labored on their feet 10–14 hours a day and only saw their families one afternoon a week.

Misrecognition

Harris-Perry's misrecognition theory (2011), an expansion of Hegel's recognition theory (Benjamin, 1990), serves as the theoretical framework for this analysis. The United States historically disregards Black women's work and value; society traditionally fails to reciprocate the appropriate recognition for equitable social status (Harris-Perry, 2011). Historically, society has dismissed Black women through such stereotypes as the Mammy, Sapphire, and Jezebel. Harris-Perry (2011) added the "Strong Black Woman" stereotype, which suggests that Black women weather any hardship, despite inadequate resources or support.

Further, middle-class white women are often misrecognized as wispy, fragile, and in need of assistance. DiAngelo (2018) highlights how white women can choose to manipulate such cultural expectations with tears and weeping. White women's tears move the community to protect her, whether she needs such protection or not. The community's move to protect the weeping white woman may satisfy her immediate quest for protection and support, yet it also reinforces a subordination that undercuts that woman's power. In contrast, when women of color express their pain and tears, the public and often their own private communities render such suffering "unnoticed and unattended to" (hooks, 1989, pp. 151–153).

These extant stereotypes elide knowledge of the disenfranchised conditions women have typically faced in abuse, rape, and housing problems, conditions the hegemony perpetuates through those "colonized" minds that adopt these domineering behaviors and assumptions (Harris-Perry, 2011; Freire, 1970). Collins (2000) stated that these stereotypes invoke a rationale for denying women's humanity. When women raise their voices in protest, they are often told to find another job or are "run off the place" (Parker, 2004). While leaving a bad situation can be valiant, not correcting the problem leaves the inequity for the next woman to fight.

Misrecognition through these stereotypes inundates both Black women and white women, creating barriers to self-determination as women can internalize and operate within the aforementioned stereotypes. Further, these stereotypes metastasize into women's hyper-invisibility, denying them the opportunity to transcend patriarchal barriers that trap both Black and white women in respective, presumed assumptions regarding behavior. In contrast to Black women, middle-class white women are stereotyped as being "weak, dependent, passive and monogamous" (Essed, 1992, pp. 32– 33); yet working-class white women are not as valued in society and are more likely to face sexual harassment than middle-class white women (Baker, 2004).

Welsh, Carr, MacQuarrie, and Huntley, (2006) point to race as a compelling factor related to women reporting sexual violence. Given the aforementioned stereotypes about Black women's sexual availability, Black women's reports of harassment, rape, and other sexual violence are not taken as seriously as when white women report being victimized by similarity behaviors (Welsh et al., 2006). Further, the study offered insight into Black women perceiving that they can handle sexual harassment on their own, whereas, in their perception, white women were less equipped to deal with sexual harassment. If a white male was the harasser, the Black woman would express her discontent and keep going with her day. However, if a Black man was the harasser, Black women were more concerned with keeping the race or family together, than reporting bad behaviors (Welsh et al., 2006). Proof positive is in Beverly Johnson's comment to a Boston Radio Station, years after the alleged assault. When asked why she waited so long to share her story, and why, Johnson replied, "it was so hard to speak out against such a powerful and positive black cultural icon (Johnson, 2014).

Hernandez (2000) reported that of Equal Employment Opportunity Commission (EEOC) complaints, Black women comprised 14.4% of sexual harassment charges, while white women were 61.9% of sexual harassment charges. However, white women in Hernandez' study were 84% of all working women and Black women were 11.5% of working women; in short, Hernandez writes (2000, p. 187) that "sexual harassers target White women as victims [at] disproportionally lower rates than women of color." These data were collected shortly after the October 1991 Anita Hill hearings. The hearings also pointed to the racialized elements in sexual harassment. As confirmed by Buchanan and Ormerod (2002), Black women are more likely to face sexual harassment, but as noted by Murrell (1996) and Richardson and Taylor (2009), Black women are less likely to be perceived as targets for sexual harassment, given the lascivious stereotypes of black women. As those who report sexual harassment become subject to retaliation and organizational isolation, and these dynamics are exacerbated for women of color (St. Jean & Feagin, 1997).

For white women, the intersection variables of class and race have an impact on their ability to speak up. In the 1970s, when women began to file more sexual harassment cases, these were typically working-class women striving to make a living. Conversely, a middle-class white woman presumably had a husband, served her family in the domestic space, and was sheltered from the consternation of day-to-day work life. The middle-class white woman was prized and protected, not seeking to leave such protection (and financial independence) for a career. Nonetheless, higher class standing can be a cloak that shields white women from sexual harassment. In comparison, Black women regardless of socioeconomic status face sexual harassment because class often is not a mitigating factor for them (Luthar, Tata, & Kwesiga, 2009).

Historical and economic markers cast women into categories of who is worthy of protection, and who is presumably available for sex; such stereotypes devalue both Black and white women through patriarchal generalizations, unfortunately, developing a profile of what is considered credible and worthy of protection. Within this continuous misrecognition paradigm, Black women and white are perpetually undervalued through the various sexist mechanisms that stifle women's self-determination.

Conclusion

Fighting sexual harassment is not just about curtailing predatory behavior; it is also about economically empowering women to fight for safe spaces. Women's economic empowerment can help keep such predators at bay. Proof positive would be the consideration that the academic community does not hear of a junior male faculty member sexually harassing a female provost; a male entry-level coordinator does not typically accost a female vice president. The organizational and financial power differentials make upward harassment unlikely, yet this differential also confirms the vulnerable position from which women typically have to fight when they are disproportionately caught in entry- and middle-level positions.

The one-two punch consists of first facing harassment and discrimination and second not having the financial gloves to fight against the threat. Those facing harassment and assault are often left in disbelief that it has happened and then contemplate next steps. Such contemplation, which would include an evaluation of one's self-worth to engage the fight, would also include the realization of the cost to mount a defense. The alternative is to flee, disrupting a career trajectory and often taking a lateral move or demotion to escape the unfair fight of sexual harassment and economic inequities.

Another viable solution is the application of ethical leadership who can mitigate pay inequity problems because they follow policy and laws (Xu, Loi & Ngo, 2016). Not only do ethical leaders follow sound policy, they strive to create and apply appropriate policy (Brown & Mitchell, 2010). Regardless of gender, conscientious leaders can serve as a critical ally in bridging the gender pay gap.

Further, the historical dynamics from which women emerge can encourage them or stifle them in the pursuit of justice. No one wants to face injustice and trauma, and then face a secondary trauma when they are silenced or discredited. Yet, the aforementioned social constructions are critical elements of a woman's propensity to fight sexual harassment.

Some preemptive strategies for women in any sector would include saving even $100 a month, if possible, to build the financial security to fight or withstand a period of unemployment. Women's groups have established a few legal defense funds, which may defer legal costs, if a woman's case is eligible. One should stay current on legal trends and recent court rulings, which can aid someone in knowing the viability of formally fighting harassment and unequal pay practices. Professional and personal networks are critical to maintain a system of colleagues who can offer objective advice about work inequities. Further, the initial conversation with legal counsel is critical in convincing that counsel to take the case. A clearly defined legal argument with data, times, dates, names, and numbers can convince a legal counsel or a civil rights agency to take a case or end the discussion after the initial consultation. With all of these strategies, a woman mounting a fight should also know that typically office friends and colleagues fade away; these colleagues might agree with the fight in theory. However in practice, if they are underpaid or have minimal job security, they may not want to lock arms and go into battle.

Without saying, these inequities create an unfair fight, where the aggrieved often have diminished resources. Adding insult to injury, the organization typically knows about such inequities and fails to rectify the problem. Just as so many people knew about Bill Cosby's behavior, a campus community knows its harassers and knows that the women are typically in a disenfranchised position to fight back. Nonetheless, though one can anticipate that the organization often responds to the complainant with aggressive disdain when a bright light is shown on organizational illegal harassment and pay issues, history has shown that such conflict, despite the odds, is necessary for the continuous fight to secure equity for women in the academy.

Process Questions and Considerations

As with any social oppression, the prongs supporting that abuse are consistent, complex, and multifaceted. Oversimplifying the problem would yield an oversimplification of the solution. Therefore, the following are offered to consider the historical intersectionality of race, gender, and class when tackling the fight against sexual harassment.

1. How can historical stereotypes compromise both Black women and white women in the fight against sexual harassment?
2. Consider, how does class have an impact on how Black women and white women respectively engage the fight against sexual harassment?
3. What steps can organizational leadership take to minimize both pay inequity and sexual harassment?
4. How could you support a friend, family member, or colleague who faces sexual harassment and/or gender-based pay inequity?
5. Whether it is sexual harassment, workplace bullying, discrimination, or other organizational abuses that hurt self-determination, what mechanisms can be put in place to curtail abuse?

References

American Council on Education. (2012). *ACE convenes discussion on women in higher education*. Retrieved from https://www.acenet.edu/news-room/Pages/Discussion-Women-Leadership.aspx

Baker, C. N. (2004). Race, class, and sexual harassment in the 1970s. *Feminist Studies*, 30(1), 7–27.

Bandura, A. (1977). Self-efficacy: Toward a unifying theory of behavioral change. *Psychological Review*, 84, 191–215.

Batty, D. (2017). Sussex University failed duty of care to assault victim, inquiry finds. *The Guardian*. Retrieved from www.theguardian.com/education/2017/jan/17/sussex-university-failed-duty-of-care-assault-victim-inquiry

Batty, D., & Cherubini, E. (2018). UK universities accused of failing to tackle sexual misconduct. *The Guardian*. Retrieved from www.theguardian.com/world/2018/mar/28/uk-universities-accused-failing-tackle-sexual-misconduct

Baxandall, R., Baxandall, R. F., Gordon, L., & Reverby, S. (Eds.). (1976). *America's working women: A documentary history, 1600 to the present*. New York, NY: Random House.

Benjamin, J. (1990). An outline of intersubjectivity: The development of recognition. *Psychoanalytic Psychology*, 7(S), 33.

Bibler, K. (2015). The pay gap is even worse for black women. And that's everyone's problem. *American association of university women*. Retrieved www.aauw.org/2015/07/21/black-women- pay- gap/

Booth, A. L., Francesconi, M., & Frank, J. (2003). A sticky floors model of promotion, pay, and gender. *European Economic Review*, 47(2), 295–322.

Brown, M. E., & Mitchell, M. S., (2010). Ethical and unethical leadership: Exploring new avenues for future research. *Business Ethics Quarterly*, 20, (4), 583–616.

Brown, S. (2018). Can colleges act more quickly to punish professors who harass? *The chronicle of higher education*. Retrieved from www.chronicle.com/article/Can-Colleges-Act-More-Quickly/242735

Collins, P. (2000). *Black feminist thought*. New York, NY: Routledge.

Davis, A. Y. (2011). *Women, race, & class*. New York, NY: Vintage.

Day, E. (2017). BBC director: 'People knew about Cosby, but they chose not to care' *The Telegraph*. Retrieved from www.telegraph.co.uk/women/life/bbc-director-people-knew-cosby-chose-not-care/

DiAngelo, R. (2018). *White fragility: Why it's so hard for white people to talk about racism*. Boston, MA: Beacon Press.

Dickerson, A., & Taylor, M. A. (2000). Self-limiting behavior in women: Self-esteem and self-efficacy as predictors. *Group & Organization Management*, 25(2), 191–210.

Doucet, C. (2011). The gender pay gap among university professors: The role of individual and organizational determinants (Dissertation/ thesis). University of Montreal.

Essed, P. (1992). Alternative knowledge sources in explanations of racist events. In M. L. McLaughlin, M. J. Cody, & S. J. Read (Eds.), *Communication: Explaining one's self to others: Reason-giving in a social context* (pp. 199–224). Hillsdale, NJ: Lawrence Erlbaum Associates, Inc.

Freire, P. (1970). *Pedagogy of the oppressed* M. B. Ramos, Trans. New York, NY: Continuum, 2007.

Harris-Perry, M. V. (2011). *Sister citizen: Shame, stereotypes, and Black women in America*. New Haven, CT: Yale University Press.

Hauge, L. J., Skogstad, A., & Einarsen, S. (2009). Individual and situational predictors of workplace bullying: Why do perpetrators engage in the bullying of others? *Work & Stress*, 23(4), 349–358.

Hernandez, T. K. (2000). Sexual harassment and racial disparity: The mutual construction of gender and race. *Journal of Gender Race & Justice*, 4, 183.

Holley, P. (2017). Reporting a hate crime is notoriously hard. Can this digital tool change that? *The Washington Post*. Retrieved from www.washingtonpost.com/news/innovations/wp/2017/09/26/reporting-a-hate-crime-is-notoriously-hard-can-this-digital-tool-change-that/?noredirect=on&utm_term=.abda9f904481

Hollis, L. P. (2015). The significance of declining full-time faculty status for community college student retention and graduation: A correlational study with a Keynesian perspective. *International Journal of Humanities and Social Science*, 5(3), 1–7.

Hollis, L. P. (2016). Socially dominated: The racialized and gendered positionality of those precluded from bullying. In *The coercive community college:*

Bullying and its costly impact on the mission to serve underrepresented populations(pp. 103–112). Bingley: Emerald Group Publishing.

Hollis, L. P. (2016a). *The coercive community college: Bullying and its Costly impact on the mission to serve underrepresented populations.* Bingley: Emerald Group Publishing.

Hooks, b. (1989). *Talking back: Thinking feminist, thinking black.* Cambridge, MA: Between the Lines.

Hutchinson, M., Vickers, M. H., Jackson, D., & Wilkes, L. (2010). Bullying as circuits of power: An Australian nursing perspective. *Administrative Theory & Praxis, 32*(1), 25–47.

Johnson, B. (2014). Cosby Accuser Beverly Johnson: He's a black man. I had to separate the Trayvon Martins and Michaels Browns from what happened to me. *WBUR Boston 90.9 radio interview.* Retrieved from www.wbur.org/onpoint/2014/12/16/bill-cosby-beverly-johnson-michael-brown-eric-garner

Johnston, H. (2016). *Pipelines pathways, and institutional leadership: An update on the state of women in higher education.* Washington, DC: American Council on Education.

Jones. J. (1985). *Labor of love labor of sorrow: Black women, work, and the family from slavery to present.* New York, NY: Basic Books.

Lerner, G. (1977). *The female experience: An American documentary.* Oxford, England: Oxford University Press on Demand.

Luthar, H. K., Tata, J., & Kwesiga, E. (2009). A model for predicting outcomes of sexual harassment complaints by race and gender. *Employee Responsibilities and Rights Journal, 21*(1), 21–35.

Mangan, K. (2018). Rochester professor at center of harassment controversy will return to teaching. *The Chronicle of Higher Education.* Retrieved from www.chronicle.com/article/Rochester-Professor-at-Center/243043

Manning, A. (1996). The equal pay act as an experiment to test theories of the labour market. *Economica*, 191–212.

Manning, A. (2003). *Monopsony in motion: Imperfect competition in labor markets.* Princeton, NJ: Princeton University Press.

McMahan, I. D. (1982). Expectancy of success on sex-linked tasks. *Sex Roles, 8,* 949–958.

Merton, R. K. (1968). The Matthew effecting science. *Science, 159,* 56–63.

Murrell, A. J. (1996). Sexual harassment and women of color: Issues, challenges, and future directions. In M. S. Stockdale (Ed.), Sexual harassment in the workplace: Perspectives, frontiers, and response strategies (pp. 51–66). Sage. Thousand Oaks, CA.

Neuburger, J. (2010). *Trends in the unequal pay of women and men across three British generations* (Doctoral dissertation). Institute of Education, University of London.

Nnedum, O. A. U., Egwu, E. U., Obinna, E. J., Ntomchukwu, M. S., & Chukwukeluo, C. B. (2011). Materialism and meaning of money (MOM): Validation of Money Metaphor Scale (MMS) in South Africa. *International Research Journal of Finance & Economics, 76,* 31–46.

Parker, P. S. (2004). *Race, gender, and leadership: Re-envisioning organizational leadership from the perspectives of African American women executives.* New York, NY: Routledge.

Reskin, B. F. (2000). Getting it right: Sex and race inequality in work organizations. *Annual Review of Sociology*, 26, 707–709.

Richardson, B. K., & Taylor, J. (2009). Sexual harassment at the intersection of race and gender: A theoretical model of the sexual harassment experiences of women of color. *Western Journal of Communication*, 73(3), 248–272.

Roig-Franzia, M. (2018). Bill Cosby sentenced to 3–10 years in state prison. *The Washington Post*. Retrieved from www.washingtonpost.com/lifestyle/style/bill-cosby-sentenced-to-3-to-10-years-in-state-prison/2018/09/25/9aa620aa-c00d-11e8-90c9-23f963eea204_story.html?utm_term=.3967861fbb75

Singer, S. (2017). I spoke up against my harasser- and paid a price. *The Chronicle of Higher Education*. Retrieved from www.chronicle.com/article/I-Spoke-Up-Against-My-Harasser/241991

Singhapakdi, A., Vitell, S., Lee, D., Nisius, A., & Yu, G. (2013). The influence of love of money and religiosity on ethical decision-making in marketing. *Journal of Business Ethics*, 114(1), 183–191.

Smith, A. (1937). *An inquiry into the nature and causes of the wealth of nations*. New York: Modern Library.

Spencer-Rodgers, J., Major, B., Forster, D. E., & Peng, K. (2016). The power of affirming group values: Group affirmation buffers the self-esteem of women exposed to blatant sexism. *Self and Identity*, 15(4), 413–431.

Srivastava, A., Locke, E., & Bartol, K. (2001). Money and subjective well-being: It's not the money, it's the motives. *Journal of Personality and Social Psychology*, 80, 959–971.

St. Jean, Y., & Feagin, J. (1997). Black women, sexism, and racism: Experiencing double jeopardy. In C. R. Ronai, B. A. Zsembik, & J. R. Feagin (Eds.), *Everyday sexism* (pp. 157–180). New York, NY: Routledge.

Tang, T. L. P., & Liu, H. (2012). Love of money and unethical behavior intention: Does an authentic supervisor's personal integrity and character (ASPIRE) make a difference? *Journal of Business Ethics*, 107 (3), 295–312.

Tippett, N., & Wolke, D. (2014). Socioeconomic status and bullying: A meta-analysis. *American Journal of Public Health*, 104(6), e48–e59.

Welsh, S., Carr, J., MacQuarrie, B., & Huntley, A. (2006). "I'm Not Thinking of It as Sexual Harassment": Understanding harassment across race and citizenship. *Gender & Society*, 20(1), 87–107.

Xu, A. J., Loi, R., & Ngo, H. Y., (2016). Ethical leadership behavior and employee justice perceptions: The mediating role of trust in organization. *Journal of Business Ethics*, 134(3), 493–504.

13 Intimate Partner Violence in Sadomasochistic Relationships

Freirean Leadership Through Disclosure and Raising Voices

Dulcinea/Alex Pitagora

> The revolution is made neither by the leaders for the people, nor by the people for the leaders, but by both acting together in unshakable solidarity. This solidarity is born only when the leaders witness to it by their humble, loving, and courageous encounter with the people.
>
> (Freire, 2005, p. 129)

If I am a leader in my communities, it is only because my communities and I have found each other and worked to support each other, to hold each other up, to be mirrors for each other, to witness our sameness and difference, to feel seen and accepted. I am a New York City psychotherapist and sex therapist, a former sex worker, and a current kinky-, poly-, queer-, and gender non-binary-identified person, and I have been told (by clients, community members, and colleagues) that I am arguably one of the most publicly self-disclosing therapists currently in practice. I do not feel revolutionary, and I do not identify as a leader of a revolution, but I do feel compelled to amplify the voices of silence sexualities, and that process includes amplifying my own voice along with their voices.

It is for this reason that these pages are written in the first person. My disclosure is a means of situating me within the marginalized communities that I work to support and amplify, and as a way to model the calculated risk that is being transparently who I am in public, instead of remaining voiceless in the margins created for us by our oppressors. As Freire noted, "I cannot be a [leader][1] if I do not perceive with ever greater clarity that my practice demands of me a definition about where I stand" (Freire, 2001, p. 93). I also feel compelled to note that I am in no way calling on anyone else to join me "out here," unless they feel safe and comfortable in doing so.

I began the journey to "out here" by discovering and honing in on my sexual identity, and finding and cultivating community. I have been a sexuality explorer since my sexual debut, starting with my internal landscape as I interacted with personal play partners.[2] My exploration expanded outward when I became as a sex worker, long before I continued the journey as a sex positive sex therapist. In hindsight, I realize that coming together as a community is the first step in giving each other support and strength. I have always felt vulnerable in being who I have been, but I have always felt it necessary to keep moving closer to being who I am, and I have found that the most direct route to being who I am is in plain view of the world around me, so that I can be in plain view of myself. A funny thing happens when leaders put themselves in plain view: More and more people see them. It follows that when more and more people see leaders, there are more and more voices to hear and to raise.

Disclosure as a Means of Participation and Leadership

Something I have never written down for public consumption: I am a survivor of childhood trauma and of intimate partner violence. I have alluded to these experiences in various contexts, and while I sometimes talk about the specifics, I rarely call myself a "survivor" because I identify more as a thriver than as a survivor. Creating my own narrative in this way, similar to narrative therapy, is a healing practice that enables me to reclaim my past experience and assume agency in moving forward (SAMHSA, 2014). For me, the word *survivor* brings with it the people who have done something to me or to those close to me, and I do not like to think about those people having had such an effect on me, though, clearly, they have. The word *survivor* is embedded with questions like *survivor of what, and of whom?* – questions that put the focus on the who (the perpetrator) and the what (the situation), instead of on my experience, thereby evoking the power that the who and what had in terms of influence they have had on my life (Singer, 2010). As a trauma-informed (by training and personal experience) therapist, when I ask iterations of these questions of my clients during intake interviews, I am particularly sensitive to the language they or I use to describe their experience (SAMHSA, 2014). The act of "pendulating" (gradually and safely facilitating) an environment in which people can reclaim the language around their trauma can be an intervention in itself (van der Kolk, 2014, p. 247).

I am a resilient person who has found a community and a healthy outlet for my trauma and means of connecting with intimacy, and I will not give credit to someone else for that. Though I don't readily identify as a survivor, I appreciate that the word *survivor* has been co-opted to replace the word *victim* in recognition of the way words like these are imbued with assumptions. I realize that the intentional move away from the use of certain words to describe oppressed people is in itself a means of interrupting that power (Stoudt, 2009), and though I applaud this effort to veer away from disempowering language, I instinctually want to continue to challenge this language. Analogous to marino's [*sic*] (1998) assertion about recursive meaning in language, the resymbolization of these words challenge me, and my reaction is to continue to challenge that resymbolization. In doing so, resymbolization becomes the reconstruction of knowledge, which can be a vehicle toward increasing self-awareness and furthering social progress (Fals-Borda, 1991), which also happen to be key ingredients in Freirean leadership (Freire, 1993).

This connection between self-awareness and social progress can be illustrated in the process that preceded and incepted this project. There is a stigma associated with being a survivor that I also never voiced before embarking on a reflective inquiry into intimate partner violence (IPV), with the intention of raising other survivors' voices in my community. This feeling rushed to consciousness abruptly in recent years, when I avoided telling the story about my mother's murder at the hands of her estranged second husband to a group of peers who, though I intuited would be supportive, I anticipated would also inadvertently project feelings of pity on me. I am aware that this is a cynical and defensive reaction to my aversion to being seen as a survivor, but I am also aware that, regardless of empathy and mindfulness of language, it is often too difficult for most people to avoid seeing survivors as victims. I have also avoided talking to people about my history of trauma because I anticipate that they will feel pain, and, as a result, I will have to feel fresh pain in a recursively empathetic reaction. It can be difficult not to experience others' empathy as demoralizing and oppressing, and after speaking to a friend about this recurring issue, I realized that I needed to investigate my defensiveness and self-censorship further. In seeking to escape the pain of oppression, I was avoiding the higher ordinal task of working toward escaping oppression itself. This process was finally addressed during clinical training on how to address countertransference, a crucial skill for any clinician enabling empathy to be experienced without internalization. Learning this skill was not solely for my own benefit. I know that my own self-censorship is an indicator that it is also occurring in others in similar ways, and that I cannot ask others to find their voice to join with mine if I have not yet found mine, and if I have not found a way to speak my truth without retraumatizing myself.

My self-censorship in talking about my history of trauma directly connects with my resistance to being reduced to one of the most common, unfounded stereotypes about sexually atypical people – that we are the way we are because of something traumatic that happened to us in childhood. This is the primary reason that I, and many others with atypical identifications, have been or stay closeted about our histories of trauma. We do not want our sexual identities, lifestyles, and subcultures reduced to a trope that is not based in scientific fact, but has been constructed by the groups in power in order to oppress and silence. In other words, as Freire (2005) asserted, the struggle for freedom is a threat not only to the oppressors and the oppressed individual, but also to the community as a whole that fears increased oppression. That this is the first time I have publicly disclosed my trauma is evidence of how effective this tactic is. It follows that I do not feel that I can embody the role of leader without full disclosure, particularly in light of Freire's (2005) assertion that individuals who have been held captive by the culture of silence must first reclaim their voices, then help prevent others from being dehumanized in the same way. Societal inoculation makes it difficult if not impossible to internalize the stigma associated with oppression (Carvalho, Lewis, Derlega, Winstead, & Viggiano, 2011). I am filled with gratitude and humility toward the communities I serve, as serving them has helped me to disentangle and release some of my own oppression. I continue to work on excavating the internalized heterosexism that oppresses me, which is in no small part accomplished through my work with others: Through disclosure to clients and peers, I am repeatedly internalizing the empowerment that occurs for me as I reframe and embody my atypical sexual identities, thereby reclaiming my identity and transcending oppression by the dominant culture.

Which brings me to Freire's (2005) concept of *conscientização*, or conscientization, an ability I discovered I had in my late 20s when I escaped from a dangerous episode of internal projective identification, followed by a period of introspection and reflective processing. Typically, projective identification is a term used to describe a sort of countertransference that can happen when a client projects painful aspects of themselves onto the therapist, and the therapist runs the risk of assuming those aspects (Agass, 2002). In my case, I had internalized my mother's death, and unconsciously projected that experience onto my current circumstances, then (as luck would have it) escaped her fate. Until that point, I had not realized that I had been trying to fill the hole in me left by the loss of my mother by assuming her identity – that I had been reliving her life and thereby seeking to relive her death by gunshot by finding a partner with a gun, to see if I could survive, to see if she could have survived. I had never engaged in therapy before then, but the authentic me that was trapped inside the living dead me made a decision to do so, not so coincidentally only weeks before the gun was pointed at me. In the very moment that a gun was pointed at me, I found the inner strength and resilience that had always been there, which I intentionally accessed for the first time as an individual conscious of my own identity. When I came back into myself, I was able to speak clearly and with strength, and was fortunate that the change in me was witnessed by and had an effect on the person holding the gun, resulting in my survival. Since then, conscientization has been instrumental in feeding my resilience, and was reinforced in my training to be a therapist, and even more so in my practice as a sex therapist.

Conscientization is a work in progress, so when I began studying intimate partner violence (IPV) during the same time period as I was learning about participatory action research (PAR) about five years ago, an alarming cacophony of feelings resurfaced that I thought I had long left behind.

I leaned into and faced my feelings. In my trainings to be a clinical social worker and clinical sexologist, I was taught to carefully consider self-reflectivity, self-disclosure – in terms of when it is valuable and when it is self-serving, and the importance of engaging with someone in a way that they can tolerate given their current state of mind and environmental context. When I look back to the inception of this project – which evolved into a collaborative investigation into the occurrence of IPV in the kink/BDSM[3] community[4] – I can see that my understanding of the positive role that self-disclosure can play in the context of participatory action research converged with an unexpected realization that I could also meet myself "where I was" in terms of self-disclosure to myself and to others. I was given permission and charged by the PAR approach to collaborate as both leader and participant, prompting me to invite people in my community to embark on an investigation of shared experiences. It was clear that self-disclosure would be a helpful, clarifying, engaging, and necessary part of the PAR process: a loop of reflecting, observing, planning, acting, collaborating, and back around to reflecting, and so on.

Reflecting in the Dark

As was part of my process, it is important at this point to share about a hidden darkness within the kink community that has nothing to do with the stereotypical darkness ascribed to the community by outsiders: Abuse happens. There is a not-so-subtle distinction between the incorrectly presumed abusive nature of BDSM interactions by those who do not understand BDSM, and the actual cases of BDSM interactions that happen to be abusive, which are exceptions to the rule that BDSM relationships and interactions are consensual by definition (Pitagora, 2013). The distinction is consent, and nonconsensual transgressions can and do happen within consensual BDSM-oriented relationships. They happen not because of the nature of the relationship, but because the kink community is a microcosm of broader society (Pitagora, 2013), and, as in broader society, there are abusers. This phenomenon is analogous to Freire's (2005) description of "cultural invasion" (p. 133), in which oppressors use manipulation and isolation to invade the cultural context of a group (in this case the BDSM community) in order to impose their own distorted and corrupt worldview, thereby stifling the creativity and expression of the oppressed group. Isolation also happens to be a common tactic used by abusers to establish dominance and control over their partners, which is then often reinforced by physical and sexual aggression (Burgess et al., 1997; Enos, 1996; Rohrbaugh, 2006). This darkness often remains hidden because of the phenomenon I described earlier – we in the kink community (as is also the case in other marginalized communities) do not want to be reduced to the stereotypes assigned us, and this makes it all the more difficult to come forward about abuse that occurs in the kink community. This also makes it all the more important that we do.

My plan to reach out and begin interviewing people in the community about their experiences of intimate partner abuse within the context of a D/s relationship[5] was an action in itself (Herr & Anderson, 2005), both in my reaction to the change within myself that I was experiencing, and the resulting desire to connect with others in the community. In the act of posting a thread using social media asking for participants, I asserted the need for action and collective voices, and invited disclosure as a means to affect change. The process of communicating with the five people that answered my post became a new act of planning and reflection that further folded into research in action. I became hyper-conscious of the language I used in communication with them prior to the interviews, driven by hyper-consciousness of my positionality in the context of the research, as well as in the community.

My positionality in this context began when I joined the NYC kink community shortly after moving to New York in 2003, and this was the first time I ever felt part of a community that accepted my intersecting (kinky, queer, poly, gender nonconforming, sex worker) identities. This was a pivotal discovery; because of the way that I grew up, I always felt like an outsider. I have a very clear childhood memory of telling another child that my mother was dead, and that child not being able to accept it, telling me that I was lying, and that I must really hate her to make up such a lie. I did not make the mistake of disclosing that information to anyone again until many years later, and then with great caution. After discovering the resonance and power I found in sexual expression in my adolescence and early adulthood, I had the new realization that I was once again an outsider, with one foot in the mainstream due to social indoctrination, and the rest of me in the fringes of exploring gender and sexual identity. After feeling like an outsider among mainstream-oriented peers, I tried becoming a part of the LGBT community, and discovered that I was an outsider in that context as well. As a female-bodied person who found power in emphasizing a hyperfeminine aesthetic (which was important to my vocation and identity as a sex worker at the time), I did not fit into the role that was expected of me. In the LGBT community during the 1990s, those who presented as more feminine were expected to partner with those who presented as more masculine – I was surprised at the extent to which this nonmainstream community reflected mainstream ideals. After continuing to explore my sexuality and expand my understanding of gender expression, I had the great fortune of finding the kink community. For the first time in my life my preferences were not questioned, and I finally felt welcomed. I became an insider.

Though I initially approached this project feeling like an insider, it quickly became apparent that various power relations were at play, and that regardless of my desire to collaborate as a peer within the community, power relations would have an effect on the way our[6] research would unfold (Herr & Anderson, 2005). Even in creating the initial post, I was reminded of my various positions within the community, which was reiterated with every conversation. I vacillated between feeling like an insider and an outsider in terms of this project and how it relates to my community. For better or worse, there tends to be an inherently hierarchical positionality within the kink community, and I hold a level of informal power within the community by virtue of my dominant BDSM-orientation. I am an insider and a peer within the community, but there is sometimes an unspoken protocol within the community to treat those who identify as dominant with deference. This phenomenon occurs all too often, though the dominant power role is meant to be confined within the context of encounters with one's intimate partners. I am an outsider in terms of being a dominant, female-bodied individual, which is a minority in every community, though it is not stigmatized in the kink community. I am both an insider and an outsider among those who have experienced IPV in the context of D/s relationships, in that I personally experienced IPV, not only in childhood but as an adult while in a dominant role, whereas my interviewees had all experienced it while in a submissive role. Finally, I am an outsider in the BDSM community in terms of my role in this project as an academic and researcher initiating this project.

I felt conscious of my dominant role within the community, and did not want this to affect the way my interviewees would relate to me or tell their stories. This was particularly highlighted when one individual contacted me from another state saying that he wanted to participate in the project. We arranged a time to talk and I had given him my phone number, and almost immediately he began texting me how devastated he was from his experiences of abuse. I was conflicted, instinctually wanting to support him, but not wanting to get involved in a way that seemed as though I was offering therapeutic services, so I made that clear. Then he began to pursue me, telling me he wanted to submit to me, so I made it clear that this also would not be possible, it was not what I was looking for or offering. I was uncomfortable, and I told him as diplomatically and gently as I could that I did not think it was a good idea for us to do the interview. He then told me that he sometimes wanted to die because of his experiences and inability to find a dominant partner that would not abuse him. I felt concern for him, and searched for local suicide hotlines based on his area code, and communicated with him that I could not directly help him, but that he could call these numbers and they would talk to him, and could provide more resources for him. He responded with vitriol, calling me a battery of offensive names, so I blocked his phone number. I was upset. I called a close friend and academic peer to tell her about the conversation and my reaction, and she validated and comforted me. She suggested that I call the suicide hotline to ask whether this was a case where mandatory reporting of suicidal ideation would call for reporting his phone number. They confirmed that I had done all I could do given the circumstances, that this was not an appropriate case for mandatory reporting, and that he had the proper information and he needed to take action. I took a deep breath and took a break from thinking about the project for two weeks until my next scheduled interviews.

The Evolution of Experiential Methodology

While a harrowing experience, dealing with that potential participant was valuable. It informed my thought process around how to communicate with the rest of my interviewees, keeping in mind my different degrees of positionality, and my responsibility to the project, (i.e., to communicate as transparently as possible while keeping them safe, and keeping myself safe). Fortunately, the rest of the participants joined the project mirroring the intention and motivation I had presented; they wanted to add their voices in support of those who had similar experiences but felt isolated and silenced. In an effort to help them feel safe, as well as to protect myself, I asked them each to sign a consent form, which stated that their identifying information provided would be kept confidential, and that interviewees would be assigned a pseudonym to protect their anonymity. The consent form also noted the possibility that the interview might be triggering, in which case I would refer them to appropriate resources as needed. It informed them that they had the right to end their participation at any time with no negative consequences. Each participant signed and emailed the form back to me.

Another great challenge in this process has been pushing against my training as a researcher, which emphasizes the idea that self-disclosure has no place in research. I have been aware of this internal conflict, however, and I believe I addressed this issue thoughtfully in an effort to offer what information I could about myself to the extent that it would make it clear that I felt on equal ground as the other participants. Having said that, I will also admit that I was not able to be as open as I expected my collaborators to be. In reaching out to people in the community to share stories of trauma and abuse, I chose not to disclose everything to everyone. During periods of introspection between interviews, I would reflect on my experience and this tendency, and realized that I was reacting to each individual in the way that I talk to therapy clients about how they share themselves differently with different people depending on where their boundaries fall with a particular person. Trusting my process, I decided to proceed with this intuitive way of disclosing information. To one participant, I explained vaguely that I had experienced childhood trauma. To another, I confided equally as vaguely that I had experienced emotional abuse by an intimate partner. To two others, I confided more specific details of both – that my mother had been shot and murdered by an estranged partner; that I had witnessed physical and verbal violence and was neglected while living with my father's parents, who as a result I can never refer to as grandparents; and that as an adult, in the context of my first D/s relationship, I was emotionally and verbally abused by my submissive partner over a period of three years.[7] At the outset of every conversation, I offered to answer any questions they had about me. While some wanted to know about my motivation and experience, others preferred to know as little as possible about me. I made conscious decisions during each interview to disclose what I felt comfortable disclosing to a given person, and that I disclosed what seemed necessary to best facilitate the interaction.

I had conducted semistructured interviews in the past, involving a list of open-ended questions that I would stray from depending on the organic flow of the conversation. This time I made a decision to avoid constructing any specific content-related questions other than asking them to tell whatever they were comfortable telling about an experience of IPV they had within the context of a D/s relationship. After answering any questions they had about me, I would then ask them demographic questions (i.e., age range, gender identification, sexual and BDSM-orientations, education level, occupation, etc.), and reiterate that they could be as anonymous as they chose to be. Sharing about my journey in this field and then allowing for others to offer basic information about themselves served as a way to become comfortable with one another. In each conversation, though, there was a pause between initial banter and the telling of their stories. Each time this happened, I told them they could tell me whatever they wanted however they wanted, and to say whatever came to mind. If they needed additional prompting, I would ask them how they met the partner that had abused them, how long they were with that partner, and to describe an example of abuse. Once they found an entry into their stories, I remained silent for the most part. Near the end of every conversation, I made a point to ask them what sort of support they had now, and how they were coping, in an effort to bring the conversation to a close emphasizing their strengths and resilience. It was difficult to end these conversations, given that I typically continue in an ongoing therapeutic support role to those who have become vulnerable while disclosing the intimate details of their life to me. With some, I talked about whether or not they would prefer to be involved in the writing of the paper, (i.e., commenting on drafts, and how we might be involved down the road). One of the participants made it clear that it was unlikely that they would be available for further input. Two of them asked to review drafts, and one of them was particularly engaged and action-oriented, and wanted to have conversations in the future about the project. This process truly felt like an experiential methodology, in that it was a productive balance of my own personal and our collective behaviors, ideas, and experiences (Fals-Borda, 1991).

During the interviews, I typed up as much of what they said verbatim as possible, sometimes asking them to repeat what they had said in order to quote them accurately, though much of it was shorthand. I began the project by asking how people felt about my recording the interviews, which I have done with in-person interviews in the past. Because my first two interviewees felt uncomfortable with the idea, I stopped asking, both to continue recording the information in a consistent way, as well as to avoid making further interviewees uncomfortable with this question. As was my practice between interviews, I reflected and recognized a similarity I have felt when doing remote sessions on the phone with therapy clients – while there is a loss of nonverbal communication when not in person, disinhibition sometimes occurs due to the additional space offered by this separation. I understood how a recording of the conversation might counteract the interviewees' ability to speak as freely.

From the first interview, themes started surfacing. From the second interview, Freire's (2005) concept of generative themes manifested. I reread my transcriptions to confirm what I had noticed was emerging from the conversations, highlighting similarities and differences among their experiences. I had to take another break because while the process of interviewing and processing my interview notes was a satisfying and edifying process, it was also an emotionally arduous and heartbreaking one. When I came back to the project a week or so later, I resolved to compare the themes that were generated by my collaborators with what existed, or did not exist as the case sometimes was, in academic literature. As mentioned earlier, I was conflicted about this process, and wanted to avoid turning my PAR project into an esoteric literature review, out of touch with the community. However, after giving myself time to process my reflections, I took solace in Fals-Borda's (1991) positing that combining academic literature with the knowledge generated from my interviews might result in a "scientific knowledge of a revolutionary nature" (p. 4). I dove into the literature using the themes that had emerged from our conversations, and found that themes in the literature merged and meshed with each person's story in a particular way. I sat down to write again, invigorated by the process.

Data Informs Literature Informs Data

If it has not yet been made clear, the voices of the peers I interviewed combine with those of my community and my own encounters to annunciate the profound effect the conspiratorial culture of silence has had on our experience(s). Paulo Freire (2005) describes "the culture of silence" (p. 12) as resulting from oppressed individuals having been trapped in situations in which they were unable to be critically aware of what was happening to them and therefore unable to respond. This imposition of silence dovetails with the isolation and a lack of transparent communication that are characteristic of systemic oppression in the macro, and of IPV on the micro; the "conspiracy of silence" has been described as a common phenomenon in cases of IPV, as well as childhood physical and sexual abuse, and incest (Boehm & Itzhaky, 2004; Butler, 1985; DiLillo, 2001; McClennen, 2005; Shea, Mahoney, & Lacey, 1997; Tigert, 2001).

I will not include here the detailed findings that were published in *Sexual and Relationship Therapy* (Pitagora, 2016), but the questions that emerged from the research my collaborators and I engaged in bear repeating: What supports and resources are needed to prevent people in the community from being oppressed and abused? What supports and resources are needed to support those in the community who have already been oppressed and abused? There is much work to be done towards creating an ideal support system for survivors of IPV in D/s relationships. There is a need for training among medical and mental health professionals on how to recognize their own biases, and understand the difference between normative expressions of BDSM and IPV. There is a need to educate the general population in this way as well, so that the difference between abuse and BDSM becomes clear and easier to recognize for those in both mainstream and BDSM communities. There is a need to employ and train law enforcement that is less aligned with patriarchal and overly moralistic attitudes and beliefs, and more empathetic and culturally competent. Finally, there is a need within the BDSM community to promote a clear understanding of the scaffolding of consent: 1. Negotiation of common interests; 2. Agreement on both a verbal and nonverbal safeword; 3. A commitment to continually attain explicit, rescindable consent; and 4. The incorporation of aftercare, not only as a means of returning to a cognitive and emotional baseline, but as a means for ensuring all parties involved were satisfied with the experience and understood it in roughly the same way.

Leadership and People, Cocreators and Re-creators of Knowledge

> Teachers and students (leadership and people), co-intent on reality, are both Subjects, not only in the task of unveiling that reality, and thereby coming to know it critically, but in the task of re-creating that knowledge. As they attain this knowledge of reality through common reflection and action, they discover themselves as its permanent re-creators.
>
> (Freire, 2005, p. 69)

After sitting down to synthesize my collaborators' accounts of abuse, weaving the academic literature with the knowledge that surfaced during our discussions, I could not help but think more about the way the literature and history related to their stories, and as Freire (2005) put it, what sort of cultural action, synthesis, and/or revolution might be enacted to address the needs of people in the BDSM community. It is clear that more information must be generated and disseminated. Modern society has come far in the last several decades in progressing towards tolerance and acceptance of individuals who may not look or act the way the statistical majority does, but human consciousness remains overwhelmingly confined by rigid heteronormative definitions of sexual orientation and gender identification, which reinforces binary stereotypes and the pathologization of individuals who identify outside of the mainstream. The enduring stigma around engaging in BDSM activities impedes the recognition and acceptance of normative D/s relationships, nullifying a context in which intimate partner violence can be recognized. In other words, when mainstream society ignores the fact that BDSM can be a healthy form of sexual expression, and conflates it with intimate partner violence, it is difficult if not impossible for someone experiencing abuse within the context of a D/s relationship to seek and receive support from healthcare providers, law enforcement, society at large, and even among peers.

The key to moving forward in unmuting the voices of those who have experienced IPV in a D/s relationship, and preventing future instances of abuse, lies in transparent and explicit communication and the raising of silenced voices. I presented the results of my research and writing to my collaborators in an effort to obtain processual consent, not only for the purpose of member checking to confirm the accuracy of my writing, but to engage them in the creation of next steps in the process (Herr & Anderson, 2005). I received one response from a collaborator who gave no feedback other than to offer compliments and ask permission to share it with a friend. I realize this in itself is a form of action, and a step in the direction of further research and participation.

I did not hear back from the others, however, bringing me to a new point of critical reflection. I was aware that they may have had difficulty relating to the subject matter in the way that I presented it, that they may have found it triggering, or that they may have felt they did what they set out to do, and were done doing it. Part of me wanted to reach out to each of them again to ask whether they would like to be further involved, what suggestions or feedback they might have, how they see the project progressing, what other action, research, and participation might be needed. My training told me, however, that their boundaries must be respected, that their silence may well be a form of self-protection, and that might be the work that they need to do for themselves right now. I did not want to run the risk of retraumatizing anyone by appearing oppressive in my diligence to pursue their participation. At the same time, I also did not want to become once again mired in the conspiratorial culture of silence. Freire (2005) addressed this plight by saying:

> A critical analysis of reality may, however, reveal that a particular form of action is impossible or inappropriate at the present time.

Those who through reflection perceive the infeasibility or inappropri-
ateness of one or another form of action (which should accordingly
be postponed or substituted) cannot thereby be accused of inaction.
Critical reflection is also action.

(p. 109)

Freire (2001) makes it clear that critical reflection is not to be confused with "fatalistic quietude" (p. 92), in which ethical transgressions
are exempted from responsibility by avoiding the type of actions that
follow critical reflection, namely the dissemination of information from
collective voices.

Conclusion

Many BDSM-oriented people, by virtue of a lifestyle that embraces
pleasure-seeking in atypical ways and through influence of the kink community, tend to be aware of and in the process of strengthening their skills
around transparency, communication, negotiation, conflict resolution, and
self-awareness (Pitagora, 2016; Taormino, 2008). Williams (2006) suggests that transparent communication and self-awareness around desires
facilitates the inclusiveness and acceptance of atypical sexual expressions
within the kink community. In turn, positive reflected appraisals and validation from peers and community may result in higher levels of sexual
pride than may be found in non-BDSM-oriented people (Pitagora, 2019).
Having said that, while some research indicates there are positive effects
of affiliation with the kink community that might also increase sexual
pride (Damm, Dentato, & Busch, 2017), the positive effects might not
be enough to mitigate sexual shame caused by discrimination and stigma
(Pitagora, 2019). This internalized shame, as reflected in my own and in
my peers' voiced experiences, can result in self-censorship, silence within
the community, and a barrier to knowledge and growth.

As noted previously, the kink community is a cross section of larger
society, and includes a diverse range of demographics, including various
age groups, ethnicities, occupations, genders, and sexual identities (Connolly, 2006; Damm et al., 2017; Pitagora, 2013; Weinberg, Williams, &
Moser, 1984). BDSM-oriented individuals with lower socioeconomic status and racial and ethnic minorities continue to be poorly represented in
research, which might relate to the need to manage multiple stigmatized
identities, and a lack of comfort in or connectedness to the kink community due to pervasive institutional classism and racism that limits the
access to community for those with less power or agency (Damm et al.,
2017; Sheff & Hammers, 2011). Research on same-sex IPV suggests
that IPV occurs at statistically similar rates in heterosexual and same-
sex relationships, as well as in other demographic groups including race/
ethnicity, class, education level, religion, and location[8] (Brown & Herman, 2015; Enos, 1996; Johnson, 2016; Rohrbaugh, 2006). Institutional

heterosexism affects all IPV survivors, mainstream or nonmainstream, regardless of gender identity, sexual orientation, or BDSM-orientation. There is, however, an intersectionality of discrimination that can exponentially affect BDSM-oriented survivors of IPV. To begin with, there is a reinforcing relationship between socially sanctioned gender roles and institutional sexism (Joseph, Pitagora, Tworecke, & Roberts, 2013). This is an issue for *all* people – regardless of gender identity, race, ethnicity, socioeconomic status, ability, immigration status, et cetera – all individuals who are subjected to IPV suffer neglect and mistreatment at the hands of patriarchal and misogynistic institutions. Likewise, when a nonmainstream sexual orientation (in this case, BDSM orientation) is added to the mix, neglect and mistreatment by the same institutions intensify.

The positionality of leaders relates to the cocreation of knowledge in the intersection of identities shared by leaders and those among them. Hopkins notes, in the author's (2007) article on negotiating ethics in practice, that this approach toward cocreating knowledge incorporates the understanding that leadership positionalities are to be reconsidered depending on context, and depending on how leaders' identities interact with peers' positionalities and identities. This approach is in contrast to the traditional methods of dictatorial hegemonic leadership, and instead relies on transparent communication of the cocreation process (Hopkins, 2007).

The type of leadership I described earlier emphasizes the importance of collective voices. Therefore, in these closing comments, the voices of other leaders in the NYC kink community (as identified by peers in the NYC kink community) who responded to my asking them what being a leader in the kink community means to them. This question was asked with no context other than my disclosure that I was working on a writing project related to sexuality leadership, community engagement, and social empowerment. I also relayed that their identities would be kept anonymous, in keeping with the same promise made to my interviewees as noted earlier. I was not surprised, though I am humbled and pleased, to report that their responses all echoed the sentiment that ethical leaders "are humble, concerned for the greater good, strive for fairness, take responsibility and show respect for each individual" (Mihelič, Lipičnik, & Tekavčič, 2010). As one leader said:

> Taking a leadership role in the kink community involves balancing an ongoing, endless devotion of energy, effort, and time to checking one's own privilege, reevaluating motivations and goals, and examining own's own desires (and the ethical implications of pursing them, under what circumstances and with whom) with a commitment to craft magical spaces (and magic circles), bring people together (both frequent, regular people and new faces), and provide opportunities for people to fulfill their own desires and get excited about new possibilities.

Another leader's humility and community pride were evident in the desire to incorporate a through line of history and tradition in art, as a means of connection to contemporaries, as well as to those who raised their voices through and despite many decades of oppression:

> Whether in the form of writing, gathering events, or creating media, my leadership is grounded in gratitude and service to the kink community. These are the people who have carved out a rich history of leather lifestyle and traditions that fuel and heal every aspect of my identity, these are the people I feel accountable to in stories, art, and activism.

Along with a nod to those who came before us, change is not only inevitable but desired in the work we do as leaders, and in ourselves as we do the work (Wadsworth, 1998). As another leader said:

> You must do work to use your platform to lift others up and uncenter yourself to showcase others. You also find that the same organization and drive that make you the planner and negotiated also put you in the position to be suited to the taking responsibility for helping to mend the deficits and harm in your community. And you feel bound (or should) to because of your privilege, access, etc. Finding a balance between creation and leadership – and holding space for – defending space for both in my heart and my calendar is a struggle [but] being a leader has changed my work and made me a better person.

In synthesis, I have learned that to be a leader in a community whose commonalities relate to atypical sexualities, I have had to learn to *tolerate vulnerability*, fortified by an understanding of how my identities intersect with my peers and with our community's historical roots, and with "emic" love – a love for those in our community that exists and persists in spite of and in contrast to those who do not understand us. In this way, my ongoing goal is to embody "Freirean leadership" (see Freire, 1993) through open disclosure and the cocreation of ideas in an attempt to engage with oppressive forces through the raising of our voices.

Process Questions and Considerations

1. What is the difference between BDSM and intimate partner violence?
2. Who is most vulnerable to intimate partner violence within the context of a BDSM-oriented relationship?

3. What might make it difficult for clients/students to talk about engaging in BDSM and/or experiencing intimate partner violence in their relationships?
4. How might a clinician/teacher facilitate open discussions about BDSM and/or abuse in their clients'/students' relationships?
5. In your profession, how might disclosure be seen as a leadership trait?
6. How would you determine whether your disclosure is in service of the client/student, or in service to countertransference/your own need to disclose for your own reasons?

Notes

1. The original quote is "I cannot be a *teacher* [emphasis added] if I do not perceive with ever greater clarity that my practice demands of me a definition about where I stand" (Freire, 2001, p. 93); I replaced "teacher" with "leader," emulating Freire's synonymous use of "teachers" and "leadership" (e.g., Freire, 2005, p. 69).
2. I use the term *play partner* to refer to people with whom I have casual or committed, short- or long-term sexual relationships, and *play* to refer to any type of sex, including BDSM.
3. The term *kink* is used throughout this chapter as synonymous with BDSM (i.e., bondage and domination/dominance and submission/sadism and masochism or sadomasochism), in reference to the vast multitude of activities that fall under the umbrella of BDSM, including, but not limited to, power exchange, the administration and receiving of pain, physical restriction, psychological humiliation, and the incorporation of fetishism, voyeurism, exhibitionism, and role play scenarios (Alison, Santtila, Sandnabba, & Nordling, 2001; Barker, 2013; Kleinplatz & Diamond, 2014; Moser & Kleinplatz, 2007; Sandnabba, Santtila, Alison, & Nordling, 2002; Sheff & Hammers, 2011; Weinberg et al., 1984; van Anders, 2015).
4. For the purposes of this chapter, I am using *kink community* to refer to the group of people who engage in BDSM, with the concession that not everyone who engages in BDSM also engages in the kink community or feels affiliated with or connected to the subculture.
5. A D/s relationship is one based on a consensual dominant/submissive power dynamic. Words like "Dominance" and "submission" are often intentionally capitalized or not capitalized by members of the BDSM community in order to emphasize their authoritative or diminutive role within a given power dynamic (Moser & Kleinplatz, 2007).
6. When I engage in participatory action research I consider the work to be "ours" instead of "mine." I used this type of language in working with people on this project to mitigate the power dynamic typically inherent between researcher and research subjects.
7. As noted in the journal article that resulted from this research: "Given that the issue of IPV in heterosexual relationships has traditionally been assumed solely to affect heterosexual women, and that stereotypical gender roles promote the assumption that the submissive partner is always female, a similar assumption follows that IPV in D/s relationships would be directed toward the

submissive partner. However, research shows that it is possible for any gender to abuse any other gender (Ard & Makadon, 2011; Enos, 1996; Rohrbaugh, 2006), and that there can be a discordance between traditional gender and power roles within D/s relationships (McClintock, 1993); therefore, it is no less plausible that dominant partners can be abused by submissive partners, regardless of gender" (Pitagora, 2015, p. 10).

8. There was, however, a statistically significantly higher rate of IPV among bisexual-identified people as compared to other sexual orientations reported in the 2010 National Intimate Partner and Sexual Violence Survey, the most recent survey to date looking at IPV prevalence by sexual orientation (as cited in Brown & Herman, 2015). There was also a statistically significantly higher rate of IPV among transgender people as compared to cisgender people reported in a 2016 study on IPV among LGBT people (Langenderfer-Magruder, Whitfield, Walls, Kattari, & Ramos, 2016). There are no consistent reports of IPV prevalence among immigrants (Gonçalves & Matos, 2016). Johnson (2016) noted that when the social disintegration factors of income, education, and never married status are controlled for, IPV among racial and ethnic groups are not statistically significantly different. While there is no research on prevalence of IPV among BDSM-oriented people, and therefore no research comparing IPV among BDSM-oriented people with other groups, it stands to reason that these groups might be affected similarly by the exponential intersectionality of discrimination.

References

Agass, D. (2002). Countertransference, supervision and the reflection process. *Journal of Social Work Practice*, 16(2), 125–133. Doi:10.1080/02650530 22000033694

Alison, L., Santtila, P., Sandnabba, K. N., & Nordling, N. (2001). Sadomasochistically oriented behavior: Diversity in practice and meaning. *Archives of Sexual Behavior*, 30(1), 1–12. Doi:10.1023/A:1026438422383

Ard, K. L., & Makadon, H. J. (2011). Addressing intimate partner violence in lesbian, gay, bisexual, and transgender patients. *Journal of General Internal Medicine*, 26(8), 630–633. Retrieved from www.ncbi.nlm.nih.gov/pmc/articles/PMC3138983/pdf/116062011_Article_1697.pdf

Barker, M. (2013). *Rewriting the rules: An integrative guide to love, sex and relationships*. New York, NY: Routledge.

Boehm, A., & Itzhaky, H. (2004). The social marketing approach: A way to increase reporting and treatment of sexual assault. *Child Abuse & Neglect*, 28, 253–265.

Brown, T. N. T., & Herman, J. L. (2015). *Violence and sexual abuse among LGBT people: A review of existing research*. Los Angeles, CA: The Williams Institute, UCLA School of Law. Retrieved from https://williamsinstitute.law.ucla.edu/wp-content/uploads/Intimate-Partner-Violence-and-Sexual-Abuse-among-LGBT-People.pdf

Burgess, A. W., Baker, T., Greening, D., Hartman, C. R., Burgess, A. G., . . . & Halloran, R. (1997). Stalking behaviors within domestic violence. *Journal of Family Violence*, 12(4), 389–403.

Butler, S. (1985). *The conspiracy of silence: The trauma of incest*. Volcano, CA: Volcano Press, Inc.

Carvalho, A. F., Lewis, R. J., Derlega, V. J., Winstead, B. A., & Viggiano, C. (2011). Internalized sexual minority stressors and same-sex intimate partner violence. *Journal of Family Violence, 26*(7), 501–509. Doi:10.1007/s10896-011-9384-2

Connolly, P. H. (2006). Psychological functioning of bondage/domination/sado masochism (BDSM) practitioners. *Journal of Psychology & Human Sexuality, 18*(1), 79–120. Doi:10.1300/J056v18n01_05

Damm, C., Dentato, M. P., & Busch, N. (2017). Unravelling intersecting identities: Understanding the lives of people who practice BDSM. *Psychology & Sexuality, 9*(1), 21–37. Doi:10.1080/19419899.2017.1410854

DiLillo, D. (2001). Interpersonal functioning among women reporting a history of childhood sexual abuse: Empirical findings and methodological issues. *Clinical Psychology Review, 21*(4), 553–576.

Enos, V. P. (1996). Prosecuting battered mothers: State laws' failure to protect battered women and abused children. *Harvard Women's Law Journal, 19*, 229–268.

Fals-Borda, O. (1991). Some basic ingredients. In O. Fals-Borda & M. A. Rahman (Eds.), *Action and knowledge: Breaking the monopoly with participatory action-research* (pp. 121–131). New York: The Apex Press.

Freire, P. (1993). *Pedagogy of the city*. New York, NY: Continuum International Publishing Group.

Freire, P. (2001). *Pedagogy of freedom: Ethics, democracy, and civic courage (Critical perspectives series: A book series dedicated to Paulo Freire)*. Lanham, Maryland: Rowman & Littlefield Publishers, Inc.

Freire, P. (2005). *Pedagogy of the oppressed*. New York, NY: Continuum International Publishing Group.

Gonçalves, M., & Matos, M. (2016). Prevalence of violence against immigrant women: A systematic review of the literature. *Journal of Family Violence, 31*(6), 697–710. Doi:10.1007/s10896-016-9820-4

Herr, K., & Anderson, G. L. (2005). *The action research dissertation: A guide for students and faculty*. Thousand Oaks, CA: Sage Publications, Inc.

Hopkins, P. E. (2007). Positionalities and knowledge: Negotiating ethics in practice. *ACME: An International E-Journal for Critical Geographies, 6*(3), 386–394. Retrieved from www.acme-journal.org/index.php/acme/article/view/787

Johnson, J. (2016). *Characteristics of intimate partner violence: Implications for prevalence rates* (Theses & Dissertations Center). Retrieved from OhioLINK Electronic.

Joseph, J. A., Pitagora, D., Tworecke, A., & Roberts, K. E. (2013). Peering into gaps in the diagnostic and statistical manual of mental disorders: Student perspectives on gender and informing education. *Society for International Education Journal: Engaging with Difference, Gender and Sexuality in Education, 7*(1), 104–127.

Kleinplatz, P., & Diamond, L. (2014). Sexual diversity. In D. L. Tolman & L. M. Diamond (Eds.), *APA handbook of sexuality and psychology: Vol. 1, person-based approaches* (pp. 245–267). Washington, DC, US: American Psychological Association. Doi:10.1037/14193-009

Langenderfer-Magruder, L., Whitfield, D. L., Walls, N. E., Kattari, S. K., & Ramos, D. (2016). Experiences of intimate partner violence and subsequent police reporting among lesbian, gay, bisexual, transgender, and queer adults in

Colorado: Comparing rates of cisgender and transgender victimization. *Journal of Interpersonal Violence, 31*(5), 855–871. Doi:10.1177/0886260514556767

Marino, D. (1998). Re-Framing: Hegemony and adult education practices. *Wild garden: Art, education, and the culture of resistance* (pp. 103–118). Toronto, ON: Between the Lines. Retrieved from https://btlbooks.com/book/wild-garden

McClennen, J. C. (2005). Domestic violence between same-gender partners: Recent findings and future research. *Journal of Interpersonal Violence, 20*(2), 149–154. Doi:10.1177/0886260504268762

McClintock, A. (1993). Maid to order: Commercial fetishism and gender power. *Social Text, 37*, 87–116. Doi:10.2307/466262

Mihelič, K. K., Lipičnik, B., & Tekavčič, M. (2010). Ethical leadership. *International Journal of Management & Information Systems, 14*(5), 31–42.

Moser, C., & Kleinplatz, P. J. (2007). Themes of SM expression. In D. Langdridge & M. Barker (Eds.), *Safe, sane, and consensual: Contemporary perspectives on sadomasochism* (pp. 35–54). Buffalo, NY: Prometheus Books.

Pitagora, D. (2013). Consent vs. coercion: BDSM interactions highlight a fine but immutable line. *New School Psychology Bulletin, 10*(1), 27–36.

Pitagora, D. (2015). Intimate partner violence in sadomasochistic relationships. *Sexual and Relationship Therapy, 31*(1), 95–108. Doi:10.1080/14681994.2015.1102219

Pitagora, D. (2016). The BDSM-poly confluence: Relationship intersectionality in marginalized communities. *Sexual and Relationship Therapy, 31*(3), 391–405. Doi:10.1080/14681994.2016.1156081

Pitagora, D. (2019). *The role of BDSM orientation on heteronormativity and shame in anoreceptive heterosexual males* (Doctoral dissertation). Chester, PA: Widener University.

Rohrbaugh, J. B. (2006). Domestic violence in same-gender relationships. *Family Court Review, 44*(2), 287–299.

SAMHSA. (2014). Tip 57. *A Treatment Improvement protocol: Trauma-Informed care in behavioral health services*. Retrieved from http://store.samhsa.gov/shin/content/SMA14-4816/SMA14-4816.pdf

Sandnabba, K. N., Santtila, P., Alison, L., & Nordling, N. (2002). Demographics, sexual behavior, family background and abuse experiences of practitioners of sadomasochistic sex: A review of recent research. *Sexual and Relationship Therapy, 17*, 39–55.

Shea, C. A., Mahoney, M., & Lacey, J. M. (1997). Breaking through the barriers of domestic violence intervention. *The American Journal of Nursing, 97*(6), 26–34.

Sheff, E., & Hammers, C. (2011). The privilege of perversities: Race, class, and education among polyamorists and kinksters. *Psychology & Sexuality, 2*, 198–223. Doi:10.1080/ 19419899.2010.537674

Singer, K. (2010). *Evicting the perpetrator: A male survivor's guide for recovery from childhood sexual abuse*. Holyoke, MA: NEARI Press.

Stoudt, B. G. (2009). The role of language & discourse in the investigation of privilege: Using participatory action research to discuss theory, develop methodology, & interrupt power. *The Urban Review, 41*(1), 7–28. Doi: 10.1007/s11256-008-0093-y

Taormino, T. A. (2008). *Opening up: A guide to creating and sustaining open relationships* (Kindle Edition). Berkeley, CA: Cleis Press.

Tigert, L. M. (2001). The power of shame. *Women & Therapy, 23*(3), 73–85. Doi:10.1300/J015v23n03_06

van Anders, S. M. (2015). Beyond sexual orientation: Integrating gender/sex and diverse sexualities via sexual configurations theory. *Archives of Sexual Behavior, 4*, 1–37. Doi:10.1007/s10508-015-0490-8

van der Kolk, B. (2014). *The body keeps the score: Brain, mind, and body in the healing of trauma.* New York, NY: Penguin Random House LLC.

Wadsworth, Y. (1998). What is participatory action research. *Action Research International.* Retrieved from www.aral.com.au/ari/p-ywadsworth98.html

Weinberg, M., Williams, C., & Moser, C. (1984). The social constituents of sadomasochism. *Social Problems, 31*, 379–389. Retrieved from www.jstor.org/stable/800385

Williams, D. J. (2006). "Different (Painful¡) Strokes for different folks: A general overview of Sexual Sadomasochism (SM) and its diversity." *Sexual Addiction & Compulsivity, The Journal of Treatment & Prevention. 13*(4), 333–346.

14 A New Renaissance

Podcasting as a Tool to Provide a Nuanced Voice to the Black Gay Male Experience

Patrick Grant

Focusing on sexuality leadership and technology, this chapter will iden-tify ways media has historically portrayed Black gay men and how these presentations have shaped general social perceptions of Black gay men. Current podcast media led by Black gay men will then be reviewed to highlight the changes that occur when Black gay men reclaim, repackage, and redistribute their narratives. Throughout this chapter, the labels of gay, queer, and same gender loving/attracted will be used interchangeably as a means of acknowledging the various sexual and romantic identities of Black men that do not align with heterosexuality.

The Harlem Renaissance is considered to be one of the most notable Black and queer creative eras to exist. Some would also argue that artists during this period opened the doors, and created the cultural shifts, in the Black community that currently exist (Busby, 2018; Villarosa, 2017). Yet the works of James Baldwin, Langston Hughes, Alaine Locke, and the like did more than provide insight into the lived experiences of Black people. Their works and lives gave consumers glimpses into the experi-ences had by Black gay men – some of the most marginalized individuals in the United States and in Black social sphere (hooks, 2004; Snorton & ProQuest, 2014). Pieces such as *Giovanni's Room* and "To F.S." high-light the yearnings and desires of Black gay men; and depict the ways Black gay men interact with various environments.

Despite being cutting edge for the time, these works still maintained a sense of respectability that continues to hinder Black queer sexual liberation today (hooks, 2004; Schwarz, 2003; Stokes, 2003; Stone, 2002). While the queer protagonist in *Giovanni's Room* embarks on a journey to understand his sexuality, his journey is made difficult by his self-inflicted moral code, or code of respectability, which challenges his desires to live freely (Stokes, 2003). Similarly, Hughes' "To F.S." com-municates romantic longing for an assumed same gendered partner, yet the writer maintains a respectable stance by shrouding the identity of his love interest (Hughes, 1925). Many of the artists from the Harlem Renaissance – while curators of work that emphasized sexual and other freedoms – tempered their participation in these freedoms with obscurities that sustained semblances of respectability (Schwarz, 2003). Yet in 1926, the publication of *FIRE!!!* – and additional works of Richard Bruce Nugent – juxtaposed the respectability presented by many Black gay male artists at the time. An impact recognizable today, Nugent's "Smoke, Lilies, and Jade" (1926) expanded upon the narratives of Black queer male bodies in the Harlem Renaissance (Glick, 2003; Ross, 2013; Stokes, 2003). Rather than conforming to the standards of Black respectability – that have defined acceptable sexuality as hetero-centric, monogamous, and purposed for reproduction – Nugent told tales of Black gay life that disrupted the commonly held perceptions of acceptable sexuality and contrasted the mainstream stereotypes of what it meant to be Black, gay, and Black and gay.

As Nugent, and other artists, are acknowledged for their contributions during the Harlem Renaissance, one may suggest that a 21st-century renaissance has occurred – a renaissance that has created space for the nuanced voices of Black gay men to reemerge. The 2000s have introduced new media outlets, which include video blogs, streaming services, and podcasts; that have given Black gay men increased avenues to expand upon their stories and experiences (Newberry, 2016). These creative spheres have also aided in the challenging of decades-long monolithic and destructive stereotypes that have been placed upon Black gay men.

In comparing the various representations of Black gay men, this chapter pulls from scholarly and technological works to highlight how Black gay male–led podcasts confront negative stereotypes placed on Black gay men by mainstream society. The current chapter will focus on the ways that homo-negativity has targeted Black gay men by conflating Black homosexuality with the HIV/AIDS virus; presenting the down-low and down-low culture as inherently negative; and juxtaposing Black homosexuality against the ideal of Black normalcy through homophobic religious rhetoric. Ways in which Black gay men use podcasting to reclaim and redistribute their stories will then be highlighted to emphasize how this medium can be used to challenge stigma.

The information in the chapter in no way intends to communicate that all commonly accepted perceptions of Black gay men are negative; nor does this chapter intend to suggest that the narratives highlighted represent all the experiences of Black gay men. While the examples provided showcase the ways some Black gay male experiences contrast stereotypical tropes projected on this cohort by the majority culture, it is recognized that some of the interpersonal and environmental experiences had by some Black gay men closely align with the potentially negative narratives presented by mainstream outlets. Nevertheless, the information presented in the chapter does not intended to investigate how Black gay male experiences parallel common narratives. This chapter instead seeks to understand the trope challenging that occurs when Black gay men tell their own stories through podcasting.

Homo-negativity and HIV/AIDS Stigma

Sexual health status may be one of the most common tools society uses to evaluate Black gay men (Carrillo & Hoffman, 2016; Moseby, 2017; Raj & Bowleg, 2012; Quinn et al., 2017; Vaughan, Rosenberg, Shouse, & Sullivan, 2014). To understand social perceptions of Black gay men is to acknowledge that they are typically viewed under a lens that intersects Blackness and gayness with sexually risky behavior and the Human Immunodeficiency Virus and/or Acquired Immune Deficiency Syndrome (HIV/AIDS) (Carrillo & Hoffman, 2016; Quinn et al., 2017; Vaughan et al., 2014). Studies state that African Americans comprise 12% of the United States population, yet carry nearly 50% of the HIV/AIDS burden (Centers for Disease Control and Prevention, 2018). Among all African Americans diagnosed with HIV/AIDS in 2016, gay and bisexual Black men represented 58% of this cohort (Centers for Disease Control and Prevention, 2018). And while research continually works to manage rates of infection among Black gay men – and among Black people in general – studies reflect that rates of infection among Black queer men in 2018 have steadily increased (Snorton & ProQuest, 2014).

While statistically supported, this data have historically made Black people the face of HIV/AIDS. They are also statistics that have aided in positioning Black gay men as agents of destruction in the Black community – individuals who assist in the eradication of the Black family through dissemination of HIV/AIDS through avenues such as promiscuity and "down-low" engagement (Moseby, 2017). From these stereotypes have emerged a homo-negativity in the Black community that has led to an ostracizing of gay Black men from many Black spheres of social support (Ward, 2005).

Literature defines homo-negativity as stigma associated with homosexuality; and links Black gay homo-negativity, and the rejection of the Black gay man from centers of social support, with sexually risky behaviors that can lead to increased chance of contracting HIV/AIDS (Jeffries, Dodge, & Sandfort, 2008; Ward, 2005). The Black church – as it stands a pillar that has aided in the Civil Rights Movement, and acts as a source of hope for many Black individuals – has noted to teach and disseminate homo-negativity (Jeffries et al., 2008; Ward, 2005; Quinn & Gomez, 2016). Through its stance of homosexuality being both sinful and an abomination, literature identifies the Black church as a paramount curator and catalyst of homo-negativity that can influence Black gay male familial and social rejection; and can then lead to consequences such as Black queer male participation in sexually risky behaviors and negative sexual health outcome experiences (Smallwood, Spencer, Ingram, Thrasher, & Thompson-Robinson, 2016). The increasing rates of HIV/AIDS infection among Black gay men, which are disproportionate to the rates of infection experienced by their white, and other raced, counterparts further support this assertion (Centers for Disease Control and Prevention, 2018; Snorton, 2014). However, investigation the history of HIV/AIDS among Black same gender loving men may present the Black church's presence, or rhetoric, as insufficient in fully highlighting how homo-negativity impacts experiences of HIV/AIDS among Black gay men (Foster, Arnold, Rebchook, & Kegeles, 2011). Literature suggests that the mechanisms in which Black gay men are presented to the public by the scientific community may also contribute to homo-negativity existing in Black community; and may give insight into the ways Black gay men perceive, experience, and navigate the HIV/AIDS virus (Moseby, 2017).

Sociologist Kevin Moseby (2017) chronicles the history of HIV/AIDS and records how the virus has historically been racialized by the Centers for Disease Control (CDC). He highlights how HIV was first characterized as a flu-like disease that impacted gay men (regardless of race) in June of 1981. By March 1983, the report of those impacted by the virus spread to include individuals that fell into four distinct categories – men who had sex with men, intravenous drug users, those of Haitian nationality, and those with chronic diseases that required blood transfusion. Although HIV/AIDS was not identified as being disproportionately experienced by Blacks until 1993, the categorization of the virus among these four specified groups in 1983 set the tone for Black people to be the face of HIV/AIDS for years to come (Moseby, 2017). In addition, bio-politicized efforts to engage minorities in health research (as evidenced by the 1995 NIH Revitalization Act) incentivized health organizations view certain cohorts through a specific health narrative (Epstern, 2007; Moseby, 2017). And while these narratives have influenced health organizations' efforts to manage HIV/AIDS rates, the commonly accepted perception of HIV/AIDS being a homosexuality-linked virus has not changed. In identifying the Black community as the disproportionate carriers of the virus, the scientific community has consequently shifted the virus from being viewed as a predominantly homosexual infection, to now being perceived as a predominantly Black homosexual infection (Moseby, 2017). The presented case is further proliferated as Black gay men are perpetually studied in health research under the lens of HIV/AIDS, which sustains stigmatic connection between Black gay men and HIV/AIDS (Carrillo & Hoffman, 2016; Moseby, 2017; Raj & Bowleg, 2012; Quinn et al., 2017; Vaughan et al., 2014).

Literature that highlights the disproportionate levels at which Black men who have sex with men experience HIV/AIDS, although empirical, aids in the stigmatization of the Black gay identity; influences internal and external homo-negativity; and also may serve as a barrier to Black gay men engaging in sexual risk prevention (Jeffries et al., 2008; Ward, 2005). What stands additionally alarming is that while there exists a plethora of research on the ways in which Black gay men navigate HIV/AIDS, there seems to be a dearth on research that highlights the general lived experiences of Black gay men unrelated to HIV/AIDS. Little research presents Black gay men as a human – as people whose existences are not centered solely around a sexual health diagnosis. This deficit of study further highlights the historical othering of Black people and emphasizes scientific efforts made to separate Blackness from humanity (hooks, 2004, Snorton & ProQuest, 2014). In recognizing the scientific community's participation in influencing the homo-negativity, and poor health outcomes, experienced by Black gay men, specific questions arise. If homo-negativity is noted to contribute to poor health outcomes for gay Black men, why has effort rarely been given to study Black gay men through purviews of homo-positivity, resilience, positive relationship building, and social normalcy? Additionally, if the connection between Black gay male social perception and negative health outcomes has been identified by literature, what incentives and barriers exist for health organizations to restructure the ways in which Black gay life is examined?

Perceptions and Functions of the Down Low

Seemingly one of the most highly endorsed fears in the Black community is that of the down-low Black man – the Black man who presents as heterosexual (as evidenced by his adherence to hegemonic masculinity and romantic and sexual engagements with women) while simultaneously participating in secret same gender loving relationships (Han, 2015). Literature exists that presents the down-low Black man as the cause for the breakdown of the Black family, as well as the source of HIV/AIDS proliferation in the Black community (arguments that obstinately ignore systemic influences on these phenomena) (Moseby, 2017). Nevertheless, there lacks widespread assessment of how secret sexual interaction has come to exist in the Black community, as well as how such engagement functions for queer Black men.

In his 2014 investigative novel, *Nobody Has to Know*, C. Riley Snorton identifies the current down-low culture among Black men as a consequence of slavery-linked generational patterns of sexual repression in the Black community. Since their capturing and transportation to the Western world, Black people have been debased, stripped of dignity, and presented as property to be used for the white wealth accumulation and sustenance (hook, 2004; Snorton & ProQuest, 2014). Snorton suggests that in effort to further distort Black humanity, Black sexualities were made exotic, unnatural, and the objects of regulation (Battle & Bennet, 2005; hooks, 2004). This trend of othering Black sexuality can be found in recent works, such as the Moynihan Reports (United States. Dept. of

Labor. Office of Policy Planning and Research 1965) (drafted by former Assistant Secretary of Labor Patrick Moynihan), in which the author presents Black sexual liberation as a hindrance of Black progression.

Many have viewed Moynihan's report as a call for Black familial improvement after years of structural and systematic attacks on Black family life. Yet further investigation of Moynihan's writings communicates a contrasting message. Moynihan's call suggests that for the Black community to thrive, members should work toward a life reflective of the white middle class – a life characterized by patriarchal heterosexual partnerships, nonlabor-based employment, and advanced education (Battle & Bennett, 2005; Snorton & ProQuest, 2014). Yet Black lives in the 1960s juxtaposed this ideal, and were therefore presented by Moynihan as that of a lower caste (Snorton & ProQuest, 2014). Many women lived and thrived independently and many Black bodies explored their sexualities without regulation (hooks, 2004; Snorton & ProQuest, 2014). Nevertheless, Moynihan's presentation of rigid hetero-patriarchal Blackness as a means of success acquisition quickly gained traction; and it led many Black individuals to reject subcultural practices, which included the expression of same gender loving interactions (Battle & Bennet, 2005; hooks, 2004; Snorton & ProQuest, 2014). Continued demonizing of same gender loving practices arose with the advent of HIV, which was initially branded the Gay-Related Immune Deficiency (GRID) (Snorton & ProQuest, 2014).

If Black gay men had no reason to hide their sexual interests due to social stigma, they were soon influenced to hide their identities based on health-related stigma (McCune, 2008; Moseby, 2017; Snorton & ProQuest, 2014). Despite the cultural shifts that have ushered the societal acceptance of same gender loving relationships, and emergence of HIV prevention and management resources, the stigma associated with having a same gender loving identity still plagues the Black community (Battle & Bennet, 2005)). Religious spheres continue to demonize Black gay men, while utilizing their talents as institutional capitol (similar to the use of Black bodies by whites during slavery) (Jefferies, Dodge, & Sandfort, 2008; Ward 2005). The stigma and social ostracizing that targets Black men who possess same gender attractions provide no incentive for Black gay men to live their sexual identities openly. Whereas literature highlights that white men may have the opportunity to explore their homoerotic desires and maintain their heterosexual identities, Black men have been noted to be held to a standard where one incident of same gender sexual interaction could significantly impact their prospects of future heterosexual engagement (Han, 2015; Hunter, 2010; Snorton, 2014).

The stigma, and negative consequences, centered around Black male same gender sexual interaction can even be observed in pop culture media. The HBO show *Insecure* presents its audience with the character Molly, a heterosexual Black woman who lives in Los Angeles. Molly is an established lawyer, a member of a prominent Black sorority, and a hopeless romantic in search of love. In season one of *Insecure*, Molly finds herself involved with Jared, a Black man who presents as rugged and caring "alpha" male who meets Molly's partner expectations. As the two become acquainted, Molly tells Jared of a time she shared a sexual experience with a woman. This does not move Jared, who expresses that he has also had a same gender sexual encounter. In contrast to Jared's reaction is Molly's disgust and stigmatization of Jared's experience. The writers of this show, focused on communicating themes that reflect perceptions of Black masculinity in today's society, use this scene to highlight that Black sexuality – particularly Black male sexuality – has been siloed into a sphere of hegemony, hyper-masculinity, non-fluidity, and rigid heteronormative performance that leaves no room for homoeroticism. If a Black man experiences interest in homoerotic interaction, he is forced to investigate this interest in secret, lest he fall victim to stigmatization that may leave him socially stunted, ostracized, and isolated (hooks, 2004; McCune, 2008; Snorton & ProQuest, 2014). One might suggest that to actualize his most genuine identities, some Black homo-interested men must make the closet, or the down-low, their norm.

Literature suggests that despite being presented as a practice that aids in HIV/AIDS proliferation, the down-low may possess a positive function for Black men (McCune, 2008). The down low is noted to have reached peak notoriety when covered in 2004 by *The Oprah Winfrey Show*. By exemplifying how the down low has impacted the lives of several women, such as author Terry McMillan, this cultural phenomenon rapidly became a focus of concern and hysteria, particularly for Black women (Snorton & ProQuest, 2014). The down low also seemingly became a scapegoat and a means to explain rising rates of HIV/AIDS among Black women (another example of highlighting one aspect of Black viral pathology without accounting for other factors such as communal networks, the impact of drugs on the community, safe sexual knowledge and practice, etc.) (Adams, 2011; Moseby, 2017; Snorton & ProQuest, 2014). Nevertheless, the function the down low plays in Black male life, outside the scope of HIV/AIDS prevention and management, has not been extensively investigated; neither has the purpose of Black men's secret homoerotic sexual encounters been added to the dialog surrounding Black male sexuality.

In his investigation of how the down low exists in the frameworks of Black male life and Black masculinity, Dr. Jeffery McCune suggests that the down low provides social nuance to the Black male identity (2004; Battle & Bennett, 2005). Whereas mainstream outlets present the down low as a deceitful practice in which Black men fulfill deviant desires unbeknownst to their female partners, McCune suggests that the down low provides Black men with an alternative to the proverbial closet (Adams, 2011; Hunter, 2010). He offers that the down low provides a space "where [Black] men negotiate issues of race, gender, class, and sexuality" (McCune, 2008, p. 299) McCune recognizes that, historically, secret Black sexual exploration occurred as a means of survival. He parallels the down low Black male experience with historical Black experiences of sexual editing to emphasize the *queer world making* that must occur in order for Black men to actualize their sexual identities without sacrificing other aspects of their functioning being (Adams, 2011; McCune, 2008).

While Eurocentric and hetero-centric culture calls for queer men to "come out," McCune's research communicates that by way of the down low culture, the same gender loving Black man experiences a "coming into" himself, where he possesses newfound freedom to explore, or not explore, his sexualities (McCune, 2008, Hunter, 2010). For some, the down low serves as a space in which some queer Black men can escape the anxiety-inducing concern that underperformance of masculine tropes will expose him gay. Many Black men perceive living on the down low as an opportunity to "chill" – to live their lives without hypervigilance, and to be sexually and emotionally vulnerable without judgment (Hunter, 2010; McCune, 2008).

This perception highlights how secret sexually affirming spaces challenge stereotyped notions of what it means to be down low. Majority culture parallels living on the down low with sexual deviance (Battle & Bennet 2005; Han, 2015; Snorton & ProQuest, 2014). It is with this perception that down low Black men have been rejected and associated with stereotypes of deceit and sexual irresponsibility – characterizations that speak to Kimberlé Crenshaw's definition of intersectionality, which states that multiple identities compound and may place certain groups at risk of experiencing increased oppression due to their layered, and typically complex, associations (Bowleg, 2012; Crenshaw, 1989, Santovec, 2017). Literature contrastingly communicates that the down low functions as a buffer against negative appraisals of same gendered sexual practice (Adams, 2011; McCune, 2008; Snorton & ProQuest, 2014). Research into the space shifting power of the down low highlights that, for Black men, the down low provides a safe and destigmatizing space that strips the conviction many same gender loving Black men feel toward participating in homoerotic behavior.

Despite the seemingly healing and affirming properties the down low may have, there exists stigma toward Black men who engage in this practice from a community that has historically had to hide and deny their sexualities from the majority (hooks, 2004; Snorton, 2014). Some literature has suggested that to exist as a Black being is to have one's sexualities perceived by society as deviant and unnatural (hooks, 2004; Lemelle, 2010; McCune, 2008; Snorton & ProQuest, 2014). Consequently, there exists a blindness – among Black heterosexual and queer persons alike – toward the connection between past Black sexual secrecy and current Black male sexual secrecy (Snorton & ProQuest, 2014). How does one reconcile between the stigmatization of the down low and consideration of the purposes it serves? What will it take for Black male sexuality to be perceived as a fluid entity? The answers to these questions may not be explicitly clear, yet clues to these inquiries may be found by unlearning oppressive norms that have been reinforced by influential institutions within the Black community.

Sexual Identity and Religion

Numerous sources recognize the significant role the institutional Black church (arguably more so than Black religiosity itself) has on Black life (Foster et al., 2011; Jeffries et al., 2008; Ward, 2005; Winder, 2015). Throughout history, and particularly after slavery, the Black church has been recognized as a physical, mental, emotional, and spiritual support for Black bodies. Nevertheless, the Black church has also been identified as a pillar of homophobia and homo-negativity in the Black community (Garrett-Walker & Torres, 2016; Foster et al., 2011; Jeffries et al., 2008; Ward, 2005; Winder, 2015).

The Black community has attempted to separate themselves from the negative sexual scripts by repressing Black sexual exploration and adhering to teachings of acceptable and unacceptable sexual performance (hook, 2004). Messages that call for Black bodies to "be fruitful and multiply" paint acceptable sexuality as a heteronormative practice that solely leads to Black reproduction (hooks, 2004; Jeffries et al., 2008; Ward, 2005; Ward, 2005). Paralleling these values are messages that call for dominance in the Black community – particularly among Black men – which result in intolerance for behaviors that could potentially be linked to femininity and vulnerability, read as powerlessness (Ward, 2005). At the crux of power through dominance (a tool the European majority used to accumulate and maintain wealth) and restricting Black sexual liberation, the Black church has used its messaging to influence the performance of hegemonic masculinity among Black men, and to aid in the rejection of those who fall outside the range of normative sexual performance (i.e., Black queer men) (Garrett-Walker & Torres, 2016; Ward, 2005).

The homo-negative rhetoric disseminated by the church has aided in maintaining the stigma-laden association between same gender loving identity and disease contraction (Garrett-Walker & Torres, 2016; Jeffries et al., 2008; Winder, 2015). These and other mindsets around same gender loving identity act as factors that contribute to Black experiences of internalized homophobia, and also present as barriers to health promotion among Black same gender loving men (Barnes & Meyer, 2012). Black churches that do not have an affirming stance toward their queer members additionally block connections between Black same gender loving men and preventive and reactive methods of HIV/AIDS treatment (Jeffries et al., 2008; Winder, 2015).

Interestingly, while non-affirming Black churches may be perceived as hindrances to the overall well-being of some Black queer people, research suggests that benefits arise when the Black queer person engages in the Black church. Some of these benefits include the potential of social bonding with those who may also identify with non-heterosexuality, potentially finding a romantic or sexual partner, using the church as an institution to build upon one's craft, or exposing oneself to potential reconciliation between one's sexual, gender, racial, and spiritual identities (Pitt, 2010; Walker & Longmire-Avital, 2013; Winder, 2015). Ethnographic literature suggests that these benefits may contribute to a higher quality of social and spiritual life specifically among Black gay men.

There nevertheless seems to exist a blindness to those Black queer men who have not experienced benefit while existing in the Black church. Some Black same gender loving men have only felt abandoned, judged, and demonized by the church for their sexual identity (McCune, 2008; Ryan & Cole, 2017b; Snorton & ProQuest, 2014). The following section in this chapter seeks to provide additional insight into the experiences of Black gay men through their use of podcasting to bring their narratives to larger audiences. It is hypothesized that the following review of podcasts produced by Black same gender loving men will bring nuanced perspectives to phenomenological and ethnographic studies focused on Black queer men. It is also hypothesized that observation of work controlled by Black gay men will produce themes that challenge the stereotypes targeted toward this cohort.

Black Gay Men as Leaders in Podcasting

The advent of podcasting has been dated to as early as 2004, when MTV video jockey Adam Curry and software developer Dave Winer created a program that enabled them to download internet radio broadcasts to their iPods (Newberry, 2016). Since then, podcasting has become a medium in which individuals can package and share their voices and perspectives on various topics. Most recently, podcasting has created a platform for Black queer people to share their experiences in ways that expound upon the ethnographic and phenomenological reviews which challenge perceptions of this cohort.

Centering on the Black queer male experience, many acknowledge Gregory A. Smith (known to most as Kid Fury) as a pioneer Black gay podcaster (Otterson, 2018). Kid Fury is noted to have started his career in media in 2006 through online and video blogging. And while all his work has contributed to his success, much of his progress has been attributed to his podcast, *The Read*. Since 2014, Fury and his costar Crissles (a self-identifying queer Black woman) have used their show to highlight their grievances toward society with a "read" (a term originated from queer people of color to denote a sophisticated art of hurling insults; made popular by the documentary *Paris is Burning*) (Livingston, Simar, & Livingston, J. (Director), 1990). In addition, Kid Fury and Crissles have given listeners access to their lived experiences – experiences that span hiding one's sexual identity from loved ones, to dealing with difficult romantic relationships. From *The Read* has arisen a montage of other podcasts that have provided a phenomenological lens into the varied experiences had by some Black same gender loving men.

Of these podcasts includes *The Hung Up Podcast*, a Philadelphia-based program hosted by the self-proclaimed "fat and femme" P. Ryan and his "masculine counterpart" E. Dante Cole. From initial presentation, the two highlight a dichotomy that appears in the Black gay community – one between masculine and feminine presenting Black gay men (Lemelle & Battle, 2004). Literature communicates that Black gay men's expressed, and internally and externally perceived, levels of masculinity can impact self-esteem, social capitol, familial bonds, and level of perceived respect by others (Lemelle & Battle, 2004; McCune, 2008). Acknowledging their contrasting presentations, and using these presentations as an introduction to their podcast, Ryan and Cole engage in dialog that many within, and outside, the gay community choose to avoid. Much of their discussions reflect on the ways these two men explore their intersecting overt (gender and racial) and covert (sexual, educational, and religious) identities. For example, the premiere episode of the *Hung Up Podcasts* recounts and unpacks Ryan and Coles experiences of negotiating their sexual identities as members of Black Greek Letter Organizations (BGLOs).

COLE: How did masculinity shape my experience? I mean, I noticed right away that it was kind of like, "Alright, Eric, you're going to have to play this kind of game" I never wanted to be someone else, or pretend to be someone else just to get in. I think there's a pseudo standard. . . . I say that only because you're expected to kind of fit into a mold.

RYAN: I'm not finna fit in what your description of masculinity is; I'm going to figure out what mine is and stick to that. I live my truth and I live it unashamedly. That will come out in subtle ways. I'm not only comfortable with myself; I'm comfortable with my body. I will wear a blazer without a shirt; or I will wear shorts, at a pool, that are super short. I'm not afraid to do that (Ryan & Cole, 2017a).

The accounts shared on the inaugural episode of *Hung Up Podcast* highlight a negotiation, or code-switching, that is expected when Black gay men enter spaces of respectability and expected masculine performance, such as the fraternal sphere (Buckley, Anderson, & Tindall, 2011; Dancy, 2011; McCune, 2008; Totten, 2015). What presents, interestingly, is that, while there exist some Black queer men who engage in this codeswitching for the sake of acceptance, Ryan and Cole's discussion emphasizes that there also exist men who refuse to participate in the politics of shrouding their sexuality (Buckley et al., 2011; Dancy, 2011; Ryan & Cole, 2017a). This inaugural dialog on Black Greek fraternal life has led to further investigations of other facets that impact Black gay men. From conversations about father-son relationships, to investigating ways in which Black gay men can interrupt ineffective generational patterns, the two hosts have assisted in reshaping the narratives created by the majority regarding Black queer men.

The Down Low as Acceptable

As literature highlights the stigma that follows Black men who engage in down low behavior, once might expect down low Black men to be poorly received within the Black queer community. Interestingly, there seems to be ambivalence in the ways in which Black queer podcasters tackle the topic of the down low, as well as variability in the perceptions expressed toward down low Black men. For the *Hung Up* hosts, having a romantic or sexual relationship with a man who identified as "discreet" or "down-low" is somewhat presented as a rite of passage, or norm, for some Black same gender loving men (McCune, 2008; Snorton & ProQuest, 2014).

COLE: Would you date someone who was on the DL?
RYAN: Yes, Eric, I would. I truly believe the DL is necessary for our community. Why? Historically, the Black man–
COLE: Black men do not have safe spaces to disclose their sexuality.
RYAN: That's it! (Ryan & Cole, 2017c)

The perspective offered from the *Hung Up Podcast* comes from a host who, although "out" with his sexual identity, recognizes the difficulty some Black queer men have in publicly living their sexual identities. His message presents the down-low identified Black man in a way that contrasts the socially portrayed perception. Ryan, through his narrative, embodies an acceptance of same gender sexual exploration with Black down low men, which literature identifies as a privilege normally experienced by White men (Carrillo & Hoffman, 2016). His willingness additionally seems to act as a tool that contrasts the marginalization and homo-negativity many Black homo-interested men are at risk of facing from the majority.

In addition to the singular viewpoint emanating from *The Hung Up Podcast*, there exists variability in the communicated perceptions queer Black men have toward those who engage in down-low behavior. Contrasting Ryan's perspective is that of interviewee Dillon, on the *Eat, Pray, Thot* podcast (hosted by Savoy Jefferson), who shares his past struggles with down-low Black men.

DJ: A lot of my younger gay experiences were with men that were discreet or down low. I feel like having to mask myself or move in a certain way to cater to their lifestyle was really hindering to who I was as a person (Jefferson, 2018).

This narrative highlights the speaker's disinterest in participating in future down-low interactions. This account emphasizes a need, within the speaker, to engage with a partner who has experienced a coming into, and a public comfortability with, his sexual identities (McCune, 2008). While the provided perspectives afford brief understanding of how Black queer men conceptualize the down low, it is interesting to note that none of the collected commentary related to down-low behavior among some Black men possessed negative connotation. Literature attributes Black male down-low behavior to rising rates of infidelity, family breakdown, and HIV/AIDS proliferation in the Black community; yet Black queer male podcasters communicate acceptance of the down-low Black man. Such acceptance provides an environment for Black men to bravely express themselves and explore their sexual identities as they choose. Could the recognized stressors some closeted Black men face from society at large act as a mediator that incites compassion and acceptance within openly queer Black men toward their discreet brothers? While the podcasted voices of some Black queer men emphasize a recognition and identification of down-low behavior as uncommon, the mechanisms that underlie this acceptance still remain unclear and deserving of further investigation.

While themes of openness to sexually and romantically engage down-low Black men appear in various Black gay male–led podcasts, discussions of the down-low are handled with vagueness. There seemingly exist no podcasts that have explicitly discussed why the down-low culture exists and how it currently functions. As literature highlights that the down-low has historically been used to gain sexually explorative freedom for some Black same gender attracted men, one must wonder if the ambivalence surrounding the down low dialog serves as an effort of openly queer Black men to protect spheres where discreet Black men can explore their sexual proclivities.

Religious Rejection and Reclamation

Observing dialog around the ways Black queer men maneuver their intersecting sexual and religious identities recaptures the communicated struggles that have been presented in literature (Ward, 2005; Winder, 2015). Research denotes how Black queer men are afforded few spaces to affirm and openly express their same gender loving identities without sacrificing some aspect of their religious social capital; and simultaneously suggests that gay Black men may elect to engage in church leadership as a way to reconcile their religious, racial, and sexual identities (Winder, 2015). Yet little research investigates what occurs when Black gay men are unable to conceal their sexual identities within the religious spheres they subscribe to. This phenomenon is nevertheless explored in the *Hung Up Podcast*'s discussion of religion, as Ryan recounts how his sexual identity expression costs him religious and social capital at church.

RYAN: I don't think I'll ever forget this night. I got a call from a [church leader] . . . he basically said somebody contacted him, and there were pictures of me online. I got this speech that "Christians don't dress like this. Christians don't pose like this." You talk about Christians but I'm not crossing any Christian [boundaries]. So I said, "The reason you brought this to me is because I'm music minister. You can keep [the leadership position]" (Ryan & Cole, 2018).

Although the position of music minister in the Black church is commonly identified as a role occupied by same gender loving individuals, Ryan's narrative hints toward the respectability standards Black queer men must adhere to in order to maintain their positions in the religious sphere (Garrett-Walker & Torres, 2016; Snorton & ProQuest, 2014; Winder, 2015). His response to the church contrasts the subservience Black queer men have used to gain acceptance from the Black church. As a result of his choice to represent himself authentically, Ryan faces rejection from the institution (Winder, 2015). The narrative of rejection from the Black church continues as Cole relays his experience with the church. Although he is not ostracized by his religious community due to his outward presentation, he experiences trauma and longstanding distress connected to homo-negative messages received from the pulpit.

COLE: One thing that I noticed when I was young . . . there were a lot of LGBTQ people in the congregation, serving the church, and the people coming to the church, in different ways. One of the things that I've noticed is . . . our community is so involved in the church yet the [Black] church has yet to really embrace us; yet we continue to unselfishly serve (Ryan & Cole, 2017b).

Cole's experience parallels the account of numerous Black queer bodies who have not been received by the Black church. These occurrences create moments of trauma that can leave Black queer men dissonant about their sexual and religious identities (Garrett-Walker & Torres, 2016; Winder, 2015). Furthermore, such experiences have been noted to counteract any recorded benefits queer Black men may receive from being exposed to the Black church – benefits that include resilience building through acquisition of spiritual coping skills, potential bonding with other LGBT-identified persons, or increasing self-esteem through mastery of a church-nurtured craft (Pitt, 2010; Walker & Longmire-Avital, 2013; Winder, 2015).

In addition to highlighting narratives of struggle in religious spaces, Black gay male podcasted stories exemplify the mechanism by which some queer Black men reclaim and transfer their religious experiences from the institutional church to their own spheres of influence (Winder, 2015). Interactions on *The Hung Up Podcast* reflect observations made by Winder (2015) in his phenomenological study and ethnographic review, and suggest that Ryan and Cole, like many Black queer men who have felt unwelcomed by their religious institutions, may have re-created their own religious space through their podcast platform.

RYAN: I was so over having to shield people from my authentic self for so long I was just like, "Take the position and I will still praise God in spirit and in truth."
COLE: Amen (Ryan & Cole, 2017b).

Whether intentional or circumstantial, many podcasts pioneered by Black same gender loving men, who have been nurtured in the Black religious' institution, seem to preserve many elements of communication that are reflective of the Black church. Call and response, investigating the status of one's spirit, and shouting when a message has impacted the listener have been identified as components of the Black spiritual experience (Winder, 2015). Observation of Black queer male podcasters emphasizes how this cohort has adopted and re-created the Black church experience. They have married church and sexuality on a platform where other Black same gender loving men can congregate, commune, and receive the spiritually lifting experience they may not experience in typical religious settings.

Black Gay Male Identity Affirmation

Transcending dialog about the down low and the reconciliation between sexual and religious identities is the sexual identity pride and acknowledgment found on podcasts created by Black gay men. Studies suggest that the intersectional stressors experienced by some Black queer men can result in experiences of internalized homophobia; yet the examination of podcasts led by queer Black men communicates a sense of self-love and community appreciation that is rarely captured by phenomenological or ethnographic studies. In light of the oppression projected on Black queer men by the majority, Black gay male–led podcasts foster an intentionally public intolerance of the negative perceptions and mistreatment geared toward this cohort. Kid Fury exemplifies this in the manner in which he addresses celebrities for berating Black gay men. In August of 2018, Fury's "read" addressed the remarks of a celebrity who used her twitter to express that she would murder her son if she discovered he was gay. According to Smith (2018), Fury said this:

> And the gays will be the only ones – when your asses are irrelevant – to still book you for Pride; and make sure that you can pay your raggedy ass lease, or whatever it is you can't afford. But y'all want to call us sissies and fags and do all of this other shit, and we're supposed to be okay with it and feel like it doesn't mean anything because y'all have gay people doing your hair and makeup; and picking out shoes; and dancing and twerking your shows. I'm tired of it!

Fury's message mirrors that of the *Hung Up Podcast*'s P. Ryan who, disheartened from learning about the suicide of Jamel Miles (a nine-year-old Black boy who chose suicide as a means to end being bullied about his sexuality), uses his platform to address homophobes. Ryan intentionally uses his message to relate the death of Miles to his personal experiences with homophobic individuals and institutions who have used prejudice and ostracizing as tools to police the assumed same gender loving sexualities of Black boys and men.

RYAN: What kills me is people are so adamant about making young [gay] folks feel like they're not worthy of life. Then these young people take their lives before they can see what's on the other side. Growing up was not easy! There were so many times when giving up was truly an option . . . but sticking it through shows you that on the other side of all this [expletive] . . . you'll one-day look at all these people and be like, "You can't even TOUCH the ground that I walk on."(Ryan & Cole, 2018)

Conclusion

The presented review highlights a support Black gay male podcasters have for their Black queer brothers; and a call for these men to be resilient in the face of prejudice. There are many ways in which Black same gender loving men have been rejected, repressed, and oppressed; yet podcasting has been used as a medium to combat this oppression and defend those who have not been supported by the majority (hooks 2004; Lemelle, 2010; Loiacano, 1989; Snorton, 2014). Amid the discussions led by the reviewed podcasts, it is interesting to note that there existed no discussions related to Black gay men being exposed to, or living with, the HIV/AIDS virus. Although some may perceive this lack of discussion as an irresponsible oversight – as Black same gender loving men have been recorded to account for 58% of documented HIV infection cases among African Americans in the United States – there lies beauty in this silence (Centers for Disease Control and Prevention, 2018). Despite the common notion that Black gay men aid in infection dissemination throughout the Black community, there exist some Black queer men whose lives transcend the experience of viral infection. Additionally, there exists an abundance of literature that investigates Black gay male life through the lens of HIV/AIDS prevention or management (Amole & Grimmett, 2015, Haile, Rowell-Cunsolo, Parker, Padilla, & Hansen, 2014; Lapinski, Braz, & Maloney, 2010). Intentionally neglecting discourse of HIV/AIDS when exploring narratives of Black same gender loving men on a public forum is a revolutionary act that challenges the narrow purview of Black queer male livelihood. Observing Black gay life beyond HIV/AIDS affords podcasters the opportunity to present Black gay men as more than transferees of disease. They have taken space to showcase Black gay men as dynamic beings whose lives are not burdened by stereotypical narratives, and whose experiences surpass sexual health diagnoses.

While podcasting serves as a valuable medium for Black gay men to reclaim and redistribute their narratives, there exist interesting challenges that accompany podcasting for some Black gay men. Seemingly most prominent is the consideration that some Black same gender loving men may not desire for their narratives to be publicized, and may hold negative perceptions toward Black gay male podcasters. An example of this negative response arises in dialog on the *Hung Up Podcast*, in which the hosts note the ways in which other Black queer men have publicly rejected the show for, "being too open" (Ryan & Cole, 2017a). To address this challenge, the Black gay male podcaster may need to appraise the costs and benefits of sharing his lived experience on a public domain, similar to the way he might weigh the costs and benefits of disclosing his sexuality in various spaces. Hosting a podcast as a Black gay man is an action that transcends coming out to one's immediate spheres of influence. This act facilitates sexual identity disclosure to any person who has internet access. While many podcast hosts have received support for their openness, they also risk inter- and intracommunal rejection (Choi, Paul, Ayala, Boylan, & Gregorich, 2013; Lasala &Frierson, 2012; Mendoza-Denton, Downey, Purdie, Davis, & Pietrzak, 2002). Nevertheless, studies highlight that while potential rejection may be an adverse effect of podcasting, Black gay men are a resilient cohort that thrive and advance their community in spite of the rejections they risk experiencing (Wilson et al., 2016).

As the Harlem Renaissance provided opportunity for Black queer creatives to share their uniquely lived experiences, the existence of podcasts has begat a new renaissance in which Black same gender loving men can offer the world novel perspectives of their lives. As the reviewed Black gay male–led podcasts highlight, there is no one presentation, experience, interaction, or characteristic that speaks to the entire Black gay community. There therefore exists value in Black same gender loving men using the podcasts as a way to continue showcasing their varied experiences. So far, use of this medium has challenged commonly held views of the down low, the intersection of Black male sexuality and religion, and the internal and external perceptions of the Black queer man. Yet podcast utilization by Black gay men maybe could also influence the acceptance of nuances within this cohort by increasing the reach of the Black gay narrative.

Podcasting provides a technological platform that affords individuals the opportunity to disseminate their experiences to anyone with internet access. Black gay men currently have the opportunity to lead in disseminating their narratives by occupying niche spaces in the podcast realm. Emil Wilbekin of *Vibe* magazine emphasizes that "[the Black gay] community is [incredibly] diverse" (Jefferson, 2019) Therefore, to solely focus on highlighting and restructuring Black gay narratives through the lenses of HIV/AIDS, the down low, and religious persecution would be to hinder Black gay voices from amassing their greatest reach. Leadership in podcasting involves a restructuring of the Black same gender loving perceptions, tropes, and stereotypes that currently exist, and includes representation of Black gay male voices in spaces where such voices are scarce. It is recommended that in addition to using podcasting to saturate spaces of pop culture, academia, and entertainment, Black queer men assert themselves, and openly relay their experiences, in novel media arenas that include comedic, religious, athletic, and other genres. Such action will allow for the presentation of Black gay men through the lenses of homo-positivity, resilience, and social normalcy; will reiterate the message that Black gay male experiences cannot be captured through monolithic, stereotype-ridden lenses; and will reinforce that the most accurate portrayal Black gay male experiences can only come from Black gay men.

Process Questions and Considerations

1. As overt and covert homo-negativity is noted to contribute to poor health outcomes for gay Black men, what factors prevent the study of Black gay male life through purviews of homo-positivity, resilience, positive relationship building, and social normalcy?
2. Since literature correlates negative health outcomes among Black gay men with the HIV-centered ways Black gay male life is investigated, what incentives and barriers exist for researchers to restructure the ways Black gay life is examined?
3. Is it possible to reconcile stigma around the down low with considerations of the benefits of down low engagement among Black men? What shifts must occur for Black male sexuality to be perceived and accepted as fluid?

4. What are some ways Black gay men, who have been rejected by their religious institutions, can further understand and nurture their religious and spiritual selves without having to endure continued institutional trauma?
5. Expanding beyond this chapter, what are further costs and benefits of Black gay men using podcasting to amplify their individual voices and narratives?
6. What privileges exist in advocating for the increase of Black gay men in the podcast sphere? How does one seek to amplify Black gay male voices without concurrently excluding members of this cohort?

References

Adams, T. E. (2011). *Narrating the closet: An autoethnography of same-sex attraction.* Walnut Creek, Calif: Left Coast Press.

Amola, O., & Grimmett, M. A. (2015). Sexual identity, mental health, HIV risk behaviors, and internalized homophobia among Black men who have sex with men. *Journal of Counseling & Development, 93*(2), 236–246.

Barnes, D. M., & Meyer, I. H. (2012). Religious affiliation, internalized homophobia, and mental health in lesbians, gay men, and bisexuals. *American Journal of Orthopsychiatry, 82*(4), 505–515.

Battle, J., & Bennett, N. (2005). Striving for place: Lesbian, gay, bisexual, and transgender (LGBT) people in *A companion to African American history* (pp. 412–438.). Malden, MA: Blackwell Publishing Ltd.

Bowleg, L. (2012). "Once you've blended the cake, you can't take the parts back to the main ingredients": Black gay and bisexual men's descriptions and experiences of intersectionality. *Sex Roles, 68*(11–12), 754–767.

Buckley, P. M., Anderson, R., & Tindall, N. T. J. (2011). *Black Greek-letter fraternities and masculinities.* Mississippi: University Press of Mississippi.

Busby, O. (2018, February 09). *Query a queer: The Harlem Renaissance and LGBT people.* Retrieved from www.thepostathens.com/article/2018/02/harlem-renaissance-whitewashed

Carrillo, H., & Hoffman, A. (2016). From MSM to heteroflexibilities: Non-exclusive straight male identities and their implications for HIV prevention and health promotion. *Global Public Health, 11*(7–8), 923–936.

Choi, K., Paul, J., Ayala, G., Boylan, R., & Gregorich, S. E. (2013). Experiences of discrimination and their impact on the mental health among African American, Asian and Pacific Islander, and Latino men who have sex with men. *American Journal of Public Health, 103*(5), 868–874.

Crenshaw, K. (1989). *Demarginalizing the intersection of race and sex: A Black feminist critique of antidiscrimination doctrine, feminist theory and anti-racist politics* (pp. 139–168). University of Chicago Legal forum. Retrieved from. http://heinonline.org/HOL/Page?handle=hein.journals/uchclf1989&div=10&g_sent=1&collection=journals

Dancy II, T. E. (2011). *Becoming men in burning sands*. Mississippi: University Press of Mississippi.

Epsterin, S. (2007). *Inclusion: The politics of difference in medical research*. Chicago: University of Chicago Press.

Foster, M. L., Arnold, E., Rebchook, G., & Kegeles, S. M. (2011). 'it's my inner strength': Spirituality, religion and HIV in the lives of young African American men who have sex with men. *Culture, Health & Sexuality, 13*(9), 1103–1117.

Garrett-Walker, J. J., & Torres, V. M. (2016). Negative religious rhetoric in the lives of Black cisgender queer emerging adult men: A qualitative analysis. *Journal of Homosexuality, 64*(13), 1816–1831.

Glick, E. F. (2003). Harlem's queer dandy: African-American modernism and the artifice of blackness. *Modern Fiction Studies, 49*(3), 414–442.

Haile, R., Rowell-Cunsolo, T. L., Parker, E. A., Padilla, M. B., & Hansen, N. B. (2014). An empirical test of racial/ethnic differences in perceived racism and affiliation with the gay community: Implications for HIV risk. *Journal of Social Issues, 70*(2), 342–359.

Han, C. (2015). No brokeback for black men: Pathologizing black male (homo) sexuality through down low discourse. *Social Identities, 21*(3), 228–243.

HIV/AIDS. (2018, July 23). *Centers for Disease Control and Prevention*. Retrieved from www.cdc.gov/hiv/group/racialethnic/africanamericans/index.html

hooks, b. (2004). *We real cool: Black men and masculinity*. New York: Routledge.

Hughes, J. M. L. (1925). "To FS". Retrieved from: http://lifeoflangstonhughes.blogspot.com.au/

Hunter, M. A. (2010). All the gays are white and all the blacks are straight: Black gay men, identity, and community. *Sexuality Research and Social Policy, 7*(2), 81–92.

Jefferson, S. (Guest, Eat, Pray, Thot, Podcast). (2019, March). Love Jones featuring Emil Wilbekin. [Audio podcast].

Jefferson, S. (Producer, Eat, Pray, Thot, Podcast). (2018, November). Trois 2 pandora's box featuring Dillon Jaden. [Audio podcast].

Jeffries, W. L., Dodge, B., & Sandfort, T. G. M. (2008). Religion and spirituality among bisexual black men in the USA. *Culture, Health & Sexuality, 10*(5), 463–477.

Lapinski, M. K., Braz, M. E., & Maloney, E. K. (2010). The down low, social stigma, and risky sexual behaviors: Insights from African-American men who have sex with men. *Journal of Homosexuality, 57*(5), 610–633.

Lasala, M. C., & Frierson, D. T. (2012). African American gay youth and their families: Redefining masculinity, coping with racism and homophobia. *Journal of GLBT Family Studies, 8*(5), 428–445.

Lemelle, A. J. (2010). *Black masculinity and sexual politics*. New York: Routledge.

Lemelle, A. J., & Battle, J. (2004). Black masculinity matters in attitudes toward gay males. *Journal of Homosexuality, 47*(1), 39–51.

Livingston, J., Simar, B. (Producers). Livingston, J. (Director). (1990). *Paris is Burning*. [DVD]

Loiacano, D. K. (1989). Gay identity issues among Black Americans: Racism, homophobia, and the need for validation. *Journal of Counseling & Development, 68*(1), 21–25.

McCune, J. Q. (2008). "Out" in the club: The down low, hip-hop, and the architecture of Black masculinity. *Text and Performance Quarterly, 28*(3), 298.

Mendoza-Denton, R., Downey, G., Purdie, V. J., Davis, A., & Pietrzak, J. (2002). Sensitivity to status-based rejection: Implications for African American students' college experience. *Journal of Personality and Social Psychology, 83*(4), 896–918.

Moseby, K. M. (2017). Two regimes of HIV/AIDS: The MMWR and the sociopolitical construction of HIV/AIDS as a 'black disease'. *Sociology of Health & Illness, 39*(7), 1068–1082.

Newberry, B. (2016). *Podcasts*

Nugent, B. (1926). "Smoke, lilies, and jade." *FIRE!!!*

Otterson, J. (2018, July 30). Kid Fury to develop HBO comedy series with Lena Waithe producing (EXCLUSIVE). Retrieved from https://variety.com/2018/tv/news/kid-fury-hbo-lena-waithe-1202888458/

Pitt, R. N. (2010). "Killing the messenger": Religious black gay men's neutralization of anti-gay religious messages. Journal for the *Scientific Study of Religion, 49*(1), 56–72.

Quinn, K., & Dickson-Gomez, J. (2016). Homonegativity, religiosity, and the intersecting identities of young black men who have sex with men. *AIDS and Behavior, 20*(1), 51–64.

Quinn, K., Voisin, D. R., Bouris, A., Jaffe, K., Kuhns, L., Eavou, R., & Schneider, J. (2017). Multiple dimensions of stigma and health related factors among young black men who have sex with men. *AIDS and Behavior, 21*(1), 207–216.

Raj, A., & Bowleg, L. (2012). Heterosexual risk for HIV among black men in the united states: A call to action against a neglected crisis in black communities. *American Journal of Men's Health, 6*(3), 178–181.

Ross, M. B. (2013). 'What's love but a second hand emotion?': Man-on-man passion in the contemporary black gay romance novel. *Callaloo: A Journal of African Diaspora Arts and Letters, 36*(3), 669.

Ryan, P., & Cole, E. (Producers, Hung Up Podcast). (2017a, April). The origin story: Wait . . . you're Black, Gay, and Greek? (feat. Eric). [Audio podcast].

Ryan, P., & Cole, E. (Producers, Hung Up Podcast). (2017b, July). Back down memory lane. [Audio podcast].

Ryan, P., & Cole, E. (Producers, Hung Up Podcast). (2017c, September). The dl convo. [Audio podcast].

Ryan, P., & Cole, E. (Producers, Hung Up Podcast). (2018, September). Nathan's story [Audio podcast]

Santovec, M. L. (2017). The necessity of intersectionality: A profile of Dr. Kimberlé Crenshaw. *Women in Higher Education, 26*(3), 8–9. Doi:10.1002/whe.20414

Schwarz, A. B. C. (2003). *Gay voices of the Harlem renaissance*. Bloomington, Indiana: Indiana University Press.

Smallwood, S. W., Spencer, S. M., Ingram, L. A., Thrasher, J. F., & Thompson-Robinson, M. V. (2016). Different dimensions: Internalized homonegativity among African American men who have sex with men in the deep south. *Journal of Homosexuality, 64*(1), 45–60.

Smith, G (Producer, The Read). (2018, August). Toy Story. [Audio podcast].

Snorton, C. R., & ProQuest (Firm). (2014). *Nobody is supposed to know: Black sexuality on the down low*. Minneapolis, Minnesota: University of Minnesota Press.

Stokes, M. (2003). Reviews: "Gay rebel of the Harlem renaissance: Selections from the world of Richard Bruce Nugent," edited by Thomas H. Wirth. *Callaloo, 26*(3), 908–913.

Stone, M. E. (2002, Nov). Life in a land of 'smoke, lilies, and jade'. *The Gay & Lesbian Review Worldwide, 9*, 38. Retrieved from https://dbproxy.lasalle.edu:443/login?url=https://dbproxy.lasalle.edu:6033/docview/1986 62299?account id=11999

Totten, P. (2015). A man should never eat a pickle in public: A black man's understanding of enactments of gender and sexuality. *Creative Approaches to Research, 8*(2), 4.

United States. Dept. of Labor. Office of Policy Planning and Research. (1965). *The negro family; the case for national action*. United States:

Vaughan, A. S., Rosenberg, E., Shouse, R. L., & Sullivan, P. S. (2014). Connecting race and place: A county-level analysis of White, Black, and Hispanic HIV prevalence, poverty, and level of urbanization. *American Journal of Public Health, 104*(7), e77–e84.

Villarosa, L. (2017, January 12). The gay Harlem Renaissance. Retrieved from www.theroot.com/the-gay-harlem-renaissance-1790864926

Walker, J. J., & Longmire-Avital, B. (2013). The impact of religious faith and internalized homonegativity on resiliency for Black lesbian, gay, and bisexual emerging adults. *Developmental Psychology, 49*(9), 1723–1731.

Ward, E. G. (2005). Homophobia, hypermasculinity and the US black church. *Culture, Health & Sexuality, 7*(5), 493–504. Doi:10.1080/13691050500151248

Winder, T. J. A. (2015). "Shouting it out": Religion and the development of black gay identities. *Qualitative Sociology, 38*(4), 375.

Wilson, P. A., Meyer, I. H., Antebi-Gruszka, N., Boone, M. R., Cook, S. H., & Cherenack, E. M. (2016). Profiles of resilience and psychosocial outcomes among young black gay and bisexual men. *American Journal of Community Psychology, 57*(1), 144–157.

15 But Did You Die? Leading Conversations About Sexuality and Loss

Jeanae Hopgood-Jones

"But did you die?" One of the famous lines from the Mr. Chow character in the *Hangover* films (Bender & Phillips, 2009), opens this chapter. The film is full of the salacious escapades that a group of friends experience during a bachelor party weekend. Much of their experiences are dangerous and bordering on illegal, while Mr. Chow provides comic relief. He often puts the characters in very risky situations to which they respond dramatically, at which point he responds, "But did you die?" His point is that none of the characters died during their experiences; therefore, they should not be upset about whatever occurred. Mr. Chow dismissed concerns, complaints, stress, sadness, and fear with a simplistic, four-word question. This reference is used to title this chapter to illustrate how experiences other than literal death are often dismissed as less significant or important.

Grief and loss challenges are the most often attributed to physical loss of a loved one due to death (Meagher & Balk, 2013). Though death is the most common way of thinking about loss and grieving, there are many other types losses that can feel just as significant as physical death. Conversations about loss pose unique opportunities to discuss experiences past, present, and future in a way that can be life-changing for the person sharing and the person facilitating. The finality of death tends to ensure it as the primary recognized loss, while other types of losses are given secondary or tertiary importance. This chapter discusses nontraditional or disenfranchised losses as they relate to issues of sexuality. It will also provide suggestions on how to lead conversations about disenfranchised losses in terms of relationships, identity, family creation, as well as power and control.

Loss Types

In facilitating conversations about loss, one must understand that there is more than one type. Losses can be divided into three main categories with any number of subcategories existing within each. For the purpose of understanding how to converse about loss, the following categories are included: traditional losses, disenfranchised losses, and abrupt or unexpected losses (Meagher & Balk, 2013). Traditional losses tend to be those associated with physical deaths, usually in relation to chronic illness or old age. These types of losses are expected, or even predicted, as well as having socially sanctioned grieving processes (Meagher & Balk, 2013). Disenfranchised losses are those that are marginalized or subjugated by society, leaving the griever feeling invalidated and alone (Doka, 1989). Individuals experiencing disenfranchised grief or a disenfranchised loss often do not feel they have the right to be perceived as or function as a bereaved person (Meagher & Balk, 2013). This type of loss can include certain forms of perinatal loss, abortion, divorce, infidelity, and LGBTQ+-specific issues including loss of support systems, identities, and sense of safety. Disenfranchised loss/grief is the area of loss on which this chapter will focus. Last, unexpected losses are those that are abrupt, or come without warning. Unexpected losses can include things such as natural disasters, murders, car accidents, and completed suicides (Meagher & Balk, 2013).

In all three of these overarching categories of loss, one must have a larger understanding of the grieving process that commonly occurs in response to such loss. The most famous stage theory explaining the process of grieving was developed by Elisabeth Kubler-Ross (1969). The five stages of grief and loss include denial, bargaining, anger, depression, and acceptance. The stages are not literal interpretations of the words as they have been commonly understood but, rather, broader contextual meaning as it relates to processing loss. For example, the stage of denial is typically associated with the griever's inability to mentally process the loss that has occurred. It is not a literal denial that the loss happened but, rather, a difficulty accepting the loss combined with a way for the brain to mentally get breaks from the pain (Kubler-Ross & Kessler, 2005). Another example is that of bargaining. This stage is not a literal attempt to create a win-win situation or gain something in exchange for another thing. Rather, it is the rumination on what the grievers could have, would have, and should have done differently that they believe might have yielded a different outcome other than the loss. This stage is often laden with feelings of guilt for the griever. Anger involves anger at self, a deity, and even sometimes the person who has passed away. This manifests as anger related to feelings of abandonment, anger about fairness and feeling the loss experience was undeserved, or anger at feeling punished. The depression stage is not necessarily associated with clinical depression, which has very specific criterion, but, rather, the general experience of sadness, loneliness, and emptiness experienced by grievers. Last, the acceptance stage represents the experience of making peace with a new reality after the loss. It does not necessarily mean people feel okay about the experience, but they may choose to no longer allow the anger or bargaining to dominate their thoughts.

Though these stages were originally, exclusively associated with death and dying, Kessler expanded these ideas to grieving as a whole and focuses on the inner (i.e., heartbreak, upset, paranormal, and reordering) and outer (i.e., rituals and ceremonies) worlds of grief (Kubler-Ross & Kessler, 2005). In addition to Kessler's interpretation of Kubler-Ross' stage model, there are several other models which will be discussed in some detail that will also be mentioned later in this chapter. When considering disenfranchised losses, like those related to sexuality (e.g., LGBTQ+ issues, perinatal loss, etc.), having a broader understanding of the ways in which grief manifests, enables more fruitful and helpful conversations towards healing.

Sexuality and Loss

Sexuality is not commonly an area associated with loss in the traditional sense; however, considering the area of disenfranchised loss and grief lends itself to expanding one's understanding of how losses effect this area of life. When initiating and leading conversations about losses and grieving as they relate to sexuality, it is beneficial to have a foundational understanding of sexual being and sexuality as a whole. Understanding sexuality in this manner helps to broaden the idea beyond that of sexual activity itself and sexual orientation factors. Dennis Dailey's (1981) model of sexual being, commonly known as the Circles of Sexuality, identifies five areas in which sexuality is experienced. The circles are identified as intimacy, sexual health and reproduction, sensuality, power and sexualization, and sexual identity (Dailey, 1981). Intimacy describes caring, love, vulnerability, and risk taking, while sexual health and reproduction describes anatomy, reproductive health, and feelings about reproductive organs. Sensuality describes body image, fantasy, and sexual response, while power and sexualization describes seduction, rape, and manipulation of sexual energy. Last, sexual identity describes sexual orientation, gender identity, and biological sex.

Broadening one's understanding of sexuality beyond what is done with genitals is imperative to leading successful and respectful conversations about sexuality and loss. Sexuality is both inter- and intra-experiential allowing for the idea that this area is also subject to feelings of grief related to experiences of deprivation. The relationships people have with themselves, and with others, are cultivated, negotiated, and lost as a result of life circumstances. Sexuality-related losses are often viewed by larger society as less significant, less impactful, and less important than traditional losses; however, despite their disenfranchised status, they can have life-long impacts on a person's life. The following subsections illustrate discussions about losses in each of Dailey's Circles of Sexuality to better elucidate this concept.

Intimacy

Intimacy is largely about relating to other people as well as to oneself. It highlights a willingness to see, and be seen by, other people both platonically and romantically. We first learn about intimacy as physical closeness in infancy (Cernero, Strawn, & Abernethy, 2017). The consistent presence of a caring other during infancy helps to form preverbal understanding of intimate relations. This is later built upon when language is involved, and the intimacy becomes bidirectional (Cernero et al., 2017). Strong and effective communication, respect, physical closeness, and feelings of emotional safety are often core components of intimacy (Cernero et al., 2017; Strong & Cohen, 2017). These components are uniquely affected by abusive interactions, abandonment, and traumatic experiences. Losing intimacy is akin to losing a sense of safety, a sense of self-worth and self-esteem, a sense of connectedness, and a sense that one matters in the world (Strong & Cohen, 2017).

Losses in intimacy can happen in friendships as well as romantic relationships. Friendships break up just as romantic partnerships do, and there are some instances in which friend break-ups feel the same, if not more significant than those of romantic relationships. Loss of connection in this way – intimacy – can lead to feelings of sadness, anxiety, and isolation; which can manifest as situational depression. An alternative consideration is that losses in intimacy can lead to a frantic desire to connect, resulting in people making rash decisions to reenter romantic relationships, try to replace best friends with acquaintances or previously undervalued friendships, or force themselves into casual relationships for their temporary likeness to true intimacy. These potential outcomes are simply attempts at reclaiming the primary sense of physical closeness as intimacy but also, the emotional connectivity (Cernero et al., 2017). Though these responses are binary in their categorization as internalizing or externalizing behaviors, they remain common outcomes as a result of losses in intimacy and are important to consider when planning for support in this area.

Sexual Health and Reproduction

Losses in this area are most associated with changes to sexual freedom (e.g., due to sexually transmitted diseases or infections [STDs/STIs]), or due to fertility challenges and perinatal loss. Autonomy over one's sexual behaviors is an area that is one of the benefits of adulthood. Who and when one chooses to have sexual encounters is significantly impacted by the presence of certain STDs; specifically those without medical cure. People living with these STDs may feel as though they have lost their sexual health due to internalized negativity and stigma, as well as societal response to their status. Those living with Human Immunodeficiency

Virus (HIV), Acquired Immune Deficiency Syndrome (AIDS), and Herpes Simplex Virus Type 2 – Genital Herpes (HSV-2) are uniquely effected by loss in this area. Though there has been significant medical advancement in recent years, social stigma still exists thereby altering relationships with potential partners, family, and friends, as well as perceptions of self.

Considering reproduction, loss in this area is incredibly common. According to the American College of Obstetricians and Gynecologists, one in four pregnancies result in miscarriage, which is defined as loss of a pregnancy prior to 20 weeks (ACOG, 2015). One in 100 pregnancies result in stillbirth (Stillbirth, 2017). Postnatal deaths in the Neo-Natal Intensive Care Unit (NICU) and deaths due to Sudden Infant Death Syndrome (SIDS) are also relatively common, and sometimes unexplainable. Aside from the actual deaths of fetuses and children, the experience of multiple attempts to conceive can also be considered losses. Individuals and couples experience similar encounters with grieving but this grief is even further dismissed when a life has not yet been created. Challenges with fertility can be linked to feelings of guilt and shame, sadness, frustration, deprivation, and anger (Black & Wright, 2012). They can also be linked to feelings of hope, resilience, perseverance, and personal growth (Black & Wright, 2012). Losses in the area of reproduction tend to challenge fundamental ideas of womanhood and manhood maintained by gender socialization practices globally. People with a uterus are socialized to want to become mothers, and both bear and rear children. People with penises are socialized to want to create children to further their own genetic lineage. When faced with physical barriers to this, as created by infertility and perinatal loss, many people are left feeling less-than, and require targeted supportive services.

Sensuality

Changes in physical ability, sexual functioning, and self-concept can lead to feelings of loss in the sensuality circle of sexuality. The ways in which one understands and values their bodies as well as those of others, is integral to how sensual one feels. Interruptions here, due to physical injury, medical challenges, weight fluctuation, and sexual function challenges such as anorgasmia or erectile dysfunction, create a unique sense of loss which is often overlooked (Pillai-Friedman & Ashline, 2014). In the first three non-sexual-activity-related areas involving physicality and physical ability, the relationship to, or the effects on, a person's sex life is usually the least important consideration. The hierarchy of importance goes first to the physical issue and increasing ability, then later, if at all, to sexual pleasure for that person. As a result, experiences of loss in this area are virtually ignored at worst, and minimized at best (Pillai-Friedman & Ashline, 2014).

In areas related specifically to sexual response, losses are associated with shame and guilt for people with penises and those with vaginas.

Pharmaceutical and natural remedies have been created to assist with erectile dysfunction, as well as increase sensitivity to make orgasm more likely to occur in males and females; however, these interventions are not 100% effective for all who use them. This can bring a sense of failure, brokenness, and lack of desire when loss is experienced in this area. Loss of sensuality is one of the most significant catalysts for individuals and couples seeking out sex therapy support. As a result of this being one of the only socially acceptable areas about which to seek help, more options are available to help address concerns.

Power and Sexualization

Loss in the area of power and sexualization tends to center around rape, harassment, and abuse. Because this circle of sexuality deals with the manipulation of sexual energy, it is strongly connected to power and control dynamics. In some ways, this manipulation can be benign, like flirting, and in other ways it can be coercive and dangerous as in the practice of sexual assault. Sexual assault as used here will encompass all derogatory practices from sexual harassment to rape. A strong sentiment of sexual assault survivors is a feeling that they have lost control of their body, their sense of safety, and their sense of knowing themselves. The relationship with themselves as well as the relationships with others can be significantly altered in response to loss in the area of power and sexualization.

This type of loss is slightly more socially sanctioned making it the least disenfranchised of the circles. Increases in social recognition of loss in this area can be attributed to the Feminist movement, and more recently, the #MeToo movement started by Tarana Burke. Burke's focus was to help women of color who have been abused, and this was later expanded to all people who have suffered sexual assault practices worldwide. The #MeToo movement has been popularized in recent years by famous actors sharing their stories of sexual abuse, assault, and harassment in the entertainment industry. The cultural acceptance that sexualization used negatively is problematic and can have lasting effects on self-esteem, self-concept, trust, intimacy, and safety makes for easier conversations regarding the grieving and healing processes that follow.

Sexual Identity

Sexual identity considers feelings of maleness and femaleness as well as other gender identities. It considers biological sex, gender identity, sexual orientation, and gender roles a person experiences (Dailey, 1981). Losses in the sexual identity sphere are often more interpersonal than intrapersonal. Loss of family and friends in response to gender identity changes or sexual orientation revelations are not uncommon. Heteronormativity (the idea that heterosexual relationships are the standard to which all other relationships must live), homophobia, and cissexism (the idea that cisgender people are superior and the marker for how everyone should be) are at the crux of many of these relationship losses. As a result of these loses occurring in core relationships, such as family, people suffer from significant feelings of deprivation, loneliness, shame and guilt, low self-esteem and worth, depression, as well as loss of their own sense of self. Identity is formed in the context of family and cultivated through years of learning, interactions with friends and peers, and exposure to the environment or society (Strong & Cohen, 2017). Removing connection to core people often raises questions of, "who am I without my [insert relationship]?" In circumstances like these, people may turn to chosen family as a means to fill to void. These relationships with fictive kin can become more significant, valued, and important than actual blood ties or old friendships (Strong & Cohen, 2017).

Leading the Conversation and Supporting Healing

Now that a broader understanding of loss has been discussed, disenfranchised loss has been highlighted, and the ways loss can be applied to sexuality have been discussed, how does one actually lead conversations about this topic area? The remainder of this chapter will discuss useful methods of engaging people in conversations, ways to support healing, and helpful things to be aware of for the person leading conversations in this content area.

What Every Conversation Leader Should Know

Though loss is a universal experience that crosses cultural, racial, and ethnic lines, it is experienced differently by everyone. Even people within homogamous groups (i.e., groups with similar characteristics to one's own identity) may cope with and understand loss in a myriad of ways. As a result, the first thing a leader can benefit from is knowing their audience. Asking questions about how the person understands loss, internalizes or externalizes loss, and makes sense of their loss is crucial to understanding and facilitation. One way to do this is to inquire about a person's spiritual and/or religious beliefs. Spiritualities, as presented by theologian John Shea (2000), can be understood as beliefs, practices, and stories that respond to a basic, shared human need to find an integrated meaning (Meagher & Balk, 2013). This is important because the morals and values associated with belief systems (organized or secular) give insight into the ways in which people make meaning of their grief.

Meaning-making as it relates to grief addresses the ways in which one makes sense of one's loss and/or one's grieving process (Kubler-Ross & Kessler, 2005; Meagher & Balk, 2013). It is part of the inner world of grief that deals with all the ways the bereaved internalize their loss. If people are in tune with their inner world enough to describe this, more than half the work is done! If they are not, this is an opportunity to offer examples of how some people make meaning of their grief, and whether those things resonate with the people with whom the leader is speaking. When considering sexuality, shame and guilt, as well as other common feelings, often abound as a result of the disenfranchised nature. Do these people believe they have done something wrong (i.e., guilt) or that they, themselves, are wrong (i.e., shame) for experiencing the loss they did? The answer to that question is often heavily linked to the meaning they are making of their experience.

A related, though separate concept, is the second area of which leaders of loss conversations in sexuality, should be aware; the assumptive world. Kubler-Ross and Kessler (2005) stress the importance of understanding what a person believes about the world and what they assume to be true. The assumptive world also consists of higher-order schemas used to help navigate the world and make sense of one's place in it (Krosch & Shakespeare-Finch, 2017). Do they believe that bad things (e.g., losses) only happen to bad people? Do they believe they will always be able-bodied? Able to conceive without challenge? That their family loves and supports them unconditionally (e.g., regardless of sexual orientation or gender identity)? That romantic partners do not sexually assault other partners? The idea here is not necessarily that people believe there is an impossibility of experiencing these types of losses, but, rather, that there is an improbability. For example, most people are aware of perinatal loss but do not expect it to happen to them . . . until it does. Therefore, when they experience a sexuality-related loss of this type, the sense of shock and devastation can be alarming. Highlighting fairly common assumptions is a way of joining (i.e., building rapport) with the listeners or audience and giving permission to own their own assumptive world ideas.

Third, it is important for conversation leaders to remember Kubler-Ross' Stages of Grief model as well as consider other models on grieving. The start of the chapter included a discussion about the Kubler-Ross stages model, which includes denial, anger, bargaining, depression, and acceptance. As a reminder, these stages are not linear and a person can experience all, or only a few, in any given order. In addition to Kubler-Ross, there are several other grief theories and theorists worth mentioning, including Freud, Wonder, Rando, and Strobe and Schut (Meagher & Balk, 2013). Freud's theory looks at mourning as the work of uncoupling and achieving detachment from the loss. Wonder's theory includes tasks culminating in finding an enduring connection with the deceased. Rando's theory also culminates in the bereaved readjusting and reinvesting in their new world post-lost. Strobe and Schut's theory posits that bereaved people focus on loss-oriented and restoration-oriented processes, as well as some oscillation between the two (Meagher & Balk, 2013). These aforementioned theories were conceived with the loss of life in mind more so than disenfranchised losses. They can loosely be applied; however, they fit more squarely into the thanatology (i.e., the study of death and dying) category. Let us now focus specifically on two theories, Lindemann and Bowlby, which can be applied to disenfranchised, sexuality-related losses.

Lindemann's grief theory addresses acute grief and the processes associated with it: somatic distress, hostility, alterations in usual patterns of conduct, and preoccupation with the loss (Meagher & Balk, 2013). Bowlby's grief theory highlights four phases of uncomplicated grieving including numbing, yearning and searching, disorganization and repair, and reorganization (Meagher & Balk, 2013). Keeping in mind the broad definitions of loss discussed, as well as the application of Kubler-Ross, Lindemann, and Bowlby's grief theories, sexuality-related losses become much easier to understand and show empathy towards. Conversation leaders benefit from a foundational understanding of grieving, and its nuance, to help increase their ability to empathize with disenfranchised losses, such as sexuality-related loss.

Last, conversation leaders benefit from having awareness of the outer world of grief (Kubler-Ross & Kessler, 2005). The outer world of grief deals with the ways in which people externalize their mourning to move towards healing. Outer world of grief activities such as ceremonies (burials, wakes, etc.), rituals, altars, and celebrations (e.g., El Dia de los Muertos, Day of the Dead in Mexico) are most often conducted as a means of connection between the living and the deceased. Awareness and knowledge in this area helps the leader to connect with the listener around cultural and social practices as they move towards healing. It is also a way for the leader to encourage the listener to conceptualize their outer-world experiences as part of their grieving process even in disenfranchised loss situations.

Using the five circles of sexuality examples previously mentioned, here are some examples of how a conversation leader could broach the outer world with listeners: Rituals in the intimacy circle can involve self-care practices such as meditation, yoga, and positive affirmations. Outer world grieving practices in the sexual health and reproduction circle can include routine testing and/or conversations about sexual health with partners, as well as yearly ceremonies or altars for lost little ones in the case of perinatal loss. Sensuality outer world grief practices may involve positive self-talk, routines and practices around preparing for sexual activity, body-positive and body-affirming practices solo, as well as with partners. Outer world grieving practices addressing loss in the power and sexualization circle may include rituals for safety in response to sexual assault (e.g., going out in pairs or always scheduling a ride). Sexual identity losses may have outer world grieving practices that include celebrations with chosen family and emotional fortifying when exposed to unsupportive biological family.

Conversation Leaders Support the Healing

There is no shortage of professionals leading conversations about thanatological topics. Loss as it relates to death and dying has been widely researched, written about, and commented on. Disenfranchised losses are less common and, in some ways, still are discussed from a position of physical death (e.g., perinatal loss and pregnancy termination). Leading conversations about the undead – not zombies, this isn't *The Walking Dead* – the losses that occur when everyone is still living, opens the door to facilitating healing in others.

So how does this facilitation of healing work exactly? Once leaders are armed with useful background information about disenfranchised losses, they can employ the PLISSIT model (Annon, 1976). The PLISSIT model is used in sex therapy practice to specifically address sexuality concerns. As a result of sexuality as a whole remaining taboo for some, this model was designed to help facilitate conversation as well as successfully move through presenting problems. PLISSIT is an acronym standing for Permission, Limited Information, Specific Suggestions, and Intensive Therapy (Annon, 1976). This model can be applied to leading conversations about sexuality-related loss, much in the same way it is used in sex therapy (Pillai-Friedman & Ashline, 2014). The facilitator grants permission to discuss the disenfranchised loss by applying the information they know to conversations had. As mentioned previously, providing examples of assumptive world beliefs, common experiences of grief stages, or simply framing an issue as a potential loss allows room (i.e., gives permission) for the people to own their experience without judgement. Many people experiencing disenfranchised losses, in general, do not feel that they have the permission or right to their feelings as a result of being marginalized.

The Limited Information and Specific Suggestions phases of the model can be addressed by the leader asking questions about meaning making and assumptive world concerns, as well as providing information about outer world of grief practices. To open dialog about sensitive topics, such as sexuality, one must inquire about a person's experience as well as provide space for people to see themselves in what is being communicated. In addition, many people experiencing sexuality-related losses feel as though they do not know where to start to move past hurt feelings. Making specific suggestions creates environments where people can choose options that feel right for them without having to do the emotional or mental labor of figuring it out for themselves in moments of grieving.

Intensive therapy can be used directly by people leading conversations if they are properly trained to do so (i.e., a clinician), or indirectly by assessing needs and making appropriate referrals to therapeutic services. If the leader or facilitator is also a therapist or clinician, here is where the bulk of healing work activities can be employed. If the leader or facilitator is not a therapist, they can aid in removing stigma about seeking support for sexuality-related losses by using psycho-education, validation and normalizing, as well as resource coordination.

Things to Watch Out For

So, you have the information you need about loss, you have broadened your understanding of it and how it applies to sexuality, and you have learned ways in which to help facilitate healing in the conversations you are leading. All is right with the world until . . . vicarious trauma. Listening to, and having conversations around, significantly emotional, traumatizing, and/or stressful content puts people at risk of vicarious trauma. McCann and Pearlman (1990) first defined vicarious trauma as the unique, cumulative, and potentially negative changes that can occur in clinicians who engage with clients empathetically. Similar terms such Secondary Traumatic Stress (STS) and Compassion Fatigue can also be applicable to facilitating conversations about sexuality-related losses. Secondary traumatic stress was originally coined to describe what occurs when professionals witness severe trauma, but do not develop or maintain an ongoing empathetic relationship with the sufferer (Figley, 1995). Compassion fatigue is similar to STS; however, it is more appropriately ascribed to loved ones overwhelmed by witnessing (verbally or physically) trauma (Figley, 1995). In both STS and compassion fatigue, the witness is also overwhelmed by a desire to provide assistance coupled with a lack of available resources to do so (Branson, 2018).

Though leading conversations about a disenfranchised loss such as a sexuality-related loss is not always literal physical death, the emotional toll this loss can take on the experiencer is significant. As mentioned throughout this chapter, losses in sexuality can carry intense feelings of guilt, shame, abandonment, loss of autonomy, failure, isolation, and disconnection (from self and/or others). It is easy for these feelings to create a sense of hopelessness and helplessness as all the details of a particular situation are unpacked (Branson, 2018). It is important for conversation leaders or facilitators in this area to be aware of their own baggage as well as be aware of how much metaphorical heaviness they are taking on from the audience. Be mindful to move the conversation along where appropriate by summarizing, highlighting important takeaways, validating feelings, and linking to the desired direction the facilitator needs to go.

The other side of the vicarious trauma coin is compassion fatigue. The indifference or apathy towards the pain and suffering of others is a risk when there is overexposure to traumatic and emotionally charged content (Branson, 2018). Compassion fatigue has the potential to lead to insensitivity and general aloofness, which is not an effective way to lead conversations about sexuality-related losses (Branson, 2018; Figley, 1995). Due to these types of losses being subjugated by larger society in many cases, leaders would do well to pay close attention to their own self-care and support systems in effort to manage both of these potential risks.

No one died physically; however, people needing to have conversations about sexuality-related losses may feel as though a part of them has died or, at minimum, like they are unable to cope with their experience. They may be experiencing their own form of "big T" trauma as a result of threatened or actual death or injury, or "little t" trauma when there are events exceeding a person's perceived ability to cope (Staggs, 2014), which may feel increasingly overwhelming for them and for you as the facilitator. Big "T" trauma experiences can include experiencing or witnessing actual death, injury, or sexual assault, while little "t" trauma can include things that are often considered disenfranchised losses, such as divorce or an abrupt loss of support systems (Staggs, 2014).

Though overwhelming feelings can arise, it is possible that they may not. For as many people debilitated by traumatic experiences, there are those who experience what is called posttraumatic growth. Posttraumatic growth is the positive psychological change one has following a traumatic event characterized by the use of the experience to facilitate positive change (Black & Wright, 2012; Calhoun & Tedeschi, 2006). This can be in the form of donations, acts of service, foundations, implementation of new healing practices, or new outlooks on life as a result of the transformative experience had. Posttraumatic growth is typically observed in perception of self, philosophy on life, and relation to others (Krosch & Shakespeare-Finch, 2017). One responsibility of people leading conversations about sexuality-related losses is to make real the concept of posttraumatic growth. Like conversations about any other type of loss, it is important to stress that whomever is on the receiving of the conversations' life is not over, despite how they may feel. There is opportunity for growth through the forced change of the loss. How one copes, heals, and continues to move forward can be an amazing source of strength and power. In addition, as the facilitator/conversation leader, you may be the only person to adopt this angle so do not miss the opportunity to help others move through their loss rather than getting stuck on their journey.

Last but certainly not least, leaders should be mindful of their own biases. The world of loss-related conversations is heavy with discussions about death and dying specifically. It is not uncommon for people to place a hierarchy of sorts around the different types of losses based on their perceived impact. Death-related loss is usually at the top of the hierarchy with disenfranchised losses, specifically those closely tied with choice (e.g., abortion), at the bottom. Clichés such as "know your audience" and "meet people where they are" cannot be overstated in this circumstance. Leading conversations about sexuality-related losses requires knowledge of sexuality beyond genitalia and sexual acts, knowledge of loss beyond physical death, and awareness of one's own judgements or biases about what constitutes a valid loss experience. Nothing can derail a productive conversation about loss more than an invalidating person at the outset. Being curious about the experiences of the people one is attempting to lead into conversation is a perfect example of leading from behind. When a leader makes room for others to communicate their needs, position, and understanding, conversations can be more targeted, productive, and fruitful.

Conclusion

Despite much advancement in the discussion of sexuality-related topics in recent years, there remains some taboo about centering these conversations. One way of removing that stigma is by expanding one's understanding of sexual being as well as both, normalizing and leading exchanges about this subject matter. Though less taboo, the topic of loss and grieving has largely held similar limitations in scope, requiring one to broaden one's understanding of the myriad of ways it can effect a person's life.

Conversation leaders of sexuality-related losses benefit from incorporating meaning-making, assessing the assumptive world of listeners or participants, highlighting the inner and outer worlds of grief, and both holding space for hard feelings as well as promoting opportunities for posttraumatic growth to occur. Concurrently, conversation leaders should practice self-care to combat vicarious traumatization (including setting personal boundaries), and self-awareness to keep biases and judgements in control.

In the age of the #MeToo movement, radical feminism, sexual liberation, and increases in community violence, leaders need to be prepared to have tough conversations about a variety of overlapping topics. The disenfranchised nature of sexuality-related losses is a prime area where fearless leadership is needed. Professionals exist in the field of sexuality education and clinical sexology. Professionals also exist in the areas of thanatology, and grief and loss. Conversation leaders and facilitators who can comfortably address both of these areas are primed to target part of the population feeling unheard, unseen, disrespected, ashamed, and alone. Sexuality cuts across racial, ethnic, cultural, socioeconomic, age, and ability lines as does grief and loss. The intersection of these two areas is no exception. This chapter unpacks sexuality using the Circles of Sexuality and one or two of many possible examples of loss in each circle. Clearly, the information provided here is not exhaustive of all potential sexuality-related losses but rather, is meant to highlight some of the most common occurrences. The PLISSIT model provides an extra framework for organizing conversations and referring out or connecting people with appropriate resources where needed.

Process Questions and Considerations

Leaders of conversations regarding sexuality-related losses should consider the following questions as part of their preparation, as well as their ongoing qualification to lead effectively:

1. What biases or judgements do you hold about sexuality and loss? What is your understanding of the grieving process as it relates to sexuality?
2. What questions would be beneficial to ask an audience when leading a conversation about a sexuality-related loss?
3. Are there current events (e.g., news, media) applicable to the type or types of sexuality-related losses you can use as examples or processing points?
4. What information have you obtained, either through reading, training, or other means, that inform your style of leading conversations about sexuality-related losses?
5. Which areas of sexuality are you most comfortable addressing and why? Which areas are you most uncomfortable addressing and why?
6. Which areas of grief and loss are you most comfortable addressing and why? Which areas are you most uncomfortable addressing and why?
7. How can you challenge yourself to have courageous conversations to address your areas of discomfort?

In the case of sexuality-related losses, more often than not, no one has physically died with the exception of perinatal loss. There are no funeral services, burial practices, or collective mourning associated with these experiences. What is associated are feelings of loss, grief, and isolated mourning in some cases. Having qualified and effective conversation leaders in this content area is necessary in facilitating understanding, eliciting empathy, and coordinating appropriate resources when needed.

References

American College of Obstetricians and Gynecologists. (2018). Early pregnancy loss. ACOG Practice Bulletin No. 200. *American College of Obstetricians and Gynecologists, 132*, e197–207.

Annon, J. S. (1976). The PLISSIT model: A proposed conceptual scheme for the behavioral treatment of sexual problems. *The Journal of Sex Education and Therapy, 2*(1), 1–15. Doi:10.1080/01614576.1976.11074483

Bender, C., (Producer) & Phillips, T. (Director). (2009). *The Hangover* (Motion Picture). USA: Warner Brothers.

Black, B. P., & Wright, P. (2012). Posttraumatic growth and transformation as outcomes of perinatal loss. *Illness, Crisis & Loss, 20*(3), 225–237. Doi:10.2190/IL.20.3.b

Branson, D. C. (2018). Vicarious trauma, themes in research, and terminology: A review of literature. *Traumatology*. Retrieved from https://doi.org/10.1037/trm0000161

Calhoun, L. G., & Tedeschi, R. G. (Eds.). (2006). *Handbook of posttraumatic growth: Research and practice*. Mahwah, NJ: Erlbaum.

Cernero, J., Strawn, B. D., & Abernethy, A. D. (2017). Embodied grief and primary metaphor: Towards a new paradigm for integrative bereavement groups. *Journal of Psychology and Christianity, 36*(4), 325–333. Retrieved from http://0-search.ebscohost.com.libcat.widener.edu/login.aspx?direct=true&db=psyh&AN=2018-15699-006&site=eds-live

Dailey, D. (1981). Sexual expression in aging. In F. J. Berghorn, D. E. Schafer, & Associates (Eds.), *The dynamics of aging* (pp. 311–333). Boulder, CO: Westview Press.

Doka, K. J. (Ed.) (1989). *Disenfranchised grief: Recognizing hidden sorrow*. Lexington, MA: Lexington Books.

Figley, C. R. (Ed.), (1995). *Compassion fatigue: Coping with secondary traumatic stress disorder in those who treat the traumatized*. New York, NY: Brummer/Mazel.

Krosch, D. J., & Shakespeare-Finch, J. (2017). Grief, traumatic stress, and posttraumatic growth in women who have experienced pregnancy loss. *Psychological Trauma: Theory, Research, Practice, and Policy, 9*(4), 425–433. Doi:10.1037/tra000183

Kubler-Ross, E. (1969). *On death and dying*. New York, NY: Macmillan.

Kubler-Ross, E., & Kessler, D. (2005). *On grief & grieving: Finding the meaning of grief through the five stages of loss*. New York: Scribner.

McCann, I. L., & Pearlman, L. A. (1990). Vicarious trauma: A framework for understanding the psychological effects of working with victims. *Journal of Traumatic Stress, 3*, 131–149. Retrieved from http://dx.doi.org/10.1007/BF00975140

Meagher, D. K., & Balk, D. E. (2013), *Handbook of thanatology* (2nd ed.). New York: Routledge

Pillai-Friedman, S., & Ashline, J. L. (2014). Women, breast cancer survivorship, sexual losses, and disenfranchised grief: A treatment model for clinicians. *Sexual and Relationship Therapy, 29*(4), 436–453. Retrieved from https://doi.org/10.1080/14681994.2014.934340

Shea, J. (2000). *Spirituality and health care: Reaching toward a holistic future*. Chicago, IL: The Park Ridge Center.

Staggs, S. (2014). The Big Deal With "Little-t traumas". *Psych Central*. Retrieved March 2, 2019, from https://blogs.psychcentral.com/after-trauma/2014/02/the-big-deal-with-little-t-traumas/

Stillbirth. (2017). Retrieved March 2, 2019 from www.marchofdimes.org/complications/stillbirth.aspx

Strong, B., & Cohen, T. F. (2017). *The marriage and family experience: Intimate relationships in a changing society* (13th ed.), Boston, MA: Cengage Learning.

16 Paradigms of Activism and Engagement for Sexuality Leadership in Faith Communities

Candace Robertson-James
and Dr. George James

Sex, Sexuality, and Relationships

In general, relationships represent vehicles through which people connect with one another and experience themselves more fully. They are the cornerstones of human interactions and fulfillment. Relationships serve as powerful tools of strength, comfort, activation, engagement, and connection. They imbue confidence, health, and freedom (Mental Health Foundation, 2016; Waldinger, Cohen, Schulz, & Crowell, 2015; Waldinger & Schulz, 2010). However, healthy, positive, strong, and fulfilling relationships don't happen by accident. They require education, discourse, modeling, and an infrastructure to support advocacy. Moreover, ill-formed, misguided, and toxic relationships and interactions lead to immense struggle, distress, trauma, and other negative and harmful outcomes (Mental Health Foundation, 2016; DeVogli, Chandola, & Marmot, 2007). Therefore, leadership models that strengthen communities and practitioners are needed to address challenges and promote healthy romantic partnerships. Furthermore, leadership is needed to address the multifaceted barriers to achieving a healthy intimate bond and sexual response, a key component of romantic relationships. This chapter provides an overview of sexuality as it relates to institutions of faith as important stakeholders and discusses the role of faith communities as collaborative partners in sexuality leadership.

Intimacy and sex remain integral components of the human romantic relational experience. Sexual desire and pleasure have the ability to either deepen intimate connections or invoke intense pain (Boston Women's Health Book Collective, 2011). Sexual expression is influenced by many factors including familial, social, cultural, religious, biological, and technological factors and healthy sexual expression may have different meanings for different groups (Claney, Hall, Anderson, & Canada, 2018; Cloete, 2012; Haffner, 2011). In fact, in honor of its 100th anniversary celebration in 2014, the American Sexual Health Association launched an initiative to ask individuals, both experts and lay communities alike, what a sexually healthy nation means to them. Perceptions of a sexually healthy nation included having 1. Access to the appropriate resources, tools, and information available to make informed decisions; 2. A healthy sexuality; 3. Healthy relationships; 4. Sexual acceptance; and 5. Understanding of one's body, sexual desire, and pleasure throughout the lifespan (American Sexual Health Association, 2014). Having access to appropriate resources, tools, and information includes access to birth control, information about sexually transmitted infections, understanding how the body changes as people age, skills to address conflict, and policies that promote healthy sexuality. A sexually healthy nation also includes acknowledgment of the sexual culture and the creation of a climate where individuals can accept themselves, their needs, desires, and imperfections. An understanding and awareness of what a healthy sexuality means is integral to sexual health as many people "remain uninformed" regarding their sexuality. Sexual health also expands beyond sex to an understanding of characteristics of healthy relationships and connections (American Sexual Health Association, 2014). There are many facets of sexual health and well-being and an agenda that is able to comprehensively address each of these areas is needed. Aspects of healthy sexuality can include behavior, functionality, expression, emotions, and cognitive components (Claney et al., 2018).

Although sexuality begins at birth, for many, adolescence marks the beginning of human sexuality and the development of intimate relationships (Claney et al., 2018). Sexuality includes expression of biological, psychological, spiritual, and social identity and integrates multiple dimensions of oneself although the behavioral dimensions are most commonly discussed (Claney et al., 2018). According to the Centers for Disease Control and Prevention, 40% of high school students surveyed in 2017 reported having sexual intercourse, with 30% reporting sexual intercourse in the past three months (Centers for Disease Control and Prevention, 2018, 2017). Overall, just under 60% (58.1%) of students have had sex by 12th grade (Ethier, Kann, & McManus, 2018) and most teens report sexual activity with a "steady" partner (Martinez, Copen, & Abma, 2011). During this time of increased exploration of sexuality, sexual risk increases. Sexually transmitted infections remain high, with disparities observed between racial/ethnic groups (CDC, 2017). In addition, 7% of teens reported being forced to have sex (CDC, 2018).

Research on adult sexual behavior suggests that most adults (>80%) report masturbation, vaginal sex, and oral sex. Additional sexual behaviors reported include anal sex, sending/receiving digital nude/seminude photos, reading erotic stories, and watching sexually explicit videos (Herbenick et al., 2017; Herbeneick et al., 2010; National Survey of Sexual Health and Behavior, 2009). Moreover, sexual activity is a key indicator for marital satisfaction as couples who frequently engage in sexual activity report higher satisfaction than those who do not (Galinsky & Waite, 2014). Although sexual activity declines as individuals age, studies show older adults continue to engage in sexual activity (Thomas, Hess, & Thurston, 2015; Galinsky, Waite, & McClintock, 2014; Lindau et al., 2007). Nevertheless, research suggests, Americans are having less sex than they were a decade or two ago due to an increasing number of individuals who are neither married or in a committed relationship and a decline in the sexual activity among those who are partnered (Twenge, Sherman, & Wells, 2017). In addition, people who struggle with sexual dysfunction, arousal, penetration, or other disorders may be reluctant to address concerns with healthcare providers, and many providers are often reluctant to conduct a comprehensive sexual history (Shindel & Parish, 2013; Maes & Louis, 2011). Moreover, one in four women and one in nine men report being victims of sexual violence (Centers for Disease Control and Prevention, 2017). Thus, many factors influence sexuality experiences and perspectives and need to be considered by sexuality leaders and practitioners.

Sexuality is influenced by sexual beliefs, attitudes, religious beliefs, and cultural and gendered sexual scripts (Claney et al., 2018). For instance, research on the role of gender norms found an association between perceptions of men's and women's roles in society and sexual behaviors (Lefkowitz, Shearer, Gillen, & Espinosa-Hernandez, 2014). This research also discussed implications for individuals of faith as others noted an association between religious individuals and gender norm stereotypes (Lefkowitz et al., 2014). Sexuality is also dynamic as its meaning, norms, and forms of expression change over time and throughout history (Carpenter, 2010). Changes in life course patterns and opportunities as well as historical events influence the construction of sexuality (Carpenter, 2010). Thus, practitioners and leaders must aptly consider the multifaceted and complex nature of sexuality and how these continue to change for diverse groups.

Sexuality and Faith

Faith institutions play an important role in communities and individuals' lives (Pew Research Center, 2016). The Religious Landscape Study conducted by the Pew Research Center in 2014 reported almost 80% of Americans identify with a religious affiliation, 71% reporting Christian. While many (77%) also rated religion as very important (53%) or somewhat important (24%) in their lives, 75% of Blacks/African Americans reported religion as very important to them (Pew Research Center, 2018). Moreover, some adults (27%) may consider themselves to be spiritual but not religious. This represents a heterogeneous group of individuals with diverse characteristics. While some (37%) of these individuals may be unaffiliated with a specific religious tradition, many (60%) do report some type of affiliation with a religion (Lipka & Gecewicz, 2017). Although the term *spirituality* means different things to different people, it generally encompasses one's concept of meaning, purpose, and connection to a higher power and may or may not be connected to identification with or practice of a specific organized religion. As religion and spirituality play important roles in many people's lives, they shape attitudes, beliefs, and some behaviors. Religion is also influenced by and integrates cultural and social norms, experiences, and perspectives (Pew Research Center, 2016). Furthermore, faith organizations have often been recruited to participate and have actively engaged in health promotion initiatives including sexual health to better meet the needs of the members of their church, mosque, parish, or synagogue (Dufour et al., 2013). Thus, religious and spiritual leaders may be uniquely positioned to shape (and influence) perspectives on sexuality (Turner & Stayton, 2014).

Faith systems influence how people live out their sexuality (Cloete, 2012). Individuals experience their sexuality through the intersecting lenses of their values, attitudes, and belief systems that are often influenced by their family, faith, culture, tradition, education, and politics (Turner & Stayton, 2014). While some may not immediately appreciate the connection between sexuality and spirituality, research suggests that faith, religious doctrines, and value systems influence sexual decisions (Stewart, 2016; Haffner, 2011). In addition, many individuals, regardless of their identification with a specific religious tradition, grapple with and have to reconcile their sense of spirituality and sexuality: their spiritual selves with their sexual selves (Freitas, 2008). The absence of spaces that allow individuals to fully reflect upon and share their spirituality and sexuality may leave them isolated (Freitas, 2008). Thus, formal and informal faith leaders from all religious traditions may play an important role in sexuality leadership that has often gone unaddressed.

Community- and faith-based organizations have provided sexuality education for many decades (Landry, Lindberg, Gemmill, Boonstra, & Finer, 2011; Haffner, 2011). The Sexuality Information and Education Council of the United States (SIECUS) provides guidance on the goals of comprehensive sexuality education, which includes information on human sexuality (development, relationships, attraction, libido, behavior, and health), exploration of sexual attitudes (values, self-esteem, relationships, exploration, obligations, and responsibilities), development of interpersonal skills (flirting, communication, foreplay, decision making, consent, safe words) and responsibility in sexual relationships (abstinence, pressure, boundaries, contraception, sexual health, pre and post intercourse procedures and hygiene) (Landry et al., 2011). Communities of faith have been actively engaged in the development of individuals, providing safety and promoting social justice. This is particularly important for sexuality and sexual health as research supports the growing role of structural inequalities, poverty, homophobism, xenophobism, incarceration, etc. in sexual health and risk (Nunn et al., 2012). Moreover, although many faith communities have historically been restrictive and limiting in their discussion of sexuality, and conservative religious groups have received much attention, there is growing recognition of the role of faith leaders in sexuality leadership. Some denominations have even established policies and curricula addressing sexuality education (The Religious Institute, 2018; Landry et al., 2011). These curricula include age appropriate comprehensive sex education that addresses attitudes and values, relationships and interpersonal skills, and responsible decision-making, and includes information about pregnancy, contraceptive options, and sexually transmitted infections. (The Religious Institute, 2018; Wise about Youth, 2013). However, recommendations for successful faith-based programs include building coalitions and partnerships to promote sexuality initiatives (Landry et al., 2011).

Faith communities routinely serve as important support systems for individuals and couples. They often include diverse groups and influence knowledge, attitudes, and beliefs (Cornelius, 2009). They supplement education and knowledge gaps of congregants (Winer, 2011) and disseminate messages on sexuality and relationships that influence attitudes and decisions. In addition, faith communities can forge important partnerships with other community organizations, have strong social network systems and an infrastructure to support programming, leadership, and advocacy (Hach & Roberts-Dobie, 2016). Moreover, faith communities play an important role in sexuality leadership as they can effectively engage in diverse and multigenerational approaches (Hach & Roberts-Dobie, 2016; Cloete, 2012). In fact, Turner and Stayton (2014) assert that faith leaders desire ways to discuss sexuality and sexual concerns with their congregations. Cloete (2012) asserts that sexuality is a spiritual issue and that spirituality and sexuality are closely related as they represent expressions of human connection. However, despite these assertions, many leaders in faith communities feel unprepared to facilitate these discussions as they may themselves have limited knowledge and may not have received formal education on sexual expression, key issues, concepts, and challenges related to sexuality (Turner & Stayton, 2014; Pichon et al., 2012). Nevertheless, congregants turn to them with questions, concerns, desires, challenges, fantasies and fears regarding their individual sexuality as well as policy issues and faith-related concerns to sexuality such as abortion and premarital sex (Turner & Stayton, 2014). Among leaders who report higher efficacy and comfort in discussing sexuality, leadership role and denomination is associated with comfort (i.e., pastors and pastors' spouses, priests, and Imans were less comfortable compared to other leader types) (Pichon et al., 2012). In addition, faith communities that are governed by their own laws and organizational structure seem to be more comfortable integrating sexuality compared to those who are accountable to a larger governance structure (Pichon et al., 2012). Leaders who are accountable to a larger governance structure may feel limitations and pressures to promote messages approved by the larger structure. The additional layer of bureaucracy may also limit their comfort with integrating sexuality.

In response to some faith leaders' limited knowledge and capacity to address sexuality issues, desires and concerns, sexuality education is increasingly recognized as a need to be addressed in seminary (Turner & Stayton, 2014). Religious doctrines that promote stigma, judgement, and condemnation are harmful as they create fear, shame, and guilt related to sex and sexuality (Haffner, 2011; Dufour et al., 2013). The messages provided by some leaders in faith communities are often narrow in scope; don't consider historical, social, and cultural norms; and may inadvertently isolate individuals and couples of faith. Moreover, some faith leaders feel ill equipped to address sexuality from a comprehensive lens as well as the complex sexual histories and experiences of their congregants. It is imperative that faith leaders understand key sexual and relational issues and challenges experienced by their congregants and their communities at large. Key partnerships with practitioners can help to address this gap.

Faith communities could also have a significant role in sexuality leadership, particularly in the area of sexual ethics (Winer, 2011). These communities contribute consciously and unconsciously to perspectives on the purpose of sex, sexual expression, sexual decision-making, consent, sexual exploration, reproductive justice, sexual violence, reproductive coercion, dysfunction, and other areas.

Efforts to build the capacity of faith leaders to effectively address issues related to sex and sexuality are needed. In fact, the Office of Adolescent Health asserts that faith-based communities are essential for teen pregnancy prevention initiatives as they support teens and families in healthy sexual development (Torres et al., 2017). Moreover, faith communities may be particularly integral for communities of color as African Americans and Latinos report high rates of church attendance (Pew Research Center, 2009).

Research investigating the role of faith leaders in sexuality has concluded that diverse aspects of sexuality should be addressed. These may include recognition of the self as a sexual being, sexual negotiation skills, sexual ethics, exploration, communication, touching, libido, honesty, relationships, fears, temptations, sexual identity, rights and responsibilities, sexuality, intimacy, consent, love, marriage, vulnerability, wellness, monogamy, non-monogamy, available resources, masturbation, STIs, sexual abuse, sexual violence, sex trafficking, anatomy and physiology, boundaries, infertility, pregnancy, commitment, infidelity, divorce, aging and sexuality, reproductive technologies, sexual dysfunction, and pornography (Hach & Roberts-Dobie, 2016; Turner & Stayton, 2014; Winer, 2011; Cornelius, 2009).

Exploring Models of Activism and Engagement: Adopting Principles and Strategies From Community-Based Participatory Research

Programming in faith institutions can vary greatly. These can include faith-based and faith-placed programs as well as collaborative partnerships. Faith-based programs are programs that originate in the church or faith institution (Hach & Roberts-Dobie, 2016; Campbell et al., 2007). These programs are often designed by and for members of the faith community. As such, these programs are able to integrate core values and principles (Stewart, 2016). Faith-placed programs originate outside of the church or faith institution but are implemented within the faith environment. As such, these programs may not include core values and doctrines of the faith. Faith communities may choose to implement the program in its entirety or parts of the program deemed most relevant (Stewart, 2016). Lastly, programs may be established through collaborative relationships, which include partnerships between faith institutions and outside community groups (Hach & Roberts-Dobie, 2016; Stewart, 2016; Campbell et al., 2007).

Many faith institutions have a legacy of providing for the needs of their communities and have also collaborated with efforts to promote health messages (Stewart, 2016). A commitment to healing, health, wellness, and addressing the needs of communities may make faith leaders ideal partners (Newlin, Dyess, Allard, Chase, & Melkus, 2012). Faith leaders are often motivated by efforts to meet the needs of their congregants and communities (Torres et al., 2017). As such, efforts to highlight sexuality as a "community need" regarding knowledge deficits, sexual dysfunction, sexual violence, reproductive justice, sexually transmitted infections, pregnancy, and the role of sexuality (multifaceted nature) in healthy intimate relationships, existing disparities, experiences, belief systems and other factors could allow faith leaders to recognize the need to address emergent sexuality issues experienced by their congregations/members. In addition, initiatives such as President Obama's National AIDS Strategy called for partnerships with faith-based organizations (Nunn et al., 2012). Research exploring effective strategies for engaging faith leaders recognizes the importance of community-based participatory research (CBPR), interfaith collaborations, adopting human rights, and restorative approaches (Nunn et al., 2012). Collaborative models of engagement have often been proven the most successful (Hach & Roberts-Dobie, 2016). Moreover, in recognition of the problem-focused programmatic and research agenda often promoted by researchers linked to disease reduction efforts, research that is useful to sexuality and other practitioners and community and faith leaders requires additional paradigms that support a more positive and holistic approach (Reece & Dodge, 2004).

Community-based participatory research (CBPR) is a participatory approach that includes community members, leaders, practitioners, and researchers as equitable partners (Israel et al., 2010). It enables researchers and practitioners to meet the needs of communities while addressing important concerns (Weiner & McDonald, 2013). CBPR aims to integrate knowledge with action and advocacy. Its core tenets include identifying opportunities to build on the strengths of communities, fostering colearning and capacity building and promoting an agenda that is mutually beneficial to all partners (Israel et al., 2010; Rhodes, Malow, & Jolly, 2010). Collaborative partnerships between faith communities, sexuality practitioners, leaders, and advocates that recognize the diversity of faith expression may lead to more integrated approaches to sexuality. Researchers and practitioners must move beyond solely engaging in faith-based and faith-placed initiatives that often involve faith leaders superficially in order to embrace a more participatory approach that engages faith leaders and communities as partners and colleagues to more effectively address issues, concerns, challenges, knowledge gaps, and understanding of sexuality (Newlin et al., 2012). Principles and strategies from community participatory research models can inform collaborative paradigms for sexuality leadership that integrate understanding of faith and sexuality. Core principles of this model include involving faith and community sexuality, sexual health, sexual violence prevention advocates and organizations in the development of a sexuality agenda.

Barriers to participatory models may include the time-intensive nature of building relationships and partnerships, money, a lack of infrastructure to support such collaboration, trust, structural inequalities such as racism, classism, sexism, and other -isms. Recognition of and respect for community voice and expertise is CBPR's greatest asset (Weiner & McDonald, 2013). CBPR recognizes the mutual ownership of products and enables multilevel action through individual agency, community advocacy, and political and social change (Rhodes et al., 2010). Participatory models that integrate communities of faith along with other practitioners and stakeholders may benefit from the development of policies and practices that address various institutional, cultural, social, and spiritual value systems that inform sexuality, sexual expression, and behaviors.

Exploring Models of Activism and Engagement

It is important for current approaches to sexuality leadership in faith communities to also include attention to the role of structural inequalities in the development of sexuality. Sexuality leaders should also be able to recognize how historical and present-day racism, sexism, and other systems of inequality influence sexual decisions, attitudes, behaviors, perspectives, sexual expression, and risk (Torres et al., 2017; Robertson-James & Jeanty, 2016). As sexuality is influenced by our social, spiritual, and cultural experiences, initiatives that consider how these factors intersect to inform sexuality for diverse populations is needed. Faith leaders can mobilize diverse communities, which are inclusive of multiple generations, in order to facilitate conversations around sexual health, healthy sexual development, sexual risk and violence, as well as contextual factors. Moreover, additional approaches that draw on action research and youth empowerment strategies may also well inform collaborative efforts in sexuality leadership. These approaches have been integral in promoting sexual health policies and programs. Strategies from these frameworks can allow faith leaders and sexuality practitioners alike to identify areas of concerns for various populations (Villa-Torres & Svanemyr, 2015). Partnerships between faith institutions and agencies such as Planned Parenthood, other local and regional sexuality resource agencies and organizations, healthcare providers, practitioners, and others to provide culturally relevant information are needed (Cornelius, 2009). Moreover, community liaisons can be great assets in serving as a bridge between faith communities and sexuality/sexual health leaders and practitioners (Torres et al., 2017).

Despite the availability of sexuality and relationship resources, many congregants continue to suffer in silence with reconciling previous sexual histories, experiences of abuse and violence, and medical and physiological issues that influence sexual experiences of pleasure and their understanding of notions of active consent, anatomy, and reproductive and relational health (Torres et al., 2017). Faith leaders can contribute to sexuality leadership through facilitating a trauma-informed culture, environment, programming, and other spaces where love, romantic relationships, dating, marriage, and sexuality (throughout the lifespan) can be explored (Torres et al., 2017; Freitas, 2008). Faith leaders who have been intimately connected with other advocacy and justice efforts can contribute their expertise to sexuality justice as they engage their congregants in discussions of responsibilities related to sex and sexuality, the multiple dimensions of sexuality (physical, ethical, social, psychological, emotional, spiritual), consent and sexual decisions, while both affirming the positive attributes of sex and sexuality and recognizing sexual risks (Haffner, 2011). Faith leaders should be considered an integral part of sexuality leadership because they play a special role in communities as they promote healing and restoration, outreach to a vast number of individuals across the lifespan, and are interested in meeting the material, spiritual, and developmental needs of communities and individuals (Briggs, Gilbert, Reece, Dodge, & Obeng, 2015; Haffner, 2011).

Process Questions and Considerations

1. How do you differentiate between spirituality and religion? What makes talking about sexuality and spirituality difficult for some leaders? What makes sexuality and religion difficult for some leaders?

2. Why might it be important that leaders be able to talk with constituents about masturbation? Abortion? Pre-marital sex? Kink?
3. Should faith-based institutions (e.g., church, mosque, synagogue, temple, etc.) be open to hosting sexuality programs even though they may not be knowledgeable about comprehensive sexuality education?
4. What do you think constituents need in order to feel comfortable talking about sexuality at their place of worship? How might sexuality programming be integrated with other health promotion or social justice initiatives?
5. In your opinion, how might religious leaders best get sexual health training?

References

American Sexual Health Association. (2014). *Creating a sexually healthy nation* (video). Retrieved December 2018, from www.youtube.com/watch?v=na7szf8u9nw

Boston Women's Health Book Collective. (2011). *Our bodies, ourselves.* New York: Simon & Schuster. Book Excerpts: Sexuality & Relationships. Our Bodies Ourselves: Information Inspires Action. Retrieved December 2018, from www.ourbodiesourselves.org/publications/our-bodies-ourselves-2011/

Briggs, L. M., Gilbert, K. R., Reece, M. D., Dodge, B. M., & Obeng, S. G. (2015). To God be the glory: Discussing sex in evangelical communities in Southern Nigeria. *African Journal of Reproductive Health, 19*(4), 41–49.

Campbell, M. K., Hudson, M. A., Resnicow, K., Blakeney, N., Paxton, A., & Baskin, M. (2007). Church based health promotion interventions: Evidence band lessons learned. *Annual Review of Public Health, 28,* 213–234.

Carpenter, L. (2010). *Gendered Sexuality Over the Lifecourse: A Conceptual Framework. Sociological Perspectives, 53*(2), 155–178.

CDC. (2016). *Sexually transmitted diseases surveillance: STDs in racial and ethnic minorities. 2017.* Retrieved November 2018, from www.cdc.gov/std/stats16/minorities.htm

CDC. (2017). Youth Risk Behavior Surveillance—United States. *MMWR Surveill Summ, 67*(SS-8), 2018. www.cdc.gov/mmwr/volumes/67/ss/ss6708a1.htm?s_cid=ss6708a1_w

CDC. (2018). *National intimate partner and sexual violence survey—2010–2012 state report.* Retrieved November 2018, from www.cdc.gov/violenceprevention/nisvs/summaryreports.html

Centers for Disease Control and Prevention. (2018). Sexual Risk Behaviors: HIV, STD, & Teen Pregnancy. *Prevention.* Retrieved November 2018, from www.cdc.gov/healthyyouth/sexualbehaviors/

Claney, C. J., Hall, M. E. L., Anderson, T. L., & Canada, A. L. (2018). Sexual without sex: A qualitative study of single emerging adult evangelical women. *Psychology of Religion and Spirituality.* Retrieved from http://dx.doi.org/10.1037/rel0000191

Cloete, A. (2012). Youth culture, media and sexuality: What could faith communities contribute? *HTS Teologiese Studies/ Theological Studies*, 68(2). Retrieved from http://dx.doi.org/10.4102/hts.v68i2.1118

Cornelius, J. B. (2009). The bees and the bible: Single African American mothers' perceptions of a faith-based sexuality education program. *Journal of Cultural Diversity*, 16(1), 21–25.

De Vogli, R., Chandola, T., & Marmot, M. G. (2007). Negative aspects of close relationships and heart disease. *Archives of Internal Medicine*, 167(18), 1951–1957

Dufour, M. K., Maiorana, A., Allen, C., Kassie, N., Thomas, M., Myers, J. (2013). How faith-based organizations' doctrines regarding sexuality affect their participation in the public health response to HIV in the Eastern Caribbean. *Sexuality Research and Social Policy*, 10, 221–232. Doi:10.1007/s13178-013-0123-8

Ethier, K. A., Kann, L., & McManus, T. (2018). Sexual intercourse among high school students—29 States and United States overall, 2005–2015. *MMWR Morbidity Mortality Weekly Report*, 66, 1393–1397. Doi:http://dx.doi.org/10.15585/mmwr.mm665152a1

Freitas, D. (2008). *Sex and the soul: Juggling sexuality, spirituality, romance and religion on America's college campuses*. Oxford: Oxford University Press.

Galinsky, A. M., & Waite, L. J. (2014). Sexual activity and psychological health as mediators of the relationship between physical health and marital quality. *Journals of Gerontology Series B*, 69(3), 482–492.

Galinsky, A., Waite, L. J., & McClintock, M. K. (2014). Sexual interest and motivation, sexual behavior and physical contact in NSHAP Wave 2. *Journals of Gerontology Series B*, 69(Suppl. 2), S83–98.

Hach, A., & Roberts-Dobie, S. (2016). Give us the words: Protestant faith leaders and sexuality education in their churches. *Sex Education*, 16(6), 619–633.

Haffner, D. W. (2011). Dearly beloved: Sexuality education in faith communities. *American Journal of Sexuality Education*, 6, 1–6.

Herbenick, D., Bowling, J., Fu, T. C., Dodge, B., Guerra-Reyes, L., & Sanders, S (2017). Sexual diversity in the United States: Results from a nationally representative probability sample of adult women and men. *PloS ONE*, 12(7), p. e0181198. Retrieved from https://doi.org/10.1371/journal.pone.0181198; https://journals.plos.org/plosone/article?id=10.1371/journal.pone.0181198

Herbenick, D., Reece, M., Schick, V., Sanders, S. A., Dodge, B., & Fortenberry, J. D. (2010). Sexual behavior in the United States: Results from a national probability sample of men and women ages 14–94. *Journal of Sexual Medicine*, 7(suppl 5), 255–265.

Israel, B. A., Coombe, C. M., Cheezum, R. R., Schulz, A. J., McGranaghan, R. J., Lichtenstein, R., Reyes, A. G., Clement, J., & Burris, A. (2010). Community based participatory research: A capacity building approach for policy advocacy aimed at eliminating health disparities. *American Journal of Public Health*, 100(11), 2094–2102.

Landry, D., Lindberg, L. D., Gemmill, A., Boonstra, H., & Finer, L. B. (2011). Review of the role of faith and community organizations in providing comprehensive sexuality education. *American Journal of Sexuality Education*, 6, 75–103.

Lefkowitz, E. S., Shearer, C. L., Gillen, M. M., & Espinosa-Hernandez, G. (2014). How gendered attitudes relate to women's and men's sexual behaviors and beliefs. *Sex Culture, 18*(4), 833–846.

Lindau, S. T., Schumm, P., Laumann, E. O., Levinson, W., O'Muircheartaigh, C. A., Waite, L. J. (2007). A study of sexuality and health among older adults in the United States. *New England Journal of Medicine, 357*(8), 762–774. Doi:10.1056/NEJMoa067423

Lipka, M., & Gecewicz, C. (2017). More Americans now say they're spiritual but not religious. *Pew research center.* Retrieved from www.pewresearch.org/fact-tank/2017/09/06/more-americans-now-say-theyre-spiritual-but-not-religious/ Accessed April 2019

Maes, C. A., & Louis, M. (2011). Nurse practitioners' sexual history-taking practices with adults 50 and older. *The Journal of Nurse Practitioners, 7*(3), 216–222.

Martinez, G., Copen, C. E., & Abma, J. C. (2011). Teenagers in the United States: Sexual activity, contraceptive use, and childbearing, 2006–2010. *National Survey of Family Growth, Vital and Health Statistics, 23*, 31, Retrieved from www.cdc.gov/nchs/data/series/sr_23/sr23_031.pdf.

Mental Health Foundation (May 2016). *Relationships in the 21st century.* London: Mental Health Foundation. Accessed January 2019. www.mentalhealth.org.uk/publications/relationships-21st-century-forgotten-foundation-mental-health-and-wellbeing

National Survey of Sexual Health and Behavior. (2009). Retrieved from https://nationalsexstudy.indiana.edu/keyfindings/index.html Accessed April 2019.

Newlin, K., Dyess, S. M., Allard, E., Chase, S., & Melkus, G. D. (2012). A methodological review of faith-based health promotion literature: Advancing the science to expand delivery of diabetes education to Black Americans. *Journal of Religion and Health, 51*(4), 1075–1097.

Nunn, A., Cornwall, A., Chute, N., Sanders, J., Thomas, G., James, G., Lally, M., Trooskin, S., & Flanigan, T. (2012). Keeping the faith: African American faith leaders' perspectives and recommendations for reducing racial disparities in HIV/AIDS infection. *PloS ONE, 7*(5), e3617.

Pew Research Center. (2014). *Religious landscape study.* Retrieved from www.pewforum.org/religious-landscape-study/. Accessed November 2018.

Pew Research Center. (2016). *Religion in everyday life.* Retrieved from www.pewforum.org/2016/04/12/religion-in-everyday-life/. Accessed January 2019

Pew Research Center. (2018). *Religion and public health. A religious portrait of African Americans, 2009.* Retrieved from www.pewforum.org/2009/01/30/a-religious-portrait-of-african-americans/ Accessed November 2018.

Pichon, L. C., Griffith, D. M., Campbell, B., Allen, J. O, Williams, T. T., & Addo, A. Y. (2012). Faith leaders' comfort implementing an HIV prevention curriculum in a faith setting. *Journal of Health Care for the Poor and Underserved, 23*, 1253–1265.

Reece, M., & Dodge, B. (2004). A study in sexual health applying the principles of community-based participatory research. *Archives of Sexual Behavior, 33*(3), 235–247.

Religious Institute. (2018). Retrieved from http://religiousinstitute.org/projects/seminaries/ Accessed January 2019

Rhodes, S. D., Malow, R. M., & Jolly, C. (2010). Community-based participatory research (CBPR): A new and not-so-new approach to HIV/AIDS prevention, care and treatment. *AIDS Education and Prevention, 22*(3), 173–183.

Robertson-James, C., & Jeanty, J. (2016). Let's talk sex: Exploring sexual risk and experiences of discrimination in African Americans. *Journal of Black Sexuality and Relationships, 2*(4), 93–113

Shindel, A. W., & Parish, S. J. (2013). Sexuality education in North American medical schools: Current status and future directions. *The Journal of Sexual Medicine, 10*(1), 3–17.

Stewart, J. (2016). Faith-Based Interventions: Pathways to health promotion. *Western Journal of Nursing Research, 38*(7), 787–789.

Thomas, H. N., Hess, R., & Thurston, R. C. (2015). Correlates of sexual activity and satisfaction in midlife older women. *Annals of Family Medicine, 13*(4), 336–342.

Torres, J., Johnson-Baker, K., Bell, S., Freeny, J., Edwards, S. Tortolero, S. R., & Swain-Ogbonno, H. I. (2017). Working with faith-based communities to develop an education tool kit on relationships, sexuality and contraception. *Journal of Applied Research on Children: Informing Policy for Children at Risk, 8*(1) Article 6. Retrieved from https://digitalcommons.library.tmc.edu/childrenatrisk/vol8/iss1/

Turner. Y., & Stayton, W. (2014). The twenty first century challenges to sexuality and religion. *Journal of Religion and Health, 53*, 483–497.

Twenge, J. M., Sherman, R. A., & Wells, B. E. (2017). Declines in sexual frequency among American adults, 1989–2014. *Archives of Sexual Behavior, 46*, 2389–2401. Doi:10.1007/s10508-017-0953-1

Villa-Torres, L., & Svanemyr, J. (2015). Ensuring youth's right to participation and promotion of youth leadership in the development of sexual and reproductive health policies and programs. *Journal of Adolescent Health, 56*, S51–S57.

Waldinger, R. J., Cohen, S., Schulz, M. S., & Crowell, J. A. (2015). Security of attachment to spouses in late life: Concurrent and prospective links with cognitive and emotional wellbeing, Clinical Psychological science, 3(4), 516–529

Waldinger, R. J., & Schulz, M. S. (2010). What's love got to do with it? Social functioning, perceived health, and daily happiness in married octogenarians. *Psychol Aging, 25*(2), 422–431.

Weiner, J., & McDonald, J. (2013). The models of community-based participatory research. *Leonard Davis Institute of Health Economics, 18*(5).

Winer, LN. (2011). Sacred choices: Adolescent relationships and sexual ethics: The reform movement's response to the need for faith-based sexuality education. *American Journal of Sexuality Education, 6*, 20–31.

Wise About Youth. (2013). Retrieved from www.hhs.gov/ash/oah/sites/default/files/ash/oah/oah-initiatives/teen_pregnancy/training/Assests/teens_faith_sexuality.pdf Accessed April 2019

17 Addressing White Fragility Through Mindfulness-Based Inquiry in Sexuality Leadership

Carole Clements and Satori Madrone

Mindfulness can be an intentional – and *steadying* – mechanism from which to develop an inclusionary practice of sexuality leadership, as it is an embodied state of non-judgmental awareness. It incorporates and advances diversity as necessary and universally beneficial, rather than a ubiquitous "add-on" and exclusionary practice focused on *marginalized* subjectivities (and their identities, desires, and behaviors) including people of color. In fact, because Western sexuality continues to evolve within a multiplicity of complex factors stemming from problematic histories of systemic inequality and privilege that perpetuate and center white, androessentialist science, research, and practice, mindfulness can serve as an exemplar for inclusionary sexuality leadership, making whiteness (and white fragility) both visible and tolerable to those who reap its privileges so that it can be dismantled.

From a long list of sexuality leaders who have guided Western sexuality discourse, some of the most noteworthy names include Freud (1932), Sanger (1938), Kinsey (Kinsey, Pomeroy, & Martin, 1948, Kinsey 1953), Masters and Johnson (1966, 1970), Gagnon and Simon (1973), and Foucault (1978). Notably, they are white and ancestrally European. While their work has been influential, their contributions should be both scrutinized and contextualized, particularly because the science of sex and the science of race arose at the same historical moment – amid a fervor of eugenics – causing the (construction of) sexuality and race to be perpetually intertwined (Laqueur, 1990). Among this bevy of contradictions, sexuality leadership is emerging as integral to the discourse to consider additional perspectives.

The discussion of sexuality leadership as an *intentional* process with an *intersectional* framework includes not only sexuality and leadership but also the embedded components of a Western epistemology and its associated power dynamics that continue to adversely impact sexuality in health, education, social work, policy-making, and all other facets of the culture. Because intersectionality situates individuals within a web of categorical identities (such as race, class, and gender) rather than a singular identity, it scrutinizes social divisions by highlighting multiple social locations and repeated and simultaneous marginalization (Taylor, 2010). As a component of sexuality leadership, intersectionality underscores how competing power structures interact in marginalized lives, illuminating for white leaders the exponential harm that ensues from unchecked assumptions and misperceptions.

The field of sexuality studies and its discourse continues to be affected and shaped by the invisibility of a nonreflexive whiteness that permeates its leadership system and anchors it to heteropatriarchal, hegemonic, and capitalist ideology. Diversity and, more recently, inclusion have been segmented into separate projects within work and management environments, targeting the integration of "out-groups" consisting of non-normative sexualities, genders, orientation, and non-white identities, into "in-groups" of homogenous representation (i.e., white, cismale, heterosexual, and able-bodied; Shore et al., 2011, p. 1263). This leads to an artificial distinction between "leadership" and "diversity and inclusion leadership" that promotes a problematic divide between white heteronormativity and everyone else. Bridging the gap requires reflexive analysis to disrupt how whiteness and white fragility impact sexuality leadership, awakening new possibilities for perceptions that facilitate change, as we address later.

This chapter situates white fragility – a decreased adeptness for tolerating racial stress that white people are socialized to have, articulated by Robin DiAngelo (2011, 2018a, 2018b), as central to an emerging sexuality leadership. Its six pillars map onto reflexive, sexuality leadership that prioritize social justice through an *inseparable* framework of diversity and inclusion. As white authors, we acknowledge that dissecting topics related to whiteness – including white fragility and white privilege – are often either intentionally or unconsciously avoided by our white colleagues in the field of sexuality studies or are otherwise maintained at a theoretical and metaphorical arm's length. In other words, while we (white) sexuality scholars, clinicians, educators, activists, policy-makers, researchers, and leaders may claim positionality as ally and/or implement intersectionality into our professional work and social lives, we often fall short of participating in ongoing reflexivity, seeking critical feedback from peers and mentors, and implementing change in all facets of our lives.

To address this transformational imperative, the second half of our chapter is devoted to providing an inclusive, mindfulness-based tool that is relevant to myriad aspects of sexuality leadership. As an improvisational present-centering method, the Five Eye Practices (Dilley, 2015) are utilized to disrupt white fragility and its normative, privileged assumptions and misperceptions. An effective leader is aware of biases and power dynamics that exist throughout the structure where leadership is facilitated, as well as within the leader's own personal positionality that informs the relationship with their collaborative team (Dworkin,

Schipani, Milliken, & Kneeland, 2018). In uncovering and confronting institutional and interpersonal biases of racism, heterosexism, ageism, ableism, and beyond, the mindful sexuality leader aims to develop awareness and compassion toward the dynamics that white fragility evokes, motivating intrapersonal, interpersonal, and systemic change. More specifically, by applying the Five Eye Practices to the challenges and dilemmas of sexuality leadership, insight into white fragility and its obstacles to cultivating diversity and inclusion inspire needed transformation.

(Re)Imagining Leadership

As the industrial economy has given way to the service industry and now the gig economy – including the multitude of freelancers and entrepreneurs – new forms of leadership have emerged that disrupt top-down hierarchies of management-style leadership and instead center collaborative relationships and community (Manthy, 2011). While certain neoliberal markets continue to thrive on white patriarchal elitism, dog-eat-dog competition, and a revolving door of replaceable cogs (Ho, 2009), other systems are venturing toward more humanizing and sustainable options (Reyes, Radina, & Aronson, 2018). The practice of *presencing* (Senge, Scharmer, Jaworski, & Flowers, 2004) and its embedded component of vulnerability – sometimes described as *radical love* – has emerged as a new best-practice approach to leadership; a strategy that has proven successful in nurturing psychological space for innovative thinking and creativity to emerge among diverse voices that might have otherwise been silenced by power dynamics and marginalization in the workplace or other environments (Reyes et al., 2018).

Within sexuality leadership, leaders are tasked with creating an intentional and inclusive space in which to facilitate discussion about culture-building for that particular project or beyond. Sometimes, a sexuality leader might be in the position to facilitate small groups, including budding non-profits, families, and even individuals. Regardless of the collective's size, each person's voice is recognized as having merit and value in that they are part of the whole (Reyes et al., 2018; Senge et al., 2004). This holistic process is enhanced by engaging in reflexivity around the performance of power, especially when engaged in topics of sexuality. While implicit cultural biases about leadership promote a hierarchy of authority within a knower-learner binary (Dworkin et al., 2018; Elbow, 1993), effective leaders explicitly dismantle the default expectations surrounding this archaic methodology to help reconfigure the environment as one that prioritizes the mindful and reflexive collaboration of all members (Senge et al, 2004).

Effective leadership focuses not only on collaboratively creating a vision for the future of the project with those involved, but works toward channeling the energy of that vision via a foundation that allows for remarkable (and often unanticipated) work to happen – focusing on what is emergent rather than *known* (Senge et al, 2004). Each participant possesses a unique brilliance that might not otherwise be evoked without intentionally establishing an operant culture that is created by the community at hand. All participants benefit by having a non-judgmental space in which to provide thoughts, ask for support and expect to give and receive feedback, which can be aided by mindfulness-based stress-management led by both individuals and the organization (Sharma & Rush, 2014; Tetrick & Winslow, 2015). This reciprocity of feedback is important to address, especially as it relates to a history of whiteness and other unearned social privileges. Due to the realities of white and masculine fragilities, people with unearned privileges are socialized to expect that their participation will be valued and their voices heard and unquestioned (DiAngelo, 2011, 2018b). Even in groups where the leader and/or community are from socially marginalized locations, the pervasiveness of white heteronormativity is typically functioning in the background, unless it is consciously identified and disrupted (DiAngelo, 2011). Therefore, while many authors center their leadership discussions around the principles and processes of effective leadership, we seek to create new conversations that prioritize how to identify and disrupt white fragility within leadership structures and systems by incorporating mindfulness-based practices. This necessitates dissecting whiteness as the operational ground in which Western-based systems of leadership and power are historically anchored.

The Strategy of Whiteness

To understand white fragility, we must first examine *whiteness*. Based in colonization, whiteness is an economic, legitimizing, hierarchal, heteropatriarchal, hegemonic, and individualizing social-organizing framework that believes in and perpetuates its own moral authority (Gabriel, 2000). It is also a fabrication that can be weakened through exposure.

> Whiteness is not a monolithic discourse, and whites are not a cohesive, homogenous ethnic group. . . . The fact that whiteness is constantly threatened by its own heterogeneity and hybridity reveals it for what it is: an intrinsically pathological discourse which has been constructed to create the fiction of a unitary and homogenous culture and people (that is, essentialist).
>
> (Gabriel, 2000, p. 68)

When allowed to remain in the shadows, the belief in whiteness infiltrates Western epistemologies and social order, saturating structures and establishing rules for temporality and space – constructing time as linear.

Mindfulness and reflexivity practices interrupt linearity by slowing the pace and requiring an in-depth, *vertical* interrogation (Kapil, 2001; Senge et al., 2004).

In the context of sexuality, whiteness claims the default for bodies, expression, behavior, and worldview. White identity is constructed to perpetuate and enact "the attainment of a position of disinterest – abstraction, distance, separation, objectivity" that is manifested by its capacity "to be everything and nothing, literally overwhelmingly present and yet apparently absent" (Dryer as cited in Ho, 2009, p. 37). And yet, the monolithic organization of whiteness is fundamentally located within embodied experiences of "being white" (Dryer as cited in Ho, 2009, p. 37). Similarly, as Ta-Nehisi Coates (2015) elaborates in a letter to his Black teenage son, the hierarchies inherent in racism are reflected in the hegemonic principles that define whiteness as an (ill)legitimate system of organizing society that effects daily lived experience, impacting *all* bodies.

> Race is the child of racism, not the father. And the process of naming "the people" has never been a matter of genealogy and physiognomy so much as one of hierarchy. Difference in hue and hair is old. But the belief in the preeminence of hue and hair, the notion that these factors can correctly organize a society and that they signify deeper attributes, which are indelible – this is the new idea at the heart of these new people who have been brought up hopelessly, tragically, deceitfully, to believe that they are white.
>
> (Coates, 2015, p. 7)

The phenomenon of whiteness impacts different racialized bodies differently, hoisting acute violence on bodies of color, particularly Black (male) bodies, as evident in *Between the World and Me*. Indeed, "racism is a visceral experience . . . it dislodges brains, blocks airways, rips muscle, extracts organs, cracks bones, breaks teeth" (Coates, 2015, p. 10). As a social construction, race lacks scientific evidence for its existence but summons strength from the gravity of shared beliefs, ideologies and social systems that maintain and reinforce it. Within a Western paradigm, race has been structured and produced by discourses of nature, morality, order, and rational thought, formulated and enforced through wealth and exertion of social influence. Historically, whiteness has been equated with freedom, whereas blackness has been associated with slavery that created a social and political hierarchy with a white ruling class (Painter, 2010). The invention and use of firearms within European warfare, for example, allowed white colonizers to perpetrate power and control over less defended bodies since 1364. Disrupting such an entrenched stronghold is no easy feat, yet it is critical for formulating conscious and just sexuality leadership.

White Fragility

Facilitating the disruption of whiteness (and its violent consequences) through mindfulness-based embodiment is a profound task for any social justice leader, including within the field of sexuality. Recognizing white fragility and its core elements is a key part of the process. According to white studies scholar, Robin DiAngelo (2011), white fragility is described as

> a state in which even a minimum amount of racial stress becomes intolerable, triggering a range of defensive moves. These moves include the outward display of emotions such as anger, fear, and guilt, and behaviors such as argumentation, silence, and leaving the stress-inducing situation. These behaviors, in turn, function to reinstate white racial equilibrium.
>
> (p. 54)

Just as whiteness is rarely made visible within predominantly white spaces where few or no people of color are present, white fragility reflects the discomfort white people experience when whiteness is brought up for examination in discussions of diversity and inclusion and social justice, especially in the presence of people of color (DiAngelo, 2011, 2018a, 2018b).

In sexuality leadership, the topic of sexuality itself necessitates reflection and analysis of the ways in which non-normative sexualities may be oppressed, given that sexuality discourse has historically arisen from binary narratives of natural-and-moral versus unnatural-and-perverse (Foucault, 1978). The white, heteropatriarchal, hegemonic history of socially unacceptable sexualities is frequently associated with bodies of color, exemplified by colonial-derived images of the "Black male rapist" (Curry, 2017) and the insatiable "Black Jezebel" female (Collier, Taylor, & Peterson, 2017). Desexualizing Asian and Native American/Indigenous men and exoticizing Asian and Native American/Indigenous women is further cultural evidence (Nagel, 2000; Seethaler, 2013).

Queering

As the overarching sociosexual discourse continues to advance – mostly unchecked – normative beliefs and ideals, stemming from Eurocentric epistemologies and the racial hierarchy, it is necessary to examine and destabilize the foundation of whiteness by targeting white fragility as the entry point for change. Relying on the implementation of *queering* practices – bending, twisting, and challenging normative assumptions – to infiltrate gender and sexuality discourses, the possibilities to exist and thrive beyond the binary become increasingly attainable (Jagose, 1996). Whiteness is a normativity practice that will benefit from similar interrogation and queering as binarism within gender and sexual orientation.

DiAngelo's Pillars of White Fragility

Again, we turn to DiAngelo's (2011, 2018a, 2018b) model of white fragility to dissect whiteness as a *centralizing* social reference – an unacknowledged and invisible racial identity that frames the white experience. White fragility is a system that is supported by unconscious ideologies that drive white cognition and behavior. DiAngelo (2018a) describes this system in terms of six pillars that support white fragility: miseducation, the good/bad binary, internalized superiority and investment in the racial order, Universalism and individualism, and segregation.

Miseducation

Miseducation is evident when white people are unaware of the processes and effects of white racial socialization (DiAngelo, 2018a), leaving them unable to perceive how citizens are socialized to equate "normal and healthy" sexuality with whiteness, heteronormativity, and monogamy. Disrupting normative sexual ideologies involves challenging ideas to include diverse sexual behaviors, identities, and expressions. It also requires "pulling back the curtain" to expose what is often invisible to white experience and comprehension of sexuality.

The Good/Bad Binary

The good/bad binary is especially problematic when inviting conversations about whiteness into sexuality leadership environments that include white people because the binary amplifies fears that white people have around acknowledging their white privilege (DiAngelo, 2018a, 2018b). Since white people commonly lack the experience of addressing their whiteness, they are generally not socially pressured to confront the systems that substantiate their unearned privilege (DiAngelo, 2011, 2018a, 2018b). Doing so can propel white people into a state of dysregulation that (at its extreme) may signal a move from emotional upset into trauma response. Because white people are socially conditioned to exist within an equilibrium of perpetual comfort, stability, and "safety" – physically, mentally, emotionally, and psychically – there is likelihood that white bodies will become dysregulated when pushed outside of their (racial) comfort zone (DiAngelo, 2011, 2018b).

For people of color, the invitation to openly discuss whiteness seems to inevitably require a chess-like strategy with skillful maneuvers where the cost is high and the payoff low, given that white people are often unable to recognize, accept, and change their complicity in a racially rigged system where they have the clear advantage. Instead, white people are culturally conditioned to claim innocence over the potential trauma that their colleagues of color commonly experience as a direct result of contrived and egregious inequities.

Internalized Superiority and Investment in the Racial Order

The "entitlement to racial comfort" (DiAngelo, 2011, p. 60) experienced by white people encompass instances when their worldviews are threatened by revelations of hidden frameworks that support unearned social status and privilege. Decentering whiteness may trigger a white person to become defensive against claims of white privilege prompting proclamations of innocence and goodness, most evident in the demonstration of "white women's tears" (DiAngelo, 2018b). Knee-jerk reactions to self-defend and recenter against (implicitly perceived) assumptions of *badness* cause white people to dismiss white privilege, since claiming whiteness is often viewed to be complicit with racism (DiAngelo, 2011, 2018a, 2018b).

Within sexuality leadership, both leaders and participants who are white do not want to be perceived and/or labeled as *bad*; therefore, whiteness goes unacknowledged so that white bodies can remain within the parameters of comfort regulated by feelings of *good*ness. It is up to sexuality leaders to be able to offer an expanded container in which to help participants and collaborators explore whiteness – with room to hold its magnitude, as the space that whiteness claims may be overwhelming.

Additionally, socioeconomic hierarchies are embedded within a capitalist, neoliberal economy to formulate status roles and power, pitting individuals and groups against one another in an evaluative social positioning process. Because of this, we develop individual and collective strategies that allow us to either remain at the status quo or move up the "ladder of success" through systems that encourage judgment and competition. This enables white people to remain unconscious of their race as a strategy, affording them privileged social status, and causing them to internalize feelings of superiority that perpetuate unconscious investment in the racial hierarchy (DiAngelo, 2011).

Whiteness maintains a comfort zone (and status quo) for white leaders and participants. Therefore, considering whiteness and white privilege to be metaphorical – rather than having actual substance and power – perpetuates an inequitable social reality and interferes with a white leader's ability to disrupt white narratives of sexuality as universal experiences with a shared history. While whiteness is constructed, and therefore artificial, its impact is real and harmful.

Universalism and Individualism

Universality is the notion that a singular monolithic story exists, including one socially accepted interpretation of sexuality in which everyone wishes to comply. In truth, only a miniscule fraction of the population is able to achieve this ideal, let alone have resources to maintain it (Marzullo, 2011). Universality perpetuates the heteropatriarchal vision of whiteness and is another pillar of white fragility (DiAngelo, 2011). Radically disrupting whiteness can confront a white leader's position of authority, opening the possibilities of sexuality leadership to emerge from non-white experiences.

The twin pillars of universality and individualism are notably similar to the balusters that construct the inequalities of neoliberalism, responsible for doling out opportunities and freedoms. According to Marzullo (2011), "those four key concepts are: autonomy, individualism, responsibility, and universality" (p. 763). In describing white fragility within a society that claims to uphold social freedoms and democracy, individualism touts that each person is unique with the means to bypass unwanted socialization to achieve what is desired, through autonomous virtue, self-responsibility, and effort (DiAngelo, 2011, 2018b). It is the wild, wild West–like notion that anyone can pull themselves up by the bootstraps, which in actuality is highly unrealistic due to social positioning inequities.

If white sexuality leaders fail to comprehend the role that racial socialization and the factors of oppression play within the complexities of sexuality, sexual development, access to sexual health and reproductive services, and freedoms of sexual expression, nonreflexive white privilege will continue to run rampant; and the destructive consequences of internalized racism and oppression for sexuality leaders of color – an intended product of white socialization – will persist.

Segregation

When white sexuality leaders fail to comprehend the grievous loss created by the absence of people of color within the white leader's professional and personal life, this is what DiAngelo (2011, 2018a) refers to as the pillar of segregation. Even when white sexuality leaders are exemplary diversity and inclusion advocates and promote reflexivity of whiteness as it affects and shapes the sexuality discourse and their role within it, living and participating in racially segregated work and social environments is harmful and antithetical to disrupting whiteness and promoting social justice.

DiAngelo's (2011, 2018a, 2018b) pillars of white fragility do not stand alone as a compartmentalized roadmap to fully comprehending how whiteness can best be disrupted, and diverse and inclusive sexuality leadership achieved, but they do lay a foundation for how to begin to examine the privilege and fragileness of whiteness. To buoy such a tenuous (and threatening) exploration, we rely on the cultivation of mindfulness. Specifically, mindfulness is introduced as an expansive framework that allows leaders and participants to develop the skills and capacities necessary for challenging white fragility through the application and engagement of Beginner's Mind, reflexivity, presence, and embodied investigatory practices such as pillow education and The Five Eye Practices.

Mindfulness

Given that white fragility compromises the ability of those with white privilege to tolerate racial stress – pushing them outside of their comfort zones – mindfulness can serve as an antidote to help build tolerance for racial discomfort, and it is essential for sexuality leaders who are committed to diversity and inclusion for the growth of *all* participants.

Jon Kabat-Zinn (2005), known for developing mindfulness-based stress reduction (MBSR) techniques and programming, considers mindfulness to be the application of purposeful attention to the immediacy of the present moment without judgment. In this context the *absence* of judgment is neither a moral stance nor a state of pleasantness, but an ongoing, inclusionary practice that relies on a view and quality of *freshness*. This "judgement-free" zone acknowledges and interrogates biases without acting on them in order to stimulate awareness and generate emergent and collaborative (as opposed to top-down) leadership and engagement. It impedes the miseducation endemic to white fragility by exposing indoctrinated beliefs that simplify, separate, and caricaturize.

Beginner's Mind

This fresh perspective-taking also aligns with the mindfulness practice of *shoshin* – which in Zen Buddhism translates to *beginner's mind* and the willingness to release preconceptions in order to harness an attitude of openness while studying; true for novice and advanced practitioners alike (Yang, 2016), implying that the work is never done. Shoshin intersects with the concept of "reflexivity" that is valued and practiced in the social sciences for its ability to expand personal and cultural awareness.

Reflexivity

Reflexivity is critical for developing an evolving diverse-and-inclusive sexuality leadership, particularly for leaders whose social positioning exhibits unearned systemic privilege, such as those identifying as white, cisgender, heterosexual, able-bodied, and/or monogamous.

Reflexivity allows for ethical and skillful consideration and responsiveness in unfamiliar and unpredictable situations, enhancing effectiveness (D'Cruz, Gillingham, & Melendez, 2007). It contains six thematic elements that mitigate a propensity toward familiarity and fixity, particularly in the face of change. As such, reflexivity 1. Distinguishes reflection from self-reflection to include emotional and intuitive knowingness, 2. Regards subjectivity and objectivity as interactive and equally valued, 3. Critiques knowledge production to include multiple explanations and "truths," 4. Incorporates introspection to continually interrogate one's biases and complicity, 5. Critically examines context, and 6. Interrogates public policy (D'Cruz et al., 2007).

Reflexivity is more broadly comprised of "centering," "decentering," and "recentering" (Breuer & Roth, 2003, para. 18). *Centering* focuses narrowly, without consideration of meta-conditions, whereas *decentering* zooms out by adopting a meta-perspective that includes awareness of the fundamental subjective nature of Western epistemology. *Recentering* is comprised of reflective actions requiring nimbleness to perceive interdependently and freshly, prompting flexibility, creativity, and innovation (Breuer & Roth, 2003). When combined, centering, decentering, and recentering enable a range of vantage points and synthesis of views for creating a better-informed and more responsive whole – akin to the mindfulness-based practice known as pillow education.

Pillow Education

Pillow education is a form of reflexivity used for solving problems by children in rural Japan (Reps, 1969). It is relevant to our discussion of mindfully aware and diverse-and-inclusive sexuality leadership, as it includes the repetition of "little disciplines" necessary to effect shifts in perception (Dilley, 2015, p. 123). Pillow education interrupts the linearity of the problem-solving process, and its conventional, horizontal flow from problem-to-solution (a.k.a. "quick fix") by slowing down the decision-making process and examining a problem from multiple perspectives (Reps, 1969).

While pillow education has no formal name, it is termed "pillow education" because "a pillow has four sides and a middle. A problem has four approaches and a middle" (Reps, 1969, pp. 17–18). Difficulties often polarize thinking, whereas pillow education is designed to engage multiple perspectives and possibilities. Specifically, pillow education asks its practitioners to consider five options, while moving their hands around each side of the pillow (positions 1–4) and into the center (position 5). They are tasked with contemplating: first, that the problem (x) is true (side 1); second, that the opposite of the problem (y) is true (side 2); third, that both x and y are true (side 3); fourth, that neither x nor y is true (side 4); and finally, that *all* possibilities are true, corresponding to the center (Reps, 1969).

In actuality, Japanese children use names instead of numbers for the five positions: *HI RI HO KEN (TEN)*, which in Japanese means "five-steps-into-universal-harmony," symbolized by hands on the middle of the pillow (Reps, 1969, p. 20). Importantly, the attainment of "universal harmony" in pillow education is achieved through consideration of multiple perspectives (and their frictions) rather than bypassing differences and difficulties. While the origin of this practice is unknown, it has been attributed to the *Chinese Book of Changes*, more commonly referred to as the *I Ching*, an ancient Chinese divination text meant to effectuate transformation (Reps, 1969). As an expansive and collaborative decision-making device, pillow education engenders embodied perspectives beyond those typically clung to as correct or "true" (Reps, 1969), making it particularly useful for sexuality leadership since it is contingent on the ability to develop complexity.

Pillow education can be practiced by sexuality leaders in order to move beyond polarizing and emotional reactivity, particularly around issues of race, and the conundrum of white fragility. To complexify the situation, we could consider, for example:

1. White fragility is *harmful*
2. White fragility is *helpful*
3. White fragility is harmful *and* helpful
4. White fragility is *neither* harmful *nor* helpful
5. White fragility is harmful, helpful, harmful, and helpful, and neither harmful or helpful

These myriad possibilities emphasize the Buddhist and Daoist principle of interdependency, which naturally include what is contrary and difficult (Reps, 1969). In this way pillow education enables conflicts to be more readily resolved by evoking a sense of "universal harmony" through shared humanity, but without bypassing difficulty or difference (Reps, 1969).

Additionally, pillow education invites its practitioners out of their heads and into their bodies by expanding awareness to include the logical as well as the *felt* sense of another person's position. By incorporating a physical practice (moving hands around the pillow and into the center) it (re) introduces (particularly for adults) an *embodied* component, in which bodies are viewed as "both physical structures and as lived, experiential structures – in short, as both "outer" and "inner," biological and phenomenological. These two sides of embodiment are obviously not opposed. Instead, we continuously circulate back and forth between them" (Varela, Thompson, & Rosch, 1993. Pp. xv–xvi). This circulatory, interdependent, embodied process requires *presence*, described as opening "beyond one's preconceptions and historical ways of making sense" to relinquish "old identities and the need to control" (Senge et al., 2004, p. 9).

Presence

> As long as our thinking is governed by habit – notably by industrial, "machine age" concepts such as control, predictability, standardization, and "faster is better" we will continue to [construct sexuality] as [it has] been, despite disharmony with the larger world, and the need of all living systems to evolve.
>
> (Senge et al., 2004, p. 9)

For white sexuality leaders it is critical to recognize that the desire to evolve can be quickly and easily short-circuited by white fragility. The anxiety and fear that accompany white fragility often cause us to revert to habituated thinking and behavior. It is crucial, therefore, to develop presence and its accompanying capacity to *suspend* (reactivity) once we realize that we are in the midst – or on the brink – of white fragility. Through mindful suspension we can recognize and disarm white fragility instead of dismissing it. In this way, white fragility can be perceived as a teachable moment around empathy, with the dual-effect of decentering privilege and engendering self-compassion.

Seeing Our Seeing

Presence deepens our awareness and activates our ability to suspend (Senge et al., 2004). It requires an interrogation of our perceptions – referred to as *seeing our seeing* – instead of blithely accepting reality as it is presented (Senge et al., 2004, p. 27). Seeing one's seeing inserts a pause into habituated thinking and response (Senge et al., 2004), fostering alignment with the kind of reflexivity necessary for developing diverse-and-inclusive sexuality leadership that relies on mind body manifesting in the present moment.

> *This very moment*, a moment when mind body are sensed in the same field of awareness, is a kinesthetic dot. In this moment you and the room and others become part of feelings and insights. It almost has no words, it changes all the time and is always the occasion.
>
> (Dilley, 2015, p. 9)

In this case, the "occasion" is the repetition of moments when white fragility rears, activating the six pillars of miseducation, universality, individualism, the good/bad binary, segregation, internalized superiority and investment in the racial order. It is also an opportunity to recognize our interdependency and capacity for change.

Theory U

Organizational learning pioneers, Senge et al. (2004) collaboratively developed the Theory U model to cultivate presence, which they perceive to be the pivotal "core capacity needed to access the field of the future" (p. 13). Acting as a transformational change agent, presence inserts pause into thinking and doing in order to cultivate intuitive and skillful responsiveness as opposed to reactivity.

A pause is inserted at the top of the (figurative) U (on the left-hand side) to interrupt the propensity to solve a problem quickly and/or linearly. Pausing enables redirection toward different and nascent possibilities, beginning with a vertical drop into uncertainty and not-knowing. This verticality invites a "deeper level of knowing" and ushers in the ensuing processes of "suspending," "redirecting," "letting go," and "letting come" that comprise the first half of Theory U, with the goal to "sense an emerging future," and invite *intention* (Senge et al., 2004, pp. 84–85).

Intention

> Perhaps the least noticed and most important capacity that sets apart some of the most successful leaders concerns their capacity to tap into and focus a larger intention. Although people are sometimes reluctant to talk about this or simply don't know how to do so, when they reflect on their own actions, a different source of action becomes evident. This source lies beyond their preconceived plans or narrow self-interest, and often beyond their past experience.
>
> (Senge et al., 2004, p. 137)

To cultivate a larger intention, the conventional approach of rational decision-making is discarded, giving way to action that arises "as a spontaneous product of the whole" (Rosch, as cited in Senge et al., 2004, p. 137). This holistic approach decenters white fragility so that a plethora of voices and experience are heard, and emerging futures are constructed within a diverse-and-inclusive framework, rather than a precarious house of cards built on white privilege and biases. To facilitate a shift away from habituated (and narrowed) perceptions toward *functioning* (rather than idealistic) wholeness, we introduce the Five Eye Practices as a mindfulness-based approach to decenter whiteness in sexuality leadership.

Five Eye Practices

The Five Eye Practices is a mindfulness-based technique developed by Barbara Dilley, Professor Emeritus of Dance at Naropa University in Boulder, Colorado meant to inform improvisational research. It was incorporated into *Naked Face*, a museum installation in 1996 to elicit embodied perspective taking. The Five Eye Practices include the following:

1. Closed eyes
2. Infant eyes
3. Peripheral seeing
4. Looking between things
5. Direct looking

(Dilley, 2015, pp. 123–124)

As with pillow education, the first four eye practices are discreet "little disciplines" meant to access an emerging whole. The fifth eye practice of direct looking (like the center of the pillow) is informed by and exceeds the preceding four, creating a *gestalt* – where the whole is greater than the sum of its parts.

Focusing on wholeness necessitates a shift in perspective between *seer* and *seen*. When the complexity of awareness begins to interrupt dualistic thinking (such as the good/bad binary) "we shift from looking 'out at the world' from the viewpoint of a detached [white] observer to looking from 'inside' what is being observed" (Senge et al., 2004, p. 41). In this way, the Five Eye Practices can serve to disrupt solidification of self and Other (white and privileged versus non-white and oppressed) creating an important observational shift from subject-object to subject-subject (Buber, 1923/1937). This shift establishes an "I-thou" relationship, according to Martin Buber (1923/1937) who coined the term, rather than an "I-it"; in which "it" is perceived to be an external and objectified Other that is separate rather than part of us. Unfortunately, the "it" is interchangeable for a person or a *thing*. An I-thou relationship cultivates intimacy where awareness is whole rather than fractured (Buber, 1923/1937), making "solutions" within the domain of sexuality leadership generative rather than fixed. Because the Five Eye Practices cultivate a fuller (more whole) way of perceiving, it challenges the fractured perception of whiteness.

Closed Eyes

Closed eyes invites participants to close their eyes, and is meant to initiate self-reflection – where the outer world temporarily recedes in order to focus on internal experience. Here, participants are encouraged to notice emotional and physiological responses and processes, such as feelings of irritation, enthusiasm, longing, disgust, etc., as well as physiological sensations, such as shallow or deep breathing, rapid or slow heart rate, dry mouth, sweaty palms, itchy feet, etc. Internal seeing is meant to relax and refresh the mind body, creating a foundation from which to explore perception more fully (Dilley, 2015).

Infant Eyes

Infant eyes coaxes oneself to see anew – *before naming*. This exercise invites participants to allow their eyes to open slowly with a soft gaze that roams around the room. Their eyes lead, inviting the head and spine follow. The impetus is toward naming (and *solidifying*) what is observed, acknowledged, and then gently released (Dilley, 2015). Rather than employing the one-dimensionality of "naming" color, for example, like red or green, participants are able to notice hues and the interplay of shadow and light. Curiosity is the hallmark of infant eyes.

Peripheral Seeing

Peripheral seeing relies on seeing from the corner of your eyes rather than straight ahead. If you hold your arms out to the side at shoulder height, while looking straight ahead, and wiggling your fingers you will locate the periphery. Peripheral seeing allows you to see the sidelines, which often go unnoticed and unattended to (Dilley, 2015). Too often what appears beyond direct perception is ignored and devalued. The role of peripheral seeing is to bring the discarded into focus. Whiteness is often intentionally and/or unintentionally discarded.

Looking Between Things

Looking between things emphasizes the importance of liminal space. For example, rather than focusing on the branches of a tree, you would look at the space between the branches. Here you might see the sky through the branches. Looking between things accentuates background and context, rather than foreground. It elaborates experience and often surprises the perceiver with discovering *something more*. Looking between things welcomes spaciousness (Dilley, 2015). Because whiteness is pervasive it saturates spaces and places, yet it is rarely observed by those who most directly benefit from it. Looking between things allows white sexuality leaders to see the impact of whiteness in every context.

Direct Looking

While looking directly is our familiar eye gaze, when it occurs following the previous four eye practices, we can return to it anew. In this way it is possible for you to observe "small, intimate aspects about what you are seeing," such as noticing previously missed "patterns in the wood on the floor, the way a light fixture is connected to the ceiling, how leaves on a tree outside the window move in the breeze" (Dilley, 2015, p. 124). Details return, refreshing static perception. No longer stale, direct perception (and the possibilities in the field) become dynamic and vast.

Application to Sexuality Leadership

The application of the Five Eye Practices to sexuality leadership can assist with developing the ability to confront white fragility in a way that bolsters presence and the capacity to suspend. Closed eyes, for example, enables leaders to calm and center themselves, amid distressing feelings (like anxiety and shame) and physiological responses (like shallow breathing and rapid pulse). This internal inventory can interrupt reactivity, and lead to more grounded responding. Infant eyes, or the practice of seeing before naming, encourages leaders and participants alike to experience the contours of white fragility before it is labeled, which frequently causes us to distance ourselves from it as it is perceived to be "bad," rather than simply "what is."

Because peripheral seeing accentuates what is on the sidelines (or margins), it is particularly relevant to sexuality leadership, given that sexual subjectivities conceived as "non-normative" are literally pushed to the margins (*margin*alized) via ideologies and policies, and devalued. Looking between things enables the sexuality leader to zoom out and acknowledge context. It situates experience within a background instead of only the foreground, thereby connecting it to other contexts, like histories, cultures, and positionalities; an example of which is intersectionality. This is particularly important for bodies of color, which have a corporeal and systemic experience that white bodies do not, threatening their daily existence with violence: "It is through the body that gender and sexuality become exposed to others, implicated in social processes, inscribed by cultural norms, and apprehended in their social meanings" (Butler, 2004, p. 20), making processes of social recognition "linked to our very sense of personhood" (Butler, 2004, p. 33).

> The body implies mortality, vulnerability, agency: the skin and the flesh expose us to the gaze of others but also to touch and to violence. The body can be the agency and the instrument of all of these as well, or the site where "doing" and "being done to" become equivocal.
>
> (Butler, 2004, p. 21)

In summary, cultivating the capacity to "discern physical and emotional reactions is a powerful practice in suspending and becoming less attached to the stories we tell ourselves about what is going on" (Senge et al., 2004, pp. 139–140). This makes it possible, particularly for the white sexuality leader, to accept white fragility as *what is*, rather than unequivocal proof of racism or *badness*. Still, leaning into what *feels* bad in part of the process. Fortunately, "moments of stress or real difficulty are 'points of power' in developing vision and integrating it into our lives" (Fritz, 2002; Senge, 2006; Senge et al., 2004, pp. 139). While the intention to identify and disrupt white fragility is a lofty goal for sexuality leaders, it is necessary for the ethical development and expansion of our field.

Process Questions and Considerations

1. Why do you think that the field of mental health (e.g., psychology, social work, sexology, etc.) have largely refused to discuss race openly and candidly?

2. What keeps some leaders from being intentional about inclusiveness as it relates to race?
3. Can people of color experience fragility when having discussions about race? If so, why? If not, please explain.
4. What keeps people from being vulnerable while discussing whiteness?
5. When should sexuality leaders begin to discuss whiteness? Elementary school, middle, high school, college? Discuss some of the developmental implications for addressing whiteness at each level.

References

Breuer, F., & Roth, W. M. (2003). Subjectivity and reflexivity in the social sciences: Epistemic windows and methodical consequences. *Forum: Qualitative Social Research*, 4(2). Retrieved from www.qualitative-research.net/index.php/fqs/article/view/698/1510

Buber, M. (1937). *I and thou*. In R. G. Smith (Trans). Edinburgh, Scotland: T & T Clark. (Original work published 1923)

Butler, J. (2004). *Undoing gender*. New York: Routledge.

Coates, T. (2015). *Between the world and me*. New York, NY: Spiegel & Grau.

Collier, J. M., Taylor, M. J., & Peterson, Z. D. (2017). Reexamining the "Jezebel" stereotype: The role of implicit and psychosexual attitudes. *The Western Journal of Black Studies*, 41(3 & 4), 92–104.

Curry, T. (2017). *The man-not: Race, class, genre, and the dilemmas of Black manhood*. Philadelphia, PA: Temple University Press.

D'Cruz, H., Gillingham, P., & Melendez, S. (2007). Reflexivity: A concept and its meanings for practitioners working with children and families. *Critical Social Work*, 8(1). Retrieved from http://www1.uwindsor.ca/criticalsocialwork/reflexivity-a-concept-and-its-meanings-for-practitioners-working-with-children-and-families

DiAngelo, R. (2011). White fragility. *International Journal of Critical Pedagogy*, 3, 54–70.

DiAngelo, R. (2018a). *Deconstructing white privilege*. [Video file]. Retrieved from https://robindiangelo.com/media/

DiAngelo, R. (2018b). *White fragility: Why it's so hard for white people to talk about racism*. Boston, MA: Beacon Press.

Dilley, B. (2015). *This very moment: Teaching thinking dancing*. Boulder, CO: Naropa University Press.

Dworkin, T. M., Schipani, C. A., Milliken, F. J., & Kneeland, M. K. (2018). Assessing the progress of women in corporate America: The more things change, the more they stay the same. *American Business Law Journal*, 55(4), 721–762. Doi:10.1111/ablj.12132

Elbow, P. (1993). The uses of binary thinking. *Journal of Advanced Composition*, 14, 22–51. Retrieved from https://scholarworks.umass.edu/eng_faculty_pubs/14/?utm_source=scholarworks.umass.edu%2Feng_faculty_pubs%2F14&utm_medium=PDF&utm_campaign=PDFCoverPages

Foucault, M. (1978). *The history of sexuality: Volume I: An introduction.* In R. Hurley, (Trans.). New York, NY: Random House. (Original work published 1976).

Freud, S. (1932). Female sexuality. *The International Journal of Psycho-Analysis, 13,* 281–297.

Fritz, R. (2002). *Your life as art.* Newfane, VT: Newfane Press.

Gabriel, J. (2000). "Dreaming of a white . . ." In S. Cottle (Ed.), *Ethnic minorities and the media* (pp. 67–83). Maidenhead, Berkshire: Open University Press.

Gagnon, J. H., & Simon, W. (1973). *Sexual conduct: The social sources of human sexuality.* Chicago, IL: Aldine Publishing Co.

Ho, K. (2009). *Liquidated: An ethnography of wall street.* Durham, NC: Duke University Press.

Jagose, A. (1996). *Queer theory: An introduction.* New York: New York University Press.

Kabat-Zinn, J. (2005). *Coming to our senses: Healing ourselves and the world through mindfulness.* New York: Hyperion Books.

Kapil (Rider), B. (2001). *The vertical interrogation of strangers.* Berkeley: Kelsey Street Press.

Kinsey, A. C. (1953). *Sexual behavior in the human female.* Philadelphia, PA: Saunders.

Kinsey, A. C., Pomeroy, W. B., & Martin, C. E. (1948). *Sexual behavior in the human male.* Philadelphia, PA: W. B. Saunders Co.

Laqueur, T. (1990). *Making sex: Body and gender from the Greeks to Freud.* Cambridge, MA: Harvard University Press.

Manthy, G. (2011). Embracing the future by transforming relationships. *Leadership, 40,* 4.

Marzullo, M. (2011). Through a glass, darkly: U.S. marriage discourse and neoliberalism. *Journal of Homosexuality, 58*(6–7), 758–774.

Masters, W. H., & Johnson, V. E. (1966). *Human sexual response.* Boston, MA: Little, Brown and Co.

Masters, W. H., & Johnson, V. E. (1970). *Human sexual inadequacy.* Boston, MA: Little, Brown and Co.

Nagel, J. (2000). Ethnicity and sexuality. *Annual Review of Sociology, 26,* 107–133.

Painter, N. I. (2010). *The history of white people.* New York, NY: W. W. Norton.

Reyes, G., Radina, R., & Aronson, B. A. (2018). Teaching against the grain as an act of love: Disrupting white Eurocentric masculinist frameworks within teacher education. *The Urban Review, 50,* 818–835.

Sanger, M. (1938). *An autobiography.* New York, NY: W. W. Norton.

Seethaler, I. (2013). "Big bad Chinese mama": How internet humor subverts stereotypes about Asian American women. *Studies in American Humor, 3*(27), 117–138.

Senge, P. M. (2006). *The fifth discipline: The art and practice of learning organization.* New York: Crown Business. (Original work published in 1990)

Senge, P. M., Scharmer, C. O., Jaworski, J., & Flowers, B. S. (2004). *Presence: Human purpose and the field of the future.* New York: Doubleday.

Sharma, M., & Rush, S. E. (2014). Mindfulness-based stress reduction as a stress management intervention for healthy individuals: A systematic review. *Journal of Evidence-Based Complementary & Alternative Medicine, 19*(4), 271–286. Doi:10.1177/2156587214543143

Shore, L. M., Randel, A. E., Chung, B. G., Dean, M. A., Ehrhart, K. H., & Singh, G. (2011). Inclusion and diversity in work groups: A review and model for future research. *Journal of Management, 37*(4), 1262–1289. Doi:10.1177/01492063 10385943

Taylor, C., & White, S. (2000). *Practising reflexivity in health and welfare: Making knowledge*. Buckingham: Open University Press.

Taylor, Y. (2010). Introduction. In Y. Taylor, S. Hines, & M. Casey (Eds.), *Theorizing intersectionality and sexuality: Genders and sexualities in the social sciences* (pp. 1–11). New York, NY: Palgrave Macmillan.

Tetrick, L. E., & Winslow, C. J. (2015). Workplace stress management interventions and health promotions. *The Annual Review of Organizational Psychology and Organizational Behavior, 2*(16), 16.1–16.21.

Varela, F. J., Thompson, E., & Rosch, E. (1993). *The embodied mind: Cognitive science and human experience*. Cambridge, MA: MIT Press.

Yang, S. (2016). Shoshin: The beginner's mind. Retrieved May 5, 2018 from https://www.allouteffort.com/2014/08/shoshin-beginners-mind.html

18 Ethical Considerations in Leadership

Dr. Tralonda Triplett

> The supreme quality for leadership is unquestionably integrity. Without it, no real success is possible, no matter whether it is on a section gang, a football field, in an army, or in an office (Eisenhower, 1965).
>
> – President Dwight D. Eisenhower (Kiisel, 2013)

Although more than six decades have passed since President Eisenhower scribed this phrase, its sentiment, its meaning, its substance is as poignant now as it was in the mid-1960s. When inquiries of ethics arise, particularly among scientists and researchers, uncomfortable discord and palatable silences often ensue. In many cases, scientists maintain implicit and often unfounded beliefs that *all* act and perform ethically in *all* cases. If not, most believe there is a very good reason for those who misstep. For some, the progress of science alone, along with financial gain and historical and social notoriety often accompanying, supersedes protections warranted by the humanity of those who volunteer to participate in research and the communities from whence participants emerge. As with other facets of public health, progression of knowledge in sexuality is innately connected to human diversities and complexities. As such leaders in sexuality study and scholarship are subject to unique levels of ethics that go beyond measures of "do no harm" espoused in the Hippocratic Oath. Population-based biomedical and behavioral sciences and the ethical responsibilities associated with them not only impact communities at large, but networks of leaders who share those objectives. To undergird sexuality research, intervention design, implementation and evaluation, and methodology and practice, explicit guidance is pivotal to set system-level parameters illustrating acceptable performance for its scientists and leaders. Establishing and monitoring integrity and ethical constructs demonstrated by sexuality intellectuals are essential to substantive progress in the field and sustained service to the populations the discipline serves.

Ethical Foundations in Health and Science

When examining historical underpinnings of factors impacting leadership and ethics in health and science, knowledge of the *Tuskegee Study of Untreated Syphilis in the Negro Male* holds tremendous credence. Beginning in January 1930, the U.S. Public Health Service (PHS) initiated the *Tuskegee Syphilis Study* in Macon County, Alabama and five other sites in the nation's Deep South. The dependent variable was whether persons with syphilis were, in fact, better off without treatment (Crenner, 2012). Although on its face, the initial premise of the study appeared plausible and valuable to U.S. populations, who at the time were enduring 35% prevalence rates of syphilis nationwide among those of reproductive age. The next four decades showed the PHS steering research permeated with blatant and deliberate acts that directly contributed to chronic harm, unnecessary suffering, and untimely death of its participants. Among the study's most prominent abuses to its 600 Black male participants included the following:

- Lack of provision or acquisition of informed consent for participation, or knowledge of known and potential dangers associated with participation
- Coercive retention of participants including requirements allowing autopsies after death in exchange for PHS provision of funds for funeral costs
- Deliberate and intentional denial of treatment, once available
- Misleading and inaccurate recruitment collateral (Brandt, 1978)

Even so, perhaps the most deleterious impact of the *Tuskegee Syphilis Study* is its persistent infamy in many communities of color that remains even to this day. Disparities in racial and ethnic minority participation in clinical trials are staggering, and greatly impacts scientific progress in health in these communities. Further, many would attest that social, cultural, and political environments that would allow and accept such widely publicized behaviors from federal agencies and their representatives have not significantly changed to date. As such, many populations of color are duly fearful that the atrocities that occurred in Macon County can happen again with little reservation by scientists or recourse for participants.

Nuremberg Code

Further, contemporary biomedical and public health ethics has also been shaped by the Nuremberg Trials and resulting Nuremberg Code. Nuremberg, Germany in 1945 and 1946 included Nazi doctors' commissions of egregious acts under the guise of "human experiments" on Jewish concentration camp prisoners. Murderous and torturous experiments under the "Doctors' Trial" endured by concentration camp attendees during World War II has had great impacts on the rights of participants in medical research. (Schuster, 1997) The resulting Nuremberg Trials and criminal indictment of doctors' acts served as bases for the Nuremberg Code.

Of specific note were the charges brought against the Nazi doctors and others, who, trial transcripts stated, were bound by the Hippocratic Oath to "first, do no harm." Because of Nazi doctors' professions as physicians and the oath, American prosecutors sought to assess the motives that would move the doctors to treat their fellow human beings as less than beasts. American prosecutors sought to extract and expose such ideas before they became "a spreading cancer in the breast of humanity" (Schuster, 1997).

In the process of the Nuremberg Trials, the Code was developed to essentially obtain real-time applications and extensions of the Hippocratic Oath for medical professionals engaged in research with human participants. The Code's ten principles included informed consent at its core but continued to establish requirements of professionals to protect the best interests of participants, and for participants to protect themselves as well. An abridged examination of the principles to be applied to sexuality research includes the following:

- Voluntary consent of the participant, with legal capacity to give consent, is essential
- Research should yield fruits for the good of society, and be neither random nor unnecessary
- Anticipated results from research should justify performance of the experiment
- Research should avoid all unnecessary physical and mental suffering and injury
- No research should occur when there is an *a priori* reason to believe that death or disabling injury will result
- Degree of risk posed by research should never outweigh determined humanitarian importance of the problem to be solved
- Proper preparation and adequate facilities should be provided to participants to remove remote possibilities of injury, disability, or death
- Research should only be performed by scientifically qualified persons
- Participants are at liberty to discontinue participation in research at any time, with no penalty
- Scientists must be prepared to terminate research at any stage if probable cause exists that continuation is likely to result in injury, disability, or death to participants (Schuster, 1997).

While the Nuremberg Code has not been adopted entirely as law by any nation, it has been referenced and serves as foundational tenants of international ethics covenants. In the five decades since its initiation, the

314 Dr. Tralonda Triplett

Nuremberg Code has greatly assisted professionals and stakeholders to advocate for human rights provisions in research implementation and evaluation.

Belmont Report

Another historical event that greatly impacted ethical principles in health research was the Belmont Report. July of 1978 brought signature of the National Research Act into law, and thereby established the National Commission for the Protection of Human Subjects of Biomedical and Behavioral Research. The Belmont Report was the result of the Commission's deliberations and detailed basic ethical principles guiding biomedical and behavioral research including human participants (Kristinsson, 2009). In contrast with principles previously presented by the Nuremberg Codes, the Belmont Report attempted to clarify ethical tenants, and enclose remaining gaps. Three comprehensive principles including respect for persons, beneficence, and justice serve as bases for the Report. Such synopses offered scientists, subjects, reviewers, and general populations greater understanding of parameters governing acceptable conduct, purpose, and implementation of biomedical and behavioral research. Further, the Report offered tangible contrasts between research and practice in these disciplines. As such, this resulting document has great impact on the subsequent study and examination of human sexuality and all of its auxiliaries.

The Belmont Report was to offer wider distribution and utility of ethical guidelines for research than previously held, and the Commission included contributions from a number of professionals from medical, law, scientific, ethics, and community sources including Dr. Dorothy I. Height of the National Council of Negro Women. Further, rather than offer the Report as a recommendation to the U.S. Secretary of Health, Education and Welfare, the Commission recommended it simply be adopted in its entirety and become a statement of the Department's policy.

While admittedly blurred, the submission of the Belmont Report offered clarity contrasting research and practice in biomedical and behavioral disciplines. *Practice*, the Report declared, refers to interventions that are designed solely to enhance the well-being of an individual patient or client and that have a reasonable expectation of success. The purpose of medical or behavioral practice, therefore, is to provide diagnosis, preventive treatment, or therapy to particular individuals. By contrast, *research* designates an activity designed to test a hypothesis, permit conclusions to be drawn, and thereby to develop or contribute to generalizable knowledge (expressed, for example, in theories, principles, and statements of relationships). Research is usually described in a formal protocol that sets forth an objective and a set of procedures designed to reach that objective. Significant departures by scientists in classification of scientific exploits from defined categories of research or practice could result in his/her investigation or intervention to not be considered research at all. The Belmont Report went on to suggest that new, fledgling investigations be considered *experimental*, yet still subject to intense scrutiny to determine safety and efficacy before implementation in human populations. (US DHHS, 1979).

Perhaps even more revolutionary was the Belmont Report's intention to devise comprehensive principles governing ethical behavior by scientists and research professionals among human participants. Shaded by the Nuremburg trials and *Tuskegee Syphilis Study of Untreated Syphilis in Negro Males* outcomes, the Belmont Report attempted to offer standard operating procedures that all research professionals should apply and adhere to regardless of role or position within scientific studies. *Respect for persons*, incorporated two ethical convictions: first, individuals should be treated as autonomous agents (that is, capable of self-motivated deliberation and decision-making of his/her volition and behalf), and second, persons with diminished autonomy were entitled to protection. The principle of respect for persons thus was divided into two separate moral requirements: the requirement to acknowledge autonomy and the requirement to protect those with diminished autonomy. Protected populations therefore included persons who lacked cognitive maturity (i.e., children), who were already ill physically or mentally, or in circumstances severely limiting liberty (i.e., incarcerated). Persons in these categories should be provided additional and extensive protections even including exclusion completely from research proceedings due to their incapacity to decide to participate without reservation and in full knowledge of potential dangers.

The Report continued by defining the concept of beneficence extending beyond general terms of kindness or charity from strict obligation. Beneficence in research, however, obliged professionals to treat research and practice participants in an ethical manner not only by respecting their decisions and protecting them from harm, but by also making deliberate efforts to secure their well-being. This guiding principle is further illustrated in the Report by establishing as an obligation to "maximize possible benefits and minimize possible harms" to research participants. This mandate in contemporary research has expanded further to include not only research participants directly, but the communities and populations to which participants belong. Contemporary researchers recognize the fragility that exists between communities and researchers particularly in underserved populations. Contemporary acknowledgements further reflect how insensitivity, disregard, and lack of integrity in publishing research outcomes that are pejorative, unfounded, or unreasonably concluded can irreparably damage subsequent studies in these populations. It is imperative, therefore, that sexuality researchers recognize cultural, familial, and humane norms not only in implementation, but also in disseminating research findings. While beneficence is not intended to pressure scientists into complimentary outcomes when they do not exist, researchers must acknowledge that research participants, particularly from underserved priority populations, have done so voluntarily. Researchers must minimize personal biases in protocol design and implementation, and exercise caution and decorum in their dissemination of research findings. Researchers must be committed to stifling stigma-inducing conclusions that may further burden populations that are already underserved.

Particularly when studying sexuality-based topics, which remain social taboos in the United States and other countries, researchers must lead with deference to communities on which inquiry was focused. While underserved populations often lack the political, social, or economic power to confront these missed steps directly, they can simply decide to no longer participate in research protocols. Such decisions further stagnate progress in addressing health inequities, and suppress the advancement of knowledge. Strict compliance to beneficence, therefore, impacts not only scientists completing research currently, but also scientists who desire to advance knowledge in similar target populations.

Institutional Review Boards

Applications resulting from the Report required researchers, and particularly those in academic institutions, to receive approval from Institutional Review Boards (IRBs) prior to implementing research protocols in human populations. Institutional Review Boards are defined as an "appropriately constituted group that has been formally designated to review and monitor biomedical research involving human subjects." *Appropriate constitution* on IRB committees has gained tremendous attention in contemporary research. In past years, IRB compositions neglected populations participating in research protocols, and therefore lacked essential sensitivities to protocol components and nuances abridging participants' rights, well-being, and welfare. Leadership in sexuality research must, therefore, ensure IRB structures reflect the spirit and underpinnings of proposed research so that adaptations and approvals are justified and supported by representatives of participant communities (US DHHS, 1979).

Protected Populations

Further, the Belmont Report yielded key ethical principles of populations whose circumstances, abilities, or other conditions impact their appreciable participation in any research at all. These "protected populations" embody clear vulnerabilities impacting their abilities to reliably respond to, or endure, potential harms associated with research of any kind. The

Federal Policy for the Protection of Human Subjects or the "Common Rule" was published in 1991 and codified in separate regulations by 15 Federal departments and agencies. This, *45 CFR part 46*, provided additional protections from participation in research to pregnant women, human fetuses and neonates, incarcerated populations, and children. In each case, populations were considered to have undue vulnerabilities to adequately respond, voluntarily consent, and physically or mentally endure research participation.

However, in recent years colleagues have yielded further classification of protected populations that sexual researchers must acknowledge. In 2016, Mrdjenovich identified special classes of research participants including students, employees, and cognitively impaired individuals who may be vulnerable in terms of their research participation. (Mrdjenovich, 2016) While these may illustrate sexuality researchers' best attempts at convenience sampling, it is foreseeable that each of these populations have factors that can greatly impact their abilities to participate in research reliably. Mrdjenvich continues to define two additional types of vulnerabilities among potential research participants that require additional protections, if not removal completely from research protocols. *Decisional impairment*, whereby potential subjects lack the capacity to make autonomous decisions in their own interest, perhaps as a result of undue influence/inducement, and *Situational/positional vulnerability*, whereby potential participants may be subjected to coercion (Mrdjenovich, 2016).

While these additional vulnerability classes may appear to closely resemble those expressed by populations in the Common Rule, these special classes are to extend ethical coverage to those who do not fit into the established categories, but can be unduly influenced or coerced into participation. Undue influence may include rewards for participants that supersede normal expenses incurred from participation, and essentially places participants in dilemmas to continue in protocols solely for compensation.

Conversely, coercion involves an "overt or implicit threat of harm or reprisal" in order to obtain compliance with a request to participate in research. In each case, research participants suffer when power imbalances with researchers interferes with their abilities to choose, act, or continue voluntarily. Sexual researchers must delicately balance including attractive incentives in protocols that adequately compensate research participants for time and expenses incurred, and exploiting the frailties of targeted populations to insure their ongoing participation.

Sexual research leaders must define if additional vulnerability classes are present within potential participant samples, define sources of additional vulnerabilities, and determine how discipline-wide standards regarding necessary protections for, or exclusion of, protected populations in subsequent sexual research. Additionally scientists from all

disciplines, and IRB committees charged with approving protocol implementation, must remain vigilant about addressing undue and/or coercive
incentives, whether intentional or unintentional. While undue influence
is relative and what may induce one individual's volition may have no
impact on another, leadership requires in-depth analyses of incentives to
maintain the sanctity of scientific inquiry.

Last, the Belmont Report offers clear guidelines on fostering justice
among research participants. Justice addresses equities in distributions
of due benefits and/or impositions of unnecessary burdens. While benefits of research ostensibly should apply to populations at large, sexuality disciplines are uniquely personal, and require additional levels of
consideration when distributing burdens of such research fairly. Justice,
therefore, must not be an afterthought or postscript to research, but a
primary foundation of protocols themselves. Leaders must ensure that
research questions are created with minimal levels of bias (both personal
and corporate) and *a priori* conclusions. In so doing, research outcomes
can be predicated on collected data and rigorous analyses only. Leaders
must ensure that enrollment, compliance, methodologies, and processes
within protocols are applied with consistency and integrity, so that outcomes can withstand criticism and social analysis. Leaders must ensure
that outcomes are articulated clearly and accurately, but with full consideration of fairness in direct and inferential conclusions to participants
and communities to which they belong.

International Conventions

As our cultures and communities continue to grow to global scales, ethical considerations in leadership extend to understanding and abiding by
international conventions. The World Health Organization (WHO) has
within its Constitution preamble a commitment to "the enjoyment of the
highest attainable standard of health is one of the fundamental rights of
every human being without distinction of race, religion, political belief,
economic or social condition" (World Health Organization, 2018). It is
feasible, then, that healthy sexual status is included in global pursuits of
this fundamental right. While cultures are not monolithic, many have
strict guidelines and normative expectations around inquiry, analysis,
dissemination, or discussion of sexual topics. It is imperative that leaders obtain credible insights from global cultural factors prior to engaging global audiences, and govern protocols and dissemination processes
accordingly.

The United Nations provides its Code of Conduct and Core Values and
Competencies and it is applied to both their staffs and consultants. These
offer additional insights and foundational principles to which leaders initiating global research should comply. Included in core values referenced
in these documents are values such as integrity, professionalism, and

respect for diversity. Integrity including "impartiality, fairness, honesty and truthfulness in all matters, for ethical decision-making when staff members face situations where applying rules may be difficult or unpopular, where a conflict between professional and private interests arises, or where special concessions are requested" (United Nations, 2018). This document provides a shared principle between national and international conventions that allows leaders to bridge and translate research between national to international audiences. Leaders are cautioned however, to explore cultural norms and/or contextual factors impacting global participating populations that may not be influencing primary populations. Leaders' willingness to pursue in-depth exploration and investigation of cultural mores when translating to global audiences is implicitly included in research integrity. As mentioned, sexuality maintains its status as a highly personal, and often socially taboo topic in many cultures. Leaders must be committed to providing information and progressing knowledge with appropriate levels of decorum and cultural humility. Otherwise, leaders' efforts to engage, inform, and empower others toward sexual health can be thwarted because they have either deliberately or accidentally offended global audiences.

This examination of cultural norms is particularly important as sexuality research produces evidence-based interventions and standards of service that have shown repetitive positive effects in pilot populations. Leaders must be mindful that while evidence-based interventions and standards of service have shown positive outcomes repeatedly, that does not render a one-size-fits-all approach to addressing the needs of diverse populations. As stated, no population, region, or culture is monolithic, so even applications of evidence-based interventions must be closely analyzed and adapted to meet the needs of target populations. Leaders must recognize differences between populations in which evidence-based interventions were piloted (including age, gender, cultures, socioeconomic contexts, locales, and governance factors) and target populations. Clear analyses of how differences between pilot populations and target populations may impact expected outcomes of evidence-based interventions and established standards of service are essential to maintaining fidelity of sexual health research and practice.

World Medical Association – Declaration of Helsinki

International conventions continue to include the World Medical Association Declaration of Helsinki. Initially adopted by the 18th World Medical Association (WMA) General Assembly in Helsinki, Finland, in June 1964, the Declaration addresses primarily physicians and focuses on ethical principles governing medical research with human participants, identifiable human material, and data. (World Medical Association, 2018) This document has remained a binding reference for medical personnel and has been amended eight times, and most recently in October 2013. Investigation of the Declaration's contents illustrates that its nuances can still greatly assist contemporary sexuality researchers to maintain and illustrate unprecedented respect for the discipline, impact, and outcomes that research is intended to require.

Principles stated in the Declaration include a requisite for physicians (and other health professionals) that "The health of my patient will be my first consideration." Further, the Declaration expresses mandates for professionals to subject medical research to ethical standards that promote and ensure respect for all human subjects and protect their health and rights. The Declaration continues to express poignant perspectives that while the primary purpose of medical research is to generate new knowledge, this goal can never take precedence over the rights and interests of individual research subjects. Contemporary researchers can keep this tenant forthright in research design, implementation, and evaluation, and recognize that participants' rights must supersede the pursuit of research outcomes.

The Declaration places responsibilities adequately to physicians (and other health professionals) who are involved in medical research to protect the life, health, dignity, integrity, right to self-determination, privacy, and confidentiality of personal information of research subjects (World Medical Association, 2018). The responsibility for the protection of research participants must always rest with the research leader and never with the research subjects, even though they have given consent for, and indicated full knowledge of the extent of, their participation. As mentioned, these protections are included in other ethical conventions, and provide reinforcement of these values to researchers seeking to bridge to international populations. As professional circles become more global in their reaches, the WMA declares that "no national or international ethical, legal or regulatory requirement should reduce or eliminate any of the protections for research subjects set forth in this Declaration" (World Medical Association, 2018). The Declaration concludes with additional shared guidance to minimize harms to research participants and other indications on conducting medical research in ways that support subsequent research in underrepresented populations. Leaders in sexuality research can certainly align contemporary ethical principles with such philosophies.

Public Health Values Statement

In ethical considerations in sexuality research and leadership, it is reasonable to frame the discipline in the context of other public and community health disciplines. To that end, Rowitz and colleagues capsulate a public health value statement that offers a firm foundation on which to tailor specific guidelines for sexuality researchers and practitioners, and to be imparted to students and partners. Their statement, "Social justice integrated with freedom, social and ethnic equality, the worth and dignity of each individual, and the brotherhood of all human beings" identifies two important facets for sexuality leadership and research (Rowitz, 2014). *Social justice* indicates fairness and equity in distribution of wealth, opportunities, and privileges within a society. *Integration* indicates seamless collaboration of the complexities of population qualities of life (Rowitz, 2014). Therefore, public health value statements infuse sexual health within the spectra of population health disciplines. Further, the statement encourages practitioners to seek social justice and to consider integrated approaches to improving sexuality as an interdependent aspect of individual (and population) wholeness. Such assertions bring with it professional connections and scientific alliances that engage sexuality research and leadership with other public health professionals.

Ethical Considerations in Sexuality Research, Program Design, and Evaluation

As sexual research continues, applications into behavioral and structural programs must also reflect ethical foundations. A key concept in sexuality program design is harm reduction. Harm reduction is a set of practical strategies and ideas aimed at reducing negative consequences associated with sexual interactions and intercourse. Leaders must ensure interventions focused on the concept of harm reduction are reasonable in their assessments, and also consider other factors where harm may be indirectly transferred. In those cases, harm is not reduced at all, but rather placed in another category of human experience. For example, public health practitioners are divided on the introduction of self-administered HIV testing to global markets. On one hand, practitioners are clear that testing is imperative to reduce harms associated with health literacy, access to quality chronic care, and secondary HIV prevention. Self-testing addresses many of the barriers public health professionals have experienced regarding participants receiving tests, but not returning for results. However, many consider that the self-administration of HIV testing takes no account for the psychological trauma and distress that can be experienced by an individual whose test results in positive outcomes. Ethical principles decry the transference of harm from not knowing HIV status, to harm resulting from positive outcomes, which may or may not be correct. As a matter of ethics, interventions must be designed to reduce harms associated with sexual interactions and intercourse. Leaders must apply due diligence to ensure harms and benefits are equitably distributed, not simply transferred from one category to another.

Further, harm reductions must be considered from both cultural and social avenues. As previously discussed, participants in research are indelibly linked to communities, cultures, and social strata from whence they emerge. As such, leaders must consider widespread impacts and implications of participations and resulting outcomes. Ethical research and program designs must not perpetuate unfounded stigma and stereotypes and maintain integrity and fidelity from inception to completion. Care must be taken to ensure both risks and benefits from sexuality research are equitably allocated, and that accurate findings are disseminated with appropriate levels of decorum and respectability.

Beneficence in Program Design and Evaluation

In intervention design, researchers can creatively illustrate beneficence without intruding on the integrity of the intervention, or on the research process. Leaders must first allocate time to thoroughly consider what benefits (and risks) exist and for whom as a result of intervention implementation. Designs must then reflect steps to balance benefits and risks among participating parties. Leaders can also ensure that research is approved for implementation by appropriate Institutional Review Boards that adequately reflect participating communities, and are sufficiently aware of the sociocultural contexts in which interventions will be implemented. During implementation, researchers demonstrate beneficence by maintaining accurate and exhaustive documentation of research protocol, preliminary outcomes, and unexpected aberrations with implications on expected outcomes and benefits. This monitoring is particularly important when implementing evidence-based interventions. While these protocols have shown effectiveness through numerous outcome evaluations, leaders must recognize differences between audiences in which such interventions have been piloted and audiences in which they are currently implementing. Marked differences in locale, gender composition, sociocultural factors, external and environmental contexts between the pilot audience and the audience of implementation can greatly impact expected outcomes. Beneficence requires leaders to document these differences and estimate their impacts on outcomes prior to implementation. This preliminary analysis will indicate additional protections audiences may need, and provides researchers with content to review during implementation.

Beneficent program design also requires researchers to adhere to research process standards. Standards exemplified by appropriate applications of classical and contemporary theories, and establishment and examination of *a priori* hypotheses which are either confirmed or rejected based on statistical analysis of collected data. In doing so, current scientists can share the credible and reliable standing that many historical scientists have leveraged to progress knowledge. Leaders must be cognizant to ensure beneficence is extended equitably to populations that enjoy benefits of research as well as those that endure the risks associated with research. Historically, these benefits have not been distributed equitably and have fostered residual skepticism and aversion for many populations to participate in current research. If unaddressed, this aversion can continue to stagnate scientific inquiry and tailored programmatic services to these populations.

Nonmaleficence in Program Design and Evaluation

Similarly, contemporary researchers are charged to emphasize nonmaleficence in protocol design, implementation, and evaluation. Researchers must remain visionary and insightful about potential risks and take definitive steps to minimize risks toward beneficial outcomes. As such, researchers are challenged to reference classical theories and contrast contemporary contexts impacting their application and appropriateness. Too often, researchers apply theories whose tenants are vastly different from current social and cultural contexts. Leaders must allocate appropriate time and labor to assess social, cultural, environmental factors then match appropriate theories, classical and contemporary, corresponding to those factors. Also, leaders must illustrate nonmaleficence in protocol and intervention designs by considering impacts of participation and outcomes on participants and their respective communities. As mentioned, sexuality remains a largely personal topic in Western cultures, and researchers must remain aware of both potential benefits and resulting stigmas participants may endure. Further, as our global communities continue to grow, researchers must remain mindful of techniques that clearly state premises under which research was implemented so that appropriate adaptations can be implemented in different populations while maintaining study fidelity.

Respect for Autonomy

Additionally, ethics in leadership and sexuality research necessitates tangible avenues to promote and respect autonomy of participants. As such, research must be a collaborative effort in which researchers exercise cultural humility to devise culturally competent approaches to establish and maintain consent of participants throughout. Researchers must also support appropriate data collection and usage procedures, and maintain privacy protections thereof. Historically, researchers have failed to protect access to, and subsequent use of, data collected simply because protocol consents did not express that data could not be used in other analyses. While the content of consent forms identified what research was permitted to do, the spirit of consent must also uphold participant's consent as the sole purpose of collected data.

Respect for autonomy in protocol and intervention design also involves researchers' appropriate induction and deduction of conclusions based on collected data. Leaders must avoid biases and preconceived notions about research outcomes and allow only collected data, statistical outcomes, and pertinent factors to impact research outcomes. Often, funding sources can directly or indirectly apply influence on researchers to create results that are conducive to preset objectives. In these cases, leaders are obliged to resist such influence, and maintain scientific and professional integrity. Leaders simply cannot succumb to pressures for research to become commercial endorsements for funders if research outcomes do not support such findings.

Further, leaders must ensure that research findings are disseminated to wider varieties of audiences. Previously, research particularly in academic institutions was isolated and shared only among academic audiences. Contemporary emphasis on cross-disciplinary and multidisciplinary approaches requires translational research dissemination to become a vital component of leadership in sexuality studies. Leaders must actively access scholarly, peer-reviewed publication options as well as media outlets targeting general populations. As effective communication skills continue to be fundamental to ethical leadership, scientists must emphasize their responsibilities to reach and inform academic, corporate, and community audiences.

In addition, researchers must acknowledge that participation in research is based solely on the volition and desires of individuals. Involvement in research is a participatory act, and therefore, contributing individuals must be considered *participants* and not *subjects*. Nomenclature and resulting inferences can make great impacts on leaders' recognition and support of the abilities of research participants to maintain or discontinue inclusion as a function of individual freedoms.

Justice

Ethics in sexuality research and leadership requires justice to emerge not as an abstract concept, but as a concrete principle illustrated in intervention and protocol design. Leaders must ensure equities in resulting risks and benefits of research. Often, vulnerable populations identified as research funding priorities are also underserved in other components of life, and often lack economic and political power. In the past, this power differential allowed scientists to essentially disregard resulting risks of research in these populations because serious ramifications were highly unlikely. While these inequities still exist in the United States and globally, ethics compels leaders to involve participating populations throughout research planning, implementation, and evaluation.

Again, effective communication plays a vital role in illustrating ethical conduct. Ethical leadership ensures accurate communication of research content, methodologies, and outcomes benefitting diverse audiences. However, ethical leaders' responsibilities to illustrate justice require communication that minimizes and eliminates stigma, stereotypes, and biases against participants and the communities to which they belong.

To accomplish this goal, leaders must practice cultural humility, address their own implicit and explicit biases, and persuade audiences to do the same. This process is imperative for fostering and sustaining lessons learned through sexuality research on population levels.

Concepts of justice, nonmaleficence, and autonomy have led much of the classical standards on ethics in research. Throughout, scientists have relied on these principles as foundations of quality research. Subsequent research has been built on previous findings, and knowledge has progressed based on new inquiries following conclusive research. Quality and sustainability of this continuum is therefore based on the viabilities of leaders to engage with participating communities equitably and to conduct research ethically. Therefore, leaders must not only prescribe to developing and implementing research that is ethical in its design and beneficial for populations-at-large themselves, but also insist upon colleagues and other professionals to do the same. As mentioned, priority populations for investigation are often underserved in numerous facets of their lives. Contemporary populations that still bear the burden of historical missed steps and inequities in research rarely participate in clinical trials and other research. So while underserved populations in the past may have been unable to leverage social, economic, or political power to confront maltreatment, they simply encouraged others not to initiate participation in new studies. When particular demographic groups are absent from research, outcomes are severely limited, knowledge is stagnated, and populations remain underserved.

Additional Consideration: Compassion – Joining Communities and Scientists

In addition, ethical considerations in sexual health research and leadership must also include compassion as a key component. Compassion as an ethical construct will support scientists' consistent application of ethical principles, and compel them to utilize appropriate measures to report misconduct. Compassion will foster professional courtesy and ensure scientists maintain ethical parameters in every facet of interaction with communities. Doing so may begin to restore credibility, reduce skepticism, and foster positive environments for continued study especially among underserved populations.

Compassion also illustrates the bidirectional dialog between organizations and communities that is the foundation for sustainability and viability to meet communities' changing needs. Compassion will allow leaders to remain capable of continuing research to further organizational missions, fortify organizational visions, build social capital, and enhance community credibility.

Further, compassion will acknowledge current protected populations described in federal legislation and extrapolate necessary protections to populations that are not included but are appropriate. Subpopulations that are already stigmatized, or represent compromised levels of autonomy (i.e., homeless populations, foster children, transgender populations, persons with histories of addictions) must be provided additional levels of protection to avoid amplifying social burdens these populations already face. Leaders must recognize human interdependence and uphold mutual respect for all populations. Such efforts will nurture necessary diversities in intervention participants, and allow research outcomes to initiate change in participating communities. By engaging compassion along with classical tenants of ethical research with human participants, scientists and leaders in sexual research will progress the discipline and its outcomes to heighten awareness, and improve status of populations around the globe.

Process Questions and Considerations

1. Do you believe the same sociocultural and political environments that allowed the Tuskegee Syphilis Study to continue for four decades uninterrupted still exist? Why or why not?
2. Does the principle of beneficence require scientists to provide research outcomes to participating populations, or engage in community-based participatory research regardless of the protocol?
3. Are scientists required to minimize stigmatizing language and inference about participating populations in research outcomes?
4. Based on initial definitions, what other populations should receive "protected" status? Why?
5. How can scientists arrive at necessary responses to research questions in populations of concern that are protected?
6. How can scientists minimize personal biases to initiate justice in distribution of research benefits and costs?
7. What factors are pivotal to bridge research completed in the United States to global audiences?
8. How can ethics-promoting measures be included in intervention designs?
9. How can leaders eliminate stigma in their communication of research information and outcomes?
10. What other ways can compassion be infused into sexuality research and leadership?
11. What impacts can compassion have on progressing sexuality research and leadership?

References

Brandt, Allan M. (1978). Racism and research: The case of the Tuskegee Syphilis study. *The Hastings Center Report, 8*(6), pp. 21–29. Retrieved from http://nrs.harvard.edu/urn-3:HUL.InstRepos:3372911

Crenner, C. (2012, April). The Tuskegee Syphilis study and the scientific concept of racial nervous resistance. *Journal of the History of Medicine and Allied Sciences, 67*(2), 244–280. Retrieved from www.jstor.org/stable/24632043

Eisenhower, Dwight D. (1965, June). What is leadership? *Reader's digest.* pp. 49–54. Retrieved from www.eisenhower.archives.gov/all_about_ike/quotes/what_is_leadership.pdf

Kiisel, Ty. (2013, February 5). Without it, no real success is possible. *Forbes,* 23–25. Retrieved from www.forbes.com/sites/tykiisel/2013/02/05/without-it-no-real-success-is-possible/#513325c6e491

Kristinsson, Sigurdur. (2009, August). The Belmont report's misleading conception of autonomy. *American Medical Association Journal of Ethics, 11*(8), pp. 611–616.

Mrdjenovich, Adam. (2016, March 21). *Unpublished manuscript.* Retrieved from https://research-compliance.umich.edu/sites/default/files/resource-download/protection_of_vulnerable_populations_in_research.pdf

National Commission for the Protection of Human Subjects of Biomedical and Behavioral Research. 1978. *The Belmont report: Ethical principles and guidelines for the protection of human subjects of research.* Bethesda, MD: US Government Printing Office.

Rowitz, Louis. (2014). *Public health leadership putting principles into practice,* New York, NY: Jones & Bartlett Learning.

Schuster, Evelyn. (1997, November 13). Fifty years later: The significance of the Nuremberg code. *New England Journal of Public Health, 337*(20), 1437–1440.

United Nations Office of Human Resource Management. (2018, November 6). *Working Together Putting Ethics to Work.* Retrieved from www.un.org/en/ethics/pdf/WorkinTogetherGuide_en.pdf

US Department of Health and Human Services, Office of the Secretary, The National Commission for the Protection of Human Subjects of Biomedical and Behavioral Research. (1979, April 18). *The Belmont report, ethical principles and guidelines for the protection of human subjects of research.* Retrieved from www.hhs.gov/ohrp/regulations-and-policy/belmont-report/index.html

World Health Organization. (2018, November 15). *Constitution.* Retrieved from www.who.int/about/mission/en/

World Medical Association. (2018, November 15). *Declaration of Helsinki,* Retrieved from www.wma.net/policies-post/wma-declaration-of-helsinki-ethical-principles-for-medical-research-involving-human-subjects/

19 WTF SAR?!

Elevating and Expanding the Sexual Attitudes Reassessment

Bianca I. Laureano

Love does not begin and end the way we seem to think it does. Love is a battle, love is a war; love is a growing up."

James Baldwin

Introduction

Professional development (PD) can be tedious, particularly for emerging professionals, who are expected to attend basic workshops prioritizing everyday interactions and tasks over more engaging activities. This might mean that significant time is devoted to things like recording a sexual health history, or highlighting and prioritizing a to-do list. Though these are clearly useful skills, when such PD opportunities are required or encouraged at the expense of more engaging programs, it is more likely for participants to feel that they are wasting their time. Clearly, losing valuable time for sexologists who may be able to do vital work helping other people is not a great PD.

This can be particularly noticeable when PD omits discussions about contemporary issues and or fails to include the experiences of Black, Indigenous, People of Color (BIPOC) and others who experience oppression, or pathologizes these experiences when they are included.

Possibility and resolution are what drive a creative, inclusive PD endeavor. There is room to dream in these spaces. Room to imagine what is possible after the war and battle for liberation and body autonomy for all. The iconic Black author and activist James Baldwin writes of love as "a growing-up." A grown-up dream for PD is one where participants have an experience that keeps them fully engaged, feeling waves of heat move through the top of their heads to the bottom of their bodies. It is a human experience where participants learn about personal values and beliefs regarding sexuality topics. It may be an uncomfortable process of laughing, and unlearning the white supremacist ways we were taught about sexuality. PD where our full selves are honored, included, and affirmed is the dream that lead to the creation of the People of Color Centered Sexual Attitudes Reassessment in 2017 (POCc SAR).

Some expectations for sexologists by society, systems, institutions, and communities are unattainable while others may be rooted in bias. Understanding how those multiple expectations of roles intersect and result in specific forms of oppression and the ways many sexologists of color in the United States have had to practice what sociologist, Iris Lopez calls "agency within constraints,"(2008) is crucial, though often overlooked.

For example, conversations about Black or Latinx people are often focused on negative impacts like HIV and STI rates of infection, transmission, death; unplanned pregnancy; or poverty. Rarely are these examinations rooted or informed by a Black feminist lens, a womanist framework, or a liberatory approach. Often when people of color are discussed in sexuality PD experiences, an assimilationist approach is used, and if any form of the feminization of poverty is presented, it is often color-free, meaning focused only on white women.

Currently, there is an increase of "diversity and inclusion" initiatives across a global span of professions (Khan et.al., 2019). Yet in PD, these endeavors may not be executed well (for example, simply including stock photos of Black and nonbinary people in a presentation without nuance [Zackary Drucker photography for The Gender Spectrum Project https://broadlygenderphotos.vice.com]).

Exclusion means using the same structures and practices to assess and affirm whiteness and applying it to people who will never be white. The ways that white supremacy is seeped into the sexuality field in the United States is extensive. It is the fertilizer that helped this field grow. Many sexologists of color have spent their entire careers being excluded, isolated, and erased. Yet a discussion of white supremacy is not often welcomed by white people in the U.S. sexuality field.

Still there is hope for change and in recent years there has been a noticeable shift. A shift where the term "racism" is not the end of a conversation and where some white people in the field are strategically using their privilege to challenge, dismantle, and destroy white supremacy. Much of this is the result of tireless work by BIPOC who long fought for this change, who helped build the movement to push the field towards recognizing and challenging how white supremacy shows up and is sustained. Many of these advocates are still working in the field today as this remains a new movement dedicated to a growing-up love for self, community, pleasure, and liberation.

Many of the BIPOC authors in this textbook are those leaders. This chapter will offer an overview of one of the PD experiences created out of that hostility and resistance in the U.S. sexuality field. What is offered is a dream put into action when the lives and experiences of BIPOC are honored. A PD experience that is needed, wanted, and required, called a Sexual Attitudes Reassessment (SAR), discusses white supremacy and its impact on the sexuality experiences for all and especially for BIPOC.

What Is a SAR?

A SAR is an extensive sexuality training and workshop that offers reflexivity. It challenges beliefs and values and grounds in one's ethics the need to understand boundaries and communicate them effectively. These practices are important when we are offering care or support to a client or patient. SARs are not only for people in the sexuality field in the United States. They can benefit anyone doing professional interpersonal work. Professionals who work with people, teaching or helping professionals, and those in interdisciplinary fields, can benefit from a SAR. When done correctly, a SAR allows all participants the opportunity to examine their own personal beliefs and understand where their boundaries exist to maintain honesty with themselves and their clients. A SAR allows professionals to be reflexive and pushes them to be honest about their feelings. SARs allows for recognition of where an individual's personal boundaries intersect with their role as providers and educators. They also facilitate the development of a referral list of providers, educators, and healers.

Currently the requirements to offer SARs includes attending a SAR, facilitating small group discussions in another SAR, and cofacilitating a SAR. Following this, one may offer SARs on their own.

Why We Need a People of Color Centered SAR

Historically, SARs in the United States have been created and lead by white people. These white people then decide who they will train to offer SARs in the future. Rumors hold that the first SAR was held in San Francisco in the early 1970s. It is thought to have focused on hours of watching various kinds of pornography. By the time the author attended a SAR in 2009, at the national American Association for Sexuality Educators, Counselors, and Therapists (AASECT) Conference, this was not the focus. However, it was clear the dominant narrative of whiteness remained. This conference highlighted the need to include more voices of people of color since out of hundreds of conference participants, only 18 women of color were in attendance. During this SAR the only time a community of color were included was during a discussion of pygmies. Once a photograph was used to show a disabled Black man, a wheelchair user, having sex with an able-bodied white woman. The facilitator was an older white man, well known to people in the field. The SAR offered the reminder that BIPOC communities are not welcome, worthy, or included, and it reflected the early research and clinical literature about sexology

Imagine an entire session on sexual violence that only presents white heterosexual able-bodied women as the recipients of harm. In such a space there is no room to discuss the way white women engage in sexual violence. A glaring example would be addressing the murder of Emmett Till, the 14-year-old Black boy visiting family in Mississippi who was murdered in 1955 because a white woman said he grabbed her and made sexually crude comments towards her. In 2017 that white woman told Duke University History professor Timothy B Tyson that her claims were false and that, "[n]othing that boy did could ever justify what happened to him" (*The Blood of Emmett Till*, 2017). Such spaces also close the door on conversations about the ways white men make the "rules" in an oppressive ableist white supremacist heteropatriarchy society such as the United States (Hurtado, 1996).

Additionally, in the traditional SAR it can be impossible to discuss how some white women and non-Black women of color in the field of sexuality have often used the labor of Black women but failed to collaborate with, cite, or include them, to publish on the sexual assault and harassment they experience while never including the voices of narratives of Black women (Hebernick et al., 2019). Imagine never having the honest conversation that white supremacy hurts us all and instead having the narratives of white and light skin women of color normalized, and only being exposed to the narratives of those women seeking protection and care from white men instead of how sexual violence is racialized, gendered, and rooted in hate. Now imagine paying $600 for that SAR experience. Not anymore.

As SARs in the United States have a history of being employed and created by racially white people, many of them have advocated for a SAR being a part of a standard experience for sexuality professionals. Attending a SAR is currently a requirement for AASECT certification. Many of these same people have created SARs, evaluated them, even written books on the topic, which a basic internet search can reveal. As white supremacy has made their writings more accessible than others, they will not be cited here. Instead, look to the citations offered in this chapter to find those who have been left out, kept out, pushed out, and all the other ways BIPOC have not been welcomed into this U.S. sexuality field. Keep in mind that white supremacy is not only a U.S. experience, but one that impacts the world because of colonization, imperialism, and capitalism; those people who are well known in the United States for the SAR experience are replicating those same harmful patterns that leave others out in other parts of the world, especially in Canada and the United Kingdom.

One of the main reasons why a SAR is important is that we need to check in with ourselves, and, following the author's 2009 SAR experience, the Women of Color Sexual Health Network (WOCSHN) was founded as a way to help make this a reality.

Why Do We Still Need Them?

What is useful about SARs is that there is an audience of self-selected people willing to learn and unlearn and who know they will be pushed. It is common for people to expect to be exposed to shocking forms of media, to hear from a panel of people who have a particular religious belief, kink, or relationship status. However, despite the boundary-pushing nature of a SAR, the images and media used invariably normalizes whiteness in ways that are often missed by white facilitators and participants. To enter into a SAR that rejects the idea that white people are the only human beings whose sexual experiences, pleasures, challenges, and cultures are worthy or valuable is to instantly commit to a different way of learning and being. People of Color centered (POCc) SARs are needed to provide a space because there is nothing in the field to host and discuss the realities and impacts of white supremacy on the lives and bodies of BIPOC.

Collaborations

ABSC

Collaboration is the way forward. There is no organizing or movement building without collaboration. The Association of Black Sexologists and Clinicians (ABSC) was the ideal choice to collaborate in hosting the pilot POCc SAR. Focusing on Black brilliance and retention, collaborators are strongest when each leader's ethics are directly in line with one another. As collaborators, ABSC leadership agreed to offer a portion of their Continuing Education (CE) units for the 2017 year to host the first and pilot POCc SAR. Historically SARs offer CE units to participants that range from the amount of time that a participant is actively engaged in the SAR. For example, a SAR that has participants engaged for a total of 10 hours (not including breaks and lunch) may offer 10 CE units, which today is the AASECT requirement for SARs and which may go up to 18 CE units. This does not include advanced SARs, which are often understood to be next level SARs that address more specific issues not featured in a traditional SAR. These advanced SARs often remain color-free as well. This is according to the guidelines of the American Association of Sexuality Educators, Counselors, and Therapists (AASECT); these may be subject to editing and updating. ABSC leadership is open to an honest representation of what is occurring for Black people and sexuality topics. Immediately creating a shift in the U.S. sexuality field by acknowledging the interdisciplinary work of Black academic and public scholars, ABSC built one of the first membership directories that featured Black people exclusively. ABSC's work and leadership embody the communal call and response "we outchea!" Translated/code-switching to mean "we are literally and figuratively out here."

ISEE

Among the plethora of institutes for higher education offering matriculation in human sexuality education, therapy, counseling, and certification, the Institute for Sexuality Education and Enlightenment (ISEE) is one of the highest quality options available in the United States. The founder and Executive Director, Dr. Rosalyn Dischiavo, has been one of the first white women colleagues to invite BIPOC to teach, and has actively heard and held their critiques, moved to action, and prioritized the lives and knowledge of BIPOC in significant ways. Dr. Dischiavo remains a colleague, friend, and mentor to the author. ISEE leadership offered mentorship on creating and building the POCc SAR, offering CEs, and maintaining the logistical information required when offered at a national conference. Dr. Dischiavo's commitment to holistic care and training are directly in line with the vision of pleasure, justice, and healing for the POCc SAR. Dr. Dischiavo lives and moves in her "deep yes" and embodies what she writes about the gift of receiving. She received our relationship and honored it with her "yes" (*The Deep Yes: The Lost Art of True Receiving*, 2016).

Woodhull Freedom Foundation

For the inaugural national POCc SAR conference experience, a strong and reputable environment for sexuality was required. The team at the Woodhull Freedom Foundation who host the Woodhull Sexual Freedom Summit has always supported the Women of Color Sexual Health Network (WOCSHN) and collaborated with them for Woodhull's inaugural focus on making their Summit more accessible to under-represented groups in the mid-2010s. Having the term *Freedom* in a national conference comes with the expectation that everyone's freedom is included. The Woodhull Freedom Foundation team has demonstrated their commitment to freedom and justice through their open acknowledgment and sharing of the shifts that occur when larger justice goals are needed. As one of the organizations in the United States seeking to make their environments more inclusive, Woodhull Freedom Foundation staff acknowledged their abilities and their challenges and understood why collaboration is important to the work they wish to continue. When proposed to collaborate, Woodhull Freedom Foundation leadership (at the time Ricci Levy and Mandy Farsace) immediately replied affirmatively. This lead to organizing a contract that outlined the room and audio equipment being offered by the Woodhull Freedom Foundation for a percentage of what other participants pay. In exchange, we offered full registration scholarships to attend the POCc SAR for Woodhull Freedom Foundation to use as they chose. They offered this scholarship to community members who identified interest and need. Sometimes sexual freedom looks and feels like supporting the dream and labor of BIPOC.

Mentioning the names and organizations of those who collaborated to allow this radical PD experience to occur is important for they must be recognized for taking the risk, the leap of faith, and the institutional responsibility of holding the POCc SAR. They trusted the author because of her work and her word. ABSC, ISEE, and Woodhull Freedom Foundation are allies in this work. They are finding ways to strategically use their privilege and access to power and resources to ensure that those of us with the desire and ability have the opportunity. Their collaboration made the reality of having BIPOC train BIPOC for offering SARs. Affirmation and trust are pillars of the sexuality field. Rarely are PD opportunities offered to witness the eloquence of theory put into practice by BIPOC. The theory of collaboration looks like trusting BIPOC to employ the brilliance of other BIPOC through attribution, analysis, and praxis.

Frameworks

This work was guided by Black womanist and feminist theories, by disability and reproductive justice frameworks, and through an intersectional analysis and praxis that examines power. The conceptualization of such a PD experience is guided by AfroFuturism (Dery, 1994), which looks at how race and technology intersect, and imagines a positive future for Black people; and by AfroPessimism (Sexton, 2006), which explores the ongoing impacts of oppression and colonization. Intersectional analysis and frameworks were applied when imagining what was possible, but doing so was not an attempt to incorporate intersectionality as a buzzword. As a scholar trained by Black and Latina feminists in a women's studies doctoral program in the early 2000s, the author and creator of the POCc SAR was a CrISP scholar, a fellow of interdisciplinary scholars using intersectional theories and analysis when doing research on race, gender, and ethnicity. The author is a trained intersectional scholar whose doctoral career prepared her to use intersectional theory, analysis, and frameworks in praxis. The manifestation of such a SAR follows the legacy of resistance BIPOC have inherited (Turman, 2019).

Recognizing how an intersectional analysis impacts learning environments requires an examination of power and how all identities are rooted in expectations and gender roles, which may be silenced, harmed, or traumatized by systems and institutions. The practice of centering Black women was and is always already at the center of the POCc SAR. Examining how Black women are often excluded impacts research in the U.S. sexuality field. Often research on Black women and sexuality focuses on negative experience; survival and institutionalization for medical issues are overly focused on at the expense of pleasure and healing and thriving. In short, the POCc SAR challenged the dehumanization framework and practice that has infested the U.S. sexuality field. A focus on values and ethics when working with communities that participants are a part of, and which they are not a part of, is vital to this practice and this PD experience.

One way we did this was to incorporate a Black Feminist framework and ask "who has power here?" What does freedom of sexual and body autonomy feel and look like for Black women and femmes? What is impacting the path to such liberation? These are common questions which have been asked by many Black women public intellectuals throughout history.

As the Combahee River Collective (1982), a group of Black feminist lesbians organized in the late 1970s, reminds us, "If Black women were free, it would mean that everyone else would have to be free since our freedom would necessitate the destruction of all the systems of oppression."

Disability Justice

A Disability Justice Framework was implemented because the creator and facilitator lives with multiple disabilities: This demonstrates leadership by one of those most impacted. There was no way to create a professional development opportunity without considering the whole entire body. How to instruct, build, and navigate during the SAR if the facilitator's body was in pain? This is sustainability. How to create a space that welcomed and honored the reality that there is no wrong way to have a body? This is recognizing wholeness. Beginning with one's own body is what a Disability Justice framework offers for a SAR experience. Often people assume Disability Justice (DJ) is only and exclusively about access in a handful of ways. This is important, but it is not the whole story. Being guided by a DJ framework goes beyond simply using videos with subtitles. We need to ask the following questions: How heavy are the doors to the training space? Are the bathrooms adequate for someone who has an assistant to comfortably access the restroom without any gender policing? What does "scent free" mean? Is this different for white people and for BIPOC? Will sex workers be safe or targeted? What safety plan is created if participants or facilitators are targeted for violence? By ignoring these questions and failing to see the entire human being as worthy of care, collective safety, or support, many organizations and PD experiences fail at DJ. This was how a dehumanization framework was rejected. One of the DJ principles is interdependence: "[w]e attempt to meet each other's needs as we build toward liberation, without always reaching for state solutions which can readily extend its control further over our lives" and asks "how do we move together as people . . . where no body/mind is left behind?" (Berne, Morales, Levins, Langstaff, & Sins Invalid, 2018).

It was DJ that lead to the exclusion of panels during a SAR. Often these panels are not well facilitated, or attended, and are done with limited compensation. Panels and demonstrations during SARs are useful and employed by many. Yet, those SARs depend on capitalism and a normalization of people's value connected to their labor, a violation of DJ. Many SAR panelists are rarely prepared or supported to speak to groups of people who ask personal and intimate questions, yet do not ask themselves such queries. Facilitation is crucial to a successful and revolutionary SAR. Many may know how to ask "how does this video make you feel?" yet not many are able to help participants understand their own values and ethics are tied to the ways their biases impact their professional and personal lives.

Reproductive Justice

Reproductive Justice is a marriage of disability justice and racial justice and it focuses on body autonomy, the right to decide when to have a child, or to not have a child, and the right to parent children in safe, sustainable communities (SisterSong.net). The framework of Reproductive Justice (RJ) was created by a group of Black women in the 1990s and was brought to a national level by the organization SisterSong, which at the time was led by activist Loretta Ross (Ross, 2017).

To facilitate a conversation that centers body autonomy of young Black women forces participants to examine power in a way that is not often possible when the focus is on white women who are often protected in ways Black women are not. Reproductive Justice allowed us an additional way to bring in the power of choice. It asks how might therapists hold bias for the ways clients have had to make difficult choices if they were never offered a PD experience to examine those biases? Access to and impact of services, systems, and institutions is another guiding justice principal. Similar to disability justice, reproductive justice forces us to ask how we collectively gain access to reproductive healthcare if we are only offered such care to limit our procreation? Since these are complex topics which require skill and a deep understanding of the history and lingering impact of the eugenics movement, excellent facilitation is required for these discussions.

Media Literacy

The use of media in a SAR has historically been a major element. However, it is also important to utilizing media literacy skills to help participants become critical media consumers. The Center for Media Literacy in Malibu, California, believes understanding these core areas are crucial in helping attain this goal:

1. All media messages are "constructed"
2. Media messages are constructed using a creative language with its own rules
3. Different people experience the same media message differently
4. Media have embedded values and points of view
5. Most media messages are organized to gain profit and/or power

They then suggest asking these five core questions:

1. Who created this message?
2. What creative techniques are used to attract my attention?
3. How might different people understand this message differently than me?

4. What values, lifestyles and points of view are represented in, or omitted from, this message?
5. Why is this message being sent?

These core concepts and questions are utilized when using media during the POCc SAR. Participants are not asked to simply passively view media. Instead, they are expected to engage with media and discuss how their values and perspectives are affirmed or challenged. Use of media can also affirm the bodies and lives of people of color from all parts of life, for example those who are queer and trans, working class, disabled, undocumented, and represent various ages. Using this framework encourages participants to assess, reflect, and act in ways that are more in line with their values and ethics.

Representation of the lives and bodies of BIPOC is an important way to affirm their reality and pleasure. Many sexologists today continue to claim that finding media including or centering people of color is a challenge. It is not. In fact, one of the many challenges we experienced in creating the POCc SAR was actually having to edit down wonderfully inclusive images and videos which we were unable to include due to time restraints. Nevertheless, it is incumbent on us all to push back against statements that further the idea that finding inclusive media is an insurmountable obstacle and expose the unexamined white supremacy that allows these statements and beliefs to thrive.

Utilizing media literacy expands opportunities for participants to recognize media justice, what is produced when media is created by those most impacted.

We need to look in some nontraditional places to find it. For example, Oakland rapper Skee-Lo's "I Wish" song and video can facilitate a conversation about Black men and fantasy. In this video, Skee-Lo fantasizes: "I wish I was a little bit taller/I wish I was a baller/I wish I had a girl who looked good, I would call her" (Skee-Lo, 1995). In this narrative we are able to explore how Black men discuss their bodies and image. As a short Black man, Skee-Lo fantasizes about having more height which would lead to athleticism and then a romantic relationship with an attractive Black women. He has complicated Black masculinity and shared a safe way to demonstrate vulnerability for heterosexual Black men interested in intra-racial dating. Also offered is a point of entry into misogyny and other forms of oppression. When SAR facilitators are not strongly guided through justice frameworks, they do not find media that is useful and thus do not always connect larger societal expectations and forms of oppression BIPOC experience and express in popular culture.

Facilitating this process in a SAR may also lead to the participants engaging in understanding their own biases in the media they create. Additionally, it can create a collective form of media that is just! This is one reason why the *pornography* presented in the POCc SAR would not be categorized as "shocking" as many SAR attendees tend to expect. In many ways the pornography used in the POCc SARs objectified and sexualized affection, consent, and foreplay among BIPOC, by showing imagery of joy and respect through communication and a range of bodies. Why is this form of Black erotica not considered "sexy" by others? Is it not shocking enough to witness a growing-up love? What forms of excitement are normalized and which are rejected or pathologized? How do BIPOC sexologists and sex professionals heal from the violence and perversion of white supremacy? May a SAR offer healing?

Healing is a focus of the POCc SAR and for this reason a range of healers, counselors, therapists, and coaches who were white and BIPOC made themselves available to offer free 30-minute sessions for participants of the POCc SAR. There was a diverse list of providers with various skills and in different time zones. The goal was to offer healing to the healers. For participants to recognize that a SAR can offer more support post-training creates an expectation of care for participants not often experienced in a SAR. It also allowed those people who could not attend or support the SAR financially to be present and offer support in other ways. The POCc SAR follows a collaboration for healing, unlearning, and revolutionary love for self, others, and the work/field.

Traditional SARs do not offer any path or guidance to much healing for pre- or post-SAR care. But being intentional about offering a list of therapists and healers for participants is more than mentioning a reminder to eat dinner, drink water, call a friend. This is not the equivalent of offering someone a free session with a healer who can support them a month or two after a SAR. This is 'trauma informed" in action. Focusing on body autonomy and liberation for Black women and femmes meant imagining needs post-SAR and the impact of exposure to white supremacy and then discussing it in a way not often offered in a professional development setting. Those harmed by white supremacy know healing is needed. Yet, it is rare to recognize when it is needed, to imagine it, create it, implement it, and to have that be both a collective and an individual experience. A next level form of collaboration was tied to healing when those who supported the POCc SAR offered a free session. They identified this as a form of solidarity and support of the revolutionary work. This resource will guide the creation of PD workshops moving forward. Acknowledging that racism and white supremacy harms us and that there must be tools and weapons to survive is essential.

Accessibility

The space that was chosen for the first POCc SAR was a rented community space in the historically Black community of Bed-Stuy, Brooklyn.

There was a door that pushed inward, seating without side arms, and affirming Black art all around. However, a small step to another room did not allow wheelchair users to access the restroom or second room. The second time the SAR was offered was in a large hotel that follows the American with Disabilities Act of 1991 in being fully accessible.

The scholarships offered were for registration to the POCc SAR only. Lodging, travel, and food were dependent on the participant. In Bed-Stuy, Brooklyn, in 2018, it was not difficult to have out-of-state participants find friends or affordable accommodations as well as local area food options to meet a variety of food needs in the immediate area. ABSC donated a variety of snacks for the POCc SAR and water. The space at the Woodhull Sexual Freedom Summit offered water and local food options.

Knowing the racialized financial violence that occurs in a capitalist society, making the POCc SAR accessible was vital. Accessibility in this context was not only the cost of the workshop, but also a transparent sharing of where the funds went, who received them, and why. The answers to those questions are as follows: directly to the facilitator/creator, who pays for the space, and buys the equipment. Payment is split fairly between cofacilitators and those in training. A donation to collaborating organizations thanking them for their support was offered.

Altar Space

An Altar space was created for the POCc SARs. This space was included for participants and facilitator to use when needing a break, shift, or grounding. When sharing the POCc SAR outline with a mentor who was told this intention about an Altar, she cried. She shared this is what she had imagined and hoped she could one day be able to participant in a PD experience. Originally created to continue the discussion of grounding oneself post-session on violence and Black bodies, the Altar was an opportunity to engage artistically and use our bodies differently. Each participant was given a votive candle, a small notebook, a small rubber frog (to represent Puerto Rico post Hurricanes Irma and Maria), external condoms, lube, and several small clothing pins. Participants lit unscented candles and touched objects as they focused on the hard work they do quietly.

As the SARs have continued so has the inclusion of the Altar space. People who are often on the margins of their communities have thanked facilitators for the Altar space, which made them feel more present and welcomed in the training space. Participants have been encouraged to think about something they would like to add to the Altar during the SAR and are invited to take what is available to share from the Altar. Often rose quartz, jade, and amethyst stones are available by the facilitator for participants to take.

Evaluation

As is standard archival requirements by AASECT, records must be kept by the CE provider for seven years. An evaluation component must be included. As the POCc SAR was created, complementary ways participants could share their experience and evaluate the SAR were considered. At a particular point in one's career there comes a time when useful critique is difficult to find. Building evaluation into the SAR from the start allowed facilitators to maintain the clarity of the outcomes and goals of the POCc SAR. Often educators and creators leave evaluation for after a program or curriculum has been established. Instead, a piece of sage advice: Invest in evaluation early. For that reason vital statistics and responses from participants for improving the SAR and how the SAR impacted their experience and learning were captured.

The POCc SAR was offered twice in 2018. Each time the groups had 11 to 13 participants, a wonderful number for deep and vital conversations. Many of the participants identified as cisgender Black women who ranged in age from 21 to 58 years old. The first POCc SAR held in Bed-stuy, Brooklyn had all participants assigned female at birth and embracing a spectrum of gender expressions and all identified as racially Black except one. There were several AfrxLatinxs, racially Black and ethnically Latinx, participants in both SARs.

ANTE UP! SAR

The time when white supremacy as a fetish and oppression are integrated into a SAR that all participants must engage with is when vital change may occur. To begin to examine how some participants may crave the comfort and safety white supremacy brings and thus choose not to resist or support oppressed people is important for those participants to know. These are the areas of growth, discomfort, and reflection that are not often provided in a SAR. It is not enough to have BIPOC bodies of color, BIPOC bodies of size, disabled BIPOC, or trans and nonbinary BIPOC represented. It requires an intentional focus and choice to challenge white supremacy: to remain in a space of consistent self-reflection. These are the essential facilitation skills for the SARs of the future because without them what else is there? How else will white sex educators and therapists be prepared to provide care to white supremacists? Aren't they the exact white people who need to be offering that point of entry? Who would they refer to if they decided they could not "handle" a white supremacist client? How will they be offered these considerations if not in a SAR?

One aspect of the POCc SAR that focused on ethics and ethical behavior was a strategic use of privilege among white and light skinned participants and those who are able-bodied, U.S. citizens, cisgender, and have class/wealth access. Many times, white people are not challenged about how they allow oppression to continue when seen or how they too participate in oppression and institutionalization that removes the body autonomy of many people. The therapeutic care sexuality therapists and counselors offer may be deeply connected to the ways Black people's joy, sexuality, and pleasure have been rejected and institutionalized. From the history of the U.S. medical industrial complex, over-medicating Black people and assuming Black people have high thresholds for pain could be a direct entry into the prison incarceration system. These systems and forms of power must be examined for a SAR to reflect the realities of many BIPOC.

Finally, the name of the SAR, specifically the POC centered part, turned many off, even when the first sentence of the registration form says "This is a SAR for all of us." As a result the title POCc SAR will be used when the SAR offered is exclusively for people of color, a SAR that will intentionally be exclusively for BIPOC. This might sound like "reverse discrimination," but that term is functionally meaning and designed to negate the real discrimination people of color face. The effect of a POC-only SAR is in fact liberation and radical acceptance.

Realizing the POCc SAR that was created was an experience unlike any other SAR or any other professional development experience. Moving beyond common practices and attempts of inclusion and diversity, this SAR combines racial justice, disability justice, reproductive justice frameworks, and practice with tools for self-analysis and embodiment. Participants are welcome to bring their full selves into a learning and an unlearning space. The intention is to make connections, be challenged, expand, and go all in for collective and individual liberation and freedom. In other words, ANTE UP!

Moving forward, the professional development experience will be titled the ANTE UP! SAR.

Process Questions and Considerations

1. Why do you think SARs have been presented in the same fashion for the last 30 years in the field of sexuality?
2. What do you think might have caused the shift or emergence of different forms of SARs in the past five years?
3. Should race be discussed during SARs? Why or why not?
4. Should sexuality leaders and educators be knowledgeable and skilled about race/racism in the field? Why or why not?
5. Describe your idea of a perfect SAR and what you would want to get out of it.

References

Berne, Patty; Morales, Aurora Levins; Langstaff, David; and Sins Invalid (2018). 10 principles of disability justice. *WSQ: Women's Studies Quarterly*, 46, (1 & 2), Spring/Summer 2018, pp. 227–230

Combahee River Collective. (1986). *The Combahee river collective statement: Black feminist organizing in the seventies and eighties.* Kitchen Table/Women of Color Press. https://combaheerivercollective.weebly.com/the-combahee-river-collective-statement.html

Dery, Mark. (1994). "Black to the Future: Interviews with Samuel R. Delaney, Greg Tate, and Tricia Rose." *Flame wars: The discourse of cyberculture* (pp. 179–222). Edited Mark Dery. Duke University Press, Durham, NC.

Dischiavo, Rosalyn. (2016). *The deep yes: The lost art of true receiving.* CreateSpace.

Herbenick, D., van Anders, S. M., Brotto, L. A., Chivers, M. L., Jawed-Wessel, S., & Galarza, J. (2019). Sexual harassment in the field of sexuality research. *Archives of Sexual Behavior* Volume 48, Issue 4, pages 997–1006.

Hurtado, Aida. (1996). *The color of privilege: Three Blasphemies on race and feminism (Critical Perspectives on Women and Gender).* University of Michigan Press, Ann Arbor, MI.

Khan, M. S., Lakha, F., Mei Jin Tan, M., Singh, S. R., Yu Chin Quek, R., Han, E., . . . Legido-Quigley, H. (2019). More talk than action: Gender and ethnic diversity in leading public health universities. *The Lancet*, *393*, (e 10171), 9–15, February 2019, pp. 594–600.

Lopez, Iris. (2008). *Matters of choice: Puerto Rican women's struggle for reproductive freedom.* Rutgers University Press, New Brunswick, NJ.

Ross, Loretta. (2017). *Reproductive justice: An introduction (Reproductive Justice: A New Vision for the 21st Century).* University of California Press, Berkeley, CA.

Sexton, Jared. (2006). Afro-Pessimism: The unclear world. *Rhizomes: Cultural Studies in Emerging Knowledge*, (29). Doi:10.20415/rhiz/029.e02.

SisterSong. www.SisterSong.net

Skee-Lo. (1995). *I wish. On I wish* [CD recording]. Scotti Bros, Sunshine Studios Hollywood, CA.

The Gender Spectrum Project https://broadlygenderphotos.vice.com

Turman, Aiesha. (2019). *There's always been an afrofuture: Black women's literature as technology of protest* (Ph.D. dissertation). Union Institute & University.

Tyson, Timothy B. (2017). *The blood of Emmett Till.* Simon & Schuster, New York, NY.

20 Sexuality Leadership and Its New Face

James C. Wadley

At a fundamental level, leadership is a relational and reciprocal process of influencing (Hickman, 2016; Koonce, 2016). Leadership in the field of human sexuality is multidimensional, fluid, and capable of painting both broad and finite strokes. There are a number of leadership models (e.g., shared, indirect, laissez-faire, distributed, transactional, etc.) that exist that describe leadership in various disciplines, but very few models capture how leadership can be demonstrated to address sensitive issues concerning sexuality. Similar to professionals in the field of counselor education, sexuality leaders have been summoned in the areas of advocacy and social justice (Heckert & Cleminson, 2011; Elia and Tokunaga, 2015; Hoefer, 2019; etc.), professional identity and advocacy (Myers, Sweeney, & White, 2002; Rocha & Rocha, 2019; Russell, 2019; etc.), relationship stewardship (Perel, 2017; Chapman, 2015; Brown, 2015; etc.); supervision (Wadley & Siegel, 2018), and community engagement (Vaccaro, Russell, & Koob, 2015; Dempsey, 2010; Rhodes, Malow, & Jolly, 2010; etc.). At this juncture of American and global politics, sexuality scholars, practitioners, and educators should begin to address the necessity of conceptualizing and demonstrating leadership that allows constituents to be affirmed and have a voice in spaces that have been traditionally reserved for a few. If this conversation among emergent and seasoned sexuality leaders does not happen, the field will continue to remain fragmented, unprepared, and possibly disempowered to handle the sophistication of addressing micro and system challenges.

This chapter discusses several components that are relative to the complexities of addressing sexuality leadership and the importance of articulating and celebrating new strategies of empowerment for clinicians, educators, and consultants within the field. The chapter addresses several traits that are needed by emergent and seasoned leaders in the field in order to initiate, create, or move towards change. The identified traits are critical in order for constituents to have access to sexuality education, growth, skill development, and possible clarity about the varying complexities of working in the field. The trait described lend themselves to the "new face" of leadership as being emancipatory and necessary for

344   *James C. Wadley*

the field to become more inclusive and relevant to the needs of constituents served.

Traits of Leadership

Since the early 1970s there have been a number of studies that have contributed to the literature of leadership (DaCosta, 2012; Wister et al., 2014; Sullivan & Syvertsen, 2019; Chammas & Hernandez, 2019; Berry, 2019; Chan, 2019; etc.). These models and theoretical postulates were developed in order to describe what was needed in order for businesses (Putra & Cho, 2019; Kroska & Cason, 2019; González-Cruz, Botella-Carrubi, & Martinez-Fuentes, 2019; etc.), healthcare (Nigro, 2018; Clarke & Berkland, 2019; Edmonstone, 2017; etc.), and formal educational systems (Tellis, 2014; Somers & Lynch, 1994; Ganser & Kennedy, 2012; etc.) to work efficiently by one, some, or many professionals. It should be noted that some of these models were born from systemic dysfunction and were needed to serve as blueprints for moving beyond or through chaos and mismanagement (Edmonstone, 2013; Humes, 1995; Sheppard, Sarros, & Santora, 2013; etc.). Other models offered strategies of engagement during sensitive circumstances or various approaches for serving underserved populations. In order for emergent leaders to address sensitive and challenging issues in complex spaces, they must have several traits that allow them to successfully navigate themselves within the framework of policy and social expectations. This is critical in the field of sexuality given its sensitivity, value laden nature, and evolving dynamic. Traits for sexuality professionals include vision, flexibility, intentionality, empathy, intuition, courage to provoke or disrupt, and collaboration. All of these traits are needed in order to engage in emancipatory leadership.

Vision

Ndalamba, Caldwell, and Anderson (2018, p. 311) offer that leadership vision is a

> profound knowledge that creates the moral and ethical capacity to conceive of a feasible and relevant plan of action that inspires and motivates others to pursue the best possible outcome; identifies the resources required and barriers to overcome in achieving a desired purpose; and unites others in understanding and carrying out that plan, despite obstacles that may arise.

Visionary leadership requires leaders to know about themselves by intentionally examining themselves and developing a heightened awareness of their natural talent (Covey, 2011). This constant self-evaluation and maintaining insight is needed by leaders so that they can exhibit authenticity to their constituents. In the field of sexuality, authenticity is expected (and usually appreciated) because it allows for students, clients, and communities to feel comfortable and safe enough to share their own experiences.

In addition to knowing oneself, visionary leadership also exhibits a commitment to others' growth. This decision to serve the welfare and growth of others is ethically responsible (Hernandez, 2008, 2012), and creates an opportunity for organizational "synergy and change" that becomes easier to go beyond individual contributions to the organization. For some sexuality leaders who are of color or represent less visible communities in mainstream organizations, there is an obligation for them to mentor, counsel, advocate, and even embrace similar professionals who may need support. To not "give back" by serving entry level professionals or people who come from disadvantaged communities seems unethical. Leaders are responsible for the advancement of those who may be less privileged.

Even though leaders may have reached a period in their lives where they are responsible for the entry and mid-level professionals, the stewardship of leaders necessitates the need for continual learning, growth, innovation, and improvement (Ndalamba, Caldwell, & Anderson, 2018). Visionary leadership requires leaders to understand the constituents they serve, their competitors, as well as their products (Hess, 2014).

It can be assumed that visionary leadership tends to be influential by its leverage of power and the necessity of change creation or implementation (Collinson, 2012). While engaging in collaborative initiatives, leaders may also engage with one another a shared vision. Kouzes and Posner (2012) share four characteristics of shared vision:

1. Imagining possible opportunities – the ability to envision what can be achieved, and barriers to overcome, creates a road map to the future (cf. Nicholson, 2013)
2. Finding a common purpose – reorganizing motivations that bring people together achieves bonding and cooperation (Rost, 1991)
3. Appealing to common ideals – this capacity includes sensitivity to the values and ethical assumptions which motivate others (Ciulla, 2014)
4. Animating the vision – making possibilities come to life and communicating their potential enables a leader to inspire others (Covey, 2005)

Flexibility

In addition to having a vision for what may be in the future, leaders should also be ideologically and behaviorally flexible enough to accommodate unforeseen circumstances. In the field of sexuality, flexibility is needed regarding curriculum development, research practices, clinical interventions, as well as consultative opportunities. Research has suggested that in order to maintain a balance with constituents, leaders must be able to adapt their leadership style to the challenges of particular circumstances or individuals (Yukl & Mahsud, 2010). Sexuality leaders must be able to embrace fast-paced environments, diversity of activities, and various competing ideologies in order to remain catalytic for change (Denison, Hooijberg, & Quinn, 1995). This position of change is sometimes complementary and at other times can be antagonistic or provocative (Baron, Rouleau, Grégoire, & Baron, 2018). Sexuality leaders must be able to balance their interventions and involvement with constituents so that cohesion and morale are maintained but remain on a path dedicated to achieving goals or something different than the current status. Flexibility in the form of tension management may allow relative parties to reflect upon past mistakes, process roles and responsibilities in the present, and move into situations that may yield more favorable affective, cognitive, or behavioral outcomes. When leaders lack balance and agility, they run the risk of creating chaos and/or alienating their constituents. Research has shown that leadership flexibility increases the likelihood of innovation from team members as well as contributes to collaborative learning and initiatives (Delia, 2012). Sexuality consultants should have a variety of tools in their professional belts in order to accommodate the demands of their constituents.

One of those demands by constituents may be that leaders become followers. Sexuality leaders must be flexible enough to allow others an opportunity to utilize their strengths in order to create change. Van Loon and Buster write:

> I have the capacity within myself to lead and follow, to take space and to give space, to tell and to ask. When we define one of these positions as better (morally higher) than the other, we may tend to swing between the polarities, rather than recognizing that both are valuable aspects of leadership.
>
> (2019, p. 74)

Sexuality leaders should be prepared to assume various roles that can shift at any time or circumstance. Their ability to adapt to their constituents and surroundings is tantamount to their capacity to initiate change.

Intentionality

With vision, leaders would need to be intentional about creating and maintaining relationships as well as achieving their goals. Being purposeful allows for constituents and team members to move with a sense of clarity towards identified aims. Establishing and articulating direction to constituents minimizes the possibility of chaos as well as satisfies the systemic need for predictability and trust. A leader's capacity to be trustworthy about his/her efforts and his/her commitment to achieve objectives fosters a sense of security and possibly increase production. For the sexuality educator, clinician, or consultant, being attentive and purposeful about advocacy efforts, community engagement, strategic planning, mentoring, and service-oriented activities is necessary in dynamic climates. Sexuality leaders should intentionally engage in principled leadership where they respond ethically in a caring fashion and exhibit a sense of duty and responsibility (McKibben, Umstead, & Borders, 2017).

West, Bubenzer, Osborn, Paez, & Desmond (2006) suggested that leaders were intentional about building consensus around a vision. Consensus building can be challenging for sexuality professionals given the level of cultural diversity within the field. In addition, power hierarchies, resource distribution inequities, hegemonic scripts of marginalization, and lack of access can sometimes make consensus building a lofty goal. Along with intentionality, sexuality professionals must be resilient and remain open to shifts that may occur within and between constituents.

Empathy

When attempting to engage with communities that have been traditionally marginalized (e.g., people of color, LGBTQAI, persons with physical or intellectual challenges, elderly, etc.), one must be able to empathic towards their experiences. Empathy is "the ability to comprehend another's feelings and to re-experience them oneself (Salovey & Mayer, 1990, pp. 194–195). Similarly, according to Plutchik (1987, p. 43), empathy is the process of sharing positive and negative emotions that enables a bond to be formed or maintained between agents."

Emotionally attuned leaders are able extend consideration to constituents in a way of caring and understanding (Goleman, 1995, p. 109). Mutual trust, respect, and support for one another's thoughts and feelings are essential for empathy to be conveyed (Ferch & Mitchel, 2001). Patton suggested that placing oneself in the position of others requires compassion and perspective taking (1998). When sexuality leaders are able to convey to their students, clients, or constituents that they completely understand their experiences, those moments become transformational in that they foster positive emotions (Håkansson & Montgomery, 2003). This positive affective investment by sexuality leaders and their constituents may allow for an unrivaled passion and commitment towards achieving personal and professional goals. When empathy is reciprocated between professionals, a sense of pride and cohesiveness may allow for the team to maneuver through and around obstructions. If sexuality leaders are not able to convey empathy appropriately, then their constituents may feel guarded or less motivated to move towards favorable outcomes because of the assumption that those in charge do not fully understand personal or environmental challenges.

Intuition

Sexuality leaders must be able to able to use collected data in a manner that enables them to predict future outcomes. Developing a sense of intuition, or an ability to foresee both positive and negative outcomes is essential to effective leadership. While there may not be enough data, time, or space to make completely informed decisions, sometimes sexuality leaders may have to make choices based upon affective or qualitative experiences that cannot be quantified. Whether it is a shift in teaching methodology, clinical intervention, consultative path, or research inquiry, sexuality leaders must be intuitive enough to shift directions or employ different strategies for those they are serving. If the course correction is wrong, then sexuality leaders must be ready and willing to demonstrate humility for healing and possible forgiveness. Sexuality clinicians may use their intention by making guesses about what may be causing a particular sexual dysfunction; educators may intuitively inquire about additional support for students who share sensitive information by means of journal writing; sexuality consultants may intuitively offer services and support to people who may be in need of medically accurate information. Sexuality leaders should be mindful of their professional experiences and how those encounters allow for greater insight into possibly helping others.

Courage to Provoke or Disrupt

Think differently. Act differently. Feel differently. Sexuality leadership may involve the courage to provoke or disrupt traditional systems that may not recognize the contributions or experiences of underrepresented or misrepresented populations. Taking calculated chances in order to enact change is needed within a field that has not traditionally provided access to all people. Disrupting the status quo enabled the evolution of contraceptive technology and reproductive rights; civil rights, women's rights, gay rights, and #metoo movements; recognition, acknowledgment, and celebration of designer relationships; shifts in understanding and mainstream of kink and alternative lifestyles; and emergence of sexuality professional organizations such as the Association of Black Sexologists and Clinicians, Women of Color Sexual Health Network, Afrosexology, and others. The expansion of the field of sexology to become more inclusive and relativistic has enable leaders and professionals to grow differently and more rapidly. Subversion of dominant paradigms and provocation for the field to transform itself has taken courage by a few for all professionals to benefit.

Collaboration

Similar to teaching (Medgyes & Malderez, 1996), collaborative leadership involves discussion, inquiry, and processing in an effort to work together towards individual and systemic change and improvement. Collaborative leadership assumes that agents are able to work with peers, extend their own conceptualization of phenomena, learn from one another, and possibly develop their expertise together (Hargreaves, 1994).

Given the entrepreneurial nature of sexology, there are a number of different organizations and entities that could possibly benefit from collaborative relationships with each other due to overlapping mission and vision statements. These entities sometimes exist and behave in silos out of the assumed fear of competing resources and interests. If systemic conversations between organizations remained tailored to individual and relational rights, healthy and consenting relationships, creating safe spaces for sharing and growth, and empowerment of marginalized groups then collaboration may not be as difficult as one might assume. Collaboration may be difficult if individual interests rival collective interests. Sexuality leaders should be clear and be willing to process what may be in the best interests of the constituents they represent.

When leaders are capable of exhibiting vision, flexibility, intentionality, empathy, intuition, courage, and collaboration, they may be engaging in emancipatory leadership.

Emancipatory Leadership

In a recent discussion between reproductive healthcare leaders in Seattle, Washington, in June 2019, it was proposed that the vision for sex education and consultation domestically and internationally in the 21st century was based upon four constructs. The first aim was devoted to access to reproductive healthcare education and commitment to developing healthy relationships. The second component of the discussion revolved around efforts to increased partnerships and collaborative efforts between sexological organizations. The third portion of the vision was that sex education and consultation would continue to become more nuanced so that it could be culturally specific to the needs of clients and constituents served. The fourth component discussed serves as the confluence of the three aforementioned areas and offers a "new face" for sexuality leadership. This emancipatory form of leadership emerged from the recognition that leaders must create and transform safe spaces for individuals, familial, communal, and global initiatives. In these new or transformed areas of growth, constituents would have an opportunity to name and describe their challenges, access resources for improvement, and use information to teach those around them. The emancipation of constituents comes from the ideology of self-determinism (Gilbert and

Kelloway, 2018; Johnson, 1999) and actualization (Wasylyshyn, 2001) where individual and collective goals can be realized and celebrated.

Emancipatory leadership is global and efficient because of how easy it is to share information quickly. Cross-border alliances and collaboration, advanced information technologies, and open market distribution have led to growth and increased and rapid transitions (Beets, 2005; Ralson, Holt, Terpstra, & Kai-Cheng, 2008). Leaders can influence constituents who they never personally come into contact with by use of social media, e-mail, or some other electronic medium. Exchanging accurate information maintains integrity and allows communities an opportunity to learn multiple perspectives for addressing issues. Ethical global engagement and leadership that creates safe spaces for learning may allow an enhanced access for engaging in problem solving.

The field of sexology is moving towards emancipation as a result of having to address systematic shifts as well as the emergence of those who have needed to create their own tables and seats that are relative to their communities. The *new face of leadership* is a mosaic of emancipated individuals and communities who have marched in the Black Lives Matter and #metoo movements, exhibited resilience and courage to share stories of victimization and alienation, advocated for the acknowledgment and celebration of gender nonbinary folks, protested recent executive and judicial decisions to erode *Roe v Wade*, and pushed for comprehensive sexuality education both domestically and abroad. Emancipated leaders are activists and hold themselves and others accountable for individual and systemic injustices. These leaders take responsibility for conceptualizing and initiating change, and, as the field continues to evolve, there will be more leaders who will emerge out of the necessity to impact and influence their surroundings in a positive way.

Process Questions and Considerations

1. What prevents some leaders from taking responsibility for their actions?
2. What might be some of the areas of leadership that you could improve upon in order to facilitate or create change?
3. Describe a moment or circumstance where you had to initiate a change in course of action?
4. Share your thoughts about whether or not community protest is a form of leadership.
5. In your opinion, who would you consider to be the best leader that you have ever encountered? Share what made/makes that person stand out to you?

References

Baron, L., Rouleau, V., Grégoire, S., & Baron, C. (2018). Mindfulness and leadership flexibility. *Journal of Management Development, 37*(2), 165–177.

Beets, S. (2005). Understanding the demand-side issues of international corruption. *Journal of Business Ethics, 57*, 65–81.

Berry, B. (2019). Teacher leadership: Prospects and promises. *Phi Delta Kappan, 100*(7), 49–55.

Brown, B. (2015). *Daring greatly: How the courage to be vulnerable transforms the way we live, love, parent, and lead.* London: Penguin Books.

Chammas, C., & Hernandez, J. (2019). Comparing transformational and instrumental leadership. *Innovation & Management Review, 16*(2), 143–160.

Chan, S. (2019). Participative leadership and job satisfaction. *Leadership & Organization Development Journal, 40*(3), 319–333.

Chapman, G. (2015). *The five love languages: The secret to love that lasts.* Chicago, IL: Northfield Publishing.

Ciulla, J. B. (2014). *Ethics, the heart of leadership.* Westport, CT: Praeger.

Clarke, P., & Berkland, D. (2019). *Paradoxes in healthcare leadership: Being-Nonbeing. nursing science quarterly, 32*(2), 116–119.

Collinson, D. (2012). Prozac leadership and the limits of positive thinking. *Leadership, 8*, 87–108.

Covey, S. R. (2005). *The 8th habit: From effectiveness to greatness.* New York: Free Press.

Covey, S. R. (2011). *The 3rd alternative: Solving life's most difficult problems.* Simon and Schuster.

DaCosta, J. (2012). Leadership models for healthcare improvement. *British Journal of Healthcare Management, 18*(11), 575–580.

Delia, E. (2012). *Complexity leadership in industrial innovation teams: A field study of leading, learning and innovating in heterogenous teams.* Ann Arbor, MI: Umi Dissertation Publishing.

Dempsey, S. E. (2010). Critiquing community engagement. *Management Communication Quarterly, 24*(3), 359–390.

Denison, D. R., Hooijberg, R., & Quinn, R. E. (1995). Paradox and performance: Toward a theory of behavioral complexity in managerial leadership. *Organization Science, 6*(5), 524–540.

Edmonstone, J. (2013). Healthcare leadership: Learning from evaluation. *Leadership in Health Services, 26*(2), 148–158.

Edmonstone, J. (2017). Escaping the healthcare leadership cul-de-sac. *Leadership in Health Services, 30*(1), 76–91.

Elia, J. P., & Tokunaga, J. (2015). Sexuality education: Implications for health, equity, and social justice in the United States. *Health Education, 115*(1), 105–120.

Ferch, S., & Mitchell, M. (2001). Intentional forgiveness in relational leadership: A technique for enhancing effective leadership. *Journal of Leadership Studies, 7*(4), 70–83.

Ganser, S., & Kennedy, T. (2012). Where it all began: Peer education and leadership in student services. *New Directions for Higher Education, 157*, 17–29.

Gilbert, S., & Kelloway, E. (2018). Self-determined leader motivation and follower perceptions of leadership. *Leadership & Organization Development Journal, 39*(5), 608–619.

Goleman, D. (1995). *Emotional intelligence: Why it can matter more than IQ.* New York: Bantam Books.

González-Cruz, T., Botella-Carrubi, D., & Martínez-Fuentes, C. (2019). Supervisor leadership style, employee regulatory focus, and leadership performance: A perspectivism approach. *Journal of Business Research, 101,* 660–667.

Hakånsson, J., & Montgomery, H. (2003). Empathy as an interpersonal phenomenon. *Journal of Social and Personal Relationship, 20*(3), 267–284.

Hargreaves, A. (1994). *Changing teachers, changing times: Teacher's work and culture in the postmodern age.* New York, NY: Teachers College Press.

Heckert, J., & Cleminson, R. (Eds.) (2011). *Anarchism & sexuality: Ethics, relationships and power.* Abingdon: Routledge.

Hernandez, M. (2008). Promoting stewardship behavior in organizations: A leadership model. *Journal of Business Ethics, 80*(1), 121–128.

Hernandez, M. (2012). Toward an understanding of psychology of stewardship. *Academy of Management Review, 37*(2), 172–193.

Hess, E. (2014). *Humility is the new smart: Rethinking human excellence in the smart machine age.* New York: Berrett-Koehler Publishers.

Hickman, G. (2016). *Leading organizations: Perspectives for a new era.* Thousand Oaks, CA: Sage.

Hoefer, R. (2019). The dangers of social justice advocacy. *Social Work, 64*(1), 87–90.

Humes, W. (1995). Coping with mismanagement. *Management in Education, 9*(5), 32–33.

Johnson, J. (1999). Leadership and self-determination. *Focus on Autism and Other Developmental Disabilities, 14*(1), 4–16.

Koonce, R. (2016). All in "the family": Leading and following through individual, relational, and collective mindsets. In R. Koonce, M. C. Bligh, M. K. Carsten, and M. Hurwitz (Eds.), *Followership in action. Cases and commentaries* (pp. 3–14). Bingley, UK: Emerald Books.

Kouzes, J. M., & Posner, B. Z. (2012). *The leadership challenge: How to make extraordinary things happen in organizations.* San Francisco, CA: The Leadership Challenge.

Kroska, A., & Cason, T. (2019). The gender gap in business leadership: Exploring an affect control theory explanation. *Social Psychology Quarterly, 82*(1), 75–97.

McKibben, W., Umstead, L., & Borders, L. (2017). Identifying Dynamics of Counseling Leadership: A Content Analysis Study. *Journal of Counseling & Development, 95*(2), 192–202.

Medgyes, P., & Malderez, A. (Eds.) (1996). Changing Perspectives in Teacher Education. Oxford: Heinemann.

Myers, J. E., Sweeney, T. J., & White, V. E. (2002). Advocacy for counseling and counselors: A professional imperative. *Journal of Counseling & Development, 80*(4), 394–402.

Ndalamba, K., Caldwell, C., & Anderson, V. (2018). Leadership vision as a moral duty. *Journal of Management Development, 37*(3), 309–319.

Nicholson, N. (2013). *The "I" of leadership: Strategies for seeing, being, doing.* West Sussex: John Wiley and Sons.

Nigro, T. (2018). The shadows in healthcare leadership. *Healthcare Management Forum, 31*(3), 97–102.

Patton, P. (1998). *Emotional intelligence: Development from success to significance.* Singapore: SNP.

Perel, E. (2017). *The state of affairs: Rethinking infidelity. A book for anyone who has ever loved.* Hachette, UK: HarperCollins Publishers.

Plutchik, R. (1987). Evolutionary bases of empathy. In N. Eisenberg, & J. Strayer (Eds.), *Empathy and its development* (pp. 38–46). New York: Cambridge University Press.

Putra, E., & Cho, S. (2019). Characteristics of small business leadership from employees' perspective: A qualitative study. *International Journal of Hospitality Management, 78*, 36–46.

Ralson, D., Holt, D., Terpstra, R., & Kai-Cheng, Y. (2008). The impact of national culture and economic ideology on managerial work values: A study of the United States, Russia, Japan, and China. *Journal of International Business Studies, 39*(1), 8–26.

Rhodes, S. D., Malow, R. M., & Jolly, C. (2010). Community-based participatory research: A new and not-so-new approach to HIV/AIDS prevention, care, and treatment. *AIDS Education and Prevention, 22*(3), 173–183.

Rocha, J., & Rocha, M. (2019). Love, sex, and social justice: The Anarcha-feminist free love debate. *Anarchist Studies, 27*(1).

Rost, J. C. (1991). *Leadership for the twenty-first century. Praeger publishers,* Westport, CT.

Russell, S. T. (2019). Social justice and the future of healthy families: Sociocultural changes and challenges. *Family Relations, 68*(3), 358–370.

Salovey, P., & Mayer, J. (1990). Emotional intelligence. *Imagination, Cognition, and Personality, 9*(3), 185–211.

Sheppard, J., Sarros, C. J., & Santora, C. J. (2013). Twenty-first century leadership: International imperatives. *Management Decision, 51*(2), 267–280.

Somers Hill, M., & Lynch, D. (1994). Future principals: Selecting educators for leadership. NASSP bulletin: *Official Journal of the National Association of Secondary School Principals, 78*(565), 81–84.

Sullivan, T., & Syvertsen, A. (2019). Conservation leadership: A developmental model. *Journal of Adolescent Research, 34*(2), 140–166.

Tellis, A. (2014). Some thoughts on education for leadership and innovation. *The Journal of General Education, 63*(2), 152–160.

Vaccaro, A., Russell, E. A., & Koob, R. M. (2015). Students with minoritized identities of sexuality and gender in campus contexts: An emergent model. *New Directions for Student Services, 152*, 25–39.

van Loon, R., & Buster, A. (2019). The future of leadership: The courage to be both leader and follower. *Journal of Leadership Studies, 13*(1), 73–74.

Wadley, J. C., & Siegel, R. (Eds.). (2018). *The art of sex therapy supervision.* Abingdon: Routledge.

Wasylyshyn, K. (2001). On the full actualization of psychology in business. *Consulting Psychology Journal: Practice and Research, 53*(1), 10–21.

354 *James C. Wadley*

West, J. D., Bubenzer, D. L., Osborn, C. J., Paez, S. B., & Desmond, K. J. (2006). Leadership and the profession of counseling: Beliefs and practices. *Counselor Education and Supervision*, 46(1), 2–16.

Wister, A., Beattie, B., Gallagher, E., Gutman, G., Hemingway, D., Reid, R., Sinden, D., & Symes, B. (2014). *Effectiveness of a Shared Leadership Model. Administration & Society*, 46(8), 863–884.

Yukl, G., & Mahsud, R. (2010). Why flexible and adaptive leadership is essential. *Consulting Psychology Journal: Practice and Research*, 62(2), 81–93.

Appendix
Graduate and Postgraduate Programs in Human Sexuality[1]

Australia

La Trobe University – Australian Research Centre in Sex, Health & Society
Melbourne
www.latrobe.edu.au/arcshs

Curtin University – Master of Sexology/Graduate Diploma of Sexology
Perth
https://study.curtin.edu.au/offering/course-pg-master-of-sexology-mc-sxlgy/?rdr=coursefinder

Belgium

Université Libre de Bruxelles – Certificat d'université en sexologie clinique
Brussels
www.ulb.ac.be/programme/FC-302/index.html

Canada

Université du Québec à Montréal – Département de Sexologie
Montréal
https://sexologie.uqam.ca/

Ireland

Dublin City University – Graduate Certificate in Relationships and Sexuality Education for People with Intellectual Disability
Dublin
www.dcu.ie/courses/Postgraduate/shhp/Graduate-Certificate-Relationships-and-Sexuality-Education-for-People

Dublin City University – Graduate Certificate in Sexuality and Sexual Health Education

Dublin
www.dcu.ie/courses/Postgraduate/snhs/Graduate-Certificate-Sexuality-and-Sexual-Education.shtml

Dublin City University – M.A. in Sexuality Studies
www.dcu.ie/courses/Postgraduate/salis/MA-Sexuality-Studies.shtml

Italy

Instituto di Sessuologia Clinica
Rome
http://sessuologiaclinicaroma.it

Istituto Scientifico di Psychosessuologio Integrata
Milano
www.ispsi.it/

Mexico

Asociación Mexicana para la Salud Sexual, A.C. (AMSSAC)
Mexico City
www.amssac.org/educacion/formacion_profesional_amssac/

Centro de Educación y Atención en la Salud y la Sexualidad A.C.
Guadalajara
www.ceassjalisco.com/

Centro de Estudios Superiores de Sexualidad (CESSEX)
Merida
http://cessex.com.mx/

Centro Integral de Sexualidad y Educación Sexual A.C (CISES)
Xalapa
https://cisesdexalapa.es.tl/

Instituto de Educación Superior en Desarrollo Humano Sustentable
Mexico City
formacion@moxviquil.org

Instituto de Estudios en Sexualidad Humana del Estado de Chiapas
(IESHECH)
Comitan
www.facebook.com/IESHECH-AC-140791123199039/

Instituto de Profesionalización y Educación en Sexología
Mexico City
www.facebook.com/IPESIAC/

Instituto Mexicano de Sexología, A.C. (IMESEX)
Mexico City
http://imesex.edu.mx/

Instituto Universitario Carl Rogers – Maestría en Sexualidad Humana
Puebla
http://unicarlrogers.com.mx/Oferta_educativa/sexualidad_humana

Universidad Autonoma de Durango – Sexualidad Clínica
Mexicali
www.uadlobos.mx/sexualidad-clinica-maestrias-mexicali.html

Universidad de Londres, Campus Queretaro – Sexualidad y Equidad
  de Género
Queretaro
http://udelondresqueretaro.com.mx/sexualidad-y-equidad-de-genero/

Universidad Iberoamericana
Mexico City
https://posgrados.ibero.mx/doctoradoenestudioscriticosdegenero

Universidad Mexicana de Estudios y Posgrados (CAS)
Morelia and several cities
http://umep.com.mx/moodle/course/index.php?categoryid=41

Universidad Nexum
Culiacan
www.nexum.edu.mx/

The Netherlands

University of Amsterdam (UvA) – Graduate School of Social Sciences
  Sociology: Gender, Sexuality and Society
Amsterdam
http://gsss.uva.nl/content/masters/sociology-gender-sexuality-and-society/
  gender-sexuality-and-society.html

Portugal

Lusófona University – Mestrado Transdisciplinar de Sexologia e Pós-
  Graduação em Sexologia
Lisbon
www.ulusofona.pt/mestrado/transdisciplinar-de-sexologia
www.ulusofona.pt/pos-graduacoes/sexologia

Sociedade Portuguesa de Sexologia Clínica
Lisbon
https://spsc.pt/index.php/o-curso/

University of Porto – Doctoral Programme in Human Sexuality
Porto
www.fpce.up.pt/pdsh/en/about.html

Spain

Instituto Superior de Estudios Psicológicos – Maestría en Sexología
Clínica y Terapia de Parejas
Madrid
www.isep.com/mx/curso/maestria-terapia-de-pareja/

Universidad de Alcalá – Máster Iberoamericano en Anticoncepción y
Salud Sexual y Reproductiva
Alcalá de Henares
http://masteriberoamericano.com/homepage-2

University de Barcelona – Clinical Sexology and Sexual Health
Barcelona
www.ub.edu/web/ub/en/estudis/oferta_formativa/masters_propis/fitxa/
C/201711890/index.html

Switzerland

Haute École de Santé Sociale Genève et Université de Lausanne –
CAS/DAS en Santé Sexuelle
Lausanne
www.hesge.ch/hets/formation-continue/formations-postgrade/diplomes-
das/das-en-sante-sexuelle-interventions-education

Université de Genève – Programme de Formation Continue Interfacul-
taire de Sexologie Clinique
Genève
www.unige.ch/formcont/site-sexologie-clinique/accueil/

Medipsy – Certificat de Sexologie Clinique et Sexothérapie
Lausanne
www.medipsy.ch/formations/

United States

American Academy of Clinical Sexology
Orlando, FL
http://esextherapy.com/

California Institute of Integral Studies
San Francisco, CA
www.ciis.edu/academics/graduate-programs/human-sexuality

Council for Relationships
Philadelphia, PA
https://councilforrelationships.org/professional-education/degree-certi
ficate-programs/sex-therapy/

Georgia State University – Women's, Gender, and Sexuality Studies
Atlanta, GA
https://wgss.gsu.edu/

Indiana University – Center for Sexual Health Promotion
Bloomington, IL
https://sexualhealth.indiana.edu/

Indiana University – Bloomington
Bloomington, IN
https://sexualitystudies.indiana.edu/

Institute for Sexual Wholeness (ISW)
http://institute.sexualwholeness.com/

Integrative Sex Therapy Institute
Washington, D.C.
www.integrativesextherapyinstitute.com/

Modern Sex Therapy Institutes
Atlanta, GA, Chicago, IL, New York, NY, Washington, D.C., West Palm
Beach, FL
www.modernsextherapyinstitutes.com/

New York University Langone Comprehensive Program in Human Sexuality
New York, NY
https://med.nyu.edu/psych/education/other-training-programs/training-
program-human-sexuality

Northwestern University – The Institute for Gender and Sexual Minority Health and Wellbeing
Chicago, IL
https://isgmh.northwestern.edu/

Ohio State University – Department of Women's, Gender, and Sexuality Studies
Columbus, OH
https://wgss.osu.edu/

San Francisco State University – Department of Sexuality Studies
San Francisco, CA
https://sxs.sfsu.edu/

Sex Coach University
Locations in California and Online
www.sexcoachu.com/

Sexual Health Alliance – California, Colorado, Illinois, Michigan, and
   Texas
Programs in many U.S. cities
https://sexualhealthalliance.com

Teacher's College Columbia University – Sexuality, Women, and Gender Certificate
New York, NY
http://swgproject.org/

Jefferson University – Couple and Family Therapy Program
Philadelphia, PA
www.jefferson.edu/university/health-professions/departments/couple-family-
   therapy/degrees-programs/ms-family-therapy/program-options.html

University of Cincinnati – Women's Gender, and Sexuality Studies
Cincinnati, OH
www.artsci.uc.edu/departments/wgss.html

University of Florida
Center for Gender, Sexualities, and Women's Studies Research
https://wst.ufl.edu/

University of Hawaii – Pacific Center for Sex and Society
Honolulu, HI
www.hawaii.edu/PCSS/

University of Minnesota – Program in Human Sexuality – Postdoc-
   toral Fellowship and Human Sexuality Certificate
Minneapolis, MN
www.sexualhealth.umn.edu/
www.sexualhealth.umn.edu/certificate

University of Iowa – Gender, Women's and Sexuality Studies
Iowa City, IA
https://clas.uiowa.edu/gwss/graduate-program

University of Michigan Sexual Health Certificate Program
Ann Arbor, MI
https://ssw.umich.edu/offices/continuing-education/certificate-courses/
   sexual-health

Washington University in St. Louis – Brown School – Sexual Health and Education Specialization
St. Louis, MO
https://brownschool.wustl.edu/Academics/Master-of-Social-Work/Pages/Sexual-Health-and Education-Specialization.aspx

Widener University – Center for Human Sexuality Studies
Chester, PA
www.widener.edu/academics/schools/shsp/hss/

United Kingdom

The Centre for Psychosexual Health
London
https://psychosexualhealth.org.uk/

Edinburgh Napier University – Graduate Certificate: Sexual and Reproductive Health
Edinburgh
www.napier.ac.uk/courses/graduate-certificate-sexual-and-reproductive-health-undergraduate-parttime

London Diploma in Psychosexual and Relationship Therapy
London
www.psychosexualtraining.org.uk/

London School of Economics & Political Science – MSc Gender (Sexuality)
London
www.lse.ac.uk/gender/postgraduate/msc/msc-gender-sexuality

Pink Therapy Foundation Certificate in GSRD Therapy
London
https://pinktherapy.org/foundation/

Tavistock Diploma in Psychosexual Therapy
London
https://tavistockrelationships.ac.uk/diploma-in-psychosexual-therapy

University of Birmingham, UK – Sexuality and Gender Studies
Birmingham
www.birmingham.ac.uk/research/activity/gender/index.aspx

University of Central Lancashire – Sexual Health Studies Msc
Preston
www.uclan.ac.uk/courses/msc_sexual_health_studies.php

University of Sussex – Sexual Dissidence M.A.
Brighton
www.sussex.ac.uk/study/masters/courses/english/sexual-dissidence-ma

University of the West Scotland – Sexual and Reproductive Health
  Graduate Certificate
Glasgow
www.uws.ac.uk/study/postgraduate/postgraduate-course-search/
  sexual-reproductive-health/

Conferences

American Association of Sexuality Educators, Counselors, and Therapists
www.aasectannualconference.com/

The Association of Black Sexologists and Clinicians
www.theabsc.com/events/

Careers in Sexuality Conference
https://careersinsexualityconference.wordpress.com/

Congresso Nacional de Educación Sexual y Sexología
www.congresofemess.org.mx/

Federazione Italiana di Sessuologia Scientifica
http://fissonline.it

Healthy Teen Network
http://conference.healthyteennetwork.org/

National Sex Ed Conference
http://sexedconference.com

Non-Monogamies and Contemporary Intimacies Conference
http://nmciconference.wordpress.com

Sex Down South
www.sexdownsouth.com/

Sex in the Middle
www.sexdownsouth.com/sex-in-the-middle

The Society for the Scientific Study of Sexuality
http://sexscience.org/

Society for Sex Therapy and Research
https://sstarnet.org/

World Association for Sexual Health
www.worldsexology.org/

YTH
http://yth.org/ythlive/

Note

1. This list was created with a great deal of input from sexologists worldwide. The document will continue to be updated in the future at Retrieved from http://bit.ly/GradProgramsInSexuality.

Index

Note: Page numbers in *italic* indicate a figure.

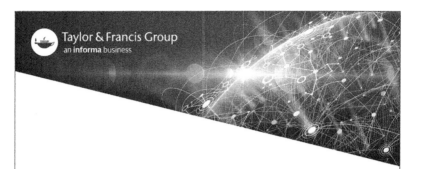

Made in the USA
Las Vegas, NV
27 September 2021